CAMBRIDGE LATIN AMERICAN STUDIES

EDITORS

MALCOLM DEAS   DAVID JOSLIN   TIMOTHY KING
CLIFFORD T. SMITH   JOHN STREET

16

CONFLICTS AND CONSPIRACIES:
BRAZIL AND PORTUGAL 1750-1808

THE SERIES

CONFLICTS
AND CONSPIRACIES:
BRAZIL AND PORTUGAL
1750–1808

KENNETH R. MAXWELL

CAMBRIDGE
AT THE UNIVERSITY PRESS
1973

Published by the Syndics of the Cambridge University Press
Bentley House, 200 Euston Road, London NW1 2DB
American Branch: 32 East 57th Street, New York, N.Y. 10022

Library of Congress Catalogue Card Number: 72–89813

© Cambridge University Press 1973

ISBN: 0 521 20053 9

Set in Great Britain at the Aberdeen University Press

Printed in the United States of America

FOR MY FATHER AND MOTHER

PREFACE

Independent Brazil, unlike most former colonial territories in the Western Hemisphere adopted a monarchical system of government, and Portuguese America unlike Spanish America did not fragment into numerous separate states. One objective of this study is to suggest an interpretive framework that might aid in explaining some of the particular circumstances which led to Brazil's special historical development. Taking a critical formative period, 1750 to 1808, I have attempted to determine how social, political and economic compulsions moulded policy and events, or were moulded by them.

Essentially the object of this work then is to delineate the broad interaction of Portugal and Brazil during the second half of the eighteenth century. I seek to explain how and why Portuguese colonial policy changed: something which can only be done with the closest attention to the complex evolution of metropolis and colony during and after the long preeminence of the Marquis of Pombal. For better or worse, therefore, Pombal and his actions form an important thread to the argument. Equally significant is Portugal's relationship with the rest of Europe, most particularly the changing pattern of her connection with Great Britain, which had far-reaching consequences for imperial policy. And as important, I seek to explain the situation in Brazil.

In the process of research questions arose concerning accepted chronology, especially in the case of the famous Minas conspiracy of 1788-9, when plotters in the interior gold mining zone attempted to foment an armed uprising against the Portuguese crown. Using the fiscal and business records of the oligarchs of Minas Gerais I was led to conclude that the historical record had been distorted, and that an important group of entrepreneurs, counting among them some of the richest and most influential men of the region, had escaped incrimination at the time, and later disappeared from history. The distortion I believe originated in the testimony of the then governor of Minas, the Visconde de Barbacena, whose reports to Lisbon and the viceroy in Rio de Janeiro were accepted in certain important aspects as an accurate account of developments. Barbacena, as I hope to demonstrate in these pages, was far from being an unbiased or disinterested witness. His story, and most particularly his dating of events, is not trustworthy. Later on circumstances served to perpetuate the governor's distortions and I seek to show how and why this happened.

I make no claim, however, to have uncovered startling new archival materials. Generations of Brazilian historians have dug deep for anything of relevance to the life and activities of Joaquim José da Silva Xavier, the *Tiradentes*, one of the key figures in the conspiracy and a man who was later to become the national hero of Republican Brazil. What I have attempted is a reassessment of multiple contemporary sources, some from archives, some from published documentary collections, some known, some unknown. I do not intend to disparage or belittle *Tiradentes* here. He was clearly a catalyst of revolution in the troubled Minas of 1788. A firm propagandist of an independent, republican, and self-sufficient Minas Gerais, he intended to initiate the revolt. Had circumstances not conspired to thwart him there can be little doubt that he, unlike some of his co-conspirators, would have taken the action he promised.

I believe, however, that in the long run, overconcentration on the role of *Tiradentes* has tended to minimize the importance of the movement of which he was a part. The conflict in Minas was, in my opinion, the result of socio-economic divergence between Minas Gerais and Portugal, and of a classic confrontation between colonial and metropolitan interest groups. The whole episode, it seems to me, was of critical importance for its impact both on the Brazilian white élite, and on the imperial policies of the metropolitan government. Thus, unlike the great Brazilian historian Capistrano de Abreu, who regarded the movement as so unimportant that it did not merit inclusion in his history of colonial Brazil, I claim that it was of central importance to the period. I have tried, therefore, to present here, based on archival research in Brazil, Portugal, Great Britain, and Spain, the broad socio-economic basis of the conspiracy and to delineate its impact.

This is no definitive study of the Minas conspiracy, a fact it is important to stress. It may well be that to write such a history is an impossible task. The subject matter consists of secret conventicles, furtive reports of even more furtive meetings, interrogations, skulduggery, and murder. I do not claim to have all the answers. What I have done is to interpret events as seems most logical and consistent with the evidence at hand. My method was to make a careful and detailed chronology of all the material available. Then I examined the individual testimony of those arrested for participation in the plot, first as a unit and afterwards against the chronology. The resulting reconstruction was then tested against the evidence obtained from public and private correspondence, fiscal, business, and administrative records.

Preface

I have been careful in the footnotes always to state exactly the time, place and circumstances of all the evidence taken from the interrogations, and in the construction of the narrative have always placed the evidence from these sources as nearly as possible in its exact chronological sequence. And if the language in these citations appears ungrammatical and the orthography inconsistent, it should be remembered that the records were subject to much redrafting, and reported verbatim the words of men who often possessed only a rudimentary education. Wherever there is any question of doubt I have cited the evidence in full, and to justify important comments in the text on the opinions and attitudes of the conspirators I have also cited in full the passage or passages on which I have based my conclusion. This may seem excessive, but with material by its nature speculative, it is essential that as complete a body of evidence as is feasible be presented. Then, where concrete statements are not possible, as for example over the mysterious death of Cláudio Manuel da Costa, the reader himself can decide.

But the Minas conspiracy is only part of the story. It is seen as one element, even if a vital one, in a wider interaction of historical circumstances. Nor are the issues discussed here peculiar to Brazil and Portugal. The second half of the eighteenth century saw much discussion of and attempts at imperial reform by all the European powers. And the epoch was also that of the American, French and Haitian revolutions, all of which had considerable impact on Portuguese America. Certainly the developments in Portugal and Brazil during these years are less well known than those elsewhere, and I hope what I have to say may be of value for those interested in comparative analysis of such phenomena as the enlightenment, colonial revolts, enlightened absolutism, slavery, economic nationalism and so on.

The limitations of this study, however, should also be borne in mind. I have remained as strictly as possible within the chronological limits, 1750 and 1808, and while developments during these years were of great importance for the consequent history of both Portugal and Brazil, it will nonetheless be necessary for much more work on the period leading up to the final break between the two countries in the 1820s before any well-informed opinion can be returned on the causes of independence. And while I have limited myself to the Luso-Brazilian system and its international connections, it may well be that my canvas is still too large, and that I have raised more questions than I have provided answers. I recognize that many of the issues discussed here await more detailed quantitative study. I hope, however, at the very least, that this book will point out the directions that such research might take.

Any historian who writes about a society and culture other than his own does so at some risk. And especially when treating a matter so intimately a part of Brazil's national heritage as the *Inconfidência Mineira* I am well aware that I tread sensitive ground. In the last resort the history of Brazil will and must be written by Brazilians. This work I offer as a contribution to that task. Hopefully Brazilians will find it useful. I trust they will be patient of my errors, and that this work will be worthy of those illustrious foreign historians of Brazil, not least my fellow countrymen from Robert Southey to Charles Boxer, who have gone before.

Coombe Water   K.R.M.
West Monkton
Somerset

September 1971

ACKNOWLEDGEMENTS

I owe a particular debt to Professor Stanley J. Stein of Princeton University for his constant encouragement and his incisive criticism. I am indebted to Lawrence W. Towner, Director of the Newberry Library, Chicago, for the opportunity of spending a year working and writing in the most ideal conditions. Research was financed by a Ford Regional Studies Fellowship 1964-6, a Princeton Regional Studies Fellowship 1966-8, and by a Newberry Library Gulbenkian Fellowship 1968-9. I am also grateful to the Calouste Gulbenkian Foundation of Lisbon and the Foundation's Director of International Projects, Dr Guilherme de Ayala Monteiro, for their support during 1964. I thank my friends, Carlos Guilherme Mota, David Davidson, Marcos Carneiro de Mendonça, Pedro Luís Carneiro de Mendonça, Orlandino Seitas Fernandes, João Gomes Teixeira, Herculano Gomes Mathias for their help and encouragement, and Dr José Honório Rodrigues for reading and criticizing the manuscript. The defects and interpretations are of course my own responsibility.

CONTENTS

Contents

Contents

ABBREVIATIONS

AAP   *Anais da Academia Portuguêsa da História*, Lisbon.

ABNRJ   *Anais da Biblioteca Nacional*, Rio de Janeiro.

ACC   *Anais do Congresso Comemorativo do Bicentenario da Transferência da Sede do Governo do Brasil da Cidade do Salvador para o Rio de Janeiro* (3 vols., Instituto Histórico e Geográfico Brasileiro, Rio de Janeiro, 1967).

ADIB   *A Inconfidência da Bahia, Devassas e Sequestros* (2 vols., Biblioteca Nacional, Rio de Janeiro, 1931).

ADIM   *Autos de Devassa de Inconfidência Mineira* (7 vols., Rio de Janeiro, 1936–8). (DMG): used to identify depositions taken from witnesses by Araújo Saldanha and Caetano Manitti in Minas devassa in Vila Rica; (DRJ) to identify depositions from witnesses taken in Vila Rica by Machado Torres and Pereira Cleto of the viceregal or Rio de Janeiro devassa.

AHN   Archivo Histórico Nacional, Madrid.

AHU   Arquivo Histórico Ultramarino, Lisbon.

AMI   *Anuário do Museu da Inconfidência*, Ouro Prêto, Minas Gerais.

AMHN   *Anais do Museu Histórico Nacional*, Rio de Janeiro.

ANRJ   Arquivo Nacional, Rio de Janeiro.

BMP   Biblioteca Municipal do Porto, [Oporto.]

APM   Arquivo Público Mineiro, Belo Horizonte, Minas Gerais.

BNLCP   Biblioteca Nacional, Lisbon, Pombal Collection.

CCANRJ   Mathias, Herculano Gomes, *A coleção da casa dos contos de Ouro Prêto* (Arquivo Nacional, Rio de Janeiro, 1966).

CCBNRJ   Casa dos Contos Collection, Biblioteca Nacional, Rio de Janeiro.

Correspondência inédita   Marcos Carneiro de Mendonça, *A Amazônia na era Pombalina. Correspondência inédita do Governador e Capitão-General do estado do Grão-Pará e Maranhão, Francisco Xavier de Mendonça Furtado 1751–1759* (Instituto Histórico e Geográfico Brasileiro, 3 vols., Rio de Janeiro, 1963).

Abbreviations

DISP   *Documentos Interessantes para a História e Costumes de
            S. Paulo*, São Paulo.
HAHR   *Hispanic American Historical Review.*
IHGB   Instituto Histórico e Geográfico Brasileiro, Arquive.
            Rio de Janeiro.
IHGB/AUC   The Arquivo Ultramarino collection of transcripts in
            the Instituto Histórico e Geográfico Brasileiro.
MHPB   Cel. Inácio Accioli de Cerqueira e Silva, *Memórias
            Históricas e Políticas* (6 vols., annotated by Braz do
            Amaral, Bahia, 1940).
PRO   Public Record Office, London (FO = Foreign Office,
            BT = Board of Trade).
RAPM   *Revista do Arquivo Público Mineiro.*
RHSP   *Revista de História*, São Paulo.
RIHGB   *Revista do Instituto Histórico e Geográfico Brasileiro*, Rio de
            Janeiro.

GLOSSARY

ALDEIA Mission village. Amerindian mission settlement supervised by the Jesuits.

ALFERES Lieutenant, ensign, standard bearer.

ALQUEIRE A measure of capacity. Equivalent to 36.27 litres in Rio while it equalled 13.80 in Lisbon.

ALVARÁ Royal decree.

ARROBA A measure of weight equal to 32 lb, or 14.75 kilograms.

CACHAÇA Sugar cane brandy.

CAIXA Treasurer.

CAPITÃO-MOR In this period most often the commandant of a company of second line militia.

CAPITANIA Captaincy, territory, an administrative unit.

CASA DE FUNDIÇÃO Smeltery, foundry-house.

CASA (or MESA) DE INSPEÇÃO Inspection board to oversee production and export of colonial staples, especially sugar and tobacco.

CASA DE SUPLICAÇÃO Supreme Court of Appeals.

COMARCA Administrative district, county.

COMMISSÁRIOS VOLANTES Itinerant traders.

COMPADRE Ritual godparent relationship.

CRUZADO Portuguese coin, worth 400 reis.

DATA Mining claim, allotment.

DESEMBARGADOR Judge, senior crown magistrate.

DERRAMA Per capita tax.

DEVASSA Judicial inquiry.

DÍZIMO Church tithe.

ENTRADAS Customs duties on merchandise, slaves and livestock entering Minas Gerais.

FAZENDA (i) Landed state estate; (ii) Treasury.

GARIMPEIRO Illicit diamond prospector.

JUNTA DA FAZENDA Captaincy exchequer board.

JUNTA DO COMÉRCIO Board of Trade, Lisbon.

OUVIDOR Crown Judge, Circuit Judge, Superior Crown Magistrate of comarca.

MESTRE DO CAMPO Colonel of infantry regiment.

MINAS GERAIS The General Mines. Region of Brazil.

Glossary

MINEIRO   (i) Miner; (ii) An inhabitant of Minas Gerais.

MISERICÓRDIA, SANTA CASA DA   Holy House of Mercy, charitable lay brotherhood.

MORGADO   Entailed estate.

PARDO   Colored man, most often mulatto.

PAULISTA   An inhabitant of São Paulo.

PROCURADOR   Person with power of attorney.

PROVEDOR   Comptroller. Superintendent of a bureaucratic office.

PROPINAS   Perquisites, emoluments, rake-offs.

QUINTO   Royal fifth.

REGIMENTO   Standing orders, instructions, rules and regulations.

RÉIS   Money of account.

RELAÇÃO   High Court of Appeals.

SARGENTO-MOR   Commissioned military officer.

SESMARIA   Concession of land.

SENHOR DE ENGENHO   Owner of a sugar mill.

TIRADENTES   Nickname of Joaquim José da Silva Xavier, literally the toothpuller.

VEREADOR   Municipal councillor.

A NOTE ON ORTHOGRAPHY

In direct transcription I have preserved the original spelling and punctuation, hence scribal inconsistencies in footnotes of this type. Elsewhere I have attempted to follow modern Brazilian form, i.e. Correia for Corrêa, Meneses for Menezes, Melo e Castro for Mello e Castro. In the English text American spelling is used.

CHAPTER I

DISPOSITIONS

It might be said, that hitherto Portugal existed only for England. She was, as it were, entirely absorbed by her. It was for her that the vine flourished at Oporto, that the tree of the Hesperides burdened itself with its golden fruit, that the olive diffused its sweet and unctuous tides; it was for her that the sun of the Brazils hardened the diamond in the bowels of the earth, and it was for her that Portugal rendered her banks and her soil inhospitable to industry.

> *Europe and America, translated from the French of the Abbé de Pradt by J. D. Williams* (2 vols., London, 1822) I, 425.

When great new dispositions are necessary they should always be put forward by ancient names and in ancient clothing.

> Manuel Teles da Silva to Sebastião José de Carvalho e Melo, Vienna, 25 Sept. 1750 *Anais da Academia Portuguesa da História*, 2nd series, vol. VI (Lisbon, 1955) 313–15.

In late July 1750, amid multifarious relics, lulled by assorted chanting ecclesiastics, João V, a moribund Portuguese *Roi Soleil* at last expired. Within three days of the accession of José I, there began the predominance in affairs of state of Sebastião José de Carvalho e Melo, later to be the Marquis of Pombal. Hardworking, taciturn, inquisitive, Carvalho e Melo had been Portuguese minister in London, then special envoy at Vienna. The political testament of Dom Luís da Cunha, delegate to the Utrecht treaty negotiation and ambassador in Paris, recommended him for his 'patient and speculative temperament'.[1] Others were not so complimentary. The British diplomat Benjamin Keene wrote: 'It is a poor Coimbrian pate as ever I met with, to be as stubborn, as dull, is the true asinine quality. [...] I shall only say that a little genius who has a mind to be a great one in a little country, is a very uneasy animal.'[2]

News of Carvalho e Melo's ascendancy in the government reached

---

[1] 'Maximas sobre a reforma...dirigidas ao Sr. D. José...por D. Luís da Cunha....' Biblioteca Nacional de Lisboa, Pombal collection (BNLCP) códice 51, folio 178v; Kenneth R. Maxwell, 'Pombal and the Nationalization of the Luso-Brazilian Economy', *The Hispanic American Historical Review (HAHR)* XLVIII, No. 4 (November 1968) 608–31.

[2] Benjamin Keene to Abraham Castres, October 1745, Sir Richard Lodge (editor) *The Private Correspondence of Sir Benjamin Keene K.B.* (Cambridge, 1933) 72. Keene had been in Lisbon from 1745 to 1749, before his appointment as envoy in Spain. Abraham Castres was (from 1746) British consul in Lisbon. Both men died during 1757.

Conflicts and conspiracies

Vienna during September of 1750. Manuel Teles da Silva, an emigré Portuguese of aristocratic lineage who had risen high within the Austrian state, wrote at once to Lisbon. 'We are not slaves of fashion and foreign practices', he told the new minister, 'we conserve unalterably the names and external practices and national establishments, but still less are we slaves of ancient habits and preoccupations. If there is puerility in fashions, there is folly in the obstinacy of old ways.' Manuel Teles da Silva, created Duke Silva-Tarouca by Charles VI in 1732, was president of the council of the Netherlands and Italy, and a confidant of the Empress Maria Theresa. He recalled his 'intimate conversations' with Carvalho e Melo, and recommended that 'when great new dispositions are necessary they should always be put forward by ancient names and in ancient clothing'.[1]

'Great new dispositions' Carvalho e Melo clearly had in mind. He was fifty years of age at the accession, and was one of a generation of open minded officials and diplomats who had given much thought to imperial organization and the mercantilist techniques believed to lie behind the startling and growing power and wealth of France and Great Britain.[2] Carvalho e Melo had written in 1742 that 'all the nations of Europe are today augmenting themselves by reciprocal imitation, each carefully watching over the actions of the others'.[3] Such careful watching was his 'most interesting duty in London', he told Cardinal da Mota.[4] The Duke Silva-Tarouca remarked in 1757: 'For eight years Your Excellency observed with a vision more secure than that of corporal eyes the constitution of Great Britain, of her forces and accidental riches, and for another period of five years in Vienna of Austria Your Excellency with equal judgement and perspicacity observed the non-accidental riches and forces of these most fertile states.'[5]

Carvalho e Melo's observation of the European situation had been

[1] [Manuel Teles da Silva] to [Sebastião José de Carvalho e Melo], Vienna, 25 September 1750, 'Correspondência entre o duque Manuel Teles da Silva e Sebastião José de Carvalho e Melo', edited by Carlos da Silva Tarouca, S.J., *Anais da Academia Portuguêsa da História* (*AAP*) 2nd series, vol. VI (Lisbon, 1955) 277–422, citations from 313–15.

[2] Manuel Nunes Dias, 'Fomento Ultramarino e Mercantilismo: A Companhia Geral do Grão Pará e Maranhão 1755–1778', I, *Revista de História* (*RHSP*), No. 66 (São Paulo, April–June 1966) 426; Moses Bensabat Amzalak *Do estudo e da evolução das doutrinas económicas em Portugal* (Lisbon, 1928) 88–98; [Teles da Silva] to [Carvalho e Melo] Vienna, 3 November 1755, *AAP*, 346–8.

[3] J. Lúcio d'Azevedo, *O marquês de Pombal e a sua época* (2nd edition, Lisbon, 1922), 40.

[4] Marcus Cheke, *Dictator of Portugal, a life of the Marquis of Pombal 1699–1782* (London, 1938) 33.

[5] [Teles da Silva] to [Carvalho e Melo], Schönbrunn, 25 July 1757, *AAP*, 379.

shrewd and systematic, and the same shrewdness was evident in his private affairs. From a family of country gentry, notorious for doctored genealogies, he had suffered personal rebuffs as a young man at court.[1] In the face of bitter opposition, however, he had married Theresa de Noronha, a widowed niece of the Count of Arcos, an arrangement which related him to the high nobility.[2] His second marriage to the Countess Daun in Austria brought the personal blessing of the Empress who counted him among her 'ancient friends'. In Vienna the Portuguese envoy's 'skill, uprightness, amiability, and especially his great patience' had won the praise of all at court according to the French minister. Maria Theresa herself told Carvalho e Melo's wife that she owed the 'preservation of the monarchy' to the Daun family.[3] It was Maria Anna of Austria, the Queen Regent of Portugal, who first recalled Carvalho e Melo from Vienna to join the ministry in Lisbon.[4]

The diminished stature of the Iberian nations in the eighteenth century had forced both Spanish and Portuguese statesmen to face the formidable problem of modernization. It became increasingly evident that governmental efficiency and imperial consolidation were essential if either country was to retain its influence in a competitive and jealous world. Carvalho e Melo was in London during the critical years between 1738 and 1745, the era of the war of the Spanish Main and Vernon's attack on Cartagena. It was a period crucial to the crystalization of imperial ideas and mythology in Britain, and inevitably brought to the forefront of Carvalho e Melo's mind those long held preoccupations about the future of the Portuguese territories. The envoy's concern was aggravated by the deep offense given to his own sensibilities by the casual way in which the British took the Anglo-Portuguese relationship for granted, and his suspicion that the 'envy of our Brazil so strong in English hearts', as he put it, would lead them to an attack on Portuguese America.[5]

Carvalho e Melo set out to investigate the causes, techniques and

[1] Ercília Pinto, *O marquês de Pombal, lavrador e autodidacta em Souré* (Coimbra, 1967) 12, 29, 34.
[2] John Athelstone Smith, *The Marquis of Pombal* (2 vols., London 1843) I, 42; Cheke, *Dictator of Portugal*, 17, 19, 60.
[3] 'Correspondence of Maria Theresa with the countess of Oeiras', appendix, Smith, *Marquis of Pombal*, II, 376–7; also I, 55–6.
[4] Antônio Ferrão, 'O marquês de Pombal e os meninos de Palhavã', Academia das Sciências de Lisboa, *Estudos Pombalinos*, 1st series, No. 1 (Coimbra, 1923).
[5] 'Ofício...[Carvalho e Melo], London, 8 July 1741, *Revista do Instituto Histórico e Geográfico Brasileiro (RIHGB)* IV (2nd edition, Rio de Janeiro, 1863) 504–14; Richard Koebner, *Empire* (2nd edition, New York, 1961) 82; Vincent T. Harlow, *The Founding of the Second British Empire 1763–1793* (2 vols., London, 1952, 1964) II, 626–30; and the classic study by Richard Pares, *War and Trade in the West Indies 1739–1763* (London, 1936).

mechanisms of British commercial and naval superiority, and during his sojourn in London succeeded in obtaining a most detailed appreciation of the British position. His remarkable library in London reflected his interests. With the books of Thomas Mun, William Petty, Charles Davenant, Charles King, Joshua Gee, Joshua Child, select reports on colonies, trade, mines, woolen manufactories, specialized tracts on sugar, tobacco, fisheries, parliamentary acts of tonnage and poundage, shipping and navigation, fraud in customs houses, the book of rates, ordinances of the British marine, and above all, with a heavy concentration of works on the English trading companies, his collection was a veritable treasure house of mercantilist classics.[1]

Out of his extensive reading and his personal observation Carvalho e Melo came to see the control Britain exercised over his country not only as the root cause of the social and economic malaise of the Portuguese nation, but also as one of the prime causes of the rapid advances of the British economy. He believed the Cromwellian treaty of 1654 had fixed on the newly independent Portugal a system of control which had made her more a slave of English interest than ever she had been of Spain. The English had achieved possession without dominion. It was a relationship which enabled them to absorb the vast riches which had come after the discovery of gold and diamonds in Brazil, and Carvalho e Melo held that the colossal capital the mines produced almost wholly passed to Britain.

This great influx of Brazilian gold to Britain had provided in Carvalho e Melo's opinion the mean for the creation of her formidable marine and vigorous arts and manufactories. The increase of bullion and circulating medium in Britain had stimulated agriculture, raised land values, and brought about the rejuvenation of manufacturing industry. And Portugal was concerned also with the results of these changes, for the Portuguese market was a guaranteed and lucrative outlet for British manufactured goods. Portugal in fact had allowed her riches to be used against herself, and the wealth of the mines were hence chimerical to her. 'The negroes that work the mines of Brazil must be clothed by England', Carvalho e Melo observed, 'thus the value of their produce becomes relative to the price of cloth.' It did not interest Britain whether the political situation in Portugal was good, indeed the opposite was the case. The effects of the system of control without responsibility had been the weakening and

---

[1] Based on the catalogues of Carvalho e Melo's books in London, BNLCP, codices 165, 167, 342, 343. Most of these works were in French editions or manuscript translations as Carvalho e Mello does not appear to have acquired enough English to read them in the originals.

discrediting of the Portuguese government machine and the moral and intellectual viability of Portuguese society.[1]

There was a great deal of truth in the new minister's diagnosis, and by placing the problems squarely into the broad imperial framework the connections and interrelationships between the issues at stake became evident. The prosperity of metropolitan Portugal in the mid-eighteenth century depended directly on the fluctuations of the colonial economy. The gold, sugar, and tobacco of Brazil formed the basis of the South Atlantic commercial complex. Sugar and tobacco provided profitable re-exports to Spain; gold a means to balance the unfavorable trade with the north and pay for the import of wood and grain.[2] 'The two cities of Lisbon and Oporto may be justly considered as the two eyes of Portugal', commented the traveller Arthur Costigan, 'for here centre the whole riches of the country and all their trade with foreign nations, and their own possessions in the Brazils; upon which last especially depends their whole existence as a people, and the immediate support of the throne.'[3] During the decade 1740–50, in the port of Lisbon alone, the annual movement of shipping surpassed 800 vessels, of which about 300 were Portuguese, and a third of these directly engaged in trade to Brazil.[4]

Specialization among the Brazilian regions was reflected by a specialization of products carried by the fleets. The Rio fleet brought gold and substantial shipments of hides and silver. From Pernambuco came wood and sugar. The fleets of the north, of Grão Pará and Maranhão carried cacao. The riches of Bahia were legendary. A fleet of thirty to forty ships left each year for Lisbon with cargoes of gold, silver, diamonds, jasper,

---

[1] This synopsis of Carvalho e Melo's views is based on a wide reading of his instructions, memorials, and observations, in particular the extracts from his writings in Smith, *Marquis of Pombal* I, 82–6, 109–26, and the 'discurso político' in the Arquivo Histórico Ultramarino Lisbon (AHU) códice 1227.

[2] For the Portuguese grain trade, Vitorino Magalhães Godinho, *Prix et Monnaies au Portugal 1750–1850* (Paris, 1955) 147–9; for Spanish–Portuguese trade, Jean François Bourgoing, *Voyage de ci-devani duc du Chatelet en Portugal...* (2 vols., Paris, 1798, 1808) I, 228; comments on the importation of wood from northern Europe, Francisco Xavier de Mendonça Furtado to Sr Fernando de Lavra, 26 January 1752, and [Mendonça Furtado] to [Carvalho e Melo], 15 July 1757, *A Amazônia na era Pombalina. Correspondência inédita do Governador e capitão-general do estado do Grão Pará e Maranhão, Francisco Xavier de Mendonça Furtado 1751–1759* (Instituto Histórico e Geográfico Brasileiro, 3 vols., Rio de Janeiro, 1963); hereinafter cited as *Correspondência inédita*, I, 214–15; III, 1119–20.

[3] Arthur William Costigan, *Sketches of Society and Manners in Portugal* (2 vols., London, 1787) I, 285.

[4] Jorge Borges de Macedo, 'Portugal e a economia "pombalina": temas e hipoteses', *RHSP*, No. 19 (July–September 1954,) 83.

cacao, balsam, cotton, tobacco and sugar.[1] So acute was the reliance on Brazil that D. Luís da Cunha foresaw the transfer of the court to Rio de Janeiro. The King would take the title 'Emperor of the West' and appoint a viceroy to rule in Lisbon. In the recommendation composed in 1736 for the use of Carvalho e Melo's uncle, Marco Antônio de Azevedo Coutinho, on his appointment as foreign secretary, D. Luís da Cunha had envisioned a Portuguese Empire in America extending from the Plata and Paraguay to north of the river Amazon. 'It is safer and more convenient to be where one has everything in abundance', he wrote, 'than where one had to wait for what one wants.'[2]

A major mechanism linking the colonial system to a developing world economy was Anglo-Portuguese commerce. By the Methuen treaty of 1703, English woolen goods entered Lisbon and Oporto free of duty, and in return, Portuguese wines received advantages on the English market. During the first half of the eighteenth century the trade was greatly in Britain's favor and the profits for individuals high.[3] Woolen cloth made up two-thirds of the total British export, and from 1756–60 Port wine composed in value 72 per cent of the total wine consumption in England.[4] Since the early 1730s the great influx of gold and diamonds from Brazil had exaggerated the imbalance of Anglo-Portuguese exchange.[5] Deficits

---

[1] For background and development of Atlantic fleet system, Frédéric Mauro, *Le Portugal et l'Atlantique au XVIIe siècle 1570–1670* (Paris, 1960); fleet specialization, Vitorino Magalhães Godinho, 'Le Portugal, les flottes du sucre et les flottes de l'or 1670–1770', *Annales-économies-sociétés-civilisations*, v année, No. 2 (April–June, 1950) 184–97; The Bahia fleet, Johan Brelim, *De passagem pelo Brasil e Portugal em 1756* (translation from Swedish by Carlos Perição de Almeida, Lisbon, 1955) 106.

[2] Academia das Sciências de Lisboa, *Instruções inéditas de D. Luís da Cunha a Marco Antônio de Azevedo Coutinho, revistas por Pedro de Azevedo e prefaciadas por Antônio Baião* (Coimbra, 1929) 211, 214, 215; C. R. Boxer, *The Golden Age of Brazil 1695–1750* (Berkeley and Los Angeles, 1962) 323–4.

[3] Background on Methuen Treaty, A. D. Francis, *The Methuens and Portugal, 1691–1708* (London, 1966); and Alan K. Manchester, *British Preeminence in Brazil* (Chapel Hill, 1933) 24; For an account of an individual merchant involved in the Portugal trade, Lucy S. Sutherland, *A London Merchant 1695–1774* (Oxford, 1933).

[4] A. B. Wallis Chapman 'The Commercial relations of England and Portugal 1487–1807', *Transactions of the Royal Historical Society*, 3rd series, vol. I, (1907) 177; Jorge Borges de Macedo, *Problemas de História da Indústria Portuguesa no século XVIII* (Lisbon, 1963) 48.

[5] 'Destinations of exports from England and Wales', Table v, and 'Sources of imports into England and Wales', Table vi, Elizabeth Boody Schumpeter with an introduction by T. S. Ashton, *English Overseas Trade Statistics* (Oxford, 1960) 17–20; Macedo, *Problemas*, 46–47, 53; H. E. S. Fisher, 'Anglo-Portuguese Trade 1700–1770', *The Economic History Review*, 2nd series, vol. XVI (1963) 229, (republished in W. E. Minchinton, ed., *The Growth of English Overseas Trade in the 17th and 18th Centuries* [London, 1969] 144–64; C. R. Boxer, 'Brazilian Gold and British Traders in the First Half of the Eighteenth Century', *Hispanic American Historical Review (HAHR)* vol. XLIX, No. 3 (August 1969) 455–72. For a more detailed discussion of Anglo-Portuguese trade see H. E. S. Fisher, *The Portugal Trade. A*

could be made up and the purchase of foreign goods facilitated by the outflow of bullion which as Henry Feilding observed, 'Portugal distributes so liberally over Europe'.[1]

Throughout the first half of the eighteenth century only Holland and Germany surpassed Portugal as consumers of British exports, and it was to be only during the most critical moments of the Seven Years' War that English shipping in the port of Lisbon fell below 50 per cent of the total.[2] The value of the Portugal trade to Britain was obvious and well known. 'By this treaty we gain a greater Ballance from Portugal, than from any other country whatsoever', wrote Charles King.[3] Others viewed the relationship with less favor. The Lisbon earthquake of 1755 could be turned to advantage claimed the pamphleteer Ange Goudar, if only Portugal took the opportunity to break away from the rapacious English connection.[4] The French foreign minister, Choiseul, wrote bluntly five years later: 'Portugal must be regarded as an English colony.'[5]

The ease with which bullion could be remitted by British Man-of-War and Falmouth packet owed much to the long tradition of British commerce in Portugal. The English factories or commercial communities in Lisbon and Oporto possessed a legal and privileged status that dated from the seventeenth century. The treaty of 1654 guaranteed the English not only the 'same liberties, privileges, and exemptions as the Portuguese in metropolitan and colonial commerce', but also provided for religious toleration and by a secret article prohibited the raising of customs duties on British goods above 23 per cent. Parts of the treaty always remained dead letters, particularly those related to the presence of English merchants in the Portuguese possessions, but the 1654 and subsequent treaties had provided a favorable environment for the creation of the state of semi-colonial dependency in which mid-eighteenth century Portugal found herself with relation to her northern ally. The factory in 1750 contained many old established and influential British companies: among them Bristow, Ward and Co., the agents of John Bristow of London; Burrell, Ducket and Hardy, the agents of Burrell and Raymond; Chase, Wilson,

---

Study of Anglo-Portuguese Commerce 1700–1770 (London, 1971) and an important theoretical and statistical analysis by S. Sideri, *Trade and Power. Informal Colonialism in Anglo-Portuguese Relations* (Rotterdam University Press, 1970).

[1] Henry Feilding, *The Journal of a Voyage to Lisbon* (editor, Austin Dobson, Oxford, 1907) 99.
[2] Schumpeter, *Trade Statistics*, 17; Macedo, *RHSP*, 90.
[3] Charles King, *The British Merchant* (3rd edition, 3 vols., London, 1748) III, 1–78.
[4] Ange Goudar, *Relation historique du tremblement de terre...* (1756).
[5] Cited by Allan Christelow, 'Economic background to the Anglo-Spanish War of 1762', *Journal of Modern History*, vol. XVIII (March, 1946), 27.

and Co., agents of T. Chase.[1] 'A great Body of His Majesty's subjects reside at Lisbon, rich, opulent, and every day increasing their fortunes and enlarging their dealings', remarked Lord Tyrawly during a special mission to Portugal in 1752.[2] 'It is a common observation of the natives', Costigan observed, 'that excepting of the lowest conditions of life, you shall not meet anyone on foot some hours of the violent heat every day, but dogs and Englishmen.'[3]

Brazilian gold was not the only link between the English and the colonial complex. 'The foreign merchant houses by means of their great capital had made themselves absolute mistress of metropolitan and colonial commerce', commented a Portuguese contemporary. 'Few or rare were the Portuguese merchants in a condition to do business with their own funds, none with goods that were not foreign. All the commerce of Brazil was made on credit and the greater part by salesmen of the foreign houses and by *commissários volantes* who took manufactures from Portugal to America and did business on the account of the foreigner receiving a commission for their work and a bonus for extra service.'[4] The *commissários volantes* – Portuguese itinerant traders – who bought goods in the metropolis, sold them personally in America, and returned with the proceeds, were one of the essential elements in the transatlantic commercial connection. These itinerant traders often traveled under false pretenses and carried merchandise in their shipboard accommodation, avoiding outlays for commissions, freight charges and warehousing.[5]

A high proportion of the British manufactured goods exported to Brazil via Portugal went straight into the Spanish colonies as contraband. The result was important, for the functioning of the system at the height of its prosperity brought silver to Britain: vital to English commerce in Asia. Bougainville estimated that at least thirty coasting vessels were

---

[1] Sir Richard Lodge, 'The English Factory at Lisbon', *Transactions of the Royal Historical Society*, 4th series, XVI (1933) 225–6; A. R. Walford, *The British Factory* (Lisbon, 1940) 20; Sutherland, *A London Merchant*, 25.

[2] Walford, *British Factory*, 20. Lord Tyrawly who had served under Marlborough was appointed envoy at Lisbon in 1728. He was to remain there for thirteen years, and was considered by Horace Walpole 'singularly licentious, even for the courts of Russia and Portugal'.

[3] Costigan, *Sketches*, II, 29.

[4] 'Súplica a Rainha para que conceda a prorogação que pede a Companhia do [Grão] Pará [e Maranhão] e não a extinga nem a de Pernambuco, com vasta exposição de motivos e alegando que o comércio do Reino para o Brasil se acha quase todo em poder das nações extrangeiras' anon., n.d., (1777?), in 'Apontamentos vários sobre a Companhia de Grão Pará e Maranhão', The Arquivo Ultramarino collection of transcripts in the Instituto Histórico e Geográfico Brasileiro, Rio de Janeiro (IHGB/AUC) I-1-8, f. 43.

[5] 'Relatório do marquês de Lavradio', *RIGHB*, IV (2nd ed., 1863) 459; J. Lúcio d'Azevedo, *Estudos de história Paraense* (Pará 1893) 74.

employed in the contraband trade between Brazil and the Plata.[1] British participation was 'very advantageous and profitable', and much of the silver returning to Europe on the Brazil fleets was re-shipped to England.[2] Nor was it only the officially favored direct contraband with Buenos Aires that brought silver into the system. Extensive fraud throughout the mining zones of the interior in the returns of the royal fifth provided the substance for an inter-American contraband of considerable proportions. In fact according to Alexandre de Gusmão, the Brazilian born secretary of the late monarch, most of the gold production escaped official fiscalization. The miners themselves were not primarily responsible for the extensive flow of contraband gold. It was in the hands of the estate owners, office holders, ecclesiastics, and preeminently the convoy merchants who supplied manufactures, horses, cattle and slaves to the mining zones, that gold evaded government control and stimulated illegal commerce. Of particular notoriety were the ecclesiastics who, owing to their exemption from search at the check points, could carry large quantities without hindrance. Contraband gold from Minas Gerais was taken to Buenos Aires or, like that of Cuiabá and Mato Grosso, into the nearby Spanish provinces. Here it was exchanged, at a favorable rate, for silver, which was returned to the Brazilian port cities and there used to purchase contraband manufactures, either from the commissaries or from the officers and seamen of the fleets.[3] A vast unofficial and illegal commerce, using the very fleet system as a cover and means for export and remittance, thus paralleled and may even at times have surpassed the legitimate traffic. It was a situation encouraged by the weakening of state power that characterized the last years of João V.[4]

[1] *A voyage round the world performed by the order of His Most Christian Majesty in the years 1766, 1767, 1768, 1769, by Lewis de Bougainville, translated from the French by John Reinhold Forster* (London, 1772) 82–3.

[2] Allan Christelow, 'Great Britain and the trades from Cadiz and Lisbon to Spanish America and Brazil 1759–1782', *HAHR*, xxvii (February 1947) 12; Olga Pantaleão, 'A penetração comercial da Inglaterra na América Espanhola 1715–1783'. *Boletim LXII da Faculdade de Filosofia Ciências e Letras da Universidade de São Paulo* (São Paulo, 1946).

[3] 'Reparos sobre a disposição da Ley de 3 de Dezembro de 1750, a respeito do novo methodo da cobrança do Quinto; abolindo a da Capitação, Escriptas para ver o Fidelissimo Senhor Rey Dom José I, por Alexandre de Gusmão', Lisbon, 18 December 1750, IHGB/AUC, 1-2-39, f. 69. Gusmão, educated in Bahia, Coimbra, and the Sorbonne, became secretary to João V in 1730. For his considerable influence on imperial policy and participation in the negotiation of the treaty of Madrid see David M. Davidson, 'How the Brazilian West was Won: Freelance and State on the Mato Grosso Frontier, *ca*. 1737–1752', *The Colonial Roots of Modern Brazil: Papers of the Newberry Library Conference 1969* (ed. Dauril Alden. Berkeley and Los Angeles, 1972); Also Jaime Cortesão, *Alexandre de Gusmão e o tratado de Madrid (1750)* (9 vols., Rio de Janeiro, 1950–1963).

[4] Jorge Borges de Macedo, *A situação económica no tempo de Pombal* (Oporto, 1951) 61, 69–9.

The great prosperity of colonial commerce and contraband and the relative freedom of trade was not without repercussions. The avoidance of freight and other charges by the *commissários volantes* allowed them to undercut the established merchants of the port cities who received consignments from their correspondents in the metropolis on a regular and legal basis. The inevitable result was the glutting of the market, and this in turn upset the credit mechanism between the colony and metropolis, with serious consequences within Brazil itself. Overstocking and price cutting in the Brazilian market was of little concern to the foreign suppliers of credit and merchandise in the metropolis, for as the factory pointed out, 'it is all one to Great Britain provided the goods are disposed of'.[1] The difficulties facing the established merchants in Brazil, however, adversely affected the agricultural producers of the hinterland. Forced to call on their credit and increase interest rates, the established merchants lacked ready cash to buy the tobacco, sugar, cattle, and leather of the interior, and their means of exchange in goods had been hopelessly debased. The interlopers lacked incentive, and the time, to deal leniently with the tobacco and sugar planters who now became their debtors. Employing judicial process and violent foreclosure their methods placed severe pressure on farmers and sugar mill owners faced with the necessity for large capital investment in processing machinery and slaves.[2] The quick profits in silver and gold which went to the itinerant traders and the foreign factors and merchants in Lisbon, of which they were little more than the hired salesmen, seriously disrupted regular colonial commerce.

The activities of the interlopers and contrabandists were not confined to the principal trading centers of Bahia, Rio de Janeiro, and Pernambuco. The illicit commerce in Amazon drugs and spices was highly profitable.[3] And the situation in Pará and Maranhão was complicated by the commercial activities of the religious orders. The colonists of the far north felt themselves shut off from the benefits of Amazon trade, and they blamed the religious orders' possessive protection of the Indian for depriving them of labor. The alternative to Indian manpower, imported

---

[1] 'Memórias do Consul e Factória Británnica na Côrte de Lisboa...' (1755–66) BNLCP, códice 94, f. 46v.

[2] 'Súplica a Rainha...', IHGB/AUC, 1-1-8, f. 43; 'Demonstrações da junta [Company of Pernambuco]', 20 April 1780, IHGB/AUC, 1-2-11, f. 31, 47; 'Discurso preliminár, histórico e introductivo, com natureza de discrição da comarca e cidade da Bahia', (*ca.* 1790) *Anais da Biblioteca Nacional*, Rio de Janeiro (*ABNRJ*) xxvii, 127–282; [Carvalho e Melo] to [Mendonça Furtado], 4 August 1755, *Correspondência inédita*, ii, 796–7.

[3] d'Azevedo, *Estudos*, 37.

African slaves, were exorbitantly priced. The Jesuits in particular, by virtue of the number and value of their properties, the temporal government of over twenty mission villages (*aldeias*), and the labor use of many other Indian settlements, possessed a capital and power feared and coveted by the inhabitants of Pará and Maranhão.[1]

Not only did the missionaries preach (for with ranches containing over 100,000 head of cattle on the island of Marajó alone, rural estates producing sugar, and the fruits of Indian collecting expeditions into the Amazon forests for native drugs, cloves, cacao, cinnamon), but they also managed a mercantile operation of great proportions resulting from years of capital accumulation, careful reinvestment and development. At the imminent arrival of the ten to eleven ship fleet from Lisbon or Oporto the commodities were conveyed by fleets of canoes to the Atlantic seaboard. Collected in the warehouse of the Jesuit *colégio*, exempt from taxation and customs dues, they were marketed by means of a fair maintained while the fleet was in port. The products were sold to ship captains and commissaries from Portugal, and a smaller portion was consigned to the metropolis in the Company of Jesus' name and under its stamp. For fifteen years Paulo da Silva Nunes, who represented the interests of the colonists of Maranhão in Lisbon, had reflected their irritation and helplessness by constant opposition to the Jesuits and propaganda against the Company.[2]

The difficulties facing the established interests in metropolis and colony were directly linked to the prosperity of those English and other foreign merchants who provided the credit and goods which in the hands of their Portuguese collaborators – the *commissários volantes*, ship

[1] [Mendonça Furtado] to [Carvalho e Melo], 24 January 1754, *Correspondência inédita*, II, 460–4; Dauril Alden, 'Economic Aspects of the expulsion of the Jesuits from Brazil: A Preliminary Report', Henry H. Keith and S. F. Edwards, eds., *Conflict and Continuity in Brazilian Society* (Columbia, South Carolina, 1969) 25–65.

[2] J. Lúcio d'Azevedo, *Os Jesuitas no Grão Pará, suas missões e a colonização* (Lisbon, 1901) 196, 200, 248–9; 'Calculo dos excessivas negociações que os Reverendos Missionarios, os seus Prelados e Communidades fazem com o serviço dos Indios e Indias nas lavradoras e fabricas que tem os 57 aldeas de S. Magde chamados as missões do Maranhão e Grão Pará junto a elles nos certões...', n.d. (1755?) IHGB/AUC, 1-1-8, f. 290–309; Manuel Nunes Dias, 'Fomento Ultramarino e Mercantilismo: A companhia Geral de Grão Pará e Maranhão', II, *RHSP*, No. 67 (July–September 1966) 96; Roberto C. Simonsen, *História económica do Brasil* 1500–1820 (5th ed., São Paulo, 1967) 324–6, 329; Arthur Cezar Ferreira Reis, *A Amazônia que os Portugueses revelaram* (Rio de Janeiro, 1956) 50; For further details of Jesuit activities in Amazonia and throughout Brazil see the monumental study by Serafim Leite, *História da companhia de Jesus no Brasil* (10 vols., Lisbon, Rio de Janeiro, 1938–50). For a judicious treatment of the expulsion of the Jesuits from Latin America as a whole see Magnus Morner's introduction to his collected readings in the Borzoi series, *The Expulsion of the Jesuits from Latin America* (New York, 1965) 3–30.

captains and crews – provided the substance of the itinerant trade and contraband connection across the Atlantic and into the interior of Brazil. Within the Atlantic commercial complex the problems of the debtors of the colonial hinterland, the unequal competition facing established merchants, and the high profits of flying commissary and contrabandist were intimately interrelated. Great prosperity and weakened state power, given the privileged position of the English and foreign merchant corporations in Lisbon and Oporto, encouraged the penetration of foreign credit and goods throughout the Luso-Brazilian system. The consequence was to upset the credit mechanism and regular exchange between Portugal and Brazil, prejudicing established interests in metropolis and colony, and producing a conflict of interests within the Luso-Brazilian entrepreneurial framework. Itinerant trader and contrabandist contributed to the increasing denationalization of Luso-Brazilian commerce. 'A sensible Portuguese writer', commented Costigan, 'compares, not unaptly, their whole Kingdom to one of that sort of spiders which has a large body (the capital) with extremely long, thin, feeble legs, reaching to a great distance, but are of no sort of use to it, and which it is hardly able to move.'[1]

The Portuguese commercial complex, however, possessed certain important characteristics, and Carvalho e Melo's recognition of them opened up possibilities of effective political action in the national interest. The fundamental metropolitan contribution to Anglo-Portuguese trade was Port wine. The colonial contribution was gold and silver bullion. Thus as far as the vast favorable balance of Britain was concerned, the principal channels of trade ran along very special lines and in a very specific direction, either to Minas Gerais, the principal gold producing region, or to the contraband network with Spanish America via Buenos Aires, or to the inter-American gold–silver network of contraband which again involved Buenos Aires and the interior mining zones. The channels of trade were not linked to the staple colonial commodities – sugar and tobacco – for these Britain obtained from her own colonies. So that in a very real way the means and direction of exchange precluded any interest of the British in the rational exploitation or valorization of the basic Brazilian staples, while the methods used for the distribution of British goods in these regions actively disrupted agricultural production.

One of the first measures of the new administration was to reform the methods of fiscalizing the gold production of the Brazilian mines. The

---

[1] Costigan, *Sketches*, I, 285.

collection of the seignorial tribute of the fifth part of the total production was to be organized according to the methods proposed by the inhabitants of Minas Gerais to the Count of Galveias in 1734. During December of 1750 the crown accepted the 1734 proposition which had offered a basic minimum contribution of 100 arrobas (1465.6 kilograms) of gold per annum, to be guaranteed by the municipal councils (*câmaras*) whose task it was to levy a per capita local tax (*derrama*) to make up the difference should the quota not be filled. In the principal place of the administrative regions (*comarcas*) were to be established foundry houses (*casas de fundição*) where all the gold was to be cast. The foundry houses were to be administered by an intendant and fiscal, chosen not from among the class of magistrates but from among the most substantial local property owners nominated by a plurality of votes in the municipal councils and approved by the superior crown magistrate (*ouvidor*) of the district. These officials were to work closely with the administrators of the contract of entrances (*entradas*), the captaincy import taxes, which had been farmed out by the overseas council to private speculators in return for an agreed sum. The royal decree setting up the new system also introduced vigorous measures for the control of contraband and provided incentives for those who cooperated with the authorities. 'All people, of whatever quality, status, or condition', discovered removing gold dust or gold bars not cast by the state from the mining zone were to lose all the contraband in their possession, a half being retained by the treasury and a half paid to the informant or discoverer of the contravention as a reward. To make fraud less easy goldsmiths were expelled from the captaincy in 1751. The foundry houses were in action by 1752 and during the coming decade this reformed method of collecting the royal fifth rendered the treasury an average of over 104 arrobas of gold per annum. In the metropolis the laws against the re-export of gold and precious stones were revived.[1] The new government also attempted to bring desperately needed protection to the commerce and producers of the two most important primary products of Brazil: sugar and tobacco. Following preliminary

---

[1] 'Alvará... para a cobrança do direito senhorial dos quintos...' 3 December 1750, coleção Josephina, BNLCP, códice 453, f. 47–50v; 'Bando publicado...para...sahirem...os Ourives', Vila Rica, 31 July 1751, IHGB, Lata 8, doc. 26; 'Coleção da casa dos Contos de Ouro Prêto, documentos avulsos', Arquivo Nacional, Rio de Janeiro, (ANRJ) Latas 99/3, 86/3, 94/2; AHU, codice 311/15; 'Regimento das Intendencias e casas de fundiçao', Coelho e Sousa, José Roberto Monteiro de Campos, ed. *Systema, ou colleção dos regimentos reaes, contem os regimentos pertencentes a fazenda real, justiças, e militares...* (7 vols., Lisbon, 1783) IV, 503–16; For previous experience with *casas de fundição* in Minas and statistics of the amount of gold handled, see C. R. Boxer, *The Golden Age of Brazil* (Berkeley and Los Angeles, 1962) 197–200, 336–8.

laws in the interests of regular production and marketing during early 1751, on 1 April, inspection houses [*casas de inspeção*] were established in Bahia, Rio de Janeiro, Pernambuco and Pará, to guarantee 'the good and just price of these two most important articles'. With royal nominees the inspectors were to include representatives of the merchant community and of the sugar and tobacco producers. The businessmen 'of those accustomed to buy the sugar and tobacco' for remission to the metropolis, the sugar mill owner (*senhor de engenho*) and tobacco planter, were selected through their respective municipal councils by a plurality of votes.[1] The government brought a more direct protection to the debtor of the hinterland. In 1752 any proprietor who owned more than thirty slaves in Minas Gerais was exempted from foreclosure.[2] Four years later legislation was enacted to prohibit the debt collecting practices which had contributed to the disruption of the sugar and tobacco industries in Pernambuco.[3]

Strategic and security problems contributed to the factors focusing the attention of the new administration on America. The treaty of Madrid, signed in January 1750, upheld the Portuguese claim to the Amazon basin. This vast region, almost a third of the land area of South America, had been penetrated and tenuously occupied by Luso-Brazilian missionaries and miners drawn into the interior of the sub-continent by visions of converting the heathen or in the search of El Dorado.[4] The Lisbon government faced the unavoidable task of implementing the agreements which called for the evacuation of the Jesuits and their Indian neophytes from the Uruguayan missions, and envisioned a survey of the line of demarcation between Spanish and Portuguese America by two joint commissions. Gomes Freire de Andrada was appointed Portuguese commissioner for the south, and to the north Carvalho e Melo's own brother, Francisco Xavier de Mendonça Furtado.[5]

The 'very secret' letter to Gomes Freire supplementing his general instructions revealed one of the most notable of Carvalho e Melo's aims and hopes for Portuguese America. 'As the power and wealth of all

[1] 'Regimento...casas de inspeção...' 1 April 1751, IHGB, lata 71, doc. 17.
[2] Simonsen, *História económica*, 280.
[3] 'Demonstrações da junta [Company of Pernambuco]', IHGB/AUC, 1-2-11, f. 47–8.
[4] Arthur C. Ferreira Reis, *O processo histórico da economia Amazonense* (Rio de Janeiro, 1944), and his *A expanção Portuguesa na Amazônia nos séculos XVII e XVIII* (Rio de Janeiro, 1959); also Simonsen, *História económica*, 303.
[5] Dauril Alden, *Royal Government in Colonial Brazil with Special Reference to the Administration of the Marquis of Lavradio, 1769–1779* (Berkeley and Los Angeles, 1968) 86–91. Gomes Freire was governor of Rio de Janeiro from 1733–63, from 1748 also exercising authority over Minas Gorais, São Paulo, Goiás, Santa Catarina, Rio Grande do Sul, and Colonia do Sacramento, a concentration of authority which in many respects foreshadowed the moving of the viceregal capital from Bahia to Rio in 1763.

countries consists principally in the number and multiplication of the people that inhabit it', he wrote, 'this number and multiplication of people is most indispensible now on the frontiers of Brazil for their defense...' As it was not 'humanly possible' to provide the necessary people from the metropolis and adjacent islands without converting them 'entirely into deserts', it was essential to abolish 'all differences between Indians and Portuguese', to attract the Indians from the Uruguay missions, and encourage their marriage with Europeans.[1]

Five months earlier the instructions to the new governor of Grão Pará and Maranhão had reflected the same compulsion. Francisco Xavier de Mendonça Furtado was recommended to secure the liberation of the Indian, to introduce married couples from the Azores, and to stimulate the commerce in African slaves. With the cooperation of the missions he was to 'cultivate, people, and secure the vast territory of Pará and Maranhão'.[2] Carvalho e Melo's brother set about his task with energy. He attempted, as he described his activity later, to implement 'positive orders for the civilization of the Indians, to enable them to acquire a knowledge of the value of money, something which they had never seen, in the interests of commerce and farming, and...familiarity with Europeans, not only by learning the Portuguese language, but by encouraging marriage between Indians and Portuguese, which were all the most proper means to those important ends and together make for the common interest and the well-being of the state.'[3]

Thus within a year of Carvalho e Melo's assumption of high office the priorities of the new government in its mercantile and imperial policy had been clearly outlined. The vital props of the Luso-Brazilian commercial system, sugar, tobacco, and gold, were to be protected by regulation and the defense of established interests. A vigorous attempt was made to rationalize and fortify the collection machinery of the major royal tribute, the royal fifth. The colonial debtor was defended from violent foreclosure. Inspection houses were established to regulate the prices of the colonial staples. And fundamental to the whole concept of the future of the American territory, the security of the colony was to be assured by population, and as this could not be realized by massive

---

[1] 'Carta secretíssima de [Carvalho e Melo] para Gomes Freire de Andrada, para servir de suplemento as instruções que lhe foram enviadas sobre a forma da execução do tratado preliminár de limites, assinado em Madrid a 13 de Janeiro de 1750', Lisbon, 21 September 1751, Marcos Carneiro de Mendonça, *O Marquês de Pombal e o Brasil* (São Paulo, 1960) 188.

[2] 'Instruções régias, públicas, e secretas para [Mendonça Furtado] capitão general do estado do Grão Pará e Maranhão', Lisbon, 31 May 1751, *Correspondência inédita*, I, 26–31.

[3] Mendonça Furtado, instructions to Conde de Cunha, 18 March 1761, *RIHGB*, XXXV, pt. I (1872) 216.

European emigration, it was to be achieved by the liberation and Europeanization of the Indian.

The measures and the preoccupations of the Portuguese administration received warm commendation from Vienna. Writing to Carvalho e Melo during August 1752, the Duke Silva-Tarouca recalled the imperial ideas of D. Luís da Cunha, his colleague at the Utrecht negotiations.

'The Kings of Portugal could come...to have an Empire like China' in Brazil, he observed, that would be 'greater than France, Germany, and Hungary if they were united in one body.' If Portugal had two million people, then Portuguese America, at least thirty times greater, might sustain sixty million, equal to Padre du Halde's calculation of the population of China. Great care, therefore, must be taken to populate Portuguese America, the Duke continued. 'Moor, White, Negro, Indian, Mulatto, or Mestizo, all serve, all are men, are good if they are governed and regulated well.' From population would follow the agricultural and commercial progress desired. The Jesuits 'could serve much the intention', but it was essential to police the backlands and frontiers more effectively. The principal families ought to be linked by favors, offices, and land grants more closely to the metropolis. Above all the vast Amazon basin should be secured by troops, fortresses and good administration. 'Population to my weak understanding is everything, many thousands of leagues of deserts serve for nothing.'[1]

It was easier to envision the possibilities, than it was to make policies that produced effective action. The new method of collecting the royal fifth provoked a bitter controversy within the overseas council. Alexandre de Gusmão felt the scheme had been 'fabricated with more zeal than experience of the mines' and would fail as all other methods had to prevent contraband and fraud. The tribute would in effect fall only on the miners he believed, virtually exempting ecclesiastics, men of government, local magnates and merchants, who in fact took most of the miners' gold in return for merchandise and foodstuffs. He saw grave danger in the process of *derrama*, the per capita tax to make up the quota, which again he believed would fall heavily on the miners.[2] It was clear also that regulation and price control of sugar and tobacco would provide no real challenge to the stranglehold of foreign credit on the Luso-Brazilian system. The inspection houses were mere palliatives which did not tackle

[1] [Teles da Silva] to [Carvalho e Melo], Vienna, 12 August 1752, *AAP*, 323–9; the above paragraph is only a sketchy and fragmentary precis of this most important letter.

[2] 'Reparos sobre a disposição de ley de 3 de Dezembro de 1750...' Lisbon, 18 December 1750, IHGB/AUC, 1-2-39, f. 65, 80–7; Marcelo Caetano, *Do conselho ultramarino ao conselho do império* (Lisbon, 1943) 34.

root causes, for the difficulties facing the established agricultural and merchant groups in the colony all too obviously lay in the dominance of the foreign merchants in the metropolis. And on the far off, vast, and ill-comprehended frontiers of Brazil the sanguine hopes that the Indians, and most especially those of the Jesuit missions, would be peacefully assimilated and Europeanized proved disastrously misplaced.

Opposition from the missions of Uruguay to the implementation of the Madrid agreements led to armed clashes with Gomes Freire in 1753, and it took a full scale campaign to dislodge them by 1756.[1] The interests of the state in the liberation of the Indian collided with the most basic philosophical tenet of the protectionist Indian policy of the Jesuits. Furthermore, as the activities of Mendonça Furtado in the north soon made evident, by removing Indian labor from the control of the missions, liberation also threatened to undermine the basic source of Jesuit wealth and predominance in Amazonia. Indeed secularization was likely to mean, as the magistrate Francisco Duarte dos Santos had foreseen in 1734, that 'the *aldeias* would remain only a memory'.[2] The members of the great missionary–mercantile complex centered around the Company of Jesus in Pará and Maranhão, would not accept easily relegation to the status of mere spiritual advisors.

In his instructions of 1751, Mendonça Furtado had been required to investigate 'with great caution, circumspection, and prudence', the reputed wealth and capital of the Jesuits.[3] After his arrival in America, the governor's relations with the 'Black Robes' steadily deteriorated. During 1754, Mendonça Furtado, in a series of letters to his brother, took up the pleas of the colonists that a commercial company be formed to facilitate the supply of African labor. He recommended the foundation of a privileged trading company. To establish prosperity in Amazonia he believed it essential to dislodge the Jesuits from the 'absolute power' their control of Indian labor and the strategic position of their settlements gave them over commerce and contraband. To assert secular authority, encourage commerce, as well as to furnish African labor on easier terms than those offered by private traders, the foundation of a company with 'solid funds' appeared a logical solution. An abundant supply of Africans would make Indian slavery unnecessary, circumvent Jesuit influence, and provide crucial labor to work the land and augment commerce. This in

1 Aurélio Porto, *História das missões orientais do Uruguai* (Rio de Janeiro, 1943) vol. 1, 429–47.
2 Cited by Dauril Alden, 'Economic Aspects of the Expulsion of the Jesuits', *Conflict and Continuity*, 38–9.
3 Instruções régias...para [Mendonça Furtado] *Correspondência inédita*, 1, 26–31.

turn would increase royal revenue and help finance the new defensive system to secure the frontiers of Portuguese America.[1]

Mendonça Furtado's proposal met with a sympathetic reception in Lisbon. Already Carvalho e Melo had attempted without success to set up a monopolistic company for Asian trade on the English model. The idea from Pará provided a practical way of realizing his long term intentions. With the advice of José Francisco da Cruz, he organized the statutes of the company of Grão Pará and Maranhão, and granted to it for twenty years an absolute monopoly of navigation and the slave trade.[2] Coincident with the establishment of the first Pombaline Brazil company, on 7 June 1755, the temporal power of ecclesiastics over the Indians was suppressed, an action that removed the Indians from a state of dependency and made them free men, at least as far as the law was concerned.[3] 'One of the great public utilities that the commercial company will bring', Carvalho e Melo wrote to his brother during August, 'is the regulation of the quantities of merchandise in proportion to consumption ... because lack of this just proportion resulted necessarily in the ruin of the commerce of the national merchants in benefit of foreign merchants and nations. For private nationals buying from the foreigners without rule or measure as much as the foreigners wished to credit them, introduced in one year goods requiring three years to consume and the national merchants were ruined because they could not sell with profit.'[4]

The company had a wider and equally significant purpose. Meeting the strategic and secular necessities of particular conditions in Brazil, the Company of Grão Pará and Maranhão also provided a way of initiating the process of breaking the stranglehold of foreign credit on the Luso-Brazilian commercial system. In December 1755 the *commissários volantes* were prohibited from engaging in colonial commerce.[5] The company and the abolition of the flying commissaries formed a two handled lever to pry open the freetrade–contraband–foreign merchant

---

[1] [Mendonça Furtado] to Diogo de Mendonça Corte Real, 18 January 1754, *Correspondência inédita*, II, 456–9; [Mendonça Furtado] to [Carvalho e Melo], 26 January 1754, *ibid.*, II, 465–70.

[2] d'Azevedo, *Estudos*, 48–9; Jacome Ratton, *Recordações* (2nd edition, Coimbra, 1920) 180; Smith, *Marquis of Pombal*, I, 75, 77; Jeronimo de Viveiros, *História do comércio do Maranhão 1612–1896* (2 vols., São Luís, 1964) I, 70.

[3] Caio Prado júnior, *A formação do Brasil contemporâneo, colônia* (7th edition, São Paulo, 1963) 89; C. R. Boxer, *Race Relations in the Portuguese Colonial Empire 1415–1825* (Oxford, 1963) 98–100.

[4] [Carvalho e Melo] to [Mendonça Furtado], 4 August 1755, BNLCP, códice 262, f. 107.

[5] 'Alvará...porque...he servido prohibir que passem ao Brasil comissários volantes...' Lisbon, 11 December 1755, BNLCP, códice 453, 79v–80.

nexus. Carvalho e Melo explained the measures to Duke Silva-Tarouca, who had written enthusiastically from Vienna on receiving the company's statutes, as being the only way 'to restore to the merchant places of Portugal and Brazil the commissions of which they were deprived, and which are the principal substance of commerce, and means by which there could be established the great houses which had been lacking in Portugal since the prevalence of the interlopers'.[1]

The establishment of the monopolistic company and the economic legislation of 1755 was a deliberate action by the state to rationalize the entrepreneurial structure in favor of the large established national merchants. It was hoped that by granting them monopoly privileges they might accumulate sufficient capital to compete effectively with foreign credit in every area of Luso-Brazilian commerce. The Company of Pará and Maranhão, Carvalho e Melo told Mendonça Furtado 'was the only way to revindicate the commerce of all Portuguese America from the hands of foreigners'.[2] Within the socio-economic situation facing the administration during the 1750s, the all-powerful minister had chosen to support the established interests in the metropolis against the interlopers and contrabandists who had disrupted regular commerce and credit and aided the penetration of foreign credit throughout the Luso-Brazilian system. And by making imperial consolidation a profitable operation, he had also linked the interests of this privileged established entrepreneurial group to the interests of Empire.

The foundation of the company brought angry reactions from the British merchants in Lisbon. A fortnight before the Portuguese government had taken action over a key and sensitive point by confiscating the gold in the possession of Humphrey Bunster about to be remitted to England. The Humphrey Bunster affair opened a long and complicated test case, and established a precedent which could not fail to concern the British merchant community in Portugal. On 1 November 1755, however, the great earthquake had laid much of Lisbon in ruins and ashes. As a consequence an extra 4 per cent import tax was levied as a contribution to the rebuilding of the city. The members of the Factory were 'sensible that a breach of treaty was the only solid foundation upon which a national complaint can be granted' and they chose to interpret the imposition as a breach of the Cromwellian treaty's secret article, and as a

---

[1] [Teles da Silva] to [Carvalho e Melo] 3 November 1755, *AAP*, 348; [Carvalho e Melo] to [Teles da Silva], no date (early 1756?) *AAP*, 419–420.

[2] [Carvalho e Melo] to [Mendonça Furtado] 4 August 1755, BNLCP, códice 626, f. 90; also in *Correspondência inédita*, II, 784–8.

means of raising their complaints against Carvalho e Melo before the London Government.[1] A strong protest was forwarded to Secretary of State Fox who immediately contacted Lord Tyrawly. The report prepared by the former ambassador was distinctly unfavorable to the pretensions of the British merchants, and in retrospect it is clear that Carvalho e Melo had acted with extreme skill and foresight. For the great profitability of Luso-Brazilian commerce and contraband had produced a serious contradiction of function among the British merchants in Portugal, and it was by the careful exploitation of this conflict within the entrepreneurial structure of the Anglo-Portuguese merchant community, that Carvalho e Melo succeeded for a time in camouflaging the real intention of his measures.[2]

The late 1740s had seen the rise of a group of merchants who, while taking advantage of the privileged position of the Factory, were in real terms only tenuously related to the traditional pattern of Anglo-Portuguese commerce. Attracted by the spoils of the Portuguese and American markets they engaged in a wide variety of exchanges which served to undermine the legitimate sale of higher priced British manufactures. The tendency of English merchants to deal in French, Dutch, and Hamburg products was encouraged by the working of the very secret article designed a century before to give British manufactures a privileged position. Faced with the competition of improved French and Dutch manufactures which had retained the low valuation imposed when they were of markedly inferior quality, the 23 per cent tariff level was ceasing to work to the advantage of British exporters.[3] Lord Tyrawly himself had noted and lamented the change in the British Factory during his 1752 visit to Lisbon. The 'traditional, regular, and frugal merchants', had been challenged by 'men of a very different character', who were 'Universal traders more than English factors', and who dealt 'More or at least as Much in French goods, Hamburg linen, Sicilian corn, and other commodities of different countries than in the Produce of their Own.' The trade of the Factory had ceased to be 'Wholly an English trade', that employed 'Our own Wool, Poor, Handicrafts, and Shops...'[4] It was not surprising then that when Lord Tyrawly returned his opinion he underlined the dichotomy within the factory between the merchant as Universal trader and the merchant as English factor, and came down

---

[1] 'Memórias do consul e Factória Británnica...' BNLCP, códice 94, f. 11v. and f. 37.
[2] 'Considerations upon the affairs of Lisbon...' Tyrawly papers, published in Walford, *British Factory*, 54–70.
[3] Sutherland, *A London Merchant*, 136–8.
[4] Walford, *British Factory*, 54–6.

solidly on the side of the factors. The 'total new modelling' he recommended to make the activities of the factory 'Wholly an English trade' was not unlike the regulation Carvalho e Melo was implementing with his commercial company and economic legislation. Tyrawly reacted against the use certain English merchants were making of the factory in much the way Carvalho e Melo reacted against the use Portuguese speculators were making of the Brazil fleets. In fact Tyrawly in his report revealed a willingness to act with Carvalho e Melo and hinted that 'new regulations' had been contemplated by them in 1752. Clearly in the changed political environment of the 1750s the universal traders were in a vulnerable position. The old established English factors in Portugal might at times have been tempted to trade in non-English merchandise, and certainly entered into arrangements with *commissários volantes*, but they also had a regular and legal access to fleet traffic backed by treaty and tradition, as well as a strong interest, once the *commissários volantes* had been abolished, in the smooth functioning of the fleet system. Thus while it was not necessarily true that only universal traders had been linked to *commissários volantes*, it was a convenient assumption, and one which could be used to political advantage.

The Company of Pará and Maranhão caused no head-on collision between the British and Portuguese governments, for despite the protests of the merchants in Lisbon, there was nothing in the Company's statutes which directly attacked vital British interests. Though administered by Portuguese subjects or naturalized citizens, investment in the Company was open to all. Foreign investment was specifically welcomed and protection was guaranteed against confiscation and reprisal in case of war between Portugal and the nation of the investor concerned.[1] As compulsory agent of exchange for the Brazilian far north the Company in no way affected the equilibrium of Anglo-Portuguese commerce, and was peripheral to the main channels of trade. The founding of the monopolistic company served indirectly to undermine the interests of English merchants in Portugal, but it avoided providing an excuse for the British government to intervene on behalf of its nationals, and it did not upset the mutually beneficial flow of Anglo-Portuguese commerce. The Company and the abolition of the *commissários volantes* was on the surface in no way detrimental to those English houses engaged in supplying British goods for regular fleet traffic, and only an attack on their interests would justify action from London.

Carvalho e Melo's policy was a practical and logical one within the

[1] Macedo, *A situação económica*, 117–18; Godinho, *Prix et Monnaies*, 326.

terms of the Anglo–Portuguese economic relationship. The balance of trade might always have been unfavorable to Portugal but it was at base an exchange of manufactured goods for Portuguese raw materials and wine and as such, though one-sided, mutually beneficial. The aim of a Portuguese economic nationalist would always be to achieve reciprocity in Anglo–Portuguese exchange not its elimination. 'It was not the treaty [of Methuen] that was the cause of such pernicious effects but the infractions and abuses', Carvalho e Melo had written in his famous account of the grievances of Portuguese subjects in England.[1] He stressed to the English that all his measures had been taken with the treaties in view. His rules and economic laws, he claimed, were intended to facilitate their object, which was 'reciprocal advantages by legal means'. Any honorable businessman could see the benefits of the provisions he had made. The opposition, he said, came from those elements among the foreign merchants in Lisbon who were linked by interest to the contrabandists, and who were abusing their privileges as British citizens. They were not worthy of the protection of Great Britain. After all, he pointed out, England's own special envoy, Lord Tyrawly, had found they did not deserve such special consideration.[2]

There was certainly no unthinking anglophobia behind Carvalho e Melo's measures, based as they were on a most careful assessment of the economic and diplomatic factors involved in the situation. His genius in the 1750s was to see that statesmanship lies as much in assessing the power and limitations of friends as in assessing that of enemies.[3] He realized that within the relationship with Great Britain there lay a large room for maneuver, and that he could safely make major policy changes – and make fundamental decisions on vital national interests – without calling the framework of the Alliance itself into question. He had no intention of altering or dispensing with the ancient connection with Great Britain. If he could maintain the distinction between 'measures rather to the disadvantage of the factory than to Great Britain', as the traveler William Dalrymple wrote, he knew that he ran no risk of a major clash with the British government.[4]

Mendonça Furtado returned from Pará in 1759. With his vast practical

---

[1] d'Azevedo, *Marquês de Pombal*, 211.

[2] 'Cartas de Londres', BNLCP, códice 611, f. 10–17.

[3] 'Memórias secretíssimas para Ministério de Londres', 16 August 1752, BNLCP, códice 610, f. 74–80. These secret instructions for his minister in London form a rare and concise summary of Carvalho e Melo's views during the early 1750s.

[4] Major William Dalrymple, *Travels through Spain and Portugal in 1774* (London, 1777), 125.

experience of Brazilian frontier conditions and intimate involvement with the affairs of the Company of Pará and Maranhão, he joined his brother's cabinet in Lisbon with direct responsibility for the colonies.[1] A month later, using the prototype of the first Brazil company, the statutes of a new commercial company received the royal approval. The state acting with the privileged established interests now brought regulation to one of the principal centers of Brazilian commerce and production: the sugar exporting captaincies of Pernambuco and Paraíba. The administrative junta of the company was to assert later that with the foundation of the company the 'fraudulent commerce many foreigners were making in the other ports of Brazil had ceased in Pernambuco, and following the laws of solid commerce the forwarding of European goods had been regulated to the value of the productions of the respective colonies'. So that it should aid and not compete with the established merchants in Pernambuco the company was allowed to sell only at wholesale in America. Customs duties in the metropolis were to be manipulated to encourage the production of those colonial commodities other than sugar which could be re-exported. The company was to stimulate the sugar mills of the region and, like its forerunner, to encourage the importation of African labor.[2]

The rationalization of the entrepreneurial structure of the Luso-Brazilian commercial community provoked repercussions throughout Portuguese society. The state, by supporting specific elements within a pattern of conflicting interests, forced those groups not favored into opposition, and at times into collusion and conspiracy. The lament of the Brazil merchant to Alonso in Thomas Atwood Digges' contemporary chronicle well represents the complaints of those who suffered from the economic policy of Carvalho e Melo during the 1750s. 'Why [resumed the merchant] until the present minister's time the trade of the Brazils was open to all his Majesty's subjects, and the community at large derived advantages from it; but the establishment of companies with such exclusive privileges has proved not only ruinous, by annihilating that spirit of enterprise and industry which results from the prospect of gain and is the support of thousands, but confines the wealth acquired by the trade of that part of the world to a few, which before was generally

---

[1] Alvará de nomeação....de [Mendonça Furtado], 19 July 1759, *Correspondência inédita*, III, 1228.

[2] 'Instituição da Companhia Geral de Pernambuco e Paraíba', Lisbon, 13 August 1759, BNLCP, códice 453, f. 275–290; 'Demonstrações da junta [Company of Pernambuco]' IHGB/AUC, 1-2-11; José Mendes de Cunha Saraiva, *Companhia Geral de Pernambuco e Paraíba* (Congresso do Mundo Português, 19 vols., Lisbon, 1940) X, 139–46.

diffused throughout the Kingdom'[1] Clearly Carvalho e Melo's measures hurt many vested interests and the reaction was swift and angry.

The promulgation of Company of Grão Pará and Maranhão's monopoly privileges and Indian emancipation from religious tutelage provoked an immediate response from the dispossessed traders and Jesuits. Both found an organ for their agitation in the *mesa do bem commum*, a rudimentary commercial association established in the late 1720s. The *mesa* formed a board of deputies representing the fraternity of Espírito Santo de Pedreira.[2] As representative of the Maranhão missions in Lisbon, Father Bento da Fonseca was in constant communication with the Pará and Maranhão commissaries. He prepared a draft from which João Tomás Negreiros formulated an extensive representation against the Company.[3] In the name of the *mesa do bem commum* its advocate, Nogueira Braga, sought an audience of the King and presented the Negreiros–Fonseca memorandum. The seven of the *mesa*'s twelve who took part in the confrontation 'indulged in the most virulent abuse of, and applied the most violent language to the Company [of Grão Pará and Maranhão], predicting the most fatal consequences to the country'.[4] Meanwhile from the pulpit of the Basilica of Santa Maria Maior, the Jesuit Manuel Ballester delivered a vehement attack on the monopoly, proclaiming that 'he who entered it would not be of the company of Christ our Lord'.[5]

The result was the violent dissolution of the commercial fraternity of Espírito Santo as prejudicial to the royal service, common interest, and commerce, and the offending deputies were condemned to penal banishment. The confiscated papers of the *mesa* revealed the extent of Jesuit involvement and Carvalho e Melo interpreted and dealt with the protest as if it were a conspiratorial uprising against royal power.[6] The *mesa do bem commum*, abolished in September 1755, was replaced by the *junta do comércio* or board of trade. The new junta was charged with the regulation of 'all affairs connected with commerce'. Headed by a *provedor*, it was to consist of a secretary, advocate and six deputies (four from Lisbon and

[1] *Adventures of Alonso: containing some striking anecdotes of the present Prime Minister of Portugal*, 2 vols., anonymously printed in London 1755 and now attributed to Thomas Atwood Digges (1741–1821) of Warburton Manor, Maryland, published in facsimile by the United States Catholic Historical Society monograph series XVII, editor Thomas J. McMohan (New York, 1943) I, 100–3.

[2] d'Azevedo, *Estudos*, 54–6; also his *Marquês de Pombal*, 138–40.

[3] d'Azevedo, *Os Jesuitas no Grão Pará*, 248–9.

[4] Conde de Carnota (John A. Smith) *Marquis of Pombal* (2nd edition, London 1871) 166–7.

[5] d'Azevedo, *Estudos*, 60.

[6] Carvalho e Melo referred to the protest as a *sublevação* in a private letter to his brother, [Carvalho e Melo] to [Mendonça Furtado] 4 August 1755, *Correspondência inédita*, II, 784–8.

two from Oporto), who were Portuguese born or naturalized subjects. The members of the junta were bound to a strict secrecy in their deliberations.[1]

The socio-economic situation in Portugal had strictly limited the group from which the future marquis of Pombal could choose his collaborators. The foreigners' dominance of commercial activity had limited the Portuguese almost exclusively to internal and colonial trade. Apparently there were only three Portuguese houses in Lisbon which had the experience of exchange business, bookkeeping methods, and general commercial expertise to engage in business with foreign markets, Bandeira and Bacigalupo, Born and Ferreira, and Emeretz and Brito, and even in these houses the Portuguese were in partnership with foreigners. It was from these merchants that Pombal found three of his most active associates. José Rodrigues Bandeira became the first provedor of the new *junta do comércio* and was a member of the direction of the Pernambuco Company. Antônio Caetano Ferreira and Luís José de Brito were both to play significant roles in the formulation and execution of economic policy. A second potent group of entrepreneurs came from the Cruz family, brought into the minister's favor by the activities of the ecclesiastic Antônio José da Cruz, who had in some way been involved in his rise to power. José Francisco da Cruz, a merchant with interests in Bahia and the tobacco trade, was closely involved in the formulation of the statutes of the Company of Pará and Maranhão, became provedor and deputy of the Company, administrator of the customs house in Lisbon, and was a close advisor on financial matters to Carvalho e Melo in many different capacities. His brother, Joaquim Inácio, who had made a most profitable marriage to an immensely rich Brazilian heiress, succeeded him in all his posts. The fourth brother, Anselmo José, succeeded to the Cruz fortune and became contractor of the royal tobacco monopoly. His daughter married Geraldo Wenceslão Braancamp, director of the Pernambuco Company and deputy to the *junta do comércio*, later to become Anselmo José da Cruz's heir.[2]

The careful farming of the royal contracts was an important part of the aid given by the state to those individuals Carvalho e Melo hoped would found the 'great houses' that he wished to see established in Portugal. Tobacco was one of the major and most lucrative of the royal

---

[1] 'Estatutos da Junta do Commércio, ordenados por El Rey...30 de Setembro de 1755, Alvará porque...he por bem confirmar os estatutos da Junta do Commércio', 16 December 1756, BNLCP, códice 453, f. 128–47.

[2] Ratton, *Recordações*, 190, 192, 257, 259, 261; d'Azevedo, *Estudos*, 50–1.

monopolies farmed out to private parties, and the tobacco trade had been one of the worst affected by the activities of the contrabandists. The tobacco merchants had a considerable interest in collaborating with the new administration. They were, moreover, in a good position to take advantage of the opportunities offered by the state, for unlike the intense international competition facing Brazilian sugar in traditional markets, the commerce in tobacco was expanding. João Gomes de Araújo and João Marques Bacalhão, close associates of the minister, were important functionaries of the tobacco junta. The office of provedor of the *junta do comércio* remained in the hands of the tobacco interest throughout the preeminence of Carvalho e Melo. José Rodrigues Bandeira was one of the major tobacco exporters in Portugal.[1]

The contracts at the disposal of the minister were not confined to the metropolis or to royal monopolies. Inácio Pedro Quintella, himself linked to the tobacco interest and a member of both Brazil companies, held the contract of tithes (*dízimos*) in Bahia. The right of collection of the *dízimos* in Brazil had been given up by the Church in return for fixed salaries paid by the state. The collection of the tax was farmed in the overseas council to private individuals, usually on a three year basis, just like any other metropolitan and colonial contract. Quintella also during 1754 and 1755 held the rights to the collection of duties on all non-fleet shipping entering Rio de Janeiro. In a similar way José Rodrigues Esteves, another director of the Pernambuco Company, held the right to the duty paid on slaves imported into Bahia.[2]

The use made of the *mesa do bem commum* by the Jesuits and the traders associated with them found a parallel in the movement by the new elements in the British community to capture control of the factory. Seeking new, far-reaching powers for the committee, they hoped to circumvent the control of the Consul, an appointee of the English crown. By doing so they would remove the most powerful obstacle to the transformation of the factory from its original function as an organization of British factors into a privileged and autonomous merchant corporation involved in the whole range of commercial speculation. Lord Tyrawly noted with disdain in his report to Secretary Fox the rise of a custom since he was 'first at Lisbon...which is that upon all matters that arise they call a meeting of the factory...where any low fellow...has as much right to talk as much nonsense as if he was the head of the best house in Lisbon'.

[1] Macedo, *A situação económica*, 141–3, 293–4.
[2] 'Livros dos contratos, dízimos reaes da Bahia, direito de dez tostois que paga cada escravo na Bahia..., contrato...do rendimento dos navios soltos...', AHU, códice 298, f. 22, 34, 93, and códice 299, f. 16, 22, 52.

William Mawman, a Lisbon merchant, in private correspondence with Lord Tyrawly described the attempt of the 'Grumbletonians' party' during a riotous general meeting in 1752 to intimidate the new consul, George Crowle, into confirming the powers they had wrung from his senile predecessor on his deathbed. The 'new powers' were so extensive as to place effective control in the hands 'of twelve men whose turbulent spirits, especially of some of them your Lordship is fully apprised of'. Crowle succeeded in thwarting the scheme but Mawman was not optimistic, reporting that 'after much squabbling the power of the new committee were reduced. Bristow and I are of the number of the new members but whilst the Sherleys, Burrells, King, and Hake are of the number I expect no good.[1]

One of the 'turbulent spirits' Mawman mentioned is of particular interest – William Shirely.[2] In 1753 Carvalho e Melo fearful that excessive demand in Spain would cause a dearth of grain in Portugal, forbade the re-export of wheat arriving in the Tagus.[3] Crowle supported the Portuguese government's measure. A violent dispute was provoked in the Factory, and the leader of the opposition was William Shirely. Crowle, acting with the Portuguese judge conservator, induced Carvalho e Melo to banish Shirely from Portugal. The Sicilian corn trade had been one of the 'universal trading' enterprises condemned by Tyrawly, and the very collusion of British representative and Portuguese government was probably exactly what the universal traders feared after the visit of Lord Tyrawly, and one of the compulsions behind their attempt to take control of the Factory. Influential pressure in London was to bring a reversal of the banishment order. The display of open faction within the British community in Portugal, involving the British crown's own representative, only served to weaken the Factory's case, to divert attention from the deeper intentions of Pombal's measures, and to confirm the aspersions of the Portuguese government and Lord Tyrawly.

The Company of Jesus was one of the more visible casualties of the events which had been set in motion by the imperial pretensions of Carvalho e Melo's administration, and by the attempts to nationalize

---

[1] Tyrawly papers, Walford, *British Factory*, 54–6.

[2] 'Sherlys' of Mawman's letter is certainly William Shirely. His name appears with those of the members of the Factory committee in a letter to Tyrawly of 17 April 1752, *ibid.*, 44–5.

[3] It is sometimes claimed that the measure had no motivation beyond the excuse for an attack on the English merchants. Crop failures in Spain during the period 1750–4 produced soaring agricultural indices, in fact the sharpest advance in agricultural prices registered in any period during the century. In 1750 the Spanish government exempted all wheat carried into Andalucia from Spanish or foreign territory from taxes on first sale, Earl J. Hamilton, *War and Prices in Spain 1651–1800* (Cambridge, Mass., 1947) 174, 198.

sectors of the Luso-Brazilian commercial system. Given the background of the effort to populate and exploit so great a tropical and sub-tropical region, to encourage European–Indian marriage, and to consolidate national territories, the clash with the Jesuits must appear an inevitable by-product. The Jesuits bestraddled the frontiers at the two most vital and sensitive points in the imperial system of D. Luís da Cunha – in the Amazon and in Paraguay and Uruguay. Pombal urged his brother in 1755 to use 'every possible pretext to separate the Jesuits from the frontier and to break all communication between them and the Jesuits of the Spanish dominions'.[1] The Indian policy of the Company of Jesus stood in the way of the desire to populate and Europeanize the interior by assimilation, and the Indian – both Mendonça Furtado and Carvalho e Melo believed – must be made to constitute the 'principal force and principal riches for the defense of the frontiers'.[2] The exemption of the missions in the far north from contribution to the state created acute tension between them and a secular administration attempting to consolidate and finance the fortification of Amazonia.

Preeminently it was the Jesuit reaction to the Madrid agreements and the measures of the new Portuguese government that made the chances of a peaceful solution remote. In opposition to the secular rulers of South America the Amerindians of the Guaraní missions took up arms. In the *mesa do bem commum* affair, Pombal was convinced that the missions of Pará and Maranhão had resorted to intrigue against a project he regarded as essential to the battle against foreign domination of the economy. Such treacherous activity in Pombal's eyes was compounded by signs of Jesuit collusion with the English, who according to the French minister in Lisbon murmured greatly at the persecution of the Jesuits with whom they had 'great and profitable commercial business'.[3] The Jesuit settlements of Paraguay were reputed to have been an area of 'beneficial commerce' for British traders.[4] Duke Silva-Tarouca reversing his earlier views on the desirability of Jesuit cooperation pointed out in February 1758 that 'it was not evangelical spirit that armed with muskets eighty or a hundred thousand Indians, and erected an intermediate power from

---

[1] [Carvalho e Melo] to [Mendonça Furtado], 17 March 1755, *Correspondência inédita*, II, 668–73.

[2] Conde de Oeiras [Carvalho e Melo] to Conde da Cunha, 26 January 1765, IHGB, lata 11, doc. 12.

[3] Sousa, Manoel de Barros (Visconde de Santarém), and L. A. Rebello da Silva, eds., *Quadro elementar das relações políticas e diplomáticas de Portugal com as diversas potencias do mundo...* (18 vols., Lisbon and Paris, 1842–60) vol. 18, 369.

[4] 'An account of the political establishment of the Jesuits in Paraguay', *The Annual Register for 1758* (London) 362–7.

the River Plate to the Amazon, which one day could be fatal to the interested and dominant powers of South America'.[1]

The social mobility of which Carvalho e Melo was himself an example, and which he facilitated by granting noble rights to the merchants with whom he had close and lucrative contacts, produced adverse reactions from the Portuguese nobility. To the aristocracy Carvalho e Melo was an upstart. In face of virulent opposition he had married into the Arcos family. His activity at the academy of history was seen as an insidious attempt to gain intelligence on the ancient houses of Portugal.[2] The Austrian envoy noted that only one of Pombal's diplomatic representatives was 'a person of distinction'.[3] And he was a threat. The minister sought to raise taxes 'without differences and without privileges whatsoever'.[4] Yet none of these factors of themselves were so significant as the explicit purpose expressed in the statutes of all his commercial companies to use the lure of ennoblement as an incentive to investment. The company's statutes not only specifically offered to non-noble investors certain exemptions and privileges which were the prerogatives of the nobility and the magistracy, but also admitted them to membership of military orders. As to the nobles who invested, the fact of participation in commercial matters was not to prejudice their status but actively to aid its advancement.[5] Incentive was also held out to the class of magistrates by permitting them to become shareholders in the companies, and making that involvement entirely compatible with the exercise of their administrative or legal functions.[6]

The *mesa do bem commum* affair, the attack on contraband, and the regulation of colonial commerce, had already brought an identity of interest between the interlopers, English universal traders, and the Jesuits. The favors bestowed on Pombal's collaborators would also tend to produce an identity of interest with the discontented nobles, for the group opposed by the interlopers and supported by Pombal also represented

---

[1] [Teles da Silva] to [Carvalho e Melo], Vienna, 10 February 1758 and Vienna, 1 April 1758, *AAP*, 386–7, 395.

[2] d'Azevedo, *Marquês de Pombal*, 148–9.

[3] Cited by d'Azevedo, *ibid.*, 125–6.

[4] For a more detailed and documented discussion of this important aspect of Carvalho e Melo's administrative and fiscal reforms see Macedo, *A situação econômica*, 50.

[5] 'Companhia Geral...do Alto Douro, instituição', paragraph xxxix, BNLCP, códice 453, f. 96–112; 'Companhia Geral de Pernambuco, instituição', paragraph 33, BNLCP, códice 453, f. 275–90.

[6] 'Alvará porque...he servido declarar que todos os ministros, e officiaes de justiça e fazenda ou guerra he permittido negociar por meyo da companhia geral do Grão Pará e Maranhão, e qualquer outros por V.M. confirmados...', 5 January 1757. BNLCP, códice 456, f. 138.

a potent challenge within the Portuguese social structure to aristocratic privilege. 'To put an end to the authority of King Sebastian it is
indispensible to destroy that of King Joseph.'[1] Such a sentiment expressed
in a letter to the Duke of Aveiro, discovered after the abortive attempt on
the King's life in 1759, was one that Jesuit, itinerant trader, English
universal trader, and aristocrat, would be tempted to support. Certainly
the news of the failure of the Távora–Aveiro assassination plot was greeted
with undisguised dismay by those interests not favored by the Pombaline
state. In Pará the Jesuits were noticeably absent from the service of thanks-
giving for the King's safety.[2] After the conspiracy trial a seventy-two
page pamphlet appeared in London refuting the accusations in detail. The
author was William Shirely, 'late of Lisbon, Merchant'.[3] The London
Annual Register, to which Shirely contributed, believed the problems of
Portugal could be resolved easily. It was to be accomplished by 'reinstating
matters on their natural basis'.[4]

During 1758 the temporal power of the Jesuits was suppressed throughout Brazil and the directory system of Indian secular control designed by
Mendonça Furtado for Pará and Maranhão made applicable in all
Portuguese America.[5] On 3 September 1759, the Portuguese government
decreed the proscription and expulsion of the Company of Jesus from the
whole Empire, prohibiting any communication either verbal or in
writing between Jesuits and Portuguese subjects.[6] In 1760 the Pará
Company's ship, *Nossa Senhora de Arrábida*, removed the last Jesuits of
Maranhão into exile.[7] While the motive for the Távoras' disaffection had
probably been an intimate personal matter – the King had taken the
young marquis' wife as his mistress – the acute state of tension produced
by the Jesuit problem aggravated the situation, and was in part responsible
for the violence of the reaction when eventually it came. From the dark
waters of the Távora–Aveiro affair, and the consequent gory extermina-

---

[1] Cited by Cheke, *Dictator of Portugal*, 146. For further details of the Távora case see *O
processo dos Távoras, publicações da Biblioteca Nacional, prefaciado e anotado por Pedro de Azevedo*
(Lisbon, 1921), and Guilherme G. de Oliveira Santos, *O Caso dos Távoras* (Lisbon n.d.).

[2] d'Azevedo, *Os Jesuitas no Grão Pará*, 306–7.

[3] *Observations on a pamphlet lately published, entitled the genuine and legal sentence pronounced by
the high court of judicature of Portugal upon the conspirators against the life of his most Faithful
Majesty...by William Shirely late of Lisbon, merchant* (London, MDCCLIX).

[4] *The Annual Register for 1770* (London), 10–11; Shirely's *Observations* had been published
by *The Annual Register for 1759* (London), 222.

[5] Prado Júnior, *A formação do Brasil contemporâneo*, 89.

[6] 'Ley porque Vossa Magastade he servida exterminar, proscrever, e mandar expulsar dos
seus Reinos e Dominios, os Religiosos da Companhia denominada de JESÚ...' 3 September
1759, BNLCP, códice 453, f. 291–4.

[7] Simonsen, *História económica*, 339.

tion by public spectacle of the leaders of the aristocratic conspiracy, there emerged a self-conscious attempt to remould the Portuguese nobility.

The attack on noble tax privileges, the qualification of commercial men for public office, the corresponding permission for public men to involve themselves in commercial matters, and the promise of ennoblement to those who invested in the privileged companies, became part of a wider policy. The College of Nobles, chartered in 1761 and endowed in 1765 (with the aid of, among other sources, the confiscated properties of the house of Aveiro and the Jesuits), was to purge the nobility of the 'false persuasion' that they could live 'independent of the virtues'. Together with Pombal's own second son, among the first pupils were the two children of the archetypal Pombal collaborator, José Francisco da Cruz, a commercial and self-made man, ennobled by investment in the Company of Pará and Maranhão, the statutes of which he inspired.[1]

Portugal in the decade following the accession of José I had seen several important initiatives. Some of them had set in motion chains of events which it would have been difficult to foresee in 1750. The new reign and the predominance of the future marquis of Pombal had brought a careful and sustained challenge to the dominating influence of the British and a determination to bring about a more balanced relationship between the two allies. Carvalho e Melo with a variety of techniques had sought to alleviate the state of semi-colonial dependency in which Portugal stood to Great Britain. To the actions of the Portuguese government he brought his careful assessment of the scope of the problem in its imperial and European contexts. Within this essentially Atlantic dimension his pragmatic approach to the issues had produced by 1755 a policy which was to have profound repercussions throughout Portuguese society.

The conflict of established interests and interlopers which had arisen within the structure of the Luso-Brazilian entrepreneurial community was paralleled by a contradiction of motivation among the British residents in Portugal. Carvalho e Melo exploited both divisions with skill. The exclusive companies, while they grew from local advice, and were intended to meet Brazilian and imperial demands, provided a practical means which, in association with economic legislation and a revitalized state, sought to break the stranglehold of foreign credit on the Luso-Brazilian commercial system. With monopoly privileges confined to a

---

[1] Rómulo de Carvalho, *História da fundação do Colégio Real dos Nobres de Lisboa 1761–1772* (Coimbra, 1959) 119–21, 182; *História dos estabelecimentos scientíficos litterários, e artísticos de Portugal nos successivos Reinados da Monarquia*, vol. 1 (Lisbon, 1871); BNLCP, códice 455, f. 69.

chosen group of collaborators, Pombal hoped to encourage capital formation in national hands, and to form great merchant houses capable of competing on terms of equality with the foreign merchants established in Portugal and by treaty inviolable.

The measures of the government indirectly attacked the interests of the foreign merchants and factors in Lisbon and Oporto, and were intended to preserve the mutually beneficial two-way traffic of Anglo-Portuguese exhange. By nationalizing sectors of Luso-Brazilian commerce, and the benefits of the processes of commerce carried on through the Portuguese and Brazilian ports, the eventual objective was to remove the necessity for the residence of foreign factors in Portugal. This long term intention was camouflaged both by the appearance that the measures were aimed mainly at the universal traders and contrabandists, and by the claim that opposition to them came only from these sources. This fiction was supported by the fact that the process began in peripheral regions, by the recommendations of Lord Tyrawly to the British government, as well as by the behaviour of the British Factory in Lisbon. Nor was the view likely to be challenged by those English factors who, like Lord Tyrawly's informant William Mawman, were quite content as long as access of British goods to American markets via legal channels and regular fleet traffic remained open. Certainly during the 1750s the English factors and the British government had no sound reasons for complaint, and between 1755–60, the value of British exports to Portugal reached the highest level and produced the greatest favorable balance of the century.[1]

[1] Schumpeter, *English Overseas Trade Statistics*, 17–20.

CHAPTER 2

CHANGE

If the commerce of Britain fails by encouraging that of France and Spain, adieu to the liberty of your Country.

> Mr Punch to the King of Portugal *Punch's Politicks* (London, 1762).

When reason allows and it is necessary to banish abuses and destroy pernicious customs to the benefit of King, Justice, and the Common Good, act with much prudence and moderation, a method which achieves more than power.

> Marquês de Pombal to Luís Pinto de Sousa Coutinho, cited by Marcos Carneiro de Mendonça, 'O pensamento da metropole em relação do Brasil', *RIHGB*, ccxxvii (October–December 1962) 54.

The Spanish invasion in 1762 brought a shattering challenge to the basic assumptions on which for a decade the government of Portugal had based its policies. Mendonça Furtado did not object to the French and English 'breaking one anothers heads' as long as Portugal was not drawn into their conflicts.[1] Both he and his brother, as well as the Duke Silva-Tarouca miscalculated the chances of Portuguese involvement in the Seven Years' War.[2] Yet the invasion had come for all that, and what was worse British assistance was required to repel it. British aid had not come without vocal protest in the House of Commons.[3] And in case the lesson of events should be lost, they were summarized by *Punch's Politicks* in an open letter to the Portuguese King. Punch foresaw that should Spain and France gain control of Lisbon, the 'previous steps taken by his *Portuguese Majesty*', would be 'an immediate withdrawing on board the *British Fleet*, with his treasures, and all that of his family and faithful subjects...to the *Brazils*'. The conquerors would be left with 'the shell to subsist on when the kernal is taken away'. Punch's 'fairy dream', for such it was described, had been intended to convey a warning. 'If the

---

[1] [Mendonça Furtado] to [Carvalho e Melo], 22 November 1755, *Correspondência inédita*, III, 876.
[2] For example [Silva-Tarouca] to [Carvalho e Melo], Vienna, 1 April 1758, *AAP*, 397.
[3] The King's message recommending support for Portugal was presented the House on 11 May 1762 and opposed by Mr Clover, spokesman of the London merchants, T. C. Hansard, *The Parliamentary History of England from the Earliest Period to the Year 1803*, xv (London, 1818) 1221, 1222, 1224.

commerce of Britain fails by encouraging that of France and Spain', Punch told the King of Portugal, 'adieu to the liberty of your country.'[1] The British minister in Lisbon, Mr Hay, reported tersely to London during October 1765: '[Carvalho e Melo] seems to lay it down for a maxim, that it is the undoubted interest of Great Britain to assist Portugal upon every emergency, at the same time that almost every innovation in the commerce for these past ten years tends evidently to the lessening of that interest.'[2]

In fact by the early 1760s British official and merchant circles had come to a very clear realization of the objectives of Pombal's commercial companies and economic legislation. During 1763 Mr Hay placed before the government in London a detailed synopsis of the Pombaline system as he saw it. Carvalho e Melo 'looks upon the Portuguese here as no more than shopkeepers, and the Brazil merchants no more than commissaries or factors to the foreigners', he pointed out. 'This put this minister upon a scheme to put the trade into the hands of the natives, and to make them the importers and wholesale traders in foreign goods....[T]he design is to establish an active trade among the subjects of Portugal, and to make foreign factors useless.'[3] The merchants of the Lisbon Factory, shaken out of their complacency, remonstrated to the Earl of Kinnoull. Their petition underlined the long term potentialities of the Portuguese government's measures, particularly if the projected companies for Bahia and Rio de Janeiro were established. These 'intended companies' the merchants reported, '...if effected will change the circulation and channel of trade from the hands of British subjects to Portuguese, and consequently we shall be deprived of the great advantage of our commission business and other profits that arise from the sale and purchase of our commodities....[...]It will force the major part of the British merchants and factors now residing in Portugal to leave the country.' And the Factory emphasized its disquiet by publishing the petition to Kinnoull as well as confidential memoranda of the past several years, doubtless in order to bring pressure to bear on the government in London.[4]

British awareness of the possible impact of the Portuguese government's

---

[1] *Punch's Politicks* (London, 1762), introduction and pp. 40–5.
[2] Quoted by Allan Christelow, 'Great Britain and the trades from Cadiz and Lisbon to Spanish America and Brazil 1759–1782', *HAHR*, XXVII (February 1947) 12.
[3] Quoted by Smith, *Pombal*, II, 46.
[4] 'Memórias do Consul e Factória Británnica', BNLCP, códice 94, f. 24, 24v,25v. 'Occasional Thoughts on the Portuguese Trade and the Inexpediency of Supporting the House of Braganza on the Throne of Portugal', (Pamphlet, London, 1767) recommended the sacrifice of Portugal in the interests of an alliance with Spain; from Greenlee Collection, Newberry Library, Chicago.

measures, together with the clear demonstration of the dependence of Portugal on Britain, served to rekindle those fears which twenty years before first led Carvalho e Melo to make his detailed and comprehensive investigation of the causes of Britain's commercial superiority. Britain's striking preponderance in world affairs at the end of the Seven Years' War turned his recurrent concern with British expansionist intentions into a near obsession about the vulnerability of Portuguese America. For the events of the early 1760s had not only narrowed the scope for policy making; they had also destroyed the confident belief that Brazil was a 'far away place' beyond the reach of European arms. The global dimension of British planning and capabilities were startlingly revealed by the daring attack on Spanish America in 1762, when Lord Albermarle took Havana and Admiral Cornish and General Draper with East India Company forces took Manila. The frightful vulnerability of the west and east coasts of the Americas to a strategy conceived in world terms, by an European power which was also becoming an Indian based Asiatic power, was clearly demonstrated. When in 1763 the British adopted a policy of expansion into the Pacific it was not only the Spaniards whose fears seemed realized.[1] The Spanish government, anxious to cement the apparent new identity of views with Lisbon, forwarded to Pombal copies of British Admiralty discussions on South America obtained by the Prince de Masserano, Spanish Ambassador in London, who had been busy bribing Admiralty clerks.[2]

Pombal wasted no time in sending the documents on to the Viceroy of Brazil. The English 'their natural arrogance' heightened by successes during the Seven Years' War, would use 'any occasion or pretext to conquer the overseas dominions of all the other European powers', he told the count da Cunha, 'Two most powerful monarchies had been laid low, and Havana, always reputed to be impregnable, taken.' The pattern was clear, first the attack on Cartagena in 1741, then the fall of Havana in 1762; how long would pass before Rio de Janeiro followed?

[1] Harlow, *Second British Empire*, I, 49,220, II, 252–5, 281, 300, 632–3; R. L. Schuyler, *The Fall of the Old Colonial System* (New York, 1945) 80–2.

[2] Pombal and the King had both expressed their wish that the two Iberian powers make common cause in the Old World and the New against the 'common enemy' the English, during conversations with the Spanish Ambassador in Lisbon, the Marqués de Almodóvar. Marqués de Almodóvar to Marqués de Grimaldi, Lisbon, 8 May 1767, Archivo Histórico Nacional, Madrid, Estado, leg. 4536 (2). Shortly thereafter Grimaldi made sure that copies of the Prince de Masserano's gleanings in London be passed on to Lisbon for Pombal's attention. Grimaldi to Almodóvar, San Ildefonso, 6 August 1767, AHN, Madrid, Estado, leg. 4536 (2) and Grimaldi to Almodóvar, San Lorenzo, 13 November 1767, AHN, Madrid, Estado, leg. 4536 (2).

'If the English establish themselves in the Rio de la Plata they would make themselves masters of all Paraguay and Tucumán, of all Chile and Peru, in a word of all Spanish America, and as a necessary consequence of all the state of Brazil.' It was essential for the Portuguese government to take every measure to deflect the threat. 'We must defend ourselves', Pombal wrote, 'first with policy, until where it will extend no further, and after, as a last resort, with force.'[1]

The careful assessment of the Anglo-Portuguese alliance which underlay Carvalho e Melo's activities and policies during the 1750s was more rational than his post war obsession. Punch in his *Politicks* had stressed that Britain 'knows her own interest too well' to search for a universal Empire. 'Commerce is her support and extent of territory, her trade neglected, must be her downfall.'[2] Subterfuge always characterized Carvalho e Melo's relations with the English, but his imputation of equal dissimulation to them in their dealings with Portugal overestimated the British government's subtlety. The 'most declared unity' he perceived between the British and the Jesuits, as well as the supposed designs of Britain on the Portuguese Empire in America had little substance in reality. The voyages of Captains Byron and Cook were in all probability genuinely motivated by a desire to penetrate and explore the Pacific; their aim was the discovery of the great southern continent that hopefully existed beyond the southern sea. So esoteric an objective for so avaricious a power only provoked contemptuous disbelief in the pragmatic mind of the Portuguese minister. The south sea objective he held was an 'appearance' only, for the expeditions were intended against Brazil and the Spanish dominions in that part of the world.[3] The British certainly harbored designs on Spanish America. Indeed, British probings at the Spanish colonies had a venerable history, dating from Walter Raleigh's attempt to open up the Orinoco basin in 1595. This was well known. The relationship with Portugal and hence with Brazil, however, was governed by quite different criteria than was the relationship with Spain and Spanish America. The acute dependency of Portugal on Great Britain meant that while all factors in the situation remained stable, it was essentially true, as Punch said, that Portugal 'can never have reasons to fear encroachment from her'.[4] Portugal was already part of that 'informal

---

[1] 'Relação das instruções de ordens que expediram ao conde da Cunha', 20 June 1767, *RIHGB*, xxxv, pt. 1 (1872) 227–326; 'Instruções officaes', 14 April 1769, Marcos Carneiro de Mendonça, *O marquês de Pombal e o Brasil* (São Paulo, 1960) 31–44.
[2] *Punch's Politicks*, 54.
[3] Carneiro de Mendonça, *Pombal e o Brasil*, 33, 36–7.
[4] *Punch's Politicks*, 54.

empire' of trade and influence which the mid-Victorian British were to consider their invention.

The dispatches of the Portuguese minister in London, Martinho de Melo e Castro, were insistent in stressing that the obsession with the English was misplaced. It was not the unreal threat of British conquest in Brazil that concerned him and the British government, but French and Spanish plans for the annexation of the Portuguese portion of America. Apparently a combined operation involving French penetration into Amazonia from Guiana, an expeditionary force against Rio de Janeiro, and a Spanish attack from the south, had been abandoned only when news arrived of the fall of Havana. For Melo e Castro the greatest happiness was that the 'precarious and sad situation of the French and Spaniards in the present situation would allow Portugal time to prepare against similar projects'.[1] The news reaching Lisbon from America made it clear that Spanish pressure on the southern frontier of Brazil would continue. It was necessary Melo e Castro recommended, to recognize that Portugal had no more 'ready or solid resources than her own forces', and that she must use all her means and facilities to make 'all her vassals of whatever estate or condition contribute for their own preservation'. As far as Britain was concerned, it would be only 'when she saw Portugal powerful and resolute that she would treat her as an ally, and not as a dependent'.[2]

To add insult to injury it was the British themselves who drew Pombal's attention to the weakness of Brazilian defenses. They forwarded to Carvalho e Melo a British officer's report on the 'deplorable condition' of the coastal fortifications. The author of this damaging indictment claimed that he would consider himself 'deserving of everlasting infamy if I do not with one Battalion of infantry make myself master of Rio de Janeiro in 24 hours'. He recommended that the 'reformation already begun there [in Portugal] be extended to the coast of Brazil', in order to prevent 'these valuable possessions from falling into the hands of the French and Spaniards'.[3]

---

[1] Martinho de Melo e Castro to Carvalho e Melo, London, 26 September 1764, BNLCP, códice 611, f. 262–6. Choiseul had intended an expedition against Brazil which would he hoped have the same effect on the trade and revenues of England as an English attack on the West Indies had upon France. At the beginning of 1762 a small expedition was to be sent against the northern provinces of Brazil, but later in the year a much larger and more important conquest was planned of Bahia and Rio de Janeiro. The instructions were dated a fortnight before the preliminaries of the peace were signed, see Pares, *War and Trade*, 594.

[2] Melo e Castro to Carvalho e Melo, 7 April 1766, BNLCP, códice 611, f. 383.

[3] Extract of a letter to Mr Grenville, dated Rio de Janeiro, 14 October 1764, BNLCP, códice 612, f. 61.

Conflicts and conspiracies

In fact the continuing Spanish threat in America made the retention of British goodwill by Portugal essential. Yet both the proto-economic nationalism of Pombal, and the changed diplomatic situation that followed the Peace of Paris, found the British very unwilling to involve themselves in a quarrel with Spain for the sake of securing Portugal in possession of her colonies. Pombal's requests that Britain require Spain to uphold the stipulations of the Peace of Paris in South America, were answered with a superb irony which could hardly have been lost on the all-powerful minister in Lisbon. 'The court of Portugal would not wish English troops to defend the mines and govern the ports and coast of Brazil', the British government observed sardonically, 'the deplorable situation of Brazil could do nothing but incite her enemies to conquer her.'[1] Pombal told the British minister in Lisbon wistfully during 1766: 'England and Portugal were like man and wife, who might have little domestic disputes among themselves, but if anybody else came to disturb the peace of the family they would joint to defend it'.[2] He was mistaken. Portugal if anything was the member of a harem. There always existed the possibility for the introduction of new and more voluptuous companions, and after all, even Spain herself might be one of them.

It was thus within a substantially changed international situation that Portugal faced the post war decade. British power was recognized, needed, and intensely distrusted. The room for maneuver within the alliance had been dramatically reduced. The Spanish continued to threaten on the frontiers. After the Peace of Paris there was clearly a need for greater circumspection and caution in dealings with Great Britain, and the first casualty was the planned extensions of the monopolistic company scheme to Bahia and Rio de Janeiro, projects the capitalization of which was doubtful anyway. The British merchants complained that such institutions would completely exclude their trade from Brazil. To placate the British in Portugal it was essential that the overall objective of the measures of 1755 be abandoned.[3]

The desire to see Portugal reestablished and in control of its own affairs, however, remained a fundamental objective. New techniques were necessary to retain that dominating aspiration within the conditions of a changed environment. The walls of the colonial system were to be made secure, the ports of Portuguese America rigorously closed to foreign

[1] Carvalho e Melo to Conde da Cunha, 18 November 1765, IHGB, lata 11, doc. 12; Melo e Castro to Carvalho e Melo, 20 March 1765, BNLCP, códice 612, f. 62–4.

[2] Quoted by Smith, *Pombal*, II, 51–2.

[3] 'Apontamentos vários sobre a Companhia do Grão-Pará e Maranhão', IHGB/AUC, 1-1-8, f. 46; 'Memórias do Consul e Factória Británnica', BNLCP, códice 94, f. 24v.

ships except for the most urgent humanitarian reasons. 'All the world knows that the overseas colonies are founded as a precious object of utility of the metropolis...from which essential certainty result infallible maxims universally observed in the practice of all nations', Mendonça Furtado commented when the British complained of actions against East Indiamen watering in Brazilian ports.[1] In place of the establishment of new monopolistic companies, the fleet system to Rio and Bahia was abolished in 1765 and ships were permitted to sail at their own convenience. The British minister at once congratulated Carvalho e Melo: 'I could not help telling him that freedom was the soul of commerce, and therefore, every liberty which could be allowed must be beneficial to the trade and credit of the nation.'[2] There was more to the deed than Mr Hay in his enthusiasm for the freedom of trade noted. Abolition of the fleets served to facilitate the access of Brazilian products to European markets and augment their competitiveness by avoiding the long delays of the old system. Brazilian producers saw quicker returns on their investment and a consequent alleviation of their debt position. Further encouragement was given in 1766 when freight charges were regulated and lowered and the freedom of intercoastal shipping decreed.[3]

Behind the 'ancient names and ancient clothing' of the 'infallible maxims' of the mercantilist colonial system, the Portuguese government and the local administration in Brazil took on some of the functions that the Brazil companies were performing in Amazonia and Pernambuco. The viceroy, the Marquis of Lavradio, was relentless in his search for new products and more efficient methods both in Bahia and Rio de Janeiro. He appointed João Hopman, a Dutch entrepreneur of thirty years residence in Brazil, as 'inspector of new plantations and farms'. Coffee plants were ordered and distributed – one to Hopman; and the viceroy sent to Santa Catarina for information on cheese and butter production. Wheat production was increased by insisting that farmers sow in proportion to their cultivated land, mulberry trees were also introduced. By guaranteeing fixed prices Lavradio employed a system of subsidy to farmers who

---

[1] 'Correspondência official da côrte de Portugal com os vice-reis do estado do Brasil', *RIHGB*, xxxiii, pt. 1 (1870) 277; 'Note and counter note', Melo e Castro to British Envoy in Lisbon, 20 March 1772, and 11 May 1772, BNLCP, códice 638, f. 210; Mendonça Furtado 'Demonstração da impossibilidade moral que obita aos navios estrangeiros de todas as nações (ainda que sejam Amigas e Alliadas) para serem recebidos nos portos dos dominios ultramarinos de Portugal', 19 April 1761, BNLCP, códice 638, f. 220–5.

[2] Quoted by Christelow, *HAHR*, xxvii, 15.

[3] Alvará, 27 September 1765, and decreto, 2 June 1766, documents in the private collection of Marcos Carneiro de Mendonça, Cosme Velho, Rio de Janeiro, Brazil; 'Discurso preliminár', *ABNRJ*, xxvii, 281–348.

experimented with new primary products, he having found that the rigidity of the colonial entrepreneurial framework did not encourage Brazilian merchants to risk the export of new products to Europe which had not been ordered in advance by their correspondents in Lisbon and Oporto.[1] In this way he stimulated indigo production and also that of cochineal–indigo to such an extent that by 1779 it formed in value 16.8 per cent of the total export from Rio de Janeiro to Lisbon, and 20.6 per cent of that to Oporto.[2]

The impetus to enterprise was not confined to primary production. With Pombal's active encouragement manufacturing establishments were set up. Lavradio in Bahia formed a company to establish a canvas factory.[3] He supported the entrepreneur Manuel Luís Vieira with his rice processing plant in Rio.[4] During 1774 the viceroy could send to Lisbon a portion of silk made from the fiber of a new species of silkworm. With Hopman, Lavradio discovered the plant *guaxima* from which a good flax for cord and canvas could be extracted. Hopman was invited to experiment, and in 1778 Lavradio forwarded to Lisbon 4 arrobas of the improved plant and three pieces of linen prepared by Hopman.[5] In the captaincy of São Paulo, the governor Luís Antônio de Sousa, Morgado de Mateus, stimulated the exploitation of the iron mines at Ipanema, and during 1765 sent Pombal a sample of the first iron forged by Domingos Ferreira Pereira at Sorocaba. Eleven years later Ferreira Pereira obtained royal permission to establish a factory with exclusive privileges to mining and smelting in the captaincy.[6] But perhaps most significant, the manufactories in America were aided directly by the Lisbon *junta do comércio*. Manuel Luís Vieira and his partner Domingos L. Loureiro received exclusive privileges for ten years in rice production during 1766. José Ferreira Leal in Bahia received junta support for the manufacture of rigging in 1767. The junta participated in the establishment of the leather factory of

[1] D. José d'Almeida, *Vice-reinado de D. Luíz d'Almeida Portugal, marquês de Lavradio* (São Paulo, 1941) 41–4; Dauril Alden, *Royal Government in Colonial Brazil with special reference to the Administration of the Marquis of Lavradio (1769–1779)* (Berkeley and Los Angeles, 1968) especially 353–87.

[2] Calculated on the basis of the tables in 'Memórias políticas e económicas...para uso de vice-rei, Luís de Vasconcellos', 1779–89, *RIHGB*, pt. 1 (1884) 25–52.

[3] d'Almeida, *Lavradio*, 15.

[4] Dauril Alden, 'Manuel Luís Vieira, an Entrepreneur in Rio de Janeiro during Brazil's Agricultural Renaissance', *HAHR*, XXXIX (November 1959) 521.

[5] d'Almeida, *Lavradio*, 42.

[6] Américo Brasiliense Antunes de Moura, *Governo do Morgado de Mateus no vice-reinado do conde da Cunha, S. Paulo restaurado* (Separata da *Revista do Arquivo Municipal*, LII, São Paulo, 1938) 130–1; *Revista do Arquivo Público Mineiro (RAPM)* VIII (1903) 1019.

Change

Feliciano Gomes Neves in Rio de Janeiro during 1760 and of Costa Moreira and Company in Pernambuco in 1772.[1]

Meanwhile the far north and the northeast of Portuguese America were making progress under the control of the privileged companies. In Pará and Maranhão capital mobilized by the crown in association with private investors provided essential credit for the import of African labor, European goods, and the initiation of new export commodities. From 1760 the export of cotton began from São Luís, and in 1767 the export of rice. Cotton production was soon in excess of metropolitan demand and provided re-exports for Rotterdam, Hamburg, Genoa, Rouen, Marseilles, and London. Exports from Belém likewise made progress. Cacao was by far the principal commodity exported from this port and capital of the state of Pará and Maranhão.[2] Company investments were used in Maranhão to establish rice processing mills and bring in skilled technicians. Even a cotton manufactory was established in Pará, in order to produce cloth for the local military forces. It was defended by the company's administrative junta on the grounds that locally produced manufactures made the purchase of similar goods from foreigners unnecessary.[3] Company ships carried European goods, Amazon products, and African slaves along trade routes that embraced Bissau, Angola, Europe, the Brazilian littoral, and the Indian Ocean.[4] As Pombal had wished, the company's activities served 'to consolidate the establishment of the Empire that the King [was] determined to found in these captaincies'.[5]

The company of Pernambuco was concerned to stimulate and augment the sugar mills within its monopoly region. Capital investment and the extension of credit brought assistance to the sugar mill owners. Direct

[1] 'Lista das fábricas instaladas com participação da junta do comércio', document 7, Macedo, *A situação econômica*; 'Alvará porque V. M. ha por bem prorogar por mais dez annos o Privilegio exclusivo concedido a fábrica de descascar Arroz, estabelecida no Rio de Janeiro que são proprietarios e Directores, Manoel Luiz Vieira e Domingos Lopes Loureiro', 8 October 1766, BNLCP, códice 456, f. 183–4.

[2] Manuel Nunes Dias, 'As frotas do cacao da amazônia 1756–1773: subsídios para o estudo do fomento ultramarino português no século XVIII', *RHSP* (April–June 1963) 363–77: and his 'Fomento e Mercantilismo: política econômica Portuguêsa na baixada Maranhense 1755–1778' v colóquio internacional de estudos Luso-Brasileiros, *Actas* (3 vols., Coimbra, 1965) II, 17–99.

[3] 'Apontamentos vários sobre a Companhia do Grão-Pará e Maranhão', IHGB/AUC, 1-1-8, f. 18; 'Correspondência official do governador do Grão-Pará', 1778–1807, IHGB/AUC, 1-1-4, f. 122.

[4] Manuel Nunes Dias, 'A tonelagem da frota da Companhia Geral do Grão-Pará e Maranhão', *RHSP* (January–March 1964) 131.

[5] Carvalho e Melo to Mendonça Furtado, 4 August 1755, *Correspondência inédita*, II, 789.

41

investment rehabilitated many *engenhos* and established new ones, the administrative junta estimating in 1780 that to the 207 mills in existence at the time of the company's establishment, including those ruined or out of action, it had added 123 mills, forming some 390 functioning and producing sugar for export. With subsidy to farmers and guaranteed prices tobacco cultivation was reestablished. Goods and slaves were advanced to farmers and sugar producers at a 3 per cent interest rate. To make Pernambucan hides competitive with those of the Spanish provinces they were exempted from duties. The government's insistence on the introduction of large numbers of African slaves met broader imperial objectives and like the Company of Pará and Maranhão, the benefits of vast investment in Brazil were considerable. The company contributed to the growing capital and influence of the privileged established interests in the metropolis.[1]

The use of a flexible tariff policy to stimulate specific interests and protect primary production was used to the benefit both of the exclusive companies and of those colonial regions outside the monopolies. Manipulation of tariffs was a vital part of the aid given to the primary production of those regions where the plan to establish companies had been abandoned. While this was important in itself, it was only a shadow of what might have been, for it was impossible to complete by these techniques the half-finished plan to nationalize the whole commercial system, as was acutely demonstrated when the bonds of the companies were declared valid as circulating medium in 1766. It was the first attempt at the emission of paper money in Portugal and an evident challenge to the financial dealings of the British houses in Lisbon, whose dominance of monetary transactions was in large measure the cause of the late development of banking in Portugal. Strong pressure from London and the rapid dispatch of William Lyttleton with special instructions to demand the modification of the law as well as to make other important demands, forced Pombal to back down. He agreed that the English should not be required to accept the companies' bonds as legal tender, and in response to Lyttleton's criticisms, he also abandoned the restrictions on the export of gold.[2]

Within the traditional framework of the colonial system revolutionary

[1] Cunha Saraiva, *Companhia Geral de Pernambuco*, 139–46; 'Demonstrações da junta [of Company of Pernambuco], 1780, IHGB/AUC, 1-2-11; Ratton, *Recordações*, 182.
[2] 'Ley para que as apólices das Companhias valhão como dinheiro da primeira plana', 21 June 1766, BNLCP, códice 454; 'Ordenando...que da publicação della em diante não seja pessoa alguma obrigada a receber em pagamento contra sua vontade as apólices das sobreditas Companhias...' 3 February 1771, BNLCP, códice 455, f. 27.

changes were also taking place in the military and fiscal structure of Portuguese America. Foreign military experts were contracted to re-organize the armed forces of Brazil. Lieutenant-General João Henrique Bohm was appointed commander-in-chief and Jacques Funck was to be chief of engineers and artillery. The troops of Portugal and Brazil were henceforth to 'constitute one...army under the same rules, with identical discipline, and without any differences whatever.' The model for the reorganization was Count Schaumburg-Lippe-Buckeburg's far reaching reforms to the Portuguese military establishment.[1] There was to be no relaxation for 'a single moment' in the creation of forces 'to guard, fortify, and people the overseas dominions'.[2] Pombal had taken the British government's gratuitous advice to heart. 'Eight unarmed British men-of-war would be sufficient to conquer Rio de Janeiro', he warned, and on the defense of that magnificent harbour and city, which in 1763 had been made the viceregal capital, 'depended the security of this precious continent.'[3]

The military rationalization of the Bohm mission was to be supplemented by forging an interdependent unit out of the diverse captaincies of Brazil. 'All the Portuguese colonies belong to his Majesty and all those who govern them are his Vassals', Pombal told the governor of São Paulo in 1775, 'and from this fact Rio de Janeiro has a pressing obligation to aid all the other captaincies of Brazil, as each of them to aid mutually one another and the said Rio de Janeiro...In this reciprocal union of power consists essentially the greatest strength of a state, and in lack of it, its weakness.'[4] The message was repeated time and again to all the governors in America, for in its realization lay 'one of the most important dispositions...for the defence, preservation, and security of all and each of them.'[5] The instructions of the Marquis of Pombal were intended, the governor of Goiás was informed in 1771, 'to establish for the government of all Portuguese America, a political, civil, and military system, applicable to all of the captaincies of that continent according to the situation and circumstances of each of them.'[6] There were no 'better instructions than those of the Marquis of Pombal', the governor of

[1] 'Relação das instruções', *RIHGB*, xxxv, pt. 1 (1872) 227–326.
[2] *Ibid.*, 212–14.
[3] 'Instruções', 20 June 1767, Carneiro de Mendonça, *Pombal e o Brasil*, 64; Lavradio, 20 February 1770, *RIHGB*, vol. ccxxv (April–June 1962) 194.
[4] 'Instrução militar para uso do governador...de São Paulo', 24 June 1775, Marcos Carneiro de Mendonça, 'O pensamento da metrópole em relação ao Brasil', *RIHGB*, vol. ccxxvii (October–December 1962) 54.
[5] 'Instruções para o governador...Minas Gerais', 1775, *ibid.*, 54–5.
[6] 'Instruções para o governador...Goiás', 1771, *ibid.*, 53.

Mato Grosso was told in the same year, 'to establish the *sistema fundamental* which today forms the government of Portuguese America.'[1] The directives from Lisbon were overoptimistic, but nevertheless important changes were achieved. At the captaincy level auxiliary cavalry and infantry regiments were raised. In Minas Gerais for example thirteen regiments of auxiliary cavalry were organized, commanded by colonels appointed from the 'principal men of greatest credit and fidelity in the captaincy'. In addition, companies of irregular foot troops were established, intended to mobilize in emergencies the numerous blacks and mulattoes of the urban and rural population. The Minas Dragoons, the captaincy's paid regular force, was reorganized into eight companies and salaries standardized.[2]

At the foundations of the new administrative military system lay a renovated fiscal structure which had grown from the establishment of the Royal Treasury in Lisbon during December 1761. The aim of the Treasury was to centralize jurisdiction for all fiscal matters in the exchequer and make it solely responsible for all the different sectors of fiscal administration from customs house revenues to the farming of royal monopolies. Carvalho e Melo became the first chancellor. The creation of the Royal Treasury marked the culmination of Carvalho e Melo's reform of the revenue and collection machinery of the state. With high salaries for officials, modern bookkeeping techniques, regular statements of balance and, like the *junta do comércio*, bound to a strict secrecy in its dealings, the new organization was controlled by José Francisco da Cruz, the first treasurer general.[3]

It was the new bookkeeping methods and the centralized overseeing functions of the Royal Treasury which had greatest impact in the colonies, for after the war the process began to establish in each Brazilian captaincy exchequer boards, or *juntas da fazenda*, each of separate competence but responsible to the Treasury for regular, standardized and, hopefully, accurate statements of receipts and expenditures. As with the Treasury in Lisbon the captaincy *juntas da fazenda* were to attract officers from among the local 'prudent and wealthy men', in particular the most opulent of

---

[1] 'Instruções para o governador...Mato Grosso', 1771, *ibid.*, 52.
[2] 'Instrucção para D. Antônio de Noronha, governador e capitão general da capitania de Minas Gerais', 24 January 1775, *Anuário do Museu da Inconfidência (AMI)* II (Ouro Prêto, 1953) 177–82; Also, 'Quadros das forças de mar e terra existentes na Capitanias de Rio de Janeiro, Sta Catharina Rio Grande, Minas Gerais, e na Praça da Colonia disponiveis para e defeza da fronteira do Sul'. 1776, IHGB, lata 44, doc. 8.
[3] *Exposição histórica do ministerio das finanças* (Lisbon, 1952) 25–6; Smith, *Pombal* II, 60; Macedo, *A situação econômica* 48–9; 'Ley sobre a cobrança da décima', 26 September 1762, BNLCP, códice 454, f. 96–9.

the local merchants, who were to be encouraged by the provision of suitably attractive salaries to bring their commercial expertise to the exercise of public affairs in the same way that the Cruz' and Bandeiras had brought theirs to fiscal and economic policy making in the metropolis.[1]

The *junta da fazenda* of Minas Gerias established in 1765 received detailed instructions on procedure during 1769 and took its final form in 1771. Expenditures were to be divided into military, ecclesiastical, civil and extraordinary lists, and the junta was to be made responsible for the disposal of the captaincy contracts, which in the case of Minas Gerais involved the important *entradas* taxes and the local *dízimos* or tithes, as well as lesser passage tariffs. Such important functions had previously been within the competence of the overseas council in Lisbon. In fact for the first time a colonial organ of government under the presidency of the local governor, which contained and welcomed local participation, became solely responsible for the regional exchequer and for all expenditure and revenue collection except that of the royal fifth. This latter tribute remained the responsibility of the foundry houses and was a revenue which could not be touched by the junta and was remitted in its entirety to the metropolis. The intendent of the foundry house, however, was *ex officio* a member of the junta.[2]

The competence of the Minas junta did not extend to the specially demarcated diamond district of the Sêrro do Frio, which since 1740 had been administered on behalf of the holders of the diamond contract as a legal and administrative fiefdom separate from and unaccountable to any colonial authority. Pombal abolished the contract system in 1771 and took the diamond administration under the direct control of the

[1] Carvalho e Melo to Lavradio, 31 March 1769, BNLCP, códice 458, f. 147–8, and códice 453, f. 328–33; also Carneiro de Mendonça *Pombal e o Brasil*, 4. Alden, *Royal Government*, 279–311.

[2] Carta régia, 6 March 1765, creation of Minas junta da fazenda, and instructions of 1769 in the collection of the casa dos contos,Biblioteca Nacional, Rio de Janeiro (CCBNRJ) 1-1-14, 1-10-3. This large and important mass of documents is as yet uncatalogued. Reference is made to the container in which the document cited is to be found, though each of these iron containers is filled with many hundreds of documents. The Ouro Prêto *casa dos contos* collection in the Biblioteca Nacional is only a third of the total collection the rest of which is at the National Archive in Rio de Janeiro and the Arquivo Público Mineiro in Belo Horizonte. Among the rich materials here are the papers of the Minas *junta da fazenda*, the foundry houses papers, the records of many of the royal contracts. For the final instructions on organization of Minas junta, letter to Conde de Valadares, 7 September 1771, AHU, códice 610, f. 69–72; In 1775 the office of *provedor* was abolished and the *ouvidor* of Vila Rica became a member of the junta. Pombal to *Junta da Fazenda*, Minas Gerais, Lisbon, 22 August 1775, CCBNRJ, 1-9, 23.

royal treasury. A restrictive set of regulations was promulgated for the management of the Diamond District and the mining and disposal of the diamonds, aimed at regulating production in keeping with the demands of the European market. The District itself was to be administered by an intendent and fiscal together with three treasurers (*caixas*). The latter were chosen from among opulent local residents and were to enjoy the same status and respect as directors of the Brazil companies.[1]

The involvement of members of the colonial plutocracy in the administrative and fiscal organs of government was characteristic of Pombal's reforms in Brazil. Local magnates had likewise been encouraged into posts of leadership in the colonial military establishment. Even within the magistracy men were appointed to powerful judicial positions within regions where they also retained widespread financial interests. Ignácio José da Alvarenga Peixoto, a Brazilian graduate of the University of Coimbra who had composed fulsome poems in honor of Pombal and his family, was appointed *ouvidor* (superior crown magistrate) of the comarca of Rio das Mortes in Minas Gerais. It was a position he himself chose specifically because of his vast landed and mining interests in the south of the captaincy.[2]

In general the quality of the men sent to Brazil as viceroys and governors was impressive, and had been foreshadowed when in 1751 Pombal's own brother had gone to the strategically crucial captaincies of the north. The Morgado de Mateus became governor of São Paulo in 1765, and the Marquis of Lavradio was appointed as governor of Bahia in 1768 and then viceroy in Rio de Janeiro in 1769. Both men were close to Pombal and his brother, and both had been profoundly influenced by the advanced military thinking of the Count Lippe. Mateus' summary of Pombal's instructions exemplified the priorities: 'The spirit...may be reduced to three principal points, the first, to secure the frontier, the second, to people it in order that it may defend itself, and third, to make profitable use of the mines and utilities which might be discovered in this vast continent.'[3] And Pombal expected much of his delegates. 'The people you go to govern', he told the governor-designate of Mato Grosso, Luís Pinto de Sousa Coutinho in 1767, 'are obedient and loyal to the King, to

---

[1] Joaquim Felício dos Santos, *Memórias do Distrito Diamantino da Comarca do Sêrro Frio* (3rd edition, Rio de Janeiro, 1956) 172–7; C. R. Boxer, *The Golden Age of Brazil 1695–1750* (Berkeley and Los Angeles, 1962) 204–25; 'Regimento para os administradores do Contrato dos Diamantes', Lisbon, 1771, BNLCP, códice 691, f. 2.

[2] M. Rodrigues Lapa, *Vida e Obra de Alvarenga Peixoto* (Rio de Janeiro, 1960) x, xxvii.

[3] Antunes de Moura, *Morgado de Mateus*, 89; For a comprehensive account of viceroyalty of Lavradio, Dauril Alden, *Royal Government in Colonial Brazil* (Berkeley and Los Angeles, 1968).

his governors and ministers, are humble, loving tranquility and peace...
Common sense teaches that forced obedience is violent and suspect and
voluntary obedience secure and firm...Do not alter anything with force
or violence...when reason allows and it is necessary to banish abuses and
destroy pernicious customs to the benefit of King, Justice and the common
Good, act with much prudence and moderation, a method which achieves
more than power....In whatever resolution your excellency intends
observe these three things: Prudence in deliberation, dexterity in preparation, perseverance in execution.'[1]

By the late sixties, however, the whole Luso-Brazilian system was
beginning to experience a sea-change. It had begun almost imperceptibly
during the first years of the decade, and as it gathered momentum was to
have repercussions of catastrophic proportions. Production in the mines
of Brazil, which a confident governor-general of Bahia at the beginning
of the eighteenth century had predicted would be 'so permanent that it
will be impossible to exhaust them as long as the world exists', had
begun to decline.[2] The exhaustion of the alluvial gold, and the failure to
devise improved techniques to meet the growing complications and
difficulties of exploitation, within an economy so dependent in specific
areas on the bullion from the Brazilian interior were bound to produce
widespread consequences.

Royal income from the gold of Minas Gerais fell sharply. The 100
arroba quota had been met and exceeded throughout the fifties. During
the following decade the fifth rendered an average per annum of only 86
arrobas of gold, and between 1774–85 the average had again fallen, this
time to 68 arrobas.[3] (See statistical appendix 1, graph B.) The impact on
minting was immediate. Fall-off in the amount of gold coin entering into
circulation was by the seventies precipitous. Monetary emission running
at 1,304,924,980 *reis* a year from 1752–61, declined by over 50 per cent to
569,010,274 *reis* during the period 1771–82.[4] (See statistical appendix 1,
graph C.) The *entradas*, one of the most sensitive indicators of the volume
of commerce between the principal mining zone and the outside world,
reflected the changing conditions by a sharp contraction which began

[1] Pombal to Luís Pinto de Sousa Coutinho, 1767, Carneiro de Mendonça, 'O pensamento da
metropole em relação do Brasil', *RIHGB*, vol. CCXXVII, 56–61.

[2] Quotation from Manuel Cardozo, 'The Brazilian Gold Rush', *The Americas*, III, no. 2
(October 1946) 137.

[3] 'Rendimento do quinto da capitania de Minas Gerais', 1752–62, 1763–73, 1774–85, AHU,
códice 311, annexes 15, 16, 17.

[4] 'Emissão de moedas de ouro e seu valor para continente', Macedo. *A situação econ ómica*, 167.

during the mid-sixties.[1] (See statistical appendix 1, graph A.) 'The diminuation of the income of Brazil is immense' reported the French envoy in Lisbon during 1772.[2] A concerned government in Lisbon directed the Minas Gerais *junta da fazenda* to insist on the immediate imposition of the *derrama* tax to make up the growing deficit under the 1750 gold quota system.[3]

The contracting gold producing sector was not the only vital area of colonial production entering into a period of depression. Competition from English, French, and Dutch colonial producers had seriously restricted traditional outlets for sugar.[4] The price of Brazilian sugar on the Amsterdam market, 0.33 guilders a pound in 1762 had fallen to 0.23 guilders a pound ten years later, and remained at that price until 1776.[5] The creeping recession was felt immediately in the metropolis where the volume of traffic in the port of Lisbon contracted and customs revenue diminished.[6] There were bankruptcies among both large and small entrepreneurs.[7] The London merchant and bullion speculator, William Braund, finding his business at Lisbon had come to an abrupt halt in 1762, withdrew altogether from Portuguese commerce.[8]

Recession did not embrace all sectors of Luso-Brazilian commerce, and the particular elements not involved had special significance. The quantity of Port wine exported increased.[9] The internal tobacco market remained stable, the tobacco export trade expanded, and the average price of an arroba of tobacco for re-export rose from 735 reis between 1756–60 to an average of 839 reis per arroba between 1774 and 1778, an increase of 14 per cent.[10] Pombal's continued security in office in face of a serious crisis of imperial commerce and state finances doubtless owed much to the fact that the major supports of the interest groups with whom

---

[1] 'Relação dos rendimentos desta capitania de Minas Gerais desde os seus descobrimentos...' Carlos José da Silva, BNLCP, códice 643, f. 204–18.

[2] Cited by Inácio José Verissimo, *Pombal os Jesuitas e o Brasil* (Rio de Janeiro, 1961) 296.

[3] Pombal to junta da fazenda, Minas Gerais, 2 August 1771, 3 June 1772, and 27 September 1773, CCBNRJ, 1-9-23.

[4] Visconde de Carnaxide, *O Brasil na administração Pombalina* (São Paulo, 1940) 78; Bourgoing, *Voyage du ci-devant Duc du Chatelet en Portugal*, 1, 228.

[5] N. W. Posthumus, *Inquiry into the History of Prices in Holland* (2 vols., Leiden, 1946, 1964) 1, 123–4. See Statistical Appendix, Graph 1.

[6] Macedo, *A situação económica*, 169; Carnaxide, *O Brasil na administração Pombalina*, 77–9.

[7] Macedo, *Problemas*, 188.

[8] Lucy S. Sutherland, *A London Merchant 1695–1774* (Oxford, 1933) 18, 26, 39.

[9] Godinho, *Prix et Monnaies*, 253.

[10] 'Movimento do mercado do tabaco na epoca pombalina, volume do comércio de tabaco no reino e fora dele. Rendimento da Alfândega do tabaco', document 8, Macedo, *A situação económica* 293–4. Godinho, *Prix et Monnaies*, 257.

he had closely linked himself and favored by government policy remained untouched. Moreover, the growing re-export of cotton to Europe, and in particular to France and Great Britain, provided the same privileged interests with further encouragement.

The collapse of the gold sector had dramatic impact on that group of interests whose channel of trade most relied on bullion for its sustenance; the vulnerable interconnection that linked the English to the gold of Minas Gerais and the gold–silver contraband network in America. In fact, the contraction of British commerce with Portugal was little short of catastrophic, as the value of the exports of British goods halved between 1760–70.[1] Only Holland and Germany had taken more English goods than did Portugal in 1760; fifteen years later, Holland, Germany, Spain, Italy, and Flanders had relegated Portugal to sixth position among Britain's foreign traders, while Africa, the East Indies, Ireland, and the American colonies far outstripped the Portuguese as buyers of English merchandise.[2] The value of English textile exports to Portugal, the great fundamental of the commerce composing some 70 per cent of total export values which had averaged over a million pounds annually in the late 1750s slumped to £709,000 in 1761–5 and £459,000 in 1766–70.[3]

The contraction of British trade was too rapid to have been due entirely to the gold crisis. British exports were also being adversely affected by a loss of markets caused by Hispano–Portuguese rivalry in South America. A high percentage of the British exports to Portugal had gone via Lisbon straight to Brazil, and from Brazil to Spanish America as contraband. In 1772 the London *Annual Register* reported: 'It must be observed that the communication between the colony of Santo-Sacramento and Buenos Aires [is] entirely cut off...the greater part of the most precious merchandizes which arrived from Europe were sent from Rio de Janeiro to that colony, from whence they were smuggled through Buenos Aires to Peru or Chile, and this contraband trade was worth a million and a half piasters of dollars annually to the Portuguese... The loss which the almost entire suppression of the contraband trade occasions cannot be calculated.'[4]

The closure of contraband was partly the result of the war against the

[1] Schumpeter, *English Overseas Trade Statistics*, 17.
[2] Manchester, *British Preeminence*, 46.
[3] H. E. S. Fisher 'Anglo-Portuguese Trade 1700–1770', *Economic History Review*, 2nd series, XVI (1963), 229; A. B. Wallis Chapman, 'The commercial relations of England and Portugal 1487–1807', *Transactions of the Royal Historical Society*, 3rd series, I, (1907) 177.
[4] *The Annual Register for 1772* (London), 155–7.

Jesuit settlements in Paraguay, and partly a consequence of the successful struggle against illegal commerce by the revived Spanish administration at Buenos Aires. A notable increase in confiscated goods occurred between 1769–75, and collection of revenue in the subtreasury of Buenos Aires more than doubled between 1773–6. The creation of the viceroyalty of the Rio de la Plata in 1776 and the comprehensive legislation of 1778 removed the *raison d'être* of contraband by opening direct trade between the Plata and Spain. Preeminently during the last years of Pombal's regime there was the Portuguese–Spanish struggle for the control of Colonia itself, the entrepôt of Plata contraband, which in the process of the campaign was obliterated.[1]

By a quirk of historical circumstance two factors totally beyond Pombal's control had achieved exactly what he had aimed to carry out by policy, and been forced to abandon by the events of the early sixties. The very special lines and very specific direction of trade which had linked Britain's vast favorable balance either to the gold of Minas Gerais or to the contraband with Spanish America via Buenos Aires were both simultaneously disrupted. The British who had only recently realized that the intention of Pombal's measures during the 1750s had been aimed at precisely such a disruption could not fail to blame the all powerful minister for the startling change in their fortunes. Violent merchant anti-Pombal propaganda in London, as well as the British Factory's publication of its confidential memorials to British ministers served to confirm the assumption.

Pombal, anxious for British support and fearful of British intentions, vainly sought to protest his innocence. The British minister complained to Pombal and his minister for foreign affairs, Luís da Cunha Manuel, the nephew of the late Paris ambassador, that 'there had been several innovations in the commerce which had affected the trade of British subjects [and] that it was a known certainty that the trade with Portugal was greatly diminished'. Luís da Cunha 'allowed this to be true'. He assigned the reasons for the diminuation of the trade, however, to 'the earthquake, the war, the burning of the customs house [1764], but particularly that the trade between Rio de Janeiro and the Nova Colonia [do Sacramento], which was formerly very considerable was now put at a stop to by the Spaniards who had blockaded Nova Colonia...and therefore the trade was entirely at a stand in the river Plate which

---

[1] Carneiro de Mendonça, *Pombal e o Brasil*, 78; John Lynch, *Spanish Colonial Administration* (London, 1958) 37; Alden, *Royal Government*, for a discussion of the complicated events in the South, especially pp. 59–275.

occasioned a great diminution in the gold [*sic*] remittance from Rio de Janeiro and in the consumption of English goods.'[1]

The ending of the golden age had positive as well as negative aspects, for the recession produced a changed environment within Portugal which offered important possibilities to the Portuguese government. Faced with an overall decline in colonial re-exports and a consequent decline in the capacity to import, but with internal demand sustained by the export of certain colonial and metropolitan products, import substitution was a natural and pragmatic solution. The recession predated and accompanied Pombal's celebrated 'industrial' development. The chronology is clear. Of the manufacturing establishments set up with the aid of the *junta do comércio* during Pombal's regime, 80 per cent were authorized after 1770.[2]

A favorable organizational and entrepreneurial framework already existed and was to facilitate greatly the creation of the new manufactories of the 1770s. The establishment of the Brazil companies had been closely linked to important initiatives concerning manufacturing industry in the metropolis. In 1757 the *junta do comércio* took over the bankrupt silk factory in the Lisbon suburb of Rato. The factory had been founded during the thirties by Cardinal da Mota and two French entrepreneurs, Robert Godin and Sibert. Capital had been raised, a company formed, and a large building constructed. The early years had been difficult and during the forties the company's deficits considerable. The royal takeover placed the *junta do comércio* in supreme control, and determined that the directors of the factory should be chosen equally from among the deputies of the junta and from the directors of the Company of Grão Pará and Maranhão. The statutes were drawn up under the influence of José Rodrigues Bandeira, and among the first directors were João Rodrigues Monteiro and José Moreira Leal representing the junta, and for the company of Pará and Maranhão, José Francisco da Cruz and Manuel Ferreira da Costa. The Factory's products during the same year were granted exemption from duties at the customs house.[3]

The type of manufacturing agglomeration envisioned for the factory

---

[1] 'Minutes of a conference with the count de Oeyras and Dom Luis da Cunha upon my taking leave of them, Friday, 28 August 1767', published by Vera Lee Brown, 'The relations of Spain and Portugal 1763–1777', *Smith College Studies in History* xv (October 1929–January 1930) 70–1. [2] Macedo, *A situação económica*, 255.

[3] 'Estatutos da Real Fábrica das Sedas, estabelecida no suburbio do Rato', Lisbon, 6 August 1757, BNLCP, códice 453, f. 158–65; 'Decreto...na Alfândega de Lisboa se duvidão sellar livres de direitas as peças de seda que se fabricão nas manufacturas destes Reynos', 2 April 1757, *ibid.*, f. 152; Jorge Borges de Macedo, *Problemas de história da indústria Portuguesa no século XVIII* (Lisbon, 1963) 70–2, 96–8.

was based partly upon the industrial configuration of the period, though it was also the result of a quite explicit policy decision based on Pombal's assessment of the causes for the success of manufacturing enterprise in England. Instead of large capital expenditure on plant and equipment such as undertaken at the foundation of the silk factory of Rato, he had seen industrial concentrations grow from individual units where initially a small outlay only had been necessary and returns immediate. The English he commented 'only study the methods to make simple or cheap the means to establish them'.[1] In 1776 the Rato factory consisted of the central building with manufacturing, accounting, and retailing functions, and an associated network of dependent individual workshops in other parts of the city. At the factory itself at least ninety-one looms were in operation and perhaps over two hundred looms dispersed in a large number of small units of production. These independent producers were integrated with the factory for marketing and dependent on it for their supply of raw materials. The concept of the manufactory as a coordinating center resting firmly on the household producer was systematically applied to the Royal Silk Factory in 1766, and of the small units of production taken under its control only part were involved in silk production *per se*.[2]

It was the close connection between the Factory and the monopolistic company which was of most significance. The presence of the same powerful directors at the head of both enterprises brought, as was no doubt intended, a close and profitable relationship between the factory and the company, and allowed for a fluidity of funds and aid which was mutually beneficial. The Company of Pará and Maranhão paid no dividend until 1759, and it is probable that capital from this source was secretly used to encourage the manufacturing enterprise.[3] The monopoly of the company also provided an assured and protected market, particularly after the establishment of the Pernambuco monopoly in an important and populated market during 1759. As the British factory complained, the 'companies have solely the permission and privilege to supply the Brazils [within their monopoly areas] and some of the directors openly declared, that their views and designs are to prefer the exportations of the commodities of their own country's produce, which consequently must find a sale, when no other goods are in competition with them, either in quality or price'.[4]

---

[1] *Ibid.*, 147.   [2] *Ibid.*, 96, 152.

[3] 'Rezumo do estado da Companhia Geral do Grão Pará e Maranhão no fim do anno de 1770'...AHU, códice 1187; 'Memórias do consul e factória Británnica', BNLCP, códice 94, f. 25v.   [4] *Ibid.*, 24.

Change

It was undoubtedly a fact that both companies took special care to favor Portuguese manufactured goods, and well they might, for it was the same group of privileged established interests which benefited at each stage of the process.[1] The growth in export of raw cotton, and the flexible interpretation of the functions of the silk factory, saw the creation of a lucrative triangle which brought profits at all points: as interest on the loans which stimulated the production of the commodities, that were to be shipped to the metropolis, and manufactured in company supported workshops, to be shipped back again on company ships to the colonial consumer, who probably bought them on company credit. The lucrative triangle was not the only part of the system (raw cotton after the Peace of Paris provided a profitable re-export business) but it was a vital core. During the early years it gave a powerful boost to both the commercial and manufacturing activities, not to mention to the capital accumulation of the privileged established interests themselves.[2] (See statistical appendix no. 2 and 3.)

Many of the manufacturing establishments founded after 1770 were dedicated to the production of luxury goods – silks, hats, chinaware, tapestry, decorative jewelry, ribbons and buttons. Often they received monopoly privileges, exemption from taxation, and the special protection of their supplies of raw materials. In addition a comparatively large number of cotton textile enterprises were set up, which were in part a response to the growing export of cotton from Brazil. Sixty per cent of the workshops set up by the direct participation of the *junta do comércio* were in Lisbon and Oporto. The cotton manufactories were almost exclusively located in coastal areas close to their seaborne raw materials. With the powerful central direction of the *junta do comércio*, and with funds for investment made available by the centralized machinery of the new Royal Treasury, often using the 4 per cent tax raised after the earthquake for the rebuilding of the city, the stimulus to development was powerful.[3]

---

[1] 'Documentos referentes a indústria de extração da seda e seu privilegio na América Portuguêsa', IHGB, lata 107, doc. 4 and doc. 10; 'Mappa de todas as fazendas que a Companhia Geral de Pernambuco e Paraíba tem extraido das fábricas do Reino e exportado para os conquistas desde o seu establelecimento até 31 de dezembro de 1777', IHGB/AUC, 1-2-11, f. 239.

[2] 'Resumo do estado da Companhia Geral do Grão-Pará e Maranhão no fim do anno de 1770', AHU, códice 1187: For Ratton's calculations of profits gained by company stockholders, Ratton, *Recordações*, 180; Manuel Nunes Dias, 'A Junta liquidatária dos fundos das Companhias do Grão-Pará e Maranhão, Pernambuco e Paraíba 1778–1837', *Revista Portuguesa de História*, x (Coimbra, 1962) 153–201.

[3] Macedo, *A situação económica*, 254–6, Macedo, *Problemas* 147, 189–90; Smith, *Pombal*, ii, 146; BNLCP, códice 256, 226. For the more urgent encouragement of silk production during the 1770s see Ratton *Recordações*, 142; *Notizie del Mondo* (16 February 1773); *Notizie del Mondo* (25 October 1774).

Conflicts and conspiracies

The model of industrial organization Pombal had applied in the Rato factory and drawn from his understanding of the English example was applied to the most important of the manufactories established: the royal woolen factory of Porto Alegre. The Porto Alegre factory, the construction of which began in 1771, was under the direct surveillance of the minister of state, Martinho de Melo e Castro, the former ambassador in London, and was financed by funds from the Royal Treasury and the *junta do comércio*. The closed economy of the metropolitan hinterland contained widespread household industry which remained isolated from the fluctuations of the urban economies of Lisbon and Oporto. Domestic production in the interior had retained its competitiveness *vis-à-vis* foreign imports, for the native linen, silk, and woolen goods outside the coastal zone could outprice foreign manufactures and would continue to do so while foreign methods of production were not sufficiently different from native methods to produce substantial differences of price. The traveller José Gorani declared that it was easier to find transport abroad or to Brazil than to Coimbra or Braga, and so long as this was true, and before technological advance transformed price differentials the domestic industry of Trás-os-Montes, Beira Alta, and Alentejo, gained a natural protection. The Porto Alegre factory, while employing seventy masters and apprentices in its weaving workshops, relied for all spinning on the surrounding area, and by 1779 of the 1,348 elements engaged by the factory 979, both spinners and weavers, were outside the establishment. The manufactory with its modified putting out system became essentially a coordinating center resting firmly on the household producer and a mechanism to facilitate the supply of hinterland production to urban demand.[1]

The Porto Alegre factory like the royal silk factory was directly administered on the royal account. In addition to re-organization and establishment of royal factories the state encouraged private industrial enterprise with exclusive or monopolistic protections.[2] There was lateral fluidity of funds between the Royal and private establishments, however. Joaquim Inácio da Cruz, for example, used funds from the Royal Silk factory to encourage the silk stocking and paper box factories in Tomar, as well as the cotton textile workshops there.[3] The labor costs of both

---

[1] José Gorani, *Portugal a côrte, e o país nos anos de 1765 a 1767* (Lisbon, 1945) 99; Macedo, *A situação económica*, 212–40, Macedo, *Problemas*, 144–52; Luís Fernando de Carvalho Dias, *História dos Lanifícios (1750–1834) Documentos* (3 vols., Lisbon, 1958–65), II, 11, 263, 322, 325.

[2] Luís Fernando de Carvalho Dias, *A relação das fábricas de 1788* (Coimbra, 1955) 21–2.

[3] Ratton, *Recordações*, 30.

royal and private privileged establishments were kept low by the imposition, sometimes violent, of a system of apprenticeship.[1] A general protective framework for both types of enterprise was provided by a flexible tariff policy of exemptions and prohibitions in favor of Portuguese production.[2]

Just as a reservoir of skill existed in the interior to be organized into more efficient groupings, so in the urban areas a large number of skilled artisans could be called upon, and whose existence made the manufacturing agglomerations of Pombal's administration a rational and workable system in the coastal zone. Demographic studies based on the tax returns of the *décima* revealed the high percentage and wide range of technical skills in eighteenth century Lisbon. Of all professional activity in the city during the sixties, at a minimum, 25 per cent was concerned with occupations of an industrial type, principally wood and leather working, but also weaving, printing, iron working and so on. Dispersed among the native tradesmen and artificers were many foreign artisans, modest men, separate from the large and influential foreign factors of the capital.[3] A substantial number of the entrepreneurs aided by the junta were foreigners, and twenty-seven of the fifty-two royal decrees issued for the foundation of new workshops went to them, and a third of these to Frenchmen.[4] Typical of the more important recipients was Jacques Ratton, born in the province of Dauphiné in 1736, shortly before his parents emigrated to Portugal to establish a business in Lisbon. Ratton, who had been one of the first to develop the re-export trade with France in Brazilian cotton after the Peace of Paris, was to engage in a whole range of manufacturing enterprises; in the production of calico, hats, of

---

[1] Carvalho Dias, *Relação*, 18; The whole system of guilds and apprenticeships was reformed after 1771. For the collected documents see Franz-Paul Langlans *As Corporações dos Ofícios Mecánicos: Subsídios para a sua história com um estudo de Marcelo Caetano* (2 vols., Lisbon, 1943).

[2] 'Alvará...fazer merce a direcção da real fábrica das sedas do indulto privativo e privilegio exclusivo do commércio da *goma copal*, produzida nos Dominios da América Portuguêsa, prohibida a entrada della nas Alfândegas destes Reinos, que até agora se introduzio de Paizes Estrangeiros, 10 Dezembro, 1770'; 'Alvará...por bem animar e protegar as fábricas da louça estabelecidas no cidade de Lisboa, e as mais, que se acham de presente. Prohibindo a entrada de toda a louça fabricada fora della, a exepção da que vier da India, e da China em Navios de propriedades portuguezas, 7 Novembro 1770'; 'Alvará, porque...he servido... prohibir a entrada de todos os chapeos fabricados fora destes Reinos, e Dominios em beneficio das fábricas que se acham estabelecidas nos mesmos Reinos, e das que para o futuro se estabelecerem, 10 Dezembro, 1770'; BNLCP, códice 453, f. 336–9, 391–3, 395–8. 'Alvará porque S. M. concedeo a João Baptista Iacatelli privilegio por tempo de dez annos de insenção de todos e qualquer direitos que nos portos do Reino e Dominios Ultramarinos diviao pagar os tecidos de Algodão simples, ou com qualquer mistura, extendedese a todos os fabricantes da mesma manufactura, 5 January 1774', BNLCP, códice 455, f. 349–50.

[3] Macedo, *Problemas*, 82–95.   [4] Macedo, *A situação econômica*, 252.

paper, and cotton textiles.[1] At Marinha, an Englishman, William Stephens, contracted by Pombal personally, and with whom Pombal was to develop a close friendship, set up a glass manufactory with junta aid and became a highly successful industrialist.[2]

The Pombaline manufactories, despite the traditional bases on which they were constructed, and although surrounded by an ancient system of privileges, monopolies and apprenticeships, were essentially a new industry, fostered by varied techniques within a protective tariff regime, and made possible by the changed economic environment. Not all the enterprises were successful. Robert Southey observed in the 1790s: 'The conego da Cruz founded a silk manufactory at Sobral, an ill-chosen situation, being a days journey from any water conveyance. His great difficulty was to keep the workmen there, who regretted the amusements and vices of the metropolis; with this view he provided plays for them, and so fully possessed by the spirit of commerce was the patriotic ecclesiastic that he even established a colony of prostitutes from Lisbon at Sobral.'[3] The project and the 'plays' were a failure, but others did make progress, the Porto Alegre factory among them. The water powered Tomar cotton textile mill produced goods of 'great beauty and at least equal to those of France and England', according to Adrien Balbi, who also praised the silks of Portugal as 'remarkable for their variety which imitate perfectly those of Lyons'.[4] Ratton was to become one of the richest industrialists in the Kingdom.

The intimate relationship between the government's means of encouragement and its recognition of the economic and technical base available to it, both in the resilient household industry of the interior, and among the skilled artisans of the coastal cities, contributed to the general success of the establishments set up after 1770. Also important was the mobility of funds and of directing personnel between the monopolistic companies, royal silk factory, *junta do comércio*, Royal Treasury, and the new manufactories. Catastrophic decline in mining output had provided the economic environment for manufacturing enterprise which had been lacking when previous eighteenth-century administrators

[1] Ratton, *Recordações*, 8, 181.

[2] 'Cartas originaes de G. Stephens dando notícias familiares e de política estrangeira', BNLCP, códice 704, f. 27–30, 87–9; Cartas inglezas, BNLCP, códice 691 [This códice is inaccurately stated in the printed catalogue to be códice 690], letters of William Stephens to Marquis of Pombal and translation of the 'Letters from Portugal' by Stephen's sister.

[3] Robert Southey, *Letters written during a Short Residence in Spain and Portugal* (2nd edition, Bristol, 1799) 403.

[4] Adrien Balbi, *Essai Statistique sur le Royaume de Portugal et d'Algarve* (2 vols., Paris, 1822), I, 451, 455.

had tried and failed to stimulate industry. And in addition the special relationships and interconnected interests which had been established during the first decade of Pombal's government – in particular between the Brazil companies and the royal silk factory – had placed his collaborators in an excellent position to take advantage of the changed economic situation.

The 1770s in fact found the privileged established interests firmly and powerfully entrenched within the body politic, and a remarkably small, compact, and interrelated group of men in positions of great power and influence. José Francisco da Cruz, and his brother Joaquim Inácio held the key post of treasurer-general of the Royal Treasury. Anselmo José da Cruz, in association with Policarpo José Machado and Geraldo Wenceslão Braancamp held the tobacco contract. Machado, a provedor of the *junta do comércio* was a stockholder of the Lisbon tobacco factory. Anselmo held the royal soap monopoly contract and had an exclusive arrangement to supply soap for industrial uses to the royal silk factory. José Francisco and Joaquim Inácio da Cruz, the latter administrator of the customs house, both held positions in the direction of the commercial companies and the manufacturing enterprises. Bandeira, who had directed the takeover of the Rato factory was a director of the Pernambuco Company, and a provedor of the *junta do comércio*. Antônio Caetano Ferreira and Luís José de Brito both became officials of the treasury and the latter a director of the silk factory. Quintella, provedor of the *junta do comércio* was a director of both Brazil companies, a stockholder in the Lisbon tobacco factory, and a member of a major tobacco exporting company to Spain. He also held the contract of *dízimos* of Bahia from 1757–63, and commencing in 1765, the exclusive rights to whaling along the whole Brazilian littoral. In 1770, he obtained the salt monopoly contract of the state of Brazil, and subsidiary Brazilian contracts such as the tax on sweet olive oil imported into Rio de Janeiro, and the right to duties on tobacco and other goods embarked at Bahia.[1] (See statistical appendix 4.)

The special protection of Pombal's collaborators continued as before. Quintella's sudden death in 1775 brought a rapid royal enactment to guarantee the orderly succession of his vast business concerns to his nephew Joaquim, who took the name Quintella and continued in all his uncle's capacities. The Quintella company was also granted special tax collection powers. The state continued to reward the new great merchant dynasties it had so carefully stimulated and aided since 1750. Joaquim

---

[1] 'Decreto para Anselmo José da Cruz ficar no contrato do tabaco 7 January 1763'; 'Decreto para Anselmo José da Cruz ser Contratador do Sabão', BNLCP, códice 454; 'Carta dos Privilegios do Contrato Geral do Tabaco de que são contratadores, Anselmo José da Cruz,

Inácio da Cruz obtained the entailed estates and title of Sobral, an ex-Jesuit possession, and the title passed to his brother Anselmo on his death. José Francisco de Cruz obtained the morgado, or entailed estates, of Alagoa, a title which became that of his sons, aspiring pupils at the college of nobles. When in 1775 the inauguration of the equestrian statue of José I 'the Magnanimous', and officially, designated Portuguese 'Caesar Augustus', took place in the great new commercial place on the waterfront of Lisbon, it was Anselmo José da Cruz who stood at the right hand of a beplumed and ceremonious Marquis of Pombal.[1]

The recession, import substitution, and the involvement of the privileged established interests in the development of the manufacturing enterprises, served to fortify a tendency set in motion by the abandonment of the Pombaline nationalization plan when only half completed, and by a rise in raw cotton exports as a result of the Pará Company's capital investment in Maranhão. The failure to dislodge the British factors in Lisbon and Oporto, and to capture from them the commercial business with Great Britain, served to concentrate the interests of Pombal's collaborators firmly in colonial commerce and the trade with continental Europe. Although the fall of Brazilian gold production had removed the means of payment for foreign manufactures, the major source of capital of the established interests – tobacco – had been unaffected by the recession. Moreover these same interests possessed through their connections with the monopolistic Brazil companies an ideal raw material for import substitution – cotton. With fiscal necessity compelling the state to invest-ment in manufacturing, the conjunction of private and state capital was a natural outcome, especially as a similar conjunction had been employed to vital national ends by the same group in the Brazil companies during the pre-crisis years.

As a consequence, important elements among the established interests took on the functions of an industrial-capitalist 'national' bourgeoisie, forming a group whose interests were rooted in the metropolis and the

Policarpo José Machado e Companhia etc.', CCBNRJ, 1-1-25; 'Contrato...do Estanco do Sal do Brazil com Joaquim Pedro Quintella, João Ferreira, etc.', CCBNRJ, 1-1-25; 'Livro de Receita e Despensa do Thesoureiro Mor do Erário Régio, Joaquim Ignácio da Cruz Sobral', CCBNRJ, 1-1-25; 'Livros dos termos de arrematação dos contractos', AHU, códices 298, 299; Myriam Ellis 'A Pesca de Baleia no Brasil Colonial', *ACC*, 71, 89–90.

[1] d'Azevedo, *Estudos*; Ratton, *Recordações*, 184–5; 'Sou servido subrogar e substituir seu sobrinho, Joaquim Tiburcio Quintella (tomando o sobrenome do falecido) para a con-tinuação e expediente daquella casa...' 8 November 1775, BNLCP, códice 456, f. 340; 'Registro de ordens para as autoridades de Minas Gerais, 1764–1799', AHU, códice 610, f. 30–1; 'Parallelo de Augusto Cesar e de Dom José, O Magnanimo Rey de Portugal', Lisbon, 1775, BNLCP, códice 456, f. 44.

Change

Luso-Brazilian commercial complex, and marking an important change from the traditional pattern of merchant oligarchy committed to extra-national commerce in conjunction with a state whose principal source of income was customs revenue. Additional recruits for this emergent entrepreneurial group came from among the modest artisan immigrants of the port cities, men paradoxically even more 'national' in outlook, like Ratton and Stephens, who were to head important enterprises. In fact it was these latter recruits who most consciously identified their interests with the state, for as Ratton explained in his memoirs, it was such an identification between his private speculations and the interest of the state that he had 'tried incessently to promote'.[1]

The emergence of this national bourgeoisie coinciding with the changed relationship with Great Britain was a factor of profound significance. The startling fall in the value of British exports to Portugal had created a more balanced commerce between the two countries. The growing re-export of raw cotton from the metropolis had also substantially altered the terms of trade with other European countries, and in particular with France, where the cotton staple had reversed the terms of trade bringing an increasingly favorable balance to Portugal.[2] (See statistical appendix 5.) The crisis, therefore, was not only creating a greater equity in Anglo-Portuguese commercial relations, but was aiding the diversification of

---

[1] Ratton, *Recordações*, 27.
[2] For example see the development of the trade between Portugal and Rouen, Pierre Dardel, *Navires et marchandises dans les ports de Rouen et du Havre au XVIIe siècle* (Paris, 1963) 550–1, and Jorge de Macedo, *O Bloqueio Continental, economia e guerra peninsular* (Lisbon, 1962) 44. Cotton exports to England and France from Portugal:

Year	Exports to England	Exports to France
	(Annual weight in arrobas)	
1776	575	13,532
1777	551	17,836
1788	4,012	56,170
1789	127,287	41,824
1796	264,581	–
1800	199,034	1,720
1801	198,872	21,234
1802	379,463	189,549
1803	302,278	149,730
1804	228,629	331,915
1805	294,838	200,027
1806	195,085	347,087
1807	102,232	330,182

Source: Macedo, *O Bloqueio Continental*, 44.

Portugal's commercial relations with the rest of Europe. In fact by the late seventies something very like Punch's 'fairy dream', and the hypothetical commercial situation he had warned against in 1762, had been created. The steep rise in cotton piece goods production which technological advance was initiating in Britain would provide a sharply rising demand for raw materials. This demand for Brazilian cotton would increasingly favor reciprocity, but at the same time bring the Luso-Brazilian Empire firmly into the orbit of a new group of interests in Britain – the Lancashire cotton manufactures and their associated merchants – who were also of all groups in Britain the most aggressive and expansionist minded.

The new situation clearly held portent of fundamental political change. The French believed as early as 1770 that in the event of a second Bourbon attack on Portugal, the British would probably content themselves with ensuring that Brazil secured virtual independence and a direct economic connection with the United Kingdom.[1] Again, as with Pombal's assessment in 1763, British intentions had been anticipated, and the French had underestimated the continuing influence of the British factors in Portugal and the traditional interests in wines and woolens with which they were associated in Britain. Yet in essence the French argument was perceptive, and the new situation was one that could only be confirmed and aggravated by the wider changes which were forcing a rapidly expanding British economy in search of larger markets, and British merchants in search of shorter credits and fewer restraints on trade.

It was a strange historical irony that cotton served to strengthen those factors which in the course of time would increase the pressures for a direct Anglo-Brazilian relationship. The Company of Pará and Maranhão had become unintentionally one of the most efficient collaborators of British industrial development, and a measure intended to strengthen the self-sufficiency and security of the Portuguese Empire had become an important element contributing to its disintegration. For Portugal, reciprocity with Britain and the diversification and growth of her commercial contacts with the rest of Europe resulted in quite opposite pressures. The privileged established interests, who as tobacco traders had always been engaged in continental as opposed to Anglo-Portuguese commerce, who as industrialists were opposed to the opening of the Portuguese market to British cotton goods, and who as entrepreneurs in cotton were interested in the profitable re-export trade, would be fortified in their opposition to any change in the exclusive character of the colonial system.

---

[1] Christelow, *HAHR*, xxvii, 24.

CHAPTER 3

DIVERGENCE

Portugal without Brazil is an insignificant power.

> Martinho de Melo e Castro to Luís de Vasconcelos e Sousa, 'instruções...acerca do governo do Brasil', [1779] *RIHGB*, xxv (1862) 479–83.

Nature made us inhabitants of the same continent and in consequence in some degree compatriots.

> *Vendek* [José Joaquim Maia e Barbalho] to Thomas Jefferson, Montpellier, 21 November 1786, *AMI*, II (1953) 11–13.

The profound changes within the Luso-Brazilian system arose from a complicated interplay of social and economic transformation, international politics and policy decision. Portugal and its colony in the New World had been brought into a new relationship. By the late 1770s, both internally within the imperial structure, and externally between the Empire and the outside world, the situation was substantially different from that which had prevailed for much of the eighteenth century. The ending of the golden age had led to the emergence of a powerfully entrenched and influential national bourgeoisie in the metropolis. The interests of this metropolitan merchant-industrial élite, although still subordinate to a broad imperial scale of priorities under the control of an all powerful minister, were becoming increasingly incompatible with the remarkably flexible mercantilism of the Pombaline state.

'The ancient names and ancient clothing' which the Duke Silva-Tarouca recommended should always disguise 'great new dispositions' had covered initiatives inconsistent with a colonial policy formulated in the exclusive interests of the metropolis. Mendonça Furtado's 'infallible maxims' concealed striking non-mercantilist features. The Lisbon *junta do comércio* directly aided manufacturing and processing enterprises in Brazil. The Company of Grão Pará and Maranhão maintained a cloth manufactory in Pará. Both the exclusive companies and the local colonial administrations used subsidy payments and guaranteed prices to stimulate new commodities. Moreover, local men, prominent for their opulence and status in society, had been drawn into the new colonial military-administrative establishment. The Portuguese government more often than not in its dealings with Brazil acted in keeping with Pombal's prudent recommendations to Luís Pinto de Sousa Coutinho.

There was some solid reasoning behind Pombal's cautionary advice to Luís Pinto. The heroic tradition of Brazilian opposition to foreign intrusion was never far from his mind. The seventeenth-century struggle of Pernambuco and Bahia against the Dutch, and the early eighteenth-century actions against the French in Rio de Janeiro, were often cited by him in diplomatic, official, and private correspondence. It was just these examples which were used to justify the wide local base given to the military establishment in the colony by the creation of numerous auxiliary regiments under the control of the local magnates.[1] The historical participation and mobilization of the Brazilians in their self-defense was also gratuitously brought to the attention of the British government faced with the revolt of their colonists in North America. The tactics of the Anglo-Americans, Pombal observed during November 1775, were identical with those of the 'good Portuguese vassals of Pernambuco and Bahia'. George III's armies would never defeat the rebels, though the loss of English America could be avoided if London acted prudently and permitted the colonists their own parliaments, which could always be controlled by royal office holders and by patronage.[2]

It was a portentous combination of circumstances that the growing conflict of interest within the imperial framework coincided with the shattering of the mercantilist system of the most powerful European colonial power. Yet despite the fact that social and economic tendencies on both sides of the Atlantic were emphasizing divergent and contradictory interests between Portugal and Brazil, Pombal continued to see external pressure on the Portuguese Empire as a far more dangerous threat than the possibility of internal disintegration. While he remained in office there was no retreat from the policies he had initiated, nor in the tolerant and flexible manner in which they were implemented.

The ferment of innovation within Brazil, however, was already raising wider questions which could only point to the pertinence of the example of the Thirteen Colonies. The viceroy, the Marquis of Lavradio, had been led to open criticism of the commercial nexus which made Brazilian merchants little more than 'simple commissaries', a situation that prevented their aiding the development of Portuguese America by reducing

[1] Martinho de Melo e Castro to D. Antônio de Noronha, 24 January 1775, *Anuário do Museu da Inconfidência (AMI)* 11 (Ouro Prêto, 1953) 178–9.

[2] Dauril Alden, 'The Marquis of Pombal and the American Revolution' *The Americas*, xvii, No. 4 (April 1961) 369–76, 377–82.

the 'commerce always to the same articles'. Lavradio believed that only with the emergence of solid merchants, acting on their own account, could this difficulty be overcome.[1] In addition, the factors which had produced import substitution in Portugal were also operative in the Americas, and with especial acuteness in the captaincy of Minas Gerais. The governor of Minas Gerais, Antônio de Noronha, reported in 1775 that numerous manufacturing establishments existed in the captaincy, and all of them were in a state of considerable growth. Their development, he observed, threatened to make the inhabitants independent of European goods.[2] Lavradio also noted the growth of manufacturing establishments in Brazil, 'private individuals having established...on their estates workshops and looms', which produced cotton, linen, woolen goods and tow, so that already 'they had become less dependent on those to whom they were debtors'. He lamented the indifference of the governors to this growth complaining that the 'greater part of the landed proprietors still continued them' despite his representations. He warned that in the case of Minas Gerais, because of the vastness of the region and the spirit of the population, such independence was a matter of great moment and might one day produce grave consequences.[3]

Growing tensions within the system were not only economic in origin. The administrative–military framework imposed in Brazil following the Peace of Paris had been forged under the stress of external threats to the territorial integrity of the colony. With the attention of the authorities riveted on the defense of the frontiers and the delineation of boundaries, great strains were placed on the new establishment and attention diverted from other equally important regions and problems. The cost of the expeditions to the south placed heavy burdens on the viceregal treasury and that of São Paulo. In both cases expenditures outpaced receipts, the subsidy for indigo lacked prompt payment, and outstanding obligations went into default.[4] During the late seventies, under the reciprocal unity system of inter-captaincy aid, troops from Minas Gerais were sent both

[1] 'Relatório do marquês de Lavradio', [1779] *RIHGB*, IV (2nd edition, 1863) 453.
[2] Quoted by Melo e Castro in 'instrução para o visconde de Barbacena', 29 January 1788, *RIHGB*, VI (1844) 19; also published in *AMI*, II (1953) 117–54.
[3] 'Relatório do marquês de Lavradio', *RIHGB*, IV, 453. Also see discussion of this matter in Alden, *Royal Government*, 383–7.
[4] Marcelino Pereira Cleto, 'Dissertação a respeito da capitania de São Paulo, sua decadéncia e modo de restabelece-la', 1782, *ABNRJ*, XXI (1899) 196; Luís de Vasconcelos e Sousa to Martinho de Melo e Castro, 15 July 1781, *RIHGB*, LI, pt. 1 (1888) 190; Vasconcelos e Sousa, *RIHGB*, IV (2nd edition, 1863) 17, 24, 30.

to the south and to Rio de Janeiro.[1] Military expenditure of the Minas *junta da fazenda* soared to unparalleled heights. The captaincy revenues were hardly sufficient for the ordinary commitments on the civil, military and ecclesiastical lists, and the obligations for food and quartering contracted by the expeditions of the 1770s remained years in arrears.[2] The startling rise in military expenditure at a time of rapidly contracting revenue sources placed added strain on the local exchequer.

Just as the lack of native entrepreneurs had been a serious obstacle to national economic development in the metropolis, even less prepared for the whole range of complicated and often far reaching reforms was the Luso-Brazilian bureaucracy. In its administrative creations on both sides of the Atlantic the Pombaline state had involved local magnates and business men in the agencies of government with a deliberation bordering on infatuation. Merchants and business men had been drawn into the administrative sections of the Royal Treasury, made deputies of the Lisbon *junta do comércio*, appointed to the colonial gold intendencies, the colonial *juntas da fazenda*, made fiscal officials of the diamond administration. Even within the magistracy Alvarenga Peixoto became superior crown magistrate with judicial and administrative functions in a region of which he was a native and where he possessed vast landed, mining, and business interests. Indeed it was because of those interests that he chose the job.[3]

Yet the intertwining of state functions and local business and landed interests worked to the interest of the state only so long as local and imperial interests coincided, and while the constant vigilance of the central government stressed the broader priorities over the personal and partisan interests of the local oligarchies. Participation by local power groups in the very mechanism of government, much in the manner the Duke Silva-Tarouca recommended during the early 1750s, did not necessarily result in the strengthening of the mutual bonds between metropolis and colony, which had been the Duke's objective, and was doubtless in Pombal's opinion the implicit corollary of the action. In

[1] Manuel Joaquim Pedroso, Vila Rica, 31 January 1782, AHU, Minas Gerais, caixa 92; Antônio de Noronha, Vila Rica, February 1780, *ibid.*; Augusto de Lima Júnior, *A capitania das Minas Gerais, origens e formação* (3rd edition, Belo Horizonte, 1965) 132.

[2] 'Extratto do balançe da receita e despeza da tezouraria G^s de V^a R^a no anno de 1769 devidida a receita de que rendimentos procede, e aos ann^s a q' pertenço com a despeza pelas folhas eclesiastica, Militar e Civil e Extraordinaria com am^{ma} divizas dos annos a q^a tãobem pertence', CCBNRJ, 1-10-3; 'Balanço da receita e Despeza dos rendimentos Reaes, que teye o Thezouro Geral da Capitania de Minas Gerais, o coronel Affonso Dias Pereira no Anno de 1799, relativo aos anos 1761–1779', Vila Rica, 1 May 1780, IHGB, lata 8, doc. 4.

[3] M. Rodrigues Lapa, *Alvarenga Peixoto*, xxviii.

fact with divergent economic motivations the very opposite might be the case.

Already during the 1770s as the old Marquis of Pombal became more lonely and suspicious in his preeminence, and the crushing burdens of the highly centralized government machine produced an immense backlog of administrative business, central direction slackened. While immediately this was of no serious consequence in Portugal, it significantly weakened the rigor of the Treasury's surveillance of the colonial *juntas da fazenda*. This state of affairs had particularly damaging consequences in Minas Gerais where the regional junta was partially responsible for the collection of the royal fifth of the captaincy, previously the most important of the crown's sources of revenue, as well as direct responsibility for the contracting of the substantial farm of the Minas *entradas*, the captaincy *dízimos*, and other revenues. By the late 1770s the stipulations of the 1750 law, in spite of the continuing failure to complete the 100 arroba annual gold quota, had been virtually abandoned. After several abortive efforts during the early 1770s the per capita tax or *derrama* to make up the amount was never imposed as was required by law.[1]

Laxity of the junta in the performance of its responsibilities towards the most important of the revenue collections to fall within its competence was encouraged by the failure of the treasury in Lisbon to answer the junta's remonstration of 1773. Because of the contraction of the mining sector the junta advised Lisbon that the retention of the old level of the fifth was impossible and the imposition of a *derrama* inadvisable, and the silence of Lisbon was conveniently interpreted as concurrence.[2] Avoidance of responsibilities in the case of the royal fifth was encouraged also by the overlapping of functions and administrative duties, where not only the *junta da fazenda*, but the intendents of the foundry houses and the municipal councils were involved. Lack of diligence could be, and was, blamed on others. While the overlapping of functions and responsibilities facilitated central control over the individual colonial administrative organs, the situation provided built in excuses for the evasion of responsibilities. And this was not only the case on the local level. The *junta da fazenda* itself, while directly responsible to the Lisbon Treasury, was composed of civil and judicial officers, such as the governor and magistrates, who were within the contol of the Secretary of State for the Overseas Dominions. The governor was *ex officio* president of the junta,

---

[1] 'Correspondência da junta da fazenda', 1771-2-3, CCBNRJ, 1-9, 23; 'Vila Rica em Câmara', 20 July 1772, *RAPM*, 11 (1897) 367-70.

[2] 'Representação da junta da fazenda', [1773] AHU, Minas Gerais, caixa 92.

which was his own most important organ of local government. When close uniformity of policy and agreement existed between the various secretaries of state and the president of the Royal Treasury in Lisbon this division of responsibility presented no problem, but such an accord on colonial affairs might not always or necessarily be the case. And these were only a fraction of the complicated and often badly defined jurisdictional overlaps which existed. The viceroy in Rio de Janeiro also retained a vaguely defined overseeing jurisdiction over the southern captaincies and Minas Gerais, not to mention the colonial and metropolitan courts and ecclesiastical bailiwicks, which paralleled, duplicated, multiplied, and superimposed jurisdictions.

Not that a clear cut system of concrete and legally defined responsibilities was any more successful in restricting fraud, corruption, and evasion of obligations. The Diamond District, meticulously regulated by the 1771 provisions and directly responsible only to the administrators and treasury in Lisbon, had become a thriving center of contrabandists and diamond smugglers. Often, if not invariably, the embezzlers carried on their activities with the connivance of the local administrative and military officers. Some important local residents, like Dr José Vieira Couto for example, whose family engaged in extensive pilfering of and contraband in diamonds, deliberately placed slaves in the military guards, doubtless with the protection of their illegal interest in mind, because the social condition of slave soldiers made them totally incapable of upholding the District's strict restrictive laws. Strict entry rules were circumvented by the liberal granting of permits to itinerant traders for the import of cachaça, a strong Brazilian sugar cane brandy. These licenses insured the traders against the attentions of the military patrols, and the cachaça was a more than acceptable bartering commodity with which to entice stolen diamonds from the workers. In contravention to the regulations a large artisan class, composed of tailors, cobblers, medical men of one type or another, tavern keepers and so on, remained in the Diamond District. Because of their close relations with the miners these men often acted as agents for contrabandists who supplied them with money for the purchase of stolen precious stones. While the district's fiscal officers might not themselves directly engage in contraband, members of their families were often among the most notorious embezzlers. Father José da Silva de Oliveira Rolim, son of the second *caixa* or treasurer of diamonds, busied himself with a bewildering range of subterfuges, from mining in prohibited areas to the illegal importation of slaves. As an official administrator of diamond washings he turned in only that portion of the total production he deemed necessary to hide the portion he retained for himself. The Dragoons, the Minas captaincy professional military troops, who shared the charge of guarding the Diamond District against the gangs of unauthorized miners and contrabandists, themselves engaged in lucrative speculations, especially if, as with the Coutos', members of the same family belonged to the officer corps while others were resident within the District itself.[1]

It was not only in the administration of the fifth and of the Diamond District where the divergence between intention and performance was monumental. The *junta da fazenda* of Minas was no more diligent in its other weighty undertakings, the contracting of the captaincy revenues from the *entradas* and *dízimos*. The contracting fees were in arrears to a high proportion of their original contract price, often years after the official returns had been due. João Rodrigues de Macedo, who held the contract of entradas for six years beginning in 1776, had paid only 298,664$798 *reis* of the contract price of 766,726$612 *reis*, by June 1786. Rodrigues Macedo also held the contract of dízimos between 1777 and 1783 for a price of 395,372$957 *reis*. By 1786, a mere third of this sum, 100,272$952 *reis*, had been paid, making him obligated to the Minas *junta da fazenda* at that time for 763,168$019 *reis*. This represented a sum which was over three times the total official captaincy revenues for 1777, and only slightly less than seventeen times the annual value to the crown of the salt-gabelle of the whole state of Brazil in the year 1776. And Rodrigues de Macedo was no exception.[2]

Intimate and lucrative interconnections between the abuses of the system and the substantial emoluments that the governor and magistrates gained from the contracts made chances of reform at the local level unlikely. Shilly shallying and bribery at the time of the disposal of contracts was predictable, but the officers of the junta also received perfectly legally by the system of *propinas* substantial sums from the contracts as contributions to their official salaries. The governor of Minas, for example,

---

[1] Luís Beltrão de Gouveia de Almeida, Intendente Geral dos Diamantes to Visconde Mordomo Mor, Lisbon, 6 July 1789. BNLCP, códice 697, f. 142–9, 155–6.

[2] *Reis* (pl. of *Real*) Portuguese money of account. 'Relação dos devedores a Real Faz[end]a por contratos arrematados, extraida na fim de Dez 1801 ',CCBNRJ 1-1-6; 'Contos correntes extrahidas no fim de Dezembro de 1795, que mostrão o que se ficou devendo a Real Fazenda da Capitania de Minas Gerais de cada hum dos contratos da mesma Capitania...' CCBNRJ, I-1-1-1 (26); 'Contrato dos dízimos de Minas Gerais arrematado a particulares, e administrado por conta da Real Fazenda desde o anno de 1747 até o de 1786 e o que deles se esta devendo', IHGB, lata 166, doc. 7; 'Relação dos contratos que rematou João Rodrigues de Macedo na Junta da Fazenda da Capitania de Minas Gerais, Carlos José da Silva', 1786, AHU, Minas Gerais, caixa 94.

obtained from *propinas* on the various Minas contracts a sum amounting to half as much again as his official remuneration, and the same was the case with the magistrates who composed the junta.[1] In addition, the propina system provided a heaven sent semi-legal cover for bribery and corruption, particularly for men like João Rodrigues de Macedo, who often acted as bankers to Minas governors, and who invariably in his mercantile and business activities extended credit facilities to ministers and officers of the captaincy administration.[2] The junta's laxity in pressing for its debts allowed men like Rodrigues de Macedo to use both the profits of the contract and the unpaid contract dues for his own speculations, while the control of the captaincy tariffs by one of the greatest local merchants facilitated manipulation and evasion of these duties to the personal advantage of the contractors' business interests.[3] Despite clear evidence of greater efficiency when the contracts were directly administered by the junta, and several denunciations of the system to the secretary of state in Lisbon, maladministration continued, and the arrears were allowed to accumulate. By 1788, on the *entradas* alone, the sum in default had reached the staggering total of 1,554,552$539 *reis*.[4]

The government's authority at the local level had always rested on a good deal of mutual tolerance between the local powerful men and the royal administration. An eighteenth-century state, however autocratic on paper, possessed in the last resort limited powers for compulsion. The Pombaline system by the recognition and officialization of this *status quo*, and lacking efficient and honest bureaucrats, took a considerable risk by intertwining the local oligarchies so closely with the government structure. In the vastness of Brazil power and wealth were untrammelled by the subtler restrictions of a more traditional society. Measures which might appear logical in a small country like Portugal, where the authority of the monarch was always close, and the benefits or the displeasures of the central government could more quickly and effectively make themselves felt, produced in the colonial setting totally opposite effects from those

---

[1] 'Propinas que vence o Governador...de Minas Gerais...quando se rematão os contratos ...' [1780?] AHU, Minas Gerais, caixa 57; 'Notícia da capitania de Minas Gerais', IHGB, lata 22, doc. 13.

[2] For example, the ouvidor of Rio das Mortes, Alvarenga Peixoto, the ouvidor of Sabará, Manitti, the governors Rodrigo José de Meneses, visconde de Barbacena, and so on, *ABNRJ*, LIV (1943) 220–1, 231, 296–7.

[3] For example the denunciation of Manuel Joaquim Pedroso to Martinho de Melo e Castro, 2 February 1782, and Pedroso to the Marquês de Angeja, 31 January 1782, AHU, Minas Gerais, caixa 92; Also the letter of João Rodrigues to Bento Rodrigues cited by Miguel Costa Filho, *A cana de açúcar em Minas Gerais* (Rio de Janeiro, 1963) 205.

[4] Junta da fazenda, Vila Rica, 11 February 1789, BNLCP, códice 643, f. 222–4.

intended. To oversee and restrain the activities of the privileged established interests in Lisbon was quite another matter from controlling those of the colonial collaborators who had been thrust into the administrative–military framework of Brazil. In Portuguese America the intended agents of royal authority were often indistinguishable from the Brazilian plutocracy, and the state, far from bending the chosen collaborators to its interests, was itself bent to the personal ambitions and greed of the men who composed the new agencies of government.

The activities of the poet-magistrate Inácio José de Alvarenga Peixoto illustrated how the high intentions were realized in practice. Alvarenga Peixoto's tangled relationships with Dr José da Silveira e Sousa, a local lawyer, and his beautiful elder daughter, the eighteen-year-old Bárbara Eliodora, by whom he had an illegitimate daughter in 1779, led to complicated litigations, denunciations, and an aggravation of the social tensions in the community under his control. Alvarenga Peixoto and Bárbara Eliodora's affair, while it produced fine poetry, also resulted in lucrative arrangements between the lawyer and the magistrate. The chicanery over the disposition of the properties of the late contractor João de Sousa Lisboa produced loud protests from the heirs and guarantors of Sousa Lisboa. In the legal dispute that ensued, Alvarenga Peixoto used the good offices of his friends and fellow poets, the eminent Vila Rica lawyer Cláudio Manuel da Costa and the Vila Rica *ouvidor* Tomás Antônio Gonzaga, and he and his would-be father-in-law retained the land and estates in question. Fulsome poetic praise, which had obtained the job for him in the first place, now lavished on successive governors, brought its reward in 1785, when Alvarenga Peixoto was made colonel of the First Auxiliary Cavalry Regiment of Rio Verde. The commission was ostensibly given in recognition of his part in preparing for and quartering the Minas troops bound for São Paulo during 1777. The obligations incurred with the farmers for fodder and *farinha* remained for years unpaid. When eventually the *junta da fazenda* authorized the sum, the transaction was made through João Rodrigues de Macedo. The Vila Rica merchant was Alvarenga Peixoto's creditor, and he retained the money intended for the farmers as partial payment of the *ouvidor's* personal debts.[1]

With the irony and tragi-comedy that was the practical result of so many of Pombal's reforms, the appointment of native born officers, magistrates and fiscal officials, only encouraged the disputes and vexations that the measures were intended to alleviate. Placing the responsibility for

[1] M. Rodrigues Lapa, *Alvarenga Peixoto*, xxxiii, xxxv, xliv, and 'documentos justicativos' 289.

vital farms into the hands of a locally constituted body, responsive to local pressures and influence, was to exaggerate the disadvantages of the contract system, the only justification of which anyway was that it offered the crown quick returns and spared it administrative expenses. In Minas by no stretch of the imagination was this the result, and the state benefited not at all. Meanwhile the contractors were as ruthless and efficient in the collection of their dues as the *junta da fazenda* was lax in pressing them for the long overdue arrears on the contracting price.[1] The system served to place great power into the hands of opulent manipulators like Rodrigues da Macedo, but it also left them dangerously and enormously obligated, in theory at least, to the royal exchequer.

Meanwhile in the metropolis the stage was being set for a repetition of the abuses which had warped the Pombaline system in Brazil. Luís Pinto de Sousa Coutinho, who had succeeded Martinho de Melo e Castro as Portuguese ambassador in London, advised Pombal confidentially during 1776, that no concrete decisions or aid could be expected from the British government, for it was convinced that José I would not survive, and with his death the whole orientation of the government in Lisbon would be altered.[2] The clear implication was that Pombal's own future would be in grave question. It had been Pombal's retention of the King's confidence which had allowed him to dominate the Portuguese government for twenty-seven years, and it was the connection between José and his minister that had always been the most vulnerable point in the power relationships which underpinned the smooth functioning of the Pombaline system. This the Duke of Aveiro's correspondent had seen clearly in 1759. The British government was correct in its assessment. With the death of the King in 1777 Pombal's position became at once untenable. The new monarch, Maria I, had been for long the focus and hope of Pombal's enemies. The pent up frustrations of those interests long discredited – the merchants who did not benefit from special privileges and protections of Pombal's collaborators, the clergy, the aristocrats who had not compromised with the regime, the English – found full play in the changed political environment.

Amid wide rejoicing and disorder, Pombal's resignation was decreed

---

[1] For complaints against the harsh methods of the collectors of the dízimos taxes see the 'consulta' of 8 May 1789, 'Registro de consultas 1786–1798', AHU, códice 302, f. 15. This consulta was in response to the representation of the camara of Mariana, the Conselho Ultramarino's ruling is to be found in 'registro das cartas, avisos, ofícios etc., para Minas Gerais 1782–1807', AHU, códice 243, f. 17v.

[2] 'Carta confidencial', Luís Pinto to Pombal, London, 10 September 1776, BNLCP, códice 695, f. 11–12.

in the Queen's name under the signature of Martinho de Melo e Castro.[1] Among her principal advisors were well-known Pombal enemies, the Marquis of Marialva, the Marquis of Angeja, and the Visconde de Vila Nova de Cerveira. Angeja had been close to José I, and was one of his lords of the bedchamber, but he had throughout Pombal's preeminence 'conducted himself so dexterously' according to the British minister in Lisbon, Robert Walpole, 'that the marquis has at times confessed that of all the noblemen he was the only one he could not penetrate'. The Marquis of Angeja was in his late sixties, and not, Walpole thought, capable of much 'laborious business'. Vila Nova had remained outside the Pombal circle throughout the previous reign. Melo e Castro, one of the few members of the new administration with wide experience, was held over from Pombal's cabinet. A younger son of the house of Galveias he had, according to the British minister, 'always been careful to pay great court to the marquis d'Angeja', and he had remained neutral during Pombal's clashes with the clergy, who now held important influence over the ultra-devout Portuguese Queen. Melo e Castro's recall from London, moreover, had not been Pombal's idea. It was the King's personal initiative, and the relationship between Melo e Castro and Pombal during the following years was not cordial. In fact, Pombal's protégé, José de Seabra e Silva, had been deliberately introduced at court to counterbalance the influence of Melo e Castro, until Seabra's own conspiring over the succession so outraged Pombal that he had been banished to Angola.[2] Melo e Castro was regarded by the British, and by Jacques Ratton, as being favorable to English interests.[3] He was, Ratton wrote later, an honest administrator, but slow in the exercise of his department, and extremely pigheaded in his opinions, over which he was not susceptible to reason.[4] He had been the minister responsible for the establishment of the Porto Alegre woolen factory. He continued as Secretary of State for the Overseas Dominions in the new administration.

Abroad, the fallen minister received credit for positive achievements. 'No one can deny him original talents and far-reaching views', commented the *Gazzetta Universale*; 'By the means of commerce, of agriculture, of population, he has laid the foundations of Portuguese independence, viewed with an envious eye by the greedy rivalry of Great Britain.'[5] It was one of the paradoxes of Pombal's image that although the

---

[1] 4 March 1777, BNLCP, códice 695, f. 36.
[2] Smith, *Pombal*, II, 142–51, 288, 299, 303.
[3] Robert Walpole to Foreign Office, Lisbon, 4 April 1795, PRO, FO, 63/20.
[4] Ratton, *Recordações*, 245. [5] *Gazzetta Universale*, 5 April 1777.

catastrophic decline in British commerce with Portugal had been caused by a profound change in the economic system and occurred after the plan to nationalize the Luso-Brazilian economy was abandoned, the memory of the bitter disputes of the 1750s associated and credited the measures Pombal had taken during that period with the consequent achievement of a more balanced trade with Britain. As a result the supposed results of the creation of privileged Brazil companies were the elements for which his regime was at the same time praised or condemned, depending on the personal interest or nationality of the observer. Defense of the measures of the 1750s in fact became tantamount to a defense of Pombal himself.

The new regime was immediately faced with the need for a decision over the future of the most famous of Pombal's creations, the Company of Grão Pará and Maranhão, and the question of the prorogation of the monopoly soon became the subject of a propaganda battle. On one side stood the Company's directors, and on the other those interests suppressed since the late 1750s and now vociferous in their hostility to all things Pombaline, backed by some of the Company's debtors in America who saw in the change of regime an opportunity to escape from their obligations. Strong pressure was brought to bear on the new ministry to extinguish the monopoly and open the trade of Pará and Maranhão to all.[1] For the Company the directors stressed the national objectives and the success of the company in reducing the dependency on Great Britain. The capital investment in America, the directors asserted, had stimulated cotton and rice production.[2] The directors of the Pernambuco Company, also faced with the threat of extinction, stressed the regulatory function that the Company had performed, and the capital investment employed to reestablish sugar and tobacco production.[3]

[1] João Pereira Caldas, Pará, 11 September 1777, 'Correspondência official do Governador do Grão-Pará 1752–1777', IHGB/AUC, 1-1-3, f. 378; 'Súplica a Rainha...lastimando a substituição da mesa do bem comum dos homens de negócio pela junta do comércio com poderes exclusivos; com lista de assinaturas de negociantes', IHGB/AUC, 1-1-8, f. 62; Arthur Cezar Ferreira Reis, 'Negadores e Entusiastas da Companhia do Comércio', *Anais do congresso comemorativo do bicentenário da transferência da sede do govêrno do Brasil da Cidade do Salvador para o Rio de Janeiro, (ACC)* Instituto Histórico e Geográfico Brasileiro, 3 vols., Rio de Janeiro, 1966) I, 11–18.

[2] 'Da junta da administração da companhia geral do Grão-Pará e Maranhão. Em que expoem a vossa magestade os motivos que obrigão a junta a supplicar a vossa magestade a prorogação da mesma companhia', Lisbon, 17 March 1777, Anselmo José da Cruz, José Ferreira Coelho, Joaquim Pedro Quintella, Domingos Lourenço, João Roque Jorge, Manoel Ignácio Pereira, Francisco José Lopes, 'Apontamentos vários sobre a companhia do Grão-Pará e Maranhão', IHGB/AUC, 1-1-8, f. 16.

[3] 'Demonstrações da junta [da administração da Companhia do Pernambuco]' Lisbon, 20 April 1780, Mauricio Cremer Vargelles, Theotónio Gomes de Carvalho, João Antônio de Amorim Vianna, Geraldo Wenceslau Braancamp de Almeida Castelo Branco, Manoel

It was precisely the Companies' investment, however, which had been the origin of the huge debts of the colonists, and the regulation of the supply of metropolitan merchandise to colonial production was blamed by the colonists for having produced high prices, shortages, and exploitation, as well as resulting in the exclusion of non-Company merchants. The planters and sugar mill owners of Pernambuco, through the municipal councils of Olinda and Recife, expressed their opposition in no uncertain terms. They reminded the Queen that they were 'the descendents of those ancient Pernambucans who at the cost of their property, blood, and lives, took this great part of America from the hands of enemies and restored it to the Portuguese Crown'.[1] The Council of State returned a majority decision favoring the abolition of the Company of Grão Pará and Maranhão, and the failure to prorogue the Pernambuco Company's monopoly was a logical consequence. The decision had been six to three, with two votes for a compromise solution. Angeja was for extinction, Melo e Castro for the extension of the privileges.[2] The new era, claimed one of the anti-monopoly memorialists, would bring the 'liberty of commerce and the competition of businessmen', and mark the end to 'private privileges, half understood taxes, and a thousand vexations'.[3]

The extinction of the Companies was a visible triumph for the free traders and the old system, as well as for the Companies' debtors in Brazil.[4] Yet the achievement was more apparent than real. The situation of 1777 was not that of the 1750s, despite the reappearance of the old debate. During the intervening years the economic system had been transformed, and the very ambivalence of the privileged established interests to Pombal's fall underscored the fact. Despite the popular hysteria that accompanied the change of regime, Pombal's collaborators were far too deeply embedded in the social structure, and too closely associated with the revenue collection and fiscal agencies of government, to disappear by the mere abolition of the monopoly privileges of the Brazil Companies. The deeper socio-economic factors which underlay their

Caetano de Melo, Francisco Polyart, Bento Alvares da Cunha, José Manuel Mendonça, José Domingos, IHGB/AUC, 1-2-11, f. 28-47.
' 'Representação que a Sua Magestade Fizerão as camaras da cidade de Olinda, Villa do Recife, e moradores de Pernambuco', 1780, *ibid.*, f. 1-8.
For the voting on this issue see IHGB/AUC, 1-1-8, f. 133.
' 'Vasta exposição de motivos a Rainha a favor da extinção das Companhias de comércio exclusivas...por José Vasques da Cunha', *ibid.*, f. 81.
For extinction of companies, Manuel Nunes Dias 'A Junta liquidatária dos fundos das Companhias do Grão-Pará e Maranhão, Pernambuco e Paraíba (1778-1837)' *Revista Portuguêsa de História* x (1962) 156-61.

position in society made the attack on the Companies, in as far as it was an attack on them as a privileged group, at best a matter of form.

Moreover, the results of the vast investment in Brazil, particularly in cotton, and the close interconnections between the Company of Grão Pará and Maranhão and the local fiscal and administrative structure, could not be obliterated by the stroke of a pen in Lisbon. In fact the 'extinct Company' remained a very real force, retaining administrators in Brazil, and actually during the 1780s engaged in trading. In Mato Grosso for example, debt collection continued guaranteed by the fact that the interior merchants still received goods on credit from the 'extinct Company'.[1] In Pernambuco, forty years after the Company of Pernambuco's abolition, Henry Koster was astonished to find the accounts had still not been wound up and a 'considerable number of the plantations were yet indebted to it'.[2]

In the metropolis the removal of a central and unchallenged focus within the government was by no means a disadvantage to the interests of the opulent merchant houses which had arisen during the Pombaline era. The most immediate result of the fall of Pombal was that the vital directing influence of the centralized administrative structure, already overburdened and backlogged, faltered. The Marquis of Angeja, who lacked administrative expertise and was uninformed on economic matters, became the president of the Royal Treasury. Under his dilatory care the role of the treasury weakened, and the previously closely supervised administrative machinery of the Treasury itself became negligent and infinitely more susceptible to corruption.[3] The debilitation of this vital central government agency, together with the lack of a clear-cut focus of power within the new regime, allowed those tendencies which had already manifested themselves in America to repeat themselves in Lisbon. The privileged interests who for so long had been encouraged, protected, and used by the state to further its nationalistic and imperial pretensions, found themselves in a position to manipulate the state in much the way that the oligarchic elements were manipulating the administrative–fiscal framework in Minas Gerais for their own advantage. Because of their key role in the royal treasury, the customs administration, their directing influence in the royal manufactories, and their personal wealth and

---

[1] I am indebted to David Davidson of Cornell University for this information based on his extensive research in the Mato Grosso and Pará archives.

[2] Henry Koster, *Travels in Brazil* (2nd edition, 2 vols., London, 1817) II, 152–3. The debt question also reemerged during the Pernambuco rising of 1817, see Carlos Guilherme Mota, *Nordeste 1817* (São Paulo, 1972), 258, 259.

[3] Ratton, *Recordações*, 121.

Divergence

influence as contract holders and opulent merchants, they were in an unassailable position which the weakness of the state served to exaggerate. Thus while Pombal's enemies tilted at the windmills of the privileged companies, Pombal's collaborators increased and strengthened their wealth and influence.

As the overseeing role of the Royal Treasury was undermined, the other great administrative agent of Pombaline governments was weakened. By the Queen's failure to reappoint deputies the *junta do comércio* membership was reduced to three, Francisco José Lopes, Jacinto Fernandes Bandeira, and the secretary, Theotônio Gomes de Carvalho.[1] The administration of the manufactories, disassociated from the junta in 1778, was placed under the care of a new body, the *junta da administração das fábricas do Reino e aquas livres*, composed of an inspector and four deputies.[2] As the title implied the new *junta das fábricas* was concerned exclusively with metropolitan establishments, and the activities of the old junta in encouraging colonial manufacturing enterprise were not repeated. The new regime witnessed the retreat of the state from direct administration of the royal manufacturing enterprises set up or reorganized during the previous reign. Again 'liberalization' was claimed to be the objective, but this did not mean the removal of privileges, the special protection of raw materials, or easy access to colonial markets. The royal establishments were alienated into the hands of those private capitalists who had been closely involved in their establishment. Through the influence of João Ferreira with the Queen's confessor, the royal factories of Covilhã and Fundão, with all their privileges, including the monopoly of the military and royal household contracts, was transferred to João Ferreira, Joaquim Inácio Quintella, Jacinto Bandeira, and Joaquim Machado. Later the Porto Alegre factory was taken over by Anselmo José da Cruz and Geraldo Braancamp, and then passed into the control of the Ferreira–Quintella–Bandeira group.[3] Meanwhile the expansion of manufacturing industry continued with added momentum. Between 1777 and 1788 over 263 new workshops were established. By comparison the previous reign had seen a mere ninety-six.[4] The new *junta das fábricas* provided a sharper focus for metropolitan industrial interests.

Thus while the reputation of Pombal 'that great man, known as such to the middle and thinking class of his nation', as Ratton wrote much later, went into eclipse, the group he had favored remained and prospered.[5]

---

[1] *Ibid.*, 202.　　　　　　　　　　[2] Macedo, *Problemas*, 224.
[3] Ratton, *Recordações*, 202; Luis F. de Carvalho Dias, *A relação das fábricas de 1788* (Coimbra, 1955) 20, 25, 63, 73.
[4] *Ibid.*, 95.　　　　　　　　　　[5] Ratton, *Recordações*, 152.

Liberalization far from undermining their power and influence served to provide a cover for the manipulation of the state in their own interests, and their takeover of most of the enterprises that the state had established. The merchant–industrial oligarchy retained the lucrative soap and tobacco monopolies from which, as the contract prices were rarely reassessed, they acquired gigantic profits. Ratton calculated that the contractor of the tobacco monopoly gained in one year more than the treasury had received from the contracts' disposal in forty years.[1] Extension of contract periods at set annual prices also advantaged the contractors to the detriment of royal revenues. The Quintella group for example was granted the salt-gabelle contract for the state of Brazil for 48,000 *milreis* per annum for thirteen years commencing in 1788.[2]

The opulence of these Portuguese noble–businessmen of the last quarter of the eighteenth century was praised by poets and pamphleteers and it impressed visiting literati. It was 'the large and magnificent houses' of the Quintellas, Braancamps and Bandeiras, that the English poet Robert Southey observed at the turn of the century, and whose 'glaring display of false taste and ill-judged magnificence' William Beckford noted in the eighties.[3] 'Is there anyone who does not do business?' asked Bernardo de Jesus Maria in his *Arte e Dicionário do Comércio e Económia Portuguêsa*, published in Lisbon during 1783. 'Good customs and much money' ran the contemporary jingle, 'make any kind of knave a gentleman.'[4] Even the crumbs that fell from the high table were worth catching, as Street Arriaga discovered on acquiring Ana, nicknamed the 'mountain of gold', widow of Joaquim Inácio da Cruz, morgado of Sobral. 'Mr. Street Arriaga', wrote Beckford in his diary, 'who is of Irish extraction, six foot high, four foot broad, a ruddy countenance, swapping shoulders, Herculean legs and all the attributes of that enterprising race who so often have the luck of marrying great fortunes...is now master of a large estate and a fubsical squat wife with a head like that of Holofernes in old tapistry, and shoulders that act the part of a platter with great exactitude. Poor Soul, she is neither Venus nor a Hebe, has a rough lip and a manly voice and is rather inclined to be dropsical.'[5] Street Arriaga doubtless joined

---

[1] See Ratton's calculations in this respect, *Recordações*, 112–202.

[2] 'Livros dos termos de arrematação dos contratos reaes da America', AHU, códices 297, 298, 299, 306.

[3] Robert Southey, *Journal of a Residence in Portugal 1800–1801* (ed. Adolfo Cabral, Oxford, 1960) 137–9; William Beckford, *The Journal of William Beckford in Portugal and Spain 1787–1788* (ed. Boyde Alexander, London, 1954) 257–8.

[4] Macedo, *Problemas*, 216.

[5] Beckford, *Journal*, 74.

Jesus Maria, dropsy or no, in his exhortation: 'Happy commerce which is the origin of so many good things.'[1]

The pervasive influence of the privileged interests after the fall of Pombal had rapid impact on the formation of colonial policy. Inácio de Pina Manique, intendent of police and administrator of the customs house, forwarded to Martinho de Melo e Castro denunciations of the extensive contraband which was taking place along the Brazilian littoral. He pointed to the damage caused to the export of metropolitan manufactured goods by the rise of textile workshops in America.[2] The president of the *junta das fábricas* also brought pressure to bare on the secretary of state and complained of the decline in the export of goods produced by the royal silk factory.[3]

It was notorious, Melo e Castro reflected, that foreign pirates and contrabandists, especially the French and English, were active along the Brazilian coasts. 'France having failed to recuperate her colonies and the English having lost a great part of theirs' would be looking with particular interest at those of their neighbors. The threat to Brazil was acute for the inhabitants were eager to cooperate.[4] The secretary of state was aware that British ships bound for Brazil were being openly insured in London, the names of the captains and sailing dates published in the public papers. Twelve British ships annually, all of over 600 tons, had been carrying British manufactures to Portuguese America.[5] Moreover, 'our Brazilian colonists have absorbed the commerce and shipping of the African coast to the total exclusion of Portugal'. This provided another route by which foreign merchandise entered Brazil, for the slavers of Bahia and Pernambuco found on the Mina coast a source of supply of foreign goods exchanged by the Dutch, English, and French for Brazilian tobacco, brandy, and sugar.[6] These factors, Melo e Castro complained, had led Brazilian sugar exporters to demand specie rather than European goods

---

[1] Macedo, *Problemas*, 216; Also see discussion of José-Augusta França, *Une Ville des Lumières* (Paris, 1965) chapter IV, especially 184–7.

[2] Diogo Inácio de Pina Manique to Martinho de Melo e Castro, Lisbon, 6 October 1784, and Manique to Melo e Castro, Lisbon, 3 December 1784, 'documentos officiaes inéditos', *RIHGB*, X (2nd ed., 1870) 225–7.

[3] Martinho de Melo e Castro, [circular to the governors in America] Ajuda, 5 January 1785, *ibid.*, 213.

[4] *Ibid.*, 214.

[5] 'Tradução de alguns paragraphos do offício que o consul geral da Grão-Bretanha por orden d'el rei seu amo apresentou n'esta côrte em o 19 de Outubro de 1784', *ibid.*, 228.

[6] José Honório Rodrigues, *Brazil and Africa* (trans. Richard A. Mazzara and Sam Hileman, Berkeley and Los Angeles, 1965) 25–9; Pierre Verger, *Flux et Reflux de la traite des nègres entre le golfe de Benin et Bahia de todos os Santos du dix-septième au dix-neuvième siècle* (Paris/La Haye, 1966).

from their metropolitan trading partners. In fact, the secretary of state sourly observed, one Brazilian business man had gone so far as to propose that a company be established for a direct trade between Britain and a part of Portuguese America.[1]

The proposition of a direct trade with Britain that would bypass the Luso-Brazilian system was not a solution any metropolitan government could easily contemplate, much less a weak administration dominated by powerful interests whose prosperity lay in the exploitation of colonial primary commodities and the retention of the colony as a protected market for their manufactured goods. For Martinho de Melo e Castro, one of the Portuguese ministers closest to the manufacturing interests of the metropolis, the remedy was clear. To meet the complaints of the *junta das fábricas* and to protect the interests of the powerful merchant-industrial oligarchy in the metropolis, the flexible Pombaline system would have to be abandoned and a more rigid and effective neo-mercantilism instituted in its place.

The removal of Pombal's broad imperial vision brought colonial policy firmly into the zone of metropolitan interest and prejudice. 'It is demonstrably certain', Melo e Castro told Lavradio's successor, Luís de Vasconcelos e Sousa, 'that Portugal without Brazil is an insignificant power.' The economic activity most proper for a colony was 'farming, navigation and commerce'. It was 'the indolence and idleness transcendent in all Brazil', he observed, which had caused the inhabitants to forget this fact.[2]

Early in January 1785 Melo e Castro circulated instructions to all the governors in Portuguese America. 'In most of the captaincies of Brazil there have been established and continue to grow various workshops and manufactories', he lamented, 'and constant and certain information had been received of excessive contraband practised in the ports and the interior of the said captaincies.' These 'pernicious transactions had caused the diminution of customs revenue and the export and profits of goods and manufactures sent to Brazil'. If action was not taken rapidly 'the consequence would be that the utilities and riches of these most important colonies will remain in the patrimony of its inhabitants and the foreign nations with whom they trade, and Portugal will conserve no more than an apparent, sterile, and useless dominion over them...It is undoubtedly certain, Brazil being most fertile and abundant in fruits and products of

---

[1] Martinho de Melo e Castro, [circular to governors in America] Ajuda, 5 January 1785, 'documentos officiaes inéditos', *RIHGB*, x, 216.

[2] 'Instruções de Martinho de Melo e Castro to Luís de Vasconcelos e Sousa acerca do governo do Brasil', *RIHGB*, xxv (1862) 479–83.

the earth that workshops and manufactories would make the inhabitants totally independent of the metropolis.' It was 'indispensably necessary' to abolish 'the said workshops and manufactories and to prevent contraband'. Attached to the circular was the *alvará* of 5 January 1785. It ordered that all textile manufactories and workshops be 'closed and abolished wherever they may be in Brazil', excepting only the manufacture of gross cloth for slaves.[1]

Melo e Castro had stated with remarkable clarity the situation that faced the metropolis in the mid-1780s. The proposition of direct trade with Britain, and the divergent pressures arising from the growth of import substituting industries in both the metropolis and Brazil, challenged the 'infallible maxims' which underlay the whole colonial system. By the 1780s the Portuguese government was faced with a choice. Either the maxims had to be abandoned, or they had to be more strictly observed. Melo e Castro's measures and attitudes were in classic mercantilist tradition.

Yet the mercantilist theory even as it was stated by the reactionary Brazilian born bishop, José Joaquim da Cunha de Azeredo Coutinho, before the Lisbon Academy of Sciences during the 1790s, involved mutual duties and obligations. It was the benefits of the mother country's 'good offices and necessary aid for the defense and security of life and property' which justified 'equal recompenses and just sacrifices', on the part of the daughter colony.[2] But on Melo e Castro's own admission, 'because the little continent of Portugal has arms most extensive, most distant and most separated one from the other, as are the overseas dominions in the four parts of the world, she cannot have the means nor the forces with which to defend them herself...' The first forces that must defend Brazil are those of Brazil.[3] It was this factor that Pombal had so often stated, and it was also, as the memorial of the câmaras of Recife and Olinda demonstrated, a factor of which Brazilians were acutely aware. The repressive measures could not fail to raise the logical alternative to

[1] Martinho de Melo e Castro, [circular to governors in America] Ajuda, 5 January 1785, 'documentos officiaes inéditos', *RIHGB*, 217–8; 'Alvará por que Vossa Magestade e servida prohibir no estado do Brasil todas as fábricas de ouro, prata, sedas, algodão, linho e la, ou os tecidos sejam fabricados de um so dos referidos generos, ou da mistura de uns com os outros, exceptuando tão somente as de fazenda grossa do dito algodão', Ajuda, 5 January 1785. *Ibid.*, 229–30; For a different interpretation see Fernando A. Novais, 'A proibição das manufacturas no Brasil e a política económica Portuguêsa do fim do século XVIII' (Separata do no. 67 da *Revista de História*, São Paulo, 1967). Also see Alden, *Royal Government*, 385.

[2] *Obras Económicas de J. J. da Cunha de Azeredo Coutinho (1794–1804)* (Ed. Sérgio Buarque de Hollanda, São Paulo, 1966) 154.

[3] 'Instruções', Martinho de Melo e Castro to Vasconcelos e Sousa, *RIHGB*, xxv (1862) 479–83.

neo-mercantilism for which the establishment of the United States had provided a shining and tantalizing example.

During October 1786, Thomas Jefferson, the envoy of the United States in France, received a letter from the ancient University of Montpellier signed only with the pseudonym *Vendek*. The writer indicated that he had a matter of great consequence to communicate, but as he was a foreigner he wished Jefferson to recommend a safe channel for correspondence. Jefferson did so at once. In a second letter *Vendek* declared himself to be a Brazilian. The slavery in which his country lay was 'rendered each day more insupportable since the epoch of your glorious independence', he told the American Revolutionary. Brazilians, he said, had decided to follow the example of the North Americans, to break the chains that bound them to Portugal and to 'relive their liberty'. To solicit the aid of the United States was the purpose of his visit to France. 'Nature made us inhabitants of the same continent', *Vendek* told Jefferson, 'and in consequence in some degree compatriots.'[1]

During May of the following year under the pretext of seeing the antiquities at Nîmes, Jefferson arranged a rendezvous with *Vendek*. The Brazilian claimed that 'the Portuguese in Brazil are few in number, mostly married there and have lost sight of their native country...and are disposed to become independent.[...]There are 20,000 regular troops, originally these were Portuguese, but as they died off they were replaced with natives, so that these compose at present the mass of the troops, and may be counted on by their native country. The officers are partly Portuguese partly Brazilian.[...]The [men] of letters are those most desirous of a revolution.[...]In fact on the question of revolution there is but one mind in that country.' What was needed *Vendek* told Jefferson, was the support of some powerful nation.

Jefferson reported to Mr Jay on his conversation from Marseilles. 'They consider the North American Revolution as a precedent for theirs', he wrote, 'they look to the United States as most likely to give them honest support and for a variety of considerations have the strongest prejudices in our favor.' Apparently Rio de Janeiro, Minas Gerais and Bahia would instigate the uprising and the other captaincies were expected to follow their example. 'The royal revenue from the fifth and diamonds, as well as the rest of the gold production could be counted on...They have an abundance of horses...They would want cannon, ammunition, ships,

---

[1] Vendek to Jefferson, Montpellier, 9 October 1786; Vendek to Jefferson, Montpellier, 21 November 1786; Jefferson to Vendek, Paris, 26 December 1786; Vendek to Jefferson, Montpellier, 5 Jan. 1787; *AMI*, II (1953) 11–13.

sailors, soldiers and officers, for which they are disposed to look to the U.S., always understood that every service and furniture will be well paid...They would want of us at all times corn, and salt fish.[...] Portugal being without either army or navy could not attempt an invasion under the twelvemonth (considering of what it would be composed it would probably never attempt a second.) Indeed this source of their wealth being intercepted, they are scarcely capable of the first effort...The Mines d'or are among mountains, inaccessible to any army, and Rio de Janeiro is considered as the strongest port in the world after Gibraltar. In case of a successful revolution a republican government in a single body would probably be established.'[1]

Vendek, José Joaquim Maia e Barbalho, a native of Rio de Janeiro, matriculated in 1783 at the University of Coimbra, where he studied mathematics.[2] He had entered the faculty of medicine at Montpellier in 1786.[3] It is possible that Maia was commissioned by merchants in Rio de Janeiro to enter into contact with Jefferson.[4] Probably he was one of the group of Brazilian students who during the early 1780s joined hands at Coimbra and vowed to work for the independence of their homeland.[5] Jefferson impressed on Maia that he had no authority to make an official commitment. He could only speak as an individual. The United States was in no condition to risk a war at the present moment. They desired to cultivate the friendship of Portugal with which they enjoyed an advantageous commerce. But a successful revolution in Brazil would obviously 'not be uninteresting to the United States, and the prospects of lucre might possibly draw numbers of individuals to their side and purer motives our officers, citizens being free to leave their own country individually without the consent of governments and equally free to go to any other'.[6]

An accurate account of Jefferson's comments reached Brazil via

---

[1] Jefferson to Mr Jay, Marseilles, 4 May 1787, *ibid.*, 13–19.

[2] 'Estudantes Brasileiros em Coimbra 1772–1872', *ABNRJ*, LXII (1940) 174.

[3] Manoel Xavier de Vasconcellos Pedrosa, 'Estudantes Brasileiros na Faculdade de Medicina de Montpellier no fim do século XVIII' *RIHGB*, CCXLIII (April–June 1959) 35–71.

[4] *Autos de Devassa da Inconfidência Mineira* (*ADIM*) (Biblioteca Nacional Rio de Janeiro, 7 vols., 1936–8) II, 81–95; It is difficult to identify with any certainty the merchants in Rio who have been involved in this enterprise or in the previous project for a direct trade with Britain. Possibly both ideas had something to do with Francisco de Araújo Pereira, for he is cited at a later date as being openly critical of the methods of the colonial administration (*ADIM*, I, 280) and was according to the viceroy Lavradio the only merchant in the city worthy of the name, the rest he dismissed as being simple commissaries (Lavradio, *Relatório*, *RIHGB*, IV, 453).

[5] *ADIM*, 84–8, II, 40.

[6] Jefferson to Mr Jay, Marseilles, 4 May 1787, *AMI*, II (1953) 17.

Domingos Vidal Barbosa, also a student at Montpellier.[1] Vidal Barbosa was a landowner at Juiz da Fora on the road between Rio de Janeiro and the capital of the captaincy of Minas Gerais, Vila Rica. He was an enthusiastic propagator of the writings of the Abbé Raynal – so much so that he was in the habit of reciting passages by heart.[2] In fact Raynal greatly influenced the thinking of many educated Brazilians during the 1780s. His *Histoire philosophique et politique des établissements et du commerce des Européens dans les deux Indes* was already an essential part of the greatest private libraries of the colony and a much quoted textbook for many of those inspired by the example of the United States.[3] Moreover, Raynal's extensive account of Brazil, his contemptuous picture of Portugal, condemnation of British political and economic influence, and recommendation that the ports of Brazil be opened to the trade of all nations, utterly contradicted the new trend of policy emanating from Lisbon.[4]

Maia and Vidal Barbosa were not alone in their educational accomplishments or their political enthusiasms. Between 1772 and 1785 300 Brazilian-born students had matriculated at the University of Coimbra.[5] Others continued their studies in France or had gone directly to the faculty of Medicine at Montpellier where fifteen Brazilian-born students matriculated between 1767 and 1793.[6] José Bonifácio de Andrada e Silva, a Paulista, who had matriculated in the same year as Maia, was writing poems during 1785 which attacked the 'horrid monster of despotism' and were heavy with a bewildering profusion of heroes, including Rousseau, Voltaire, Locke, Pope, Virgil, and Camoes.[7] José Álvares Maciel, son of a wealthy Vila Rica merchant and landowner, and a contemporary of Maia at Coimbra, travelled to England.[8] Maciel spent a year and a half in Britain, studied manufacturing techniques, and whenever possible bought accounts of the American Revolution. He discussed the possibility of

[1] 'Estudantes Brasileiros na faculdade de medicina de Montpellier', *RIHGB*, CCXLIII, 41, 48–50.
[2] *ADIM*, II, 59.
[3] The influence of Raynal in the thinking of Luís Vieira da Silva, the owner of one of the finest libraries in Minas Gerais, and among the members of the Literary Society of Rio de Janeiro are but two examples, *ADIM*, I, 445–65; II, 95; IV, 207; and *ABNRJ*, LXI (1939) 384, 409–12, 435.
[4] Raynal (l'abbé Thomas Guillaume François), *Histoire philosophique et politique des établissements et du commerce des Européens dans les deux Indes* (4 vols., Amsterdam, 1770).
[5] 'Estudantes Brasileiros em Coimbra', *ABNRJ*, LXII, 141–81.
[6] 'Estudantes Brasileiros...Montpellier', *RIHGB*, CCXLIII, 40.
[7] Octavio Tarquínio de Sousa, *História dos Fundadores do Império do Brasil, vol. 1, José Bonifácio* (Rio de Janeiro, 1960) 63.
[8] Maciel matriculated in 1782 and graduated in 1785, Maia matriculated in 1783, 'Estudantes Brasileiros em Coimbra', *ABNRJ*, LXII, 172, 174.

Brazilian independence with sympathetic English merchants.[1] Even on the far frontiers of Portuguese America ideas and opinions subversive to the colonial system were aired, though they were not always approved. José de Lacerda e Almeida, a Paulista, who had matriculated at Coimbra in 1772, denounced his colleague on the border commission in Mato Grosso for his rebellious discourses. António Pires da Silva Ponte the informer told Melo e Castro in September 1786, had claimed that his homeland, Minas Gerais, would become 'the head of a great kingdom'.[2]

By the 1780s tensions within the Luso-Brazilian system were clearly causing a growing divergence between colony and metropolis. While imperial policy remained tolerant, and firm control existed in Lisbon, the involvement of powerful metropolitan and colonial interest groups in the functions of government did not necessarily nor inevitably threaten a confrontation between them. But following the fall of Pombal, and with contradictory economic motivations, the situation was dramatically changed. The increasing rigidity of a colonial policy framed in terms of a strict neo-mercantilism, and the coincident growth of enthusiasm among Brazilians for the example of the successful colonial rebellion in North America, made the chances of avoiding a crisis in imperial relations slim indeed.

---

[1] *ADIM*, ii, 40, 251; iv, 400.
[2] José de Lacerda e Almeida to Martinho de Melo e Castro, 24 September 1786, AHU, Mato Grosso, maço 12. I am grateful to David Davidson for drawing my attention to this most important letter.

CHAPTER 4

CONFRONTATION

Among all the peoples that make up the different captaincies of Brazil, none perhaps cost more to subjugate and subdue to the just obedience and submissiveness of Vassals to their Sovereign, as have those of Minas Gerais.

> Martinho de Melo e Castro to the visconde de Barbacena, Salvaterra de Magos, 29 January 1788, *AMI*, II (1953) 126.

They are worthy of attention.

> Inácio José de Alvarenga Peixoto, 'Canto Genetlíaco', 1782, M. Rodrigues Lapa, *Vida e Obra de Alvarenga Peixoto* (Rio de Janeiro, 1960) 37.

To approach Minas Gerais from the Atlantic seaboard is to traverse the bastions of a great natural fortress. From Espírito Santo to Paraná the continent presents a line of high mountains to the ocean, and before them lies an inhospitable coast. South of Cape Frio where the Bay of Guanabara opens up behind a bottleneck entrance, the mountains of the sea are fortified by the moat of the Paraíba river valley and the barbarous ranges of Mantiqueira. Virgin forests, the *matas*, scarcely touched in the late 1770s, continued deep into Minas. Vila Rica, the rich town of black gold, lay some fifteen days by mule train from the viceregal seat of Rio de Janeiro. The road to the Brazilian highlands passing through dense tropical forest and twisting around precipitous scarps was hazardous and spectacular.[1]

The traveler crossed the Bay of Guanabara by small boat to the mouth of the River Inhomerin where at the Porto de Estrella a convoy of fifty to seventy mules waited. Close to the captaincy boundary the mule train, subdivided into lots of seven animals in order to negotiate the difficult trail and river crossings, was assessed for customs taxes by the agents of the *entradas* contractors. Dry goods – a category comprising all non-edible items – were subject to a uniform 1,125 *reis* per arroba charge,

---

[1] Fortress analogy borrowed from João Camillo de Oliveira Torres, *História de Minas Gerais* (5 vols., Belo Horizonte, 1962) I, 104; Description of journey, topography, and time needed to reach Vila Rica, from Luís Albuquerque de Melo Pereira's account, 30 November 1775, BNLCP, códice 170; João Maurício Rugendas, *Viagem pitoresca através do Brasil* (trans., Sérgio Milliet, 5th edition, São Paulo, 1954) 25–34; 'Narrativa de Viagem de um naturalista Inglês ao Rio de Janeiro e Minas Gerais', *ABNRJ*, LXII (1940) especially 53–68; John Mawe, *Travels in the interior of Brazil...* (London, 1812) 141–64; Auguste de Saint-Hilaire, *Voyage dans les Provinces de Rio de Janeiro et de Minas Gerais* (2 vols., Paris, 1830) I, 58–74, 113–37. Also see Enéas Martins Filho, 'Os três caminhos para as Minas Gerais', *ACC*, I, 169–212.

and wet goods – foodstuffs and drink – paid 750 *reis* for each 2–3 arrobas weight.[1] The merchants generally passed credits in lieu of cash payments – a factor partially responsible for the chronic state of indebtedness of the *entradas* contracts.[2] On the perilous road over the steep Mantiqueira mountains the convoy would encounter detachments of the Minas Dragoons. These cavalry troopers, ostensibly on the lookout for diamond smugglers and contrabandists, were often engaged in their own speculative peculations. After Igreja Nova (today Barbacena), a place famed for its numerous and persistent mulatta prostitutes, the country changed.[3] Undulating hills of the region called the *campos* presented an open landscape which lacked continuous tree coverage. Soon the high mountains of the Serra do Espinhaço appeared. Here were the boom towns of eighteenth-century Brazil, built close to the gold-rich streams where a mere two generations before there had existed only unexplored wilderness.

The urban centers were relatively close to one another and hugged the edges of the range from São João d'El Rei in the south to Sabará and Tejuco in the north. Because of the high altitude the climate of the mountain cities was equable, and they were subject to damp mists and low clouds – even on occasion to white frosts. Vila Rica, close to the lofty boulder of *Itacolumí*, was by 1780 a spider's web of paved, winding streets over steep hillsides. The town had long ceased to be a graceless mining camp. Elegant two-storied town houses abounded, with terraced gardens where flowers and vegetables grew in profusion.[4] Perched on hill summits or facing open squares were innumerable finely proportioned Baroque churches, their interiors rich with golden altars and lavish ornament. 'The precious pearl of Brazil', the author of the *Triunfo Eucharístico* had called Vila Rica in 1734.[5]

From the central spine of Minas the São Francisco River runs north into Bahia and Pernambuco, and the Rio Grande and Rio das Mortes flow to the basin of the River Plate. The gold towns straddled the divide, and the vital intercommunication these river valleys afforded between the northeast and the south of Portuguese America. There was no easy access to the Atlantic. The River Doce valley was the undisputed territory of the ferocious Aimores Indians, and the River Jequintinhonha, rigorously restricted by the diamond regulations, likewise offered no easy alternative route to the coast. Lack of an easy natural outlet to the Atlantic from the

[1] *AMI*, II (1953) 142.
[2] Junta da fazenda, Vila Rica, 31 January 1789, BNLCP, códice 642, f. 222f.
[3] Saint-Hilaire, *Voyage*, I, 123.   [4] Mawe, *Travels*, 166.
[5] Cited by Robert C. Smith Jr, 'Colonial Architecture of Minas Gerais', *Art Bulletin*, XXI (1939) 113.

mining zone gave the difficult trail from Rio de Janeiro great strategic importance.

The population of Minas Gerais in 1776, excluding Indians, was over 300,000, which accounted for 20 per cent of the total population of Portuguese America, and represented the greatest agglomeration of the colony. Census takers classified the population by racial groupings, though they did not provide statistics of the proportion of slaves to free men. Over 50 per cent of the population was black, composed of imported African or native born slaves of pure African heritage. The remaining proportion was composed of roughly equal percentages of whites, and *pardos*. The latter group included mulattoes and other racial mixtures wholly American born.[1]

Between the captaincy's administrative divisions the population was unevenly distributed. The comarca of Sêrro Frio, a substantial portion of which was taken up by the Diamond District, had least people, principally due to the fact that the diamond regulations imposed strict limitations on the area. Sabará, a region of extensive cattle ranges where a series of rich gold strikes occurred, although it had the smallest proportion of white men, possessed the greatest number of blacks and was the most heavily populated comarca of the captaincy. In the comarca of Rio das Mortes the balance was markedly different. Here there existed by the late eighteenth century a more balanced and diversified local economy, and the comarca was populated by the most white men and almost half the total number of white women in the whole of Minas Gerais. Disproportion between men and women in all the comarcas was great, and within the racial groups only *pardas* outnumbered *pardos*. Ten years later, in 1786, the number of free men in Minas Gerais was placed at 188,712 and of slaves at 174,135. Black, and especially *pardo*, freemen thus made up as much as a quarter of the total population during the last quarter of the eighteenth century. In addition the population of the captaincy was experiencing considerable internal migration, and growth among the four comarcas was uneven. The comarca of Vila Rica during the four decades following the census of 1776 suffered an overall decline of population. Rio das Mortes, however, in the same period very nearly tripled its population, from 82,781 in 1776 to 213,617 in 1821.[2]

---

[1] 'Taboa das habitantes da capitania de Minas Gerais', 1776, in 'notícia da capitania de Minas Gerais', IHGB, lata 22, doc. 13; Dauril Alden, 'The population of Brazil in the late Eighteenth Century: A Preliminary Survey', *HAHR*, XLIII, No. 2 (May 1963) 173–205.

[2] 'População da província de Minas Gerais, 1776–1823', and 'Mappa da população da província de Minas Gerais tirado no anno de 1821', from 'Noticias e Reflexões Estatísticas da Província de Minas Gerais por Guilherme Barão de Eschwege', *RAPM*, IV (1899)

Population shift to the south was indicative of the profound change in economic fortune and functions Minas Gerais experienced after the 1760s. The decline of Vila Rica and the rise of the south reflected the waning of the dominant role of mining and the increasing importance of agricultural, pastoral and plantation activities. Change was gradual, and the transformation of a predominantly mining into a predominantly agricultural economy, did not mean that either the former or the latter had ever been mutually exclusive. Indeed the process of change itself, especially by the 1780s, had created a remarkable diversification of the regional economy, which although it could not be a permanent phenomenon was during the last quarter of the eighteenth century a fact of great significance.

Rural Minas Gerais from the earliest years presented features which contrasted markedly with the plantation and latifundian economy of the littoral. The gold strikes created for the first time hundreds of miles from the coast new markets for products such as brandy and sugar, which until then had only been exported. Very soon the miners themselves had begun to produce locally certain basic commodities essential to the provisioning of the expanding mining camps. Although it required a longer growing period to produce sugar in Minas than nearer the coast, the first two decades of the eighteenth century saw a rapid growth in the number of sugar mills, and an expanding production of sugar and cachaça for local consumption. The metropolitan government sought to prevent the erection of sugar mills fearful that they would entice workers from the gold washings, and in 1714 the construction of new mills had been prohibited in the comarca of Vila Rica. Like all such cataclysmic laws it was in practice only shakily implemented, if only because of the fragility of any authority in the early gold rush years.[1]

With the establishment of sugar mills in Minas and the substantial urban demand, a special type of rural landed estate came into existence, different both from the great monoculture plantations of the coastal zones, and the cattle ranches of those interior areas settled in previous expansions. The Minas *fazenda* often combined sugar mill with mine, or mine with cattle raising, or sugar mill with cattle. Many Minas estates had gold washings, plantations, cattle ranges, and sugar and *farinha* mills.[2]

294–5, 737; Saint-Hilaire, *Voyage*, I, 58–74; 'Colleção das memórias archivadas pela Câmara da Vila do Sabará', *RIHGB*, IV (1844) 249–76; See Statistical appendix, No. 7, Population tables of Minas Gerais.

[1] Costa Filho, *A cana de açúcar*, 79, 106, 117, 175.

[2] *Ibid.*, 159, 162, 164–5, 352; For a description of the fazenda do Barro, Mawe, *Travels*, 183–4.

Alvarenga Peixoto's extensive holding in the south of Minas was just such a horizontally integrated estate, possessing extensive gold washings, a sugar mill, cane fields, coffee plantation, and cattle ranges.[1] The holdings of the wealthy vicar of São José in Rio das Mortes, Carlos Correia de Toledo e Melo, encompassed mineral workings, plantations, maize and bean fields, and a sugar mill.[2] The nearby *fazendas* of Colonel Francisco Antônio de Oliveira Lopes also had plantations and a sugar mill as well as mineral workings, cattle (some 300 head), pigs, and poultry. His lands, like those of the vicar, were enclosed by stone walls, a characteristic of farming in Minas and a distinctive feature in Portuguese America, indicative of the more advanced techniques of land use employed in the captaincy.[3] The Vila Rica lawyer, Cláudio Manuel da Costa, was in partnership in mineral workings and raised cattle and pigs on his *fazenda* near Vila Rica.[4]

The system of land grants and the mode of granting mining rights encouraged the type of diversified activity encompassed within many Minas landed properties. Although absolute rights to mining were alienated to the individual miner, the right to extraction did not of itself guarantee property rights to the surface area. This was governed by the traditional letter of *sesmaria*. Thus in theory two private proprietors could possess the same land, and to avoid this it was customary to obtain a *carta de data* with the right to extract gold for the same land held by *carta de sesmaria*.[5]

The products of the Minas *fazendas* fed a commerce both within the captaincy and along the river valley routes into the neighboring captaincies. Traders bringing animals from São Paulo returned with Minas cotton, cloth, and sugar.[6] The contractor João Rodrigues de Macedo engaged in extensive commerce in sugar within Minas. His

---

[1] Sequestro, Inácio José de Alvarenga Peixoto, *ADIM*, I, 385–6; Sequestro, Alvarenga Peixoto, *ADIM*, I, 411–32; 'Traslado do sequestro de...Alvarenga Peixoto', *ADIM*, v, 351–421.

[2] Sequestro, Carlos Corrêa de Toledo e Melo, *ADIM*, I, 386–403; 'Traslado do sequestro do vigário Carlos Corrêa de Toledo', *ADIM*, v, 335–47.

[3] 'Traslado do sequestro feito a Francisco Antônio de Oliveira Lopes', *ADIM*, v, 233–47; 'Autos de deposito do capitão Pedro Joaquim de Melo pelos bens do inconfidente Francisco Antônio d'Oliveira Lopes', 1811, IHGB, lata 3, doc. 4.

[4] 'Traslado...do sequestro, Dr. Cláudio Manoel da Costa', *ADIM*, I, 356–64, 375; 'Traslado dos sequestros feitos ao Doutor Claudio Manoel da Costa', *ADIM*, v, 263–76.

[5] 'Memória de observações fisíco-económicas acerca da extração do ouro do Brasil por Manuel Ferreira da Câmara', Marcos Carneiro de Mendonça, *O Intendente Câmara, Manuel Ferreira da Câmara Bethencourt e Sá, Intendente Geral das Minas e dos Diamantes, 1764–1835* (São Paulo, 1958) 499–523.

[6] Simonsen, *História económica*, 231.

agency in São João d'El Rei, for example, bought large stocks of sugar there to be shipped to Vila Rica and Sabará for sale in his retail shops in those cities.[1] There was extensive internal commerce in brandy, sweets, Minas cheese, in local cotton from the Montes Claros region, and in linen and flax from the Rio Grande and the Rio das Mortes.[2] Rio das Mortes, by the time the English geologist John Mawe passed through São João d'El Rei in the first decade of the nineteenth century, had become the 'granary of the district', and produced maize, beans, and a little wheat in its rich and fertile lands, while cheese, lard, poultry, sugar, cotton, and cachaça were exported to the other camarcas and to Rio de Janeiro. At São José, nearby, local cotton was manufactured into gross cloth for slaves or fine cloth for tableware.[3] Indeed many of the estates possessed looms, as had so often been denounced to the secretary of state in Lisbon. The vicar of São José, Carlos Correia, owned one, as did the Vila Rica lawyer Cláudio Manuel da Costa.[4]

The regional economy with its horizontally integrated landed estates was especially suited to absorb the shock of the transformation which followed the exhaustion of alluvial gold. Both were capable of responding to the stimulation which came to the internal economy as the vast external trade which had flowed along the route from Rio de Janeiro withered away in direct proportion to the decline in gold output. After the 1760s any local product stood in a favorable relationship to imported articles, and the resilience of the regional economy in face of a catastrophic contraction in the volume of external trade was reflected in the differing fortunes of the *dízimos* and the *entradas*, for while the decline of the latter is by now notorious, the former retained a level of returns which had seen little substantial change since the 1750s.[5]

The growing expense of imported articles served to increase the miners' difficulties as the era of easy and inexpensive exploitation of the surface and stream deposits passed, and mining shifted to deeper diggings and shaft mining. More complicated demands required greater capital outlays, a wider use of iron and steel tools, as well as more rational and scientific exploitation. High priced iron and gunpowder, imported under unfavorable terms of trade from Europe, and subject to prohibitive duties,

---

[1] Costa Filho, *A cana de açúcar*, 200–1.
[2] Augusto de Lima Júnior, *A Capitania de Minas Gerais*, 200–1; Inácio Correia Pamplona to Carlos José da Silva, mid-April 1789, *ADIM*, I, 37–8; Mawe, *Travels*, 149, 156, 206, 207, 239.   [3] Mawe, *Travels*, 273.
[4] Sequestro, Carlos Correia de Toledo e Melo, *ADIM*, I, 389; Sequestros, Cláudio Manuel da Costa, *ADIM*, v, 269.
[5] 'Relação dos rendimentos...' (1800) BNLCP, códice 643, 204–18; See statistical appendix, I, graph f.

confronted the miner with a situation in which all the essentials – capital, imported labor and tools – became more and more difficult to obtain on reasonable terms. The mining economy had in fact become locked in its own self perpetuating downward spiral, from which it would be excessively difficult to escape. An imperative need to lower costs of production increasingly obliged entrepreneurs and bureaucrats to search for local substitutes. As far as iron was concerned these lay close at hand.[1]

Dom Rodrigo José de Meneses, a son of the Marquis of Marialva, six months after taking up the post of governor in 1780 wrote a detailed exposition on the economic situation in Minas Gerais to Martinho de Melo e Castro.[2] Minas Gerais, he pointed out, was, properly speaking, neither an agricultural nor a commercial captaincy. The miner, he continued, deserved special attention and protection. He proposed the establishment of an iron foundry, which 'although at first sight might appear to be opposed to the spirit of the system of this captaincy', would be seen on further reflection to be a matter of great public utility. The Governor informed Lisbon that he had already given license for an experimental test to be conducted which demonstrated the quality of the local ore. Furthermore he recommended that the prohibition on construction of new sugar mills be abolished, and a fund be set up on the royal account to lend gold to miners so that they might have sufficient capital for exploitation and the improvement of techniques.

Minas Gerais, however, was and remained during the last quarter of the eighteenth century essentially an urban society, and the development of the regional economy was itself the result of urban demand. Minas society in the eighteenth century was never composed only of masters and slaves, at least not in the sense that those terms could be applied to the vast plantations of the coastal regions. In Minas the urban settings of the mountain cities provided a different environment, and while the more wealthy urban whites retained extensive interests in mining and agriculture outside the municipalities, the town house was the cultural focus of their activities and ethos. Nor was society so exclusively patriarchal as that of the other regions. The powerful influence of extended

[1] 'Memória sobre o estado da Capitania de Minas Gerais por José Eloi Ottoni', 1798, *RHSP*, XXVI (April–June 1956) 463; 'Memória sobre as minas de ouro do Brasil por Domingos Vandelli', *ABNRJ*, XX (1898) 266–79; Mawe, *Travels*, 208; 'Instrução para o govêrno da Capitania de Minas Gerais por José João Teixeira Coelho, Desembargador da relação do Porto', 1780, *RAPM*, VIII (1903) especially 499–511.

[2] 'Exposição do governador D. Rodrigo José de Menezes sobre o estado de decadência da capitania de Minas Gerais e meios de remedial-o', Vila Rica, 4 August 1780, *RAPM*, II (1897) 311–25.

kinship relationships was a vital part of the social structure. Yet in Minas the urban focus, and the pervasive involvement in assorted economic activities made the plutocratic values of the Minas magnates something different in quality from the patriarchial spirit of the rest of the colony. The magnates of Minas, typified by the opulent contractor, João Rodrigues de Macedo, or the great landowner Alvarenga Peixoto, or the Vila Rica lawyer, Cláudio Manuel da Costa, were involved in a myriad of economic functions, and were increasingly linked to the regional economy in a way that the great producers of colonial staples elsewhere in Portuguese America could never be.

Moreover, the transformation of the regional fiscal and administrative organs of government into concentrated centers of local interest had fortified this tendency. The Minas *junta da fazenda*, as a constituted body of great influence, was challenged by no other authority of equal stature. Vila Rica possessed no High Court, house of inspection, or independent customs administration, such as existed in the coastal captaincies with authoritative competences.[1] The Minas junta since the 1760s had been solely responsible for the farming of contracts of great importance, and no local contracts were held by metropolitan entrepreneurs in Minas Gerais, unlike the coastal captaincies where some contracts were still farmed in Lisbon itself.[2] These factors together with the notorious abuses of the system made the junta an organ wherein were focused the most powerful local economic interests. The result was that the vital concerns of a Portuguese immigrant merchant like João Rodrigues de Macedo became deeply rooted in and inseparable from the local process in a way unthinkable to the port city commissary or import–export entrepreneur.

Among the white minority in Minas Gerais the values and modes of the northern Portuguese provinces, especially Minho, Trás-os-Montes, Oporto, Douro and the Beiras, were predominant, rarely did the immigrants come from Lisbon and the South.[3] Reflected in speech and in ecclesiastical and domestic architecture, this dominant northern influence provided a powerful element in the consolidation of society, and encouraged a rapid and successful transplantation of Portuguese cultural

---

[1] For comparison with the situation in Rio de Janeiro see 'Almanaque da cidade do Rio de Janeiro', 1792, *ABNRJ*, LIX (1937) 198–263.

[2] The *dízimos* of Rio de Janeiro, Rio Grande, and Santa Catarina, for example, were farmed in Lisbon during the 1790s, 'livros dos termos da arrematação dos contratos', AHU, códice 306, f. 23v; codice 307, f. 12, 37v. Also see colonial contracts held by Quintella, statistical appendix 4.

[3] M. Rodrigues Lapa, *As 'Cartas Chilenas', Um problema histórico e filológico, com prefácio de Afonso Pena Júnior* (Rio de Janeiro, 1958) 64; Lima Júnior, *A capitania de Minas Gerais*, 123. José Ferreira Carrato, *Igreja, Iluminismo e Escolas Mineiras Coloniais* (São Paulo, 1968) 3, 7.

mores into the highly volatile and unstable social and economic environment of the mining zone. Society in Minas, however, was a complicated mosaic of groups and races, of new white immigrants and second and third generation native Americans, of new slaves and native born captives not to mention the ubiquitous Açorians. Race consciousness was a powerful, even a predominant element in social relationships. African influence was powerful, especially in the subcultures of fetishism, folklore, and dance.[1] Moreover, the *pardo* offspring of the early miscegenation had rapidly ascended into municipal and judicial office. Unfavorable reactions from more recently arrived Portuguese immigrants to this mobility had been quick to develop. During 1725 the Lisbon overseas council in response to local complaints declared the admission of mulattoes to municipal office to be 'indecorous' and admonished the inhabitants to leave descendants who were not 'infected, defective and impure'.[2] The latter recommendation was hardly likely to be fulfilled while the numbers of white women remained miniscule and heavily concentrated in the southern zone of the captaincy and concubinage was widely practiced.

Stratification of society corresponded to the division between racial groups. As elsewhere in Brazil, militia, auxiliary regiments, and the majority of lay religious brotherhoods, were rigorously exclusivist. The tertiary order of São Francisco of Vila Rica by the first statute of its 1765 institutions prohibited the admission of 'mulattoes, jews, moors, and heretics, or their descendents to the fourth generation'.[3] The brotherhood of Carmo of Ouro Prêto accepted only those of 'clean blood, good life and customs, and who could pay the annual subscription'.[4] Although such white, pardo and black regiments and brotherhoods were not peculiar to Minas Gerais these racially exclusivist social organisms played an especially important role in Minas society. This had resulted from the expulsion, during the second decade of the eighteenth century, of all regular monastic and religious orders from the mining zone. These expulsions, which included the Jesuits, Franciscans, and Carmelites, were the result of the dominant role played by renegade friars in the turbulent clashes and challenges to royal authority which had marked the early history of the colonization of the interior, and was indicative of the

---

[1] Aires da Mata Machado Filho, *O Negro e o Garimpo em Minas Gerais* (2nd edition, Rio de Janeiro, 1964) 60.
[2] Augusto de Lima Júnior, 'A formação social das Minas Gerais', *Congresso do Mundo Português*, Vol. 10 (Lisbon, 1940) 400–2.
[3] Cônego Raimundo Trindade, *São Francisco de Assis de Ouro Prêto* (Rio de Janeiro, 1951) 23.
[4] Francisco Antônio Lopes, *Historia da construção da Igreja do Carmo de Ouro Prêto* (Rio de Janeiro, 1942) 405.

metropolitan government's jealous protection of its treasure trove from all potential competitors.[1] In the absence of the regular orders the Minas lay religious associations – brotherhoods, and tertiary orders – took a dominant position in society by performing the functions and community tasks which in Minas had by default devolved on to the people.

Black and brown men were not denied the right to organize lay corporations. Miners, merchants, mulatto artisans, even the slaves, grouped themselves into legally constituted organizations, which as powerful and often very rich sodalities involved themselves in a myriad of religious and secular activities. The period of 1740–80 witnessed the greatest burst of activity by all types of brotherhood, from the fraternity of Our Lady of the Rosary of Blacks at the one extreme, to the white tertiary orders of São Francisco and Carmo, composed of merchants, intellectuals and high functionaries, at the other. In the euphoric ostentation of the new gold-rich society the sodalities competed and disputed with vigorous persistence to provide the most spectacular festivals, to join the great religious processions in more prestigious positions, and above all to construct the greatest and richest churches. The Minas brotherhoods commissioned architects, craftsmen, and musicians, employed the most famous preachers, ran hospitals and systems of mutual aid.[2] If they became especially wealthy they served as credit agencies for their members, even on occasion made loans to the captaincy exchequer.[3]

It was in architectural achievement that the activity of the brotherhoods was most remarkable. As early as 1750 Minas took the lead in architectural development in the colony, and the coincident shift in concentration from parochial churches to those of the brotherhoods was responsible for a remarkable maturing of colonial architecture in Minas Gerais. Free from the imported models that dominated the littoral, the existence of competing and wealthy lay sponsors liberated colonial creativity in Minas as nowhere else in Brazil. Under the patronage of the brotherhoods a brilliant generation of native artisans, architects, and painters emerged who graced the sprawling gold rush towns with elegant baroque churches, breathtaking sculpture and artifacts. Great advantage was taken of the

---

[1] José Ferreira Carrato, *As Minas Gerais e os Primordios do Caraça* (São Paulo, 1963) 57, 62.

[2] Fritz Teixeira de Salles, *Associações Religiosas no ciclo do ouro* (Belo Horizonte, 1963), 27, 36, 65, 71; Silvio de Carvalho Vasconcellos, 'A architectura colonial Mineira', *Ia Seminário de estudos Mineiros, Universidade de Minas Gerais* (Belo Horizonte, 1956) 67; Francisco Curt Lange, 'Musica Religiosa de Minas Gerais', *MEC* (Ministério da Educação e Cultura, Rio de Janeiro, May–June 1958) 19–25. Francisco Curt Lange, 'A Musica Barroca', *História Geral da civilização Brasileira* (directed by Sérgio Buarque de Holanda, São Paulo, 1960) I, 2, 121–40.

[3] Lopes, *História da construção*, 96.

local materials, particularly the soapstone, a soft blueish variety of
steatite. While the neo-classical dominated in Lisbon, in Minas Gerais the
baroque was refined and disciplined to greater elegance and unity.[1]

The special genius of the mulatto, Antônio Francisco Lisboa, the
Aleijadinho, was to give the Minas urban centers some of the world's
finest rococo churches. It was no accident that it was his design for the
church of the order of São Francisco of Ouro Prêto in the Minas capital,
begun in 1766, where the extraordinary development of the Minas
baroque was most clearly demonstrated. *Aleijadinho*, who preferred to
call himself an 'ornamental sculptor', was the illegitimate son of the
Portuguese architect Manuel Francisco Lisboa and a slave. He was
crippled and worked with a hammer and chisel strapped to his arms.
São Francisco of Ouro Prêto proposed new solutions of plan and façade
and produced a unified whole which Germain Bazin has numbered among
'the most perfect monuments of Luso-Brazilian art'.[2]

The vigorous competition between the sodalities because of their
composition was also a racial competition. Probably in the long term this
fact acted more as a harmonizer than as a divisive agent in the community, by channeling energies of racially exclusivist groupings into
constructive competition. Moreover, the sodalities by long tradition
arbitrated their disputes through legal channels. In addition the strict
ordering of society on racial lines did not preclude the employment of
talented individuals across the racial divide. It was the brotherhood of
Our Lady of the Rosary of Blacks which had sponsored the publication of
the *Triumpho Eucharístico* in Lisbon in 1734, and the lily white order of
São Francisco engaged the mulatto Antônio Francisco Lisboa to design
and execute sculpture in their churches in Vila Rica and São João d'El Rei.[3]
The numerous skilled musicians, painters, sculptors (many of them
pardos) formed an urban artisan class which stood between the slaves and

[1] Germain Bazin, *L'Architecture Religieuse Baroque au Brésil* (2 vols., Paris, São Paulo, 1956) I,
173–213; Robert C. Smith Jr, 'The Arts in Brazil: Baroque Architecture', *Portugal and
Brazil* (editor, Harold Livermore, Oxford, 1963) 349, and *Art Bulletin*, XXI, 110–42; George
Kubler, Martin Soria, *Art and Architecture in Spain and Portugal and their American Dominions
1500–1800* (Pelican History of Art, 1959); There is a large bibliography on the Minas
baroque to which the works mentioned here provide an excellent introduction.

[2] Bazin, *l'Architecture Religieuse Baroque*, I, 213: J. B. Bury, 'The Aleijadinho', *Cornhill
Magazine* (Summer 1949), and 'Estilo Aleijadinho and the Churches of Eighteenth Century
Brazil', *Architectural Review* LXI (1952); Germain Bazin, *Aleijadinho et la sculpture baroque au
Brésil* (Paris, 1963).

[3] Boxer, *Golden Age*, 177; Bazin, *l'Architecture Religieuse Baroque*, II, 97, 111; For some
interesting observations on the mulatto freeman in Brazil see Herbert S. Klein, 'The
Colored Freedman in Brazilian Slave Society', *Journal of Social History*, III, No. 1 (1969)
30–52.

the white minority, which had become an influential native articulator, especially in the visual arts and music, of the distinctive character of the region.

Among the Brazilian-born whites existed a highly literate élite who themselves were increasingly articulating the special quality of their society. For forty years rich *Mineiros* had been sending their sons to the University of Coimbra. In 1786, twelve of twenty-seven Brazilians matriculated at Coimbra were from Minas, and in 1787, ten out of nineteen.[1] Doyen of the older generation of Brazilian-born graduates was the ageing, gracious, and bespectacled advocate Cláudio Manuel da Costa. The wealthy lawyer had been educated at the Jesuit college in Rio de Janeiro where he had been sent at the age of fifteen. He had entered Coimbra during 1749. In Portugal he rapidly acquired a reputation as a poet, and after his return to Brazil a few years later to establish a legal practice in Vila Rica composed dramatic poems for receptive audiences in the theaters of the captaincy and those of Rio de Janeiro. During 1759 he was elected a member of the *Academia Brasilica dos Renascidos* of Bahia, a short lived literary and historical association, and one of the few enterprises which had genuinely sought to embrace the whole of Portuguese America as its parish. The successful young Brazilian caught the eye of Gomes Freire de Andrada who appointed him secretary to the government of Minas, a post he held between 1762 and 1765 and again from 1769 to 1773. In 1771 he was appointed attorney to the Tertiary Order of São Francisco of Vila Rica. He had applied for the habit of the order of Chirst in 1761 paying eight arrobas of gold to the royal exchequer. A delay of ten years ensued before the honor was bestowed, for the existence of an olive-oil vending grandfather proved an embarrassing impediment. The order was eventually confirmed though it was painfully evident, especially to the sensitive recipient, that his nobility was conferred because he was rich and not because of his birth. Cláudio Manuel da Costa was in fact a very wealthy man with important clients, slaves, a partnership in gold washings, a *fazenda* with cattle and pigs, and a considerable money lending business. His spacious town house in Vila Rica was the gathering point for the intellectuals of the captaincy.[2]

---

[1] 'Estudantes Brasileiros em Coimbra', *ABNRJ*, LXII, 181–7.

[2] Alberto Lamego, *Mentiras Históricas* (Rio de Janeiro, 1947) 113–20; Alberto Lamego, *Autobiografia e inédito de Cláudio Manuel da Costa* (Brussels/Paris, nd); Sequestro, Cláudio Manuel da Costa, *ADIM*, I, 356–64; 'Traslado dos sequestros', *ADIM*, V, 263–76; Rodrigues Lapa, *Cartas Chilenas*, 28, 37; Lúcio José dos Santos, *A Inconfidência Mineira: Papel de Tiradentes na Inconfidência Mineira* (São Paulo, 1927) 234–9; Carrato, *Igreja, Iluminismo e Escolas Mineiras Coloniais*, 83, 85, 184–5.

Among the poet's most regular visitors during the 1780s was Tomás Antônio Gonzaga, the *ouvidor* of Vila Rica, an ambitious and fastidious legalist, son of one of Pombal's confidants. His father was a Brazilian-born magistrate who had served as *ouvidor* of Pernambuco, as judge of the Bahian high court, intendent general of gold and first minister of the Inspection House of Bahia, and then as judge of the high court of Oporto. He had personally presented to Pombal his son's dissertation on the natural law, a treatise dedicated to the marquis, 'that hero and lover of true science'. Tomás Antônio Gonzaga, born in Oporto, was brought up almost wholly in Brazil, where he attended the Jesuit college in Bahia, witnessing the expulsion of the 'black robes' in 1759. He was nephew to Feliciano Gomes Neves, one of the entrepreneurs aided by the Pombaline *junta do comércio*. Appointed *juiz de fora* of Beja in 1779, he had been nominated ouvidor of Vila Rica in 1782. Long an admirer of the works of Cláudio Manuel da Costa, he was himself a poet of merit and originality. The two men formed the center of a group which embraced the intendent of Vila Rica, Francisco Gregório Pires Bandeira, the contractor, João Rodrigues de Macedo, the ex-*ouvidor* of São João d'El Rei, Alvarenga Peixoto, and two priests, Carlos Correia de Toledo e Melo, vicar of the wealthy parish of São José in Rio das Mortes, and canon Luís Vieira da Silva of the cathedral of Mariana.[1]

Carlos Correia de Toledo, a strong willed Paulista in his mid-fifties was a man of fortune, a slaveowner with *fazendas* and mineral workings. When in Vila Rica he stayed as the guest of the *ouvidor*, Gonzaga. His household in Rio das Mortes contained a respectable library, he employed a mulatto musician, and the vicar stood at the head of a large dependency.[2] Luís Vieira da Silva was a well known and persuasive preacher, much in demand on solemn or festive occasions. An erudite and thoughtful cleric in his early fifties he possessed a fine and up-to-date library of over 600 volumes. During his numerous visits to the Minas capital he stayed as the guest of João Rodrigues de Macedo. After studying at the Jesuit college in São Paulo he had been appointed to the chair of philosophy in the seminary at Mariana in 1757, and was Carlos Correia's predecessor as vicar of São José. He had been elected commissary of the order of São

---

[1] *Obras Completas de Tomás Antônio Gonzaga*, I, *Poesias, Cartas Chilenas* (editor, M. Rodrigues Lapa, Rio de Janeiro, 1957) ix–xv; 'Auto de inquiração summario de testemunhas', Vila Rica, 26 May 1789, *ADIM*, II, 441–52; 'Direito Natural accommodado ao estado civil catholica, offerecida ao Illᵃ— e Exᵃ—Snʳ Sebastião José de Carvalho e Melo, Marquês de Pombal, por Tomáz Antônio Gonzaga', BNLCP, códice 29.

[2] Letter of appointment, 22 June 1776, AHU, Minas Gerais, caixa 93; Sequestro, *ADIM*, I, 386–403; Sequestro, *ADIM*, V, 335–47.

Francisco of Vila Rica in 1770, through the influence of the then governor, the count of Valladares, the 'protector' of the order. Luís Vieira was outspoken in his enthusiasm for the events in North America. He held that the European powers had no right to dominion in America. The Portuguese monarchy had spent nothing in its conquest and the Brazilians themselves had restored Bahia to the crown from the Dutch, and bought Rio de Janeiro from the French. Luís Vieira, a man who had never left Brazil was close in opinion to those conspiratorial students who had joined hands in Coimbra and vowed to see their country free of the yoke of Portugal.[1]

The Vila Rica circle was not the only group of like-minded and intelligent men who regularly and informally met to discuss poetry, philosophy, and the events in Europe and the Americas. Similar groups of lawyers and writers met in São João d'El Rei and elsewhere in the captaincy for conversations or cards.[2] The members of the Vila Rica circle, however, by the quality of their poetry, and by their position, influence, and wealth stood at the apex of Minas society, with lines of family, friendship, or economic interest linking them to a network of similar if less articulate men throughout the captaincy. In their capacities as lawyers and judges, as *fazendeiros*, merchants, and money lenders, as the officers of powerful lay brotherhoods, they typified the diversified but intensely American interests of the Minas plutocracy.

The powerful economic forces obliging entrepreneurs and bureaucrats to become self-sufficient, together with the urban ethos, and the obvious success of the transplanted culture in finding its own distinctive solutions in art, architecture, and music, were, in conjunction, the factors which led even an exiled Mineiro like Silva Ponte to exclaim in 1786 that his homeland would become 'the head of a great Kingdom'. During the early 1780s the comarcas had begun the proud cataloguing of all the major buildings of their districts.[3] The history of the capital became the theme of Cláudio Manuel da Costa's epic poem *Vila Rica*, and subject of a lengthy

---

1 Trindade, *São Francisco*, 197–200, 222–8; 'Avaliação dos livros sequestrados, conego Luís Vieira da Silva', *ADIM*, I, 445–65; 'Auto de perguntas', Rio de Janeiro, 20 November 1789, *ADIM*, IV, 292–3; 'Auto de continuação de perguntas', Rio de Janeiro, 21 July 1790 [*sic* – This must be 1791 for Vasconcelos Coutinho the interrogating judge in this instance did not arrive in Rio until the end of December 1790] *ibid.*, 304; witness, Vicente Vieira da Mota, Vila Rica, 23 June 1789, *ADIM*, I, 110–11; witness, Vieira da Mota, Vila Rica, 3 August 1789, *ADIM*, III, 336; Auto de perguntas, Rio de Janeiro, 19 July 1791, *ADIM*, V, 19–21; *AMI*, II (1953) 68; Carrato, *Igreja, Iluminismo, e Escolas Mineiras Coloniais*, 112–14; Eduardo Frieiro, *O diabo na livraria do cônego* (Belo Horizonte, M. G., 1957).

2 Rodrigues Lapa, *Alvarenga Peixoto*, xxxii.

3 Bazin, *l'Architecture Religieuse Baroque*, I, 173.

prose dissertation by him, replete with statistical tables.[1] During 1781 Alvarenga Peixoto reflected this powerful self-awareness in his *canto genetlíaco*. The poem was an enthusiastic apology for the riches, men, and promise of the Brazilian land. He compared the deeds of the *Mineiros* to those of Hercules, Ulysses, and Alexander. The transplantation of the Portuguese race was, in better physical conditions, creating a great civilization, and he did not fail to include the slaves, 'duros e valentes', in his panegyric. In a portentous phrase which could well have applied to the rest of his countrymen the poet asserted: 'They are worthy of attention.'[2]

Social and economic conditions in Minas Gerais during the 1780s contradicted everything that the concept of colonial dependency then current among policy makers in Lisbon held to be self-evident. The condition was transient – an agricultural economy would in time predominate and with it the urban focus of the eighteenth century would be weakened and the power of the distinctive Minas plutocracy be supplanted by that of rural patriarchs more characteristic of the rest of Brazil. Nor was the economic regionalism of Minas Gerais and the quest for self-sufficiency representative of the whole of Portuguese America – especially the Northern captaincies with the export orientation of their sugar and cotton economies. Yet the developments which had taken place in Minas were the antithesis of what the official mind in Lisbon believed to be the functions of a colonial captaincy, and especially one which had for so long been the most vital source of Portugal's colonial wealth. The local compulsions which led D. Rodrigo José de Meneses to propose the establishment of an iron foundry was anathema to those formulating the new and rigid neo-mercantilism emanating from the post-Pombaline administration. Just as João Rodrigues de Macedo stood at the elbow of the Governor of Minas – the two men were on terms of intimate familiarity – so the opulent metropolitan merchant-industrialists stood behind that of Martinho de Melo e Castro, and by the 1780s the interests of the Minas plutocracy and the Metropolitan oligarchs had become totally incompatible.[3] None of the Governor's proposals were implemented, and the whole thrust of policy from Lisbon moved inexorably toward the structures of the alvará of January 1785. In October 1783, the able and intelligent D. Rodrigo José de Meneses, to whose son the poem *canto*

---

[1] 'Notícia da Capitania de Minas Gerais por Cláudio Manuel da Costa', IHGB, lata 22, doc. 13.

[2] Rodrigues Lapa, *Alvarenga Peixoto*, xli, 33–8.

[3] For the close relationship between the two men see D. Rodrigo José de Meneses to Sr João Roiz' de Macedo, Bahia, 7 February 1789, *ABNRJ*, lxv, 231.

genetlíaco had been dedicated by Alvarenga Peixoto in 1782, was moved to Bahia.[1]

The new governor could not have been a stronger contrast to his predecessor. Luís da Cunha Meneses was a stylish martinet with an entourage of venal sycophants and hangers-on. He was a man who viewed his prerogatives as supreme and brooked no opposition to his whims and authority, or those of his favorites. His pleasure in appearances and loyalty to his cronies outweighed his sense of justice. Previously governor of Goiás, he took no pains to disguise his disdain for the local native-born whites. In Vila Boa, Brazilians had been unceremoniously removed from lucrative posts to make way for his friends. Lavish in the distribution of military commissions – a process lucrative to his personal secretary – he had offended the racial susceptibilities of colonial society by appointing black and *pardo* officers.[2]

In Minas the governor immediately ran headlong into a series of bitter disputes. These focused around the two most sensitive elements in the captaincy's administrative–fiscal system – the *junta da fazenda*, and the Diamond District. In 1784 Cunha Meneses clashed with the *ouvidor* Gonzaga and the *intendent* Bandeira over the merits of their respective clients for the farm of the *entradas*. The magistrates insisted that the governor's client, José Pereira Marques, was in no way suited to hold the contract, lacking the financial and social status required by law. Carlos José da Silva, the junta's secretary, appointed after the reform of 1771, pleaded in vain that the *entradas* be administered directly on the royal account, pointing out that this method had proved much more profitable and effective to the exchequer. The proposition was opposed by Gonzaga and Bandeira. Both they and the governor stood to lose substantial emoluments should such a proposal be accepted. The governor used his presidency of the junta to overrule the objections and granted the contract to Pereira Marques.[3]

The clash with the magistrates and the partisan battle over the contract

---

[1] 'Governo de Minas Gerais, período colonial', *RAPM*, I (1896).

[2] 'Queixa de Luís Henrique da Silva contra arbitrariedades cometidas em Goiás por Luís da Cunha Menezes', Vila Boa, 22 July 1782, Rodrigues Lapa, *Cartas Chilenas*, 230–2; 'Queixa do vigário de Vila Boa de Goiás contra o Governador', Vila Boa, 29 May 1782, *ibid.*, 223–9; 'Representação do presidente da camara de Vila Boa contra abusos do Governador', Vila Boa, 6 May 1782 *ibid.*, 216–22; 'Representação do ouvidor de Goiás contra o Governador', Vila Boa, 15 April 1782, *ibid.*, 204–15.

[3] 'Acta da junta da administração e arrecadação da Real Fazenda, presidente o capitão-general Luís da Cunha Menezes', 3 December 1784, *AMI*, II (1953) 193–201; Luís da Cunha Meneses to M. de Melo e Castro, Vila Rica, 5 January 1785, Rodrigues Lapa, *Cartas Chilenas*, 246–9; M. de Melo e Castro to visconde de Barbacena, 29 January 1788, *AMI*, II (1953) 151.

began an acrimonious dispute. Cunha Meneses granted to Pereira Marques and to the former contractor of *entradas* Silvério dos Reis – who according to Gonzaga was lavish with bribes at the governor's palace – special powers in debt collection and foreclosure which circumvented the courts and the magistrates.[1] The result was to deny important court costs and legal fees to the magistracy. Previously the *ouvidor* had granted any special debt collecting privileges and received the benefits from the resulting litigation – Gonzaga had granted for example, special rights of foreclosure and apprehension of goods and chattels to João Rodrigues de Macedo in July 1783.[2] The reason given by Cunha Meneses for bypassing legal process was the disastrous financial state in which he found the *dízimos* and *entradas*. Ninety cases had been heard by the judge in 1784 he claimed, and not one of them had brought any benefit to the royal coffers – the only ones to gain had been the judge and scribe. He encouraged the contractors to use the military in debt collection and denied legal recourse to the debtors.[3] His actions hurt Gonzaga in particular. The *ouvidor* was not a wealthy man and he had borrowed 1,549$000 *reis* to cover the expenses of his journey to Vila Rica in 1782.[4]

The involvement of the governor's cronies in the lucrative diamond smuggling network became a matter of public scandal. Embezzlement and malpractice within the District had long been common. The difference during the 1780s was that backed by the governor's unswerving and unquestioned support, his favorites were able to monopolize smuggling and flout the authority of the District's judicial officers – the intendent and fiscal – with impunity. Smuggled diamonds had previously come from two sources. For long the mountains of the Sêrro do Frio had been infested with gangs of illegal miners, the *garimpeiros*, who in league with small itinerant merchants, the *capangueiros*, provided a portion of the precious stones which by various routes reached the European market.[5] The rest had come from embezzlement within the District, generally by the well-placed relatives of the Brazilian-born treasurers or by members of the military guards, especially those with family connections with Tejuco residents. These illegal shipments had left Minas with the connivance of the contractors, the Minas Dragoons, and perhaps the magistracy.

---

[1] Rodrigues Lapa, *Cartas Chilenas*, 147–8, 264; Order of Luís da Cunha Meneses, Vila Rica, 24 September 1785, *ibid.*, 250–1.

[2] Order of Tomás Antônio Gonzaga, 14 July 1783, CCBNRJ, I-1-2-1, doc. 3.

[3] Gonzaga, *Obras completas*, I, xviii.

[4] 'Conta com documentos e obrigações de Tomás Antônio Gonzaga', IHGB, lata 116, doc. 5.

[5] Machado Filho, *O Negro e o Garimpo*, 13–14; For the diamond trade to Amsterdam, H. I. Bloom, *The Economic Activities of the Jews of Amsterdam* (Philadelphia, 1937) 40.

The priest José da Silva de Oliveira Rolim, for example, son of the principal treasurer of diamonds, and one of the most notorious embezzlers, was a close friend of the sixty-year-old contractor of *dízimos*, Domingos de Abreu Vieira.[1] Abreu Vieira, a Portuguese from Braga and lieutenant-colonel of the auxiliary cavalry of Minas Novas, was in turn the protector and godfather to the illegitimate daughter of the *alferes*, Joaquim José da Silva Xavier, commandant during the early 1780s of the crucial Dragoons detachment that patrolled the road to Rio de Janeiro over the Mantiqueira mountains between Mathias Barbosa and Igreja Nova.[2] Silva Xavier, nicknamed the toothpuller (*Tiradentes*), after his part-time occupation of removing teeth and fitting new ones of bone, had, before entering the military in 1775, been an unsuccessful prospector in Minas Novas. He was hoping for the hand of Oliveira Rolim's niece in marriage.[3] The embezzling cleric sent gifts to the *ouvidor* Gonzaga through Abreu Vieira, and Gonzaga in his house in Vila Rica had a store of precious stones.[4] The aging contractor was closely associated with Cláudio Manuel da Costa with whom he had extensive credit transactions. He retained the famous poet as his lawyer for forty oitavas of gold per annum to represent his interests in the matter of his contract, which most often, of course, involved cases appearing before their mutual friend the *ouvidor* Gonzaga, superior crown magistrate of Vila Rica and *ex-officio* deputy of the *junta da fazenda*.[5]

With the arrival of Cunha Meneses these harmonious and doubtless lucrative relationships between the magistracy and smugglers were upset, for another group of peculators entered the scene. The military commandant of the Diamond District, José de Vasconcelos Parada e Sousa, in association with Bazilio de Brito Malheiro, a heavily indebted *fazendeiro* in the Sêrro do Frio, together with one of the governor's favorite officers, José de Sousa Lobo, commandant of the mountains of Santo Antônio, came to dominate the illegal commerce. Sousa Lobo, Portuguese like Bazilio de Brito and Parada e Sousa, had been rapidly promoted to the rank of *sargento-mor*.[6] The military detachment of Santo Antônio and

---

[1] José da Sᵃ e Carvᵃ Rollim to Sʳ Domingos de Abreu Vieira, and José da Sᵃ to Sʳ Domingos de Abreu, Tejuco 20 April 1789, *ADIM*, I, 71–4. [2] Mathias, *CCANRJ*, 25–6.

[3] 'Auto de perguntas...Padre José da Silva de Oliveira Rolim', Vila Rica, 3 March 1790, *ADIM*, II, 473–6; 'Auto de perguntas feitas ao Sargento-Mor Alberto da Silva e Oliveira Rolim', Vila Rica, 20 February 1790, *ADIM*, II, especially 460–1.

[4] José da Silva to Domingos de Abreu Vieira, Tejuco 30 March 1789, *ADIM*, I, 71–3; Sequestro, Gonzaga, *ADIM*, V, 305.

[5] 'Sequestro em creditos e obrigações, Cláudio Manuel da Costa', *ADIM*, I, 356.

[6] Witness, Bazilio de Brito Malheiro do Lago, Vila Rica, 18 June 1789, *ADIM*, I, 98; witness, José de Sousa Lobo, Vila Rica 14 June 1790, *ADIM*, I, 278; witness, José de Vasconcellos

that of Tejuco were the most important commands of the Dragoons.[1] Secure in the governor's favoritism, Sousa Lobo, instead of persecuting the *garimpeiros* as was his charge, entered into a pact which guaranteed them the free exercise of their illegal mining in return for the profit of controlling contraband.[2]

The lucrative control of the contraband in diamonds by the governor's lackeys in both the Diamond District and Santo Antônio cut out many who had previously benefited – especially the Brazilian-born officers of the Dragoons with relatives or friends in the District. The dissension within the Dragoons was more acute, for by 1780 Brazilians outnumbered Portuguese by twenty-six to twenty-one within the officer corps, and eighteen of the Brazilian officers were Minas born.[3] Moreover, Sousa Lobo had replaced Baltasar João Mairinque, whose eldest daughter Maria Doroteia was the object of the *ouvidor* Gonzaga's amorous and poetic attentions.[4] The *alferes* Silva Xavier was so outraged by the governor's favoritism, his removal from the command of the Mantiqueira patrol and lack of promotion, that he talked openly of rebellion. The governor on being informed of his seditious statements dismissed them as being the jealous chatter of a knave (*mariola*).[5]

When the Intendent of the Diamond District, José Antônio de Meireles Freire, sent instructions to Gonzaga to arrest Bazilio de Brito Malheiro in Vila Rica on the charge of murder, the governor at the prompting of his military favorites countermanded the order, released the accused, and allowed him to withdraw to his estates.[6] Sousa Lobo

---

Parada e Sousa, Vila Rica 26 June 1789, *ADIM*, I, 125–6; Dez°r Intendente Geral dos Diamantes, Antônio Barrozo Pereira to M. de Melo e Castro, Tejuco, 15 May 1789, Rodrigues Lapa, *Cartas Chilenas*, 344–5; Beltrão, Tejuco, 16 May 1789, *ibid.*, 345–9; Antônio Coelho Pares de França, Tejuco 27 June 1788, *ibid.*, 328–32; also *ibid.*, 191–3.

[1] 'Regimento de cavalaria regular de Vila Rica', July, August, September, October, November, December 1788, CCBNRJ, I-I-19.

[2] Luís Beltrão de Gouveia d'Almeida, fiscal dos diamantes to M. de Melo e Castro, Tejuco, 20 January 1789, Rodrigues Lapa, *Cartas Chilenas*, 281–7.

[3] 'Officiais e Off⁵ inferiores – Cavalaria paga de Minas Gerais', AHU, Minas Gerais, caixa 92.

[4] Gonzaga, *obras completas*, I, xvi; D. Maria Doroteia Joaquina de Seixas was the famous Marília de Dirceu of Gonzaga's poems, Tomás Antônio Gonzaga, *Marília de Dirceu e mais poesias* (editor, M. Rodrigues Lapa, Lisbon 1944), xiii.

[5] 'Auto de continuação de perguntas feitas ao Alferes Joaquim José de Silva Xavier', Rio de Janeiro 18 January 1790, *ADIM*, IV, 45–6; witness, Vicente Vieira da Mota, Vila Rica 3 August 1789, *ADIM*, III, 335–6; José Aires Gomes to visconde de Barbacena, Vila Rica, 1 August 1789, *ADIM*, II, 429.

[6] For comments on the *intendent* see Santos, *Memorias*, 197; On the arrest and release, José Antônio de Meireles Freire to M. de Melo e Castro, Tejuco, 5 July 1784, Rodrigues Lapa, *Cartas Chilenas*, 240–3; Minuta, Dr Tomás Antônio Gonzaga, Vila Rica, 8 April 1784, Gonzaga, *obras completas* II, 188.

meanwhile openly defied and publicly humiliated the magistrates of the District, and had José Ferreira Cioto, nicknamed 'The Ear' (*o Orelha*), murdered before he could give evidence against the smugglers and their military accomplices.[1] The fiscal of the District, Luís Beltrão de Gouveia, formerly a counselor to D. Rodrigo José de Meneses, and a friend of the contractor João Rodrigues de Macedo and the Vila Rica magistrates Gonzaga and Bandeira, protested to Lisbon that the law was powerless in face of the breakdown of relations between the governor and the magistracy.[2] The governor considered his jurisdiction unlimited, he complained, and viewed the magistrates as so many enemies. The arbitrary rule of Cunha Meneses brought 'unheard of barbarities to a land that has religion and laws'.[3]

The outrage of the ouvidor was no less. The tension between the autocratic governor and the magistrate became acute. The contrast between the licentious Cunha Meneses with his sycophantic court and numerous concubines, and Tomás Antônio Gonzaga, the prim middle-aged poet who wooed from afar the teenage beauty of his 'Marília de Dirceu', could not have been greater. The aversion between the executive head of the Minas government and the chief judicial officer of the captaincy, forced to meet regularly at the sessions of the *junta da fazenda*, was mutual, bitter, and in the conditions of Minas Gerais in the 1780s catalytic. Gonzaga, a stubborn and self-righteous man whose father had stood close to the inner circle of Pombal's advisers, was a formidable match for the martinet in the governor's palace. Thwarted over the contracting of the *entradas*, denied lucrative fees by the bypassing of the courts, he forwarded a series of outspoken denunciations to Lisbon against the governor's 'notorious despotism'. Cunha Meneses, he claimed, 'recognized no other law or reason than the dictates of his own will and those of his cronies'.[4]

Gonzaga in his treatise on the natural law, which attacked democracy as the worst system of government, had praised monarchy for its contractual nature. 'The King', the young Gonzaga had written, 'was a mandatory of the people, a minister of God, the end of whose rule was

---

[1] Rodrigues Lapa, *Cartas Chilenas*, 183–188.

[2] For relationships between Beltrão and João Rodrigues de Macedo and Gonzaga and Bandeira, see *ibid.*, 135; Beltrão while in Vila Rica stayed as a guest at Rodrigues de Macedo's townhouse, see José Aires Gomes to Visconde de Barbacena, Vila Rica, 1 August 1789, *ADIM*, II, 429.

[3] Luís Beltrão de Gouveia d'Almeida to M. de Melo e Castro, Tejuco, 20 January 1787, Rodrigues Lapa, *Cartas Chilenas*, 281–7.

[4] Minute, Dr Tomás Antônio Gonzaga, Vila Rica, 8 April, 1784, Gonzaga, *obras completas*, II, 185–9; Minute, Gonzaga, Vila Rica, 21 March 1787, *ibid.*, 194.

the utility of the people.' It was clear from Gonzaga's representations of the 1780s that he regarded the Crown's representative in Minas Gerais as being a man who had blatantly ignored both the well-being of the people and the restraints of law, tradition and justice. In face of the arbitrary nature of Cunha Meneses' rule the *ouvidor* sharpened his attack by using the time honored medium of polemic verse. He composed and circulated an audacious poetic libel. A more sophisticated form of the scurrilous pasquins – scandalous personal attacks in verse and doggerel common in Minas Gerais during the eighteenth century – the *cartas chilenas*, probably written during 1786 and 1787, were a thinly disguised assault on the governor's rule. Ostensibly set in Chile, the thirteen letters were in reality a detailed and formidable arraignment against Cunha Meneses, his friends, and his deeds.[1]

The recourse of the superior crown magistrate of Vila Rica to the methods of the ballad makers of the streets moved the controversy into quite a different category from the confidential letters to the Queen, a standard and accepted recourse to dissatisfied jurists. During July 1786 Cunha Meneses ordered a search of the fazenda belonging to the capitão-mor of Vila Rica, José Álvares Maciel.[2] The intendent Bandeira who undertook the search with diligence could find no incriminating papers. If the objective had been to uncover copies of Gonzaga's letters the search was to no avail, but the cavalier disregard for the person of one of the captaincy's wealthy and distinguished magnates was typical of Cunha Meneses high-handed actions. The daughter of José Álvares Maciel was betrothed to the commanding officer of the Minas Dragoons, Francisco de Paula Freire de Andrade, illegitimate son of José Antônio Freire, brother of Gomes Freire de Andrada.[3] The capitão-mor's three sons had all matriculated at Coimbra in 1782. They were contemporaries of José Joaquim Maia who three months after the search of the Maciel *fazenda* composed his first letter at Montpellier to Thomas Jefferson. The capitão-mor's second son and namesake, José Álvares Maciel was in England avidly buying reports on the American revolution.[4]

---

[1] There is a vast bibliography on the *cartas chilenas*, their attribution, identification of the characters, and so on. Hardly a major literary scholar or historian in Portugal and Brazil has not at some stage discussed the work. I have relied heavily on M. Rodrigues Lapa's masterly *As 'Cartas Chilenas': Um Problema histórico e filológico* (Rio de Janeiro, 1958), though it is unlikely that even this profound and careful study will prove to be the definitive work.

[2] 'Busca ordenada por D. Luís da Cunha e Menezes em casa do Cel. José Alves Maciel', CCBNRJ, 1-1-13: also in *ABNRJ*, LXV (1943) 218–19.

[3] 'Auto de perguntas feitas a Francisco de Paula Freire de Andrade', Rio de Janeiro, 16 November 1789, *ADIM*, IV, 205; Santos, *Inconfidência*, 179.

[4] 'Estudantes Brasileiros em Coimbra', *ABNRJ*, LXII, 171–2.

The acrimonious dispute over the contracting of the *entradas*, however, had focused the attention of the Lisbon government on the fiscal and administrative affairs of the captaincy. During June 1786 Carlos José da Silva, the *junta da fazenda*'s secretary, forwarded to Martinho de Melo e Castro a detailed account of the debts owed to the royal exchequer by the two ex-contractors, João Rodrigues de Macedo and Joaquim Silvério dos Reis. These two men alone, the secretary of state discovered, were obligated for the vast sum of almost a million *milreis*.[1] This was twice as much as the total value of the average annual monetary issue in Portugal during the period (See Statistical appendix, Graph C). Later in the year da Silva forwarded a detailed list of the state of arrears on all contracts farmed since the late 1740s.[2] When in September, Cunha Meneses discovered that these damaging reports had gone to Lisbon, he wrote to Melo e Castro in self justification. He admitted the figures to be accurate, but pointed out that in the case of João Rodrigues de Macedo the deadline for payment was not due until July 1788, and that there were other contracts, some twenty and thirty years old, which also had great sums outstanding. The case of Rodrigues de Macedo he claimed was different for these older contracts, for the captaincy owed to the opulent contractor double what he owed to the exchequer. The same factors applied to the case of Silvério dos Reis. This was not so with the older contracts and in fact he had instituted proceedings against the capitão-mor of Vila Rica, who had been *caixa* for some of these older farms and was the only representative still alive.[3]

The governor's explanation of his actions carried little conviction in Lisbon, although it further alienated the Maciel family with its important kin in Brazil. Moreover, Melo e Castro's secretariate was not the only metropolitan organ of government concentrating its attentions on the affairs of the captaincy. The harsh and oppressive demands of the extra-legal and military methods used in debt collection had provoked the câmara of Mariana into an appeal to the overseas council which had

[1] 'Relação dos contratos que rematão João Roiz' de Macedo na junta da fazenda da capitania d'Minas Gerais', Carlos José da Silva, 26 June 1786; 'Relação dos contratos...' Joaquim Silvério dos Reis, AHU, Minas Gerais, caixa 94.

[2] 'Contratos de Minas Gerais, particularmente o contrato das entradas e dividas a real fazenda', AHU, Minas Gerais, caixa 94; 'Relação dos contratos que se achão por pagar e pertenecentes a esta capitania de Minas Gerais, cujos restos de cada hum deles se verificão feitas as contas no dia 22 de Septembro de 1786', Carlos José da Silva, *AMI*, II (1953) 201–4.

[3] Luís da Cunha Meneses to M. de Melo e Castro, Vila Rica 23 September 1786, Rodrigues Lapa, *Cartas Chilenas*, 275–7. It is possible that the search of July was connected with the papers of the contract. There is no suggestion, however, in the document as to the type of papers sought.

begun an investigation of the situation.[1] The chaotic state of the Diamond District and the competition facing the royal contract by contraband diamonds reaching the Amsterdam market from Brazil by unofficial channels was also causing concern to the Royal Treasury. The high court judge, Antônio Dinis da Cruz e Silva, was dispatched from Rio de Janeiro to conduct a *devassa* or judicial inquiry into conditions in Tejuco.[2] To impress the visiting judge, Cunha Meneses ordered Parada e Sousa to expel Oliveira Rolim from the District and the captaincy. His action, like that against the capitão-mor, struck at an important Brazilian magnate – Oliveira Rolim was the son of the first *caixa* of the Diamond District. Neither Álvares Maciel or Oliveira Rolim were innocents, but they were being clearly and blatantly made scapegoats for others. The removal of the avaricious priest – who according to Gonzaga refused to pay off the governor's private secretary who had demanded several thousand *cruzados* from him – also extinguished one of the major native-born competitors to the Portuguese contrabandists who thrived under the governor's protection.[3]

Cunha Meneses and Tomás Antônio Gonzaga were replaced in 1786. The Visconde de Barbacena was appointed governor designate and Gonzaga nominated to be a judge (*Desembargador*) of the High Court of Bahia.[4] The extensive investigations underway in Lisbon led to an inordinate delay in the arrival of the successors of both men and in the interim period relations between the judiciary and the executive branch of the government in Minas Gerais remained virtually paralyzed. The actions of the governor's favorites became more blatant and notorious and Cunha Meneses himself no less arbitrary in his actions. He ordered the retiring intendent of the Diamond District Meireles Freire arrested in Mathias Barbosa, searched, and the gold he was carrying confiscated as contraband.[5] And Lisbon remained badly informed of events in Minas, for Melo e Castro's spy in the Governor's secretariate, José Onório de Valadares e Aboim, was carefully kept from all matters of importance on

---

[1] 'Representação q'fizerão a Sua Maga os Offes os da Câmara da Cide de Marianna, 1789' Registro de consultas 1786–1798', AHU, códice 302, f. 15.

[2] Dr Antônio Dinis da Cruz e Silva left Minas after completing his investigations on 11 August 1786, Luís da Cunha Meneses, to M. de Melo e Castro, Vila Rica, 7 September 1786, Rodrigues Lapa, *Cartas Chilenas*, 274.

[3] Order to José de Vasconcellos Parada e Souza, 27 June 1786, Gonzaga, *Obras completas*, I, note 77, 258; for identification of Matúsio, Rodrigues Lapa, *Cartas Chilenas*, 165–9.

[4] 'Nomeação do visconde de Barbacena', 10 August 1786, *ibid.*, 265; 'Houve por bem fazer merce ao Bacharel Tomás Antônio Gonzaga de hum lugar ordinario de Dezembargador da Relação de Bahia', 7 November 1786, AHU, Minas Gerais, caixa 92. Gonzaga had requested position in Bahia and was approved 11 October 1786 by Overseas Council, see *ABNRJ*, XXXII (1910) 594–5.   [5] Rodrigues Lapa, *Cartas Chilenas*, 197–8.

the specious grounds that he was both deaf and blind, an assertion he strenuously but uselessly denied.[1] Indeed while the bureaucrats deliberated, the conditions in Minas became dangerously unsettled and the reports of the various inquiries being conducted in Lisbon had disquieting effects on the exchequer's debtors in Brazil. The priest Oliveira Rolim before his expulsion had broken into the visiting judge's quarters in Tejuco and examined his secret dispatches to Lisbon, which condemned him in particular, and severely criticized the employment of men of local origin in the positions of *caixas* and administrators.[2]

Eventually, by January 1788, Melo e Castro had completed his vast instruction to the governor-designate. The massive directive ran to 123 paragraphs and was accompanied by over twenty annexes in justification. It represented a comprehensive formulation of policy, strictly within the framework set up four years before by the alvará of January 5 1785. It applied Lisbon's neo-mercantilism with obsessive detail to the captaincy's affairs. The instruction went through several drafts. 'The Captaincy of Minas Gerais is because of its situation and productions one of the most important of all those that make up the dominions of Brazil and Portuguese America', Melo e Castro began.[3] One of the earlier formulations had been even more explicit. The secretary of state called the captaincy the 'soul' of the Portuguese empire in America.[4]

Barbacena's orders covered the whole spectrum of life in the captaincy. 'An entire and general reform of the abuses' of the clergy was to be instituted, and new regulations imposed to limit parochial and ecclesiastical emoluments. The annual salary paid to the parish priests was reduced from 200 *milreis* to 50 *milreis*, the deducted monies being applied to churches and parishes elsewhere in Brazil.[5] The magistrates had the authority to judge in total independence of the governor, Melo e Castro told Barbacena. But at the same time, magistrates must respect and know the governor as their legitimate superior, and if the governor ordered actions contrary to the law then the magistrate was to tell the governor with moderation and respect that this was the case. There was to be no dispute or contestation, if these representations were ignored, but instead a confidential report

---

[1] José Onório de Valladares e Aboim to M. de Melo e Castro, Vila Rica, 26 June 1785, *ibid.*, 253–4.

[2] Witness, Joaquim Silvério dos Reis, Rio de Janeiro, 18 May 1789, *ADIM*, III, 247.

[3] 'Instrucçam para o visconde de Barbacena, Luís António Furtado de Mendonça', 1788, AHU, códice 610, f. 114–59.

[4] 'Minutas de instruções de M. de Melo e Castro para o Governador e capitão-general de Minas Gerais, visconde de Barbacena', 29 January 1788, AHU, Minas Gerais, caixa 94.

[5] 'Instrução para o visconde de Barbacena, Luís António Furtado de Mendonça, Governador e capitão general da capitania de Minas Gerais, [1788] *AMI*, II (1953) 117–54, paragraphs 1–5, 6, 20–22, 117–23.

to the Queen, to whom the governor was responsible for his good or bad comportment.[1]

'It is certain', Melo e Castro commented, 'that a great part of the abuses and prevarications that have perverted and pervert the order and regularity of the government of Minas have their origin in the violences and injustices that the magistrates practice in their corrections and diligences in the interior of the captaincy....' In addition, by indirect means magistrates, lawyers and others associated with the administration of justice, had multiplied processes for venal ends. The omission and negligence of the intendents in their actions against the contrabandists and defrauders was likewise, he claimed, due to the valuable emoluments and fees that accrued from eternal proceedings in court. The processes and executions of the royal exchequer itself, Melo e Castro observed, were not exempt from these prevarications.[2]

Fifty-two of the 123 paragraphs of instruction dealt with the state of the captaincy revenues and the comportment of the Minas *junta da fazenda*. All the means of collecting the quinto, Melo e Castro complained 'had been eluded by the inhabitants of Minas'. The 'affected and sinister asserverations and declarations of the inhabitants seeking to persuade that the mines were exhausted' he dismissed as subterfuge to disguise the abuses and the fraud practised in the captaincy. The fall off in gold returns since 1762 proceeded 'from the great relaxation of those whose charge was the inviolable observance of the laws'. Despite the continuing failure to fill the quota 'not a single word had been mentioned about a *derrama* which was, and is, the legal method to make up the losses'.[3]

Melo e Castro instructed Barbacena on his arrival in Minas to assemble the *junta da fazenda* and read to the deputies the alvará of 3 December 1750. He was to draw their attention to its essential stipulations. First, that the peoples of Minas were obliged to guarantee to the royal exchequer 100 arrobas of gold per annum. Second, that to satisfy this quota the people were to take all gold extracted from the mines to the foundry houses. Third, that if the quota was not filled then the people were to make up the arrears by means of a per capita tax, the *derrama*, and that this last stipulation was the essential security and complement of the first, and was always to be exactly and inviolably observed.[4] He was to warn the members of the junta that they were responsible in their persons and property for the losses incurred by the exchequer, especially if these were the result of omission or negligence. The *junta da fazenda*, Melo e Castro

[1] Paragraphs 23–4, *ibid.*, 123.
[2] Paragraph 25, *ibid.*, 123–4.
[3] Paragraphs 52–68, *ibid.*, 131–6.
[4] Paragraphs 69–70, *ibid.*, 137–8.

declared, had in its 'indolence watched tranquilly as one of the most important branches of the royal patrimony was reduced to almost a half of its value', and no effort had been made to prevent the inhabitants of Minas from totally extinguishing the contribution. Due to the junta's negligence the people of the captaincy were indebted by 538 arrobas of gold, or 3,305,472$000 *reis*, to the Royal Treasury.[1] Barbacena was to insist that the exchequer be indemnified, and that until it had been decided how this payment would be made, the greatest care should be taken to assure that the debt was not increased. The stipulations of the alvará of 3 December 1750, particularly with respect to the *derrama*, were to be entirely observed.[2]

Melo e Castro then turned to the *entradas*. Some reform of the system was indispensible he noted. Duties on the productions of the metropolis, such as salt, wine, vinegar, and olive oil, was so great as to render them prohibitively expensive in Minas. It was essential that all the instruments necessary for the exploitation of the mines and the cultivation of the land be obtainable at reasonable prices. As it was duties were levied according to weight, and iron goods, for example, suffered a much greater impost than did silk finery. In fact '[the] method actually established for the valuing of the duties of entrance into Minas Gerais is the most absurd and most diametrically opposed to the interests of the royal exchequer and the prosperity of the inhabitants', the secretary of state concluded.[3] Barbacena was ordered to consult with the viceroy in Rio de Janeiro on his arrival in Brazil and draw up a new list of rates. Instruments of necessity for the mines and agriculture should be favored, as well as cloth for Negroes and the poor, while luxury items were to be subject to much greater duties. When he reached Minas the governor was to take special note of such goods and effects of the captaincy as might be identical with those produced elsewhere in Brazil. It was unjust, Melo e Castro declared, that goods imported into Minas were subject to duties when the same items internally produced remained exempt, especially considering that the imported effects had to pay transportation costs. 'It is indispensably necessary that the captaincy of Minas conserve some dependence on the other captaincies with respect to consumption and the flow of its commerce', he concluded, 'because the alternative would end communication between them and extinguish the mutual advantages that reciprocally they might lend one another.'[4]

Finally the governor-designate was to examine the state of the various

---

[1] Paragraph 71, *ibid.*, 138–9.   [2] Paragraphs 72–7, *ibid.*, 139–41.
[3] Paragraphs 82–9, *ibid.*, 142–4.   [4] Paragraphs 90–100, *ibid.*, 144–7.

contracts farmed since 1754. He was to investigate especially the enormous abuses which had occurred in the farming of the contracts and the failure of the *junta da fazenda* to collect outstanding debts. João Rodrigues de Macedo still owed 466,454$480 *reis*, on a contract which ended in 1781, the secretary of state observed, and Joaquim Silvério dos Reis, whose contract ended in 1784, owed 220,423$149 *reis*. The *dízimos* and *entradas* combined, Melo e Castro pointed out, represented debts to the exchequer of 2,420,055$689 *reis*.[1] 'One could not view without indignation a junta established...with no other end than the good administration and revenue collection of the royal exchequer, which had instead of this obligation cared only for its own self interest and those of its clients, with irreparable prejudice to the exchequer', Melo e Castro lamented. In the case of the farming of the Pereira Marques contract 'the royal treasury in the midst of scandalous contestations, orphan and abandoned, served only as a pretext for each of the two parties to promote the interests of its clients'. Out of thirty-one contracts farmed, there was not one in which the royal exchequer was not a creditor. On his arrival in Minas Barbacena was instructed to declare the present contracts void and to substitute a direct administration on the royal account. Any protests that the decadent state of the captaincy had caused the arrears were to be ignored, and legal proceedings instituted against the debtors of the treasury 'of whatever quality they may be'.[2]

The magistrates charged with these diligences, Melo e Castro added, should administer prompt and impartial justice. If they failed in this the governor was to make clear to them in no uncertain terms 'the just punishment and the severity with which the crown proceeded against those who failed to comply with the indispensible obligations of their offices, especially in a matter so important as the indemnification of the royal exchequer'. Especially as 'omission, negligence, protections, and perhaps vile, sordid and abominable self-interest' had been responsible for the present deplorable situation.[3]

The treasury in Lisbon returned an indictment no less severe than that contained in Melo e Castro's instructions to the Visconde de Barbacena. The Diamond District had 'become a residence of contrabandists and thieves of diamonds enjoying in scandalous impunity and security the fruits of their crimes', the investigators concluded. In even clearer terms than those of Melo e Castro the treasury asserted that the indolence, corruption and malpractices of the *caixas*, administrators, and overseers,

---

[1] Paragraphs 101–112, *ibid.*, 147–50. [2] Paragraphs 113–23, *ibid.*, 151–4.
[3] Paragraphs 123, *ibid.*, 154.

'had proceeded from the choice of men born in the country for these positions'. The precarious authority of the ministers arose because decisions were reached 'by a plurality of votes, including those of the native-born *caixas*, who attended more to the demands of friendships, sons and relations', than to the regulations of the District. Moreover the 'unlimited greed and arbitrary and violent behavior of the Dragoons of Vila Rica' had powerfully contributed to the defrauding of the treasury and to contraband and clandestine mining.[1]

After years of neglect the metropolitan government had completed what amounted to a colossal reassessment of the state of the captaincy of Minas and its administration. The decisions embodied in the instructions to Barbacena represented a root and branch reform of the whole fiscal system, and in terms so uncompromising as to produce an unfavorable reaction from even the Queen. She insisted that Melo e Castro tell Barbacena not to proceed with the severity indicated without first informing himself whether the people of Minas were in a state to support the *derrama*, and that when imposed some hope be held out that exact compliance would be the most effective way to achieve the pardon of the vast outstanding debt.[2] Yet on one fundamental issue Melo e Castro had miscalculated, and as a result his whole policy was based on a mistaken assumption. Nowhere in the instruction to the governor designate would he admit the fact of the contraction of gold production. Repeatedly he dismissed the claims that the captaincy was economically 'decadent' as being pernicious subterfuges to hide the enormities of the contraband and fraud in gold returns. He was confident that 'abuses' had caused the decline in the royal fifth.

There was no excuse for the assumption that it was only the perversity of the inhabitants of Minas which caused the special socio-economic conditions of the captaincy in 1788. Melo e Castro's own secretariate possessed ample documentation of the profound economic problems which existed, not least the reports and recommendations of D. Rodrigo José de Meneses. Moreover, during 1780, José João Teixeira Coelho, a judge of the High Court of Oporto, had asserted that it was impossible to collect the gold quota by means of the *derrama*, and stressed the inadvisability of attempting to do so.[3] It was precisely this, however, which Melo

---

[1] Visconde Mordomo Mor to Sr Luís Beltrão de Gouveia de Almeida, Intendente Geral dos Diamantes, BNLCP, códice 697, f. 142–9, 155–6.

[2] M. de Melo e Castro to visconde de Barbacena, Ajuda, 7 February, 1788, AHU, códice 610. f. 160.

[3] 'Instrução para o governo da Capitania de Minas Gerais por José João Teixeira Coelho, Desembargador de Relação do Porto, 1780', *RAPM*, VIII (1903) 399–581, especially his 'reflexão unica', 511. Also published in *RIHGB*, XV (1852) 257–476.

e Castro expected. Not to mention his threat that the colossal debt of 538 arrobas of gold, arising from the arrears on unfilled quotas since 1762, would be redeemed as soon as a suitable method had been devised.

Melo e Castro was, as Ratton explained, rigid in his opinions and impervious to logical argument on certain issues.[1] Undoubtedly his strong prejudices against Brazilians, nowhere more evident than in his instructions to Barbacena, encouraged him in the belief that the decline of the fifth was exclusively the result of fraud and prevarication. Perhaps behind Melo e Castro's interpretation lay the unspoken assumption that the economic changes of the previous twenty years had been caused by factors other than the decline in gold production. He had been one of the few who had opposed the extinction of the monopoly companies after the fall of the Marquis of Pombal. Many saw in Pombal's economic policies the cause of the profound transformation of the social and economic structure of the Empire, and such a view would tend to hide from the secretary of state the real causes of the changes. Moreover, the peculiar circumstances of Cunha Meneses governorship had served to exaggerate the abuses and the most blatant malpractices, and it was these factors which forced the reassessment of policy with respect to Minas. Certainly there was truth in Melo e Castro's assertions. The Minas *junta da fazenda* had been criminally negligent in its affairs. The magistracy had been influenced by venal, selfish, and personal interests. There had been official connivance with contrabandists and smugglers. But so totally to reject any notion that the mining economy was waning a full twenty years after the decline of gold returns had first become discernible, and when the economic relationships between Portugal and Brazil and Portugal and Great Britain had been transformed largely as a result, is little short of incredible. Perhaps behind the aversion of Melo e Castro to the malpractices in Minas lay the fierce self-righteousness of an honest man who had labored too long within a corrupt and venal system.

The reform of the *entradas* was in itself long overdue. But the actual proposals suggested ran contrary to the whole trend of development in Minas during the 1780s. Melo e Castro wished to see Minas more dependent on the other captaincies and ultimately on Portugal. He intended that iron tools and other necessary items for mining and agriculture be made more abundantly and cheaply available, and that metropolitan products should obtain a wider market by a reduction in retail prices. This was to be achieved by tariff manipulation, which in effect would transform the Pombaline military reciprocal aid scheme into

---

[1] Ratton, *Recordações*, 245.

an economic system where, with the aid of a variety of fiscal devices, the Brazilian captaincies would be made economically dependent on one another and on Portugal. The motivation was essentially the same as that which had inspired the alvará of January 1785 against Brazilian textile manufactories. Not a word was mentioned about the exploitation of the natural resources of the captaincy, nor about the establishment of iron foundries, both of which had been accepted by Brazilian entrepreneurs and by bureaucrats like D. Rodrigo José de Meneses, as the only sensible solution to the economic problems of the region. The reason why propositions such as those of the former governor received no support in Lisbon was clear. They were diametrically opposed to the concept of dependency.

By a deliberate policy decision even the more conciliatory aspects of Melo e Castro's instructions were kept from the inhabitants of Minas. It was evident in the wording of the directive that the secretary of state thought the stipulations of the *alvará* of 3 December 1750, to be unsatisfactory. Yet because he had not the slightest confidence in the good intentions of the *Mineiros*, the public aspect of the policy was to display a rigid demand for the exact execution of existing laws. Suggestions and arguments about possible reform of the tributary system were to be discussed in secret and in Lisbon. In addition Melo e Castro had specifically designated for attack some of the captaincy's richest and most powerful men, and he had directed that no excuses be accepted from them and no quarter shown to them by the magistrates charged with the redemption of the vast sums they owed to the royal exchequer.

Sixty days out from Lisbon, on 24 May 1788, *Our Lady of Bethlehem* dropped anchor in the Bay of Guanabara.[1] There had been a brief call at Bahia. The Visconde de Barbacena, his wife and family, had traveled from Portugal in the company of the governors-designate of Bahia, D. Fernando José de Portugal, and of São Paulo, Bernardo de Lorena.[2] Once in Rio de Janeiro, in keeping with his instructions, the new governor entered into conference with the viceroy, his uncle, Luís de Vasconcelos e Sousa. The two men discussed the reform of the Minas *entradas* and the state of the royal fifth.[3] Proceeding to Vila Rica, Barbacena took formal possession of the government on 11 July.[4] He established his residence at Cachoeira do Campo, four leagues northeast of Vila Rica, where the Minas governors

---

[1] Luís de Vasconcelos e Sousa, Rio de Janeiro, 14 April 1789, *RIHGB*, xxxvi, pt. 1 (1873) 149–55.
[2] Barbacena to M. de Melo e Castro, Vila Rica, 14 July 1788, *AMI*, ii (1953) 40.
[3] Vilhena, *Cartas*, i, 441.
[4] Barbacena to M. de Melo e Castro, Vila Rica, 14 July 1788, *AMI*, ii (1953) 40.

possessed a delightful country residence, renovated by D. Rodrigo José de Meneses, and linked by a new road to the capital. The barracks of the Dragoons constructed by Antônio de Noronha in 1779 was nearby.[1]

The fiscal Beltrão wrote that the arrival of the new governor promised an end to disorder and augured the reestablishment of public tranquility.[2] The magistrate's optimism was premature. Without delay Barbacena set in action a thorough investigation of the captaincy's exchequer. Five days after his investiture he convoked the *junta da fazenda*. He delivered the reprimand from Lisbon, insisted on the imposition of the *derrama*, and annulled the contracts.[3] The governor's words fell like a bombshell. Barbacena, a youngish, ambitious, and intelligent protégé of Melo e Castro, had been one of the first students at the college of nobles and at the reformed University of Coimbra. He had been secretary of the recently established and prestigious Lisbon Academy of Sciences.[4] Unfortunately for the magnates of Minas Gerais not only were they faced with the fulminations of a distant secretary of state in Lisbon, but by a new governor taking up his first administrative post who gave every indication of carrying out his instructions to the letter.

In the imperial setting a conflict of classic proportions was in the making. Melo e Castro's colonial policy, growing out of the circumstances of the post-Pombaline years and in the broadest sense servant to the interests of the powerful merchant–industrial oligarchy of the metropolis, had been brought in 1788 to a very specific confrontation with the colonial plutocrats who even before the fall of Pombal had directly or indirectly taken over the government in Minas Gerais. Indeed, there was not one part of the power élite of Minas which would not in some way be affected by Melo e Castro's directives, or by the imminent shakeup in the administration of the Diamond District. And underlying the confrontation of interest groups was the deeper confrontation between a society growing in self-awareness and self-confidence within an economic environment that encouraged and stressed self-sufficiency, and a metropolis bent on the retention of dependent markets and the safeguarding of a vital producer of precious stones, gold, and revenue.

[1] Dos Santos, *A Inconfidência Mineira*, 42–3.
[2] Luís Beltrão de Gouveia d'Almeida to M. de Melo e Castro, Tejuco, 28 June 1788, Rodrigues Lapa, *Cartas Chilenas*, 318–20.
[3] Junta da Fazenda, 16 July 1788, AHU, Minas Gerais, caixa 92.
[4] Romulo de Carvalho, *História da fundação do colégio real dos nobres de Lisboa*, 186; *Livro de Oiro da Nobreza* (3 vols., Braga, 1932) I, 226.

CHAPTER 5

CONSPIRACY

There is no form of government which has the prerogative to be immutable. No
political authority, which created yesterday, or a thousand years ago, may not be
abrogated in ten years' time or tomorrow. No power, however respectable, however
sacred, that is authorized to regard the state as its property. Whoever thinks otherwise
is a slave.

> The Revolution of America by the Abbé Raynal (London, 1781) 40.

The Abbé Raynal had been a writer of great vision, for he prognosticated the
uprising of North America, and the captaincy of Minas Gerais with the imposition
of the derrama was now in the same circumstances...

> 'Auto de perguntas feitas a Francisco de Paula Freire de Andrade,
> Tenente Coronel da Tropa paga de Minas Gerais', Rio de
> Janeiro, 16 November 1789, ADIM, IV, 207.

At about eight o'clock on a cold and rainy evening in late December
1788 a message bearer hurried down the steep Rua Direita of Vila Rica
and turned into a wider Rua São José.[1] The recently constructed town
house of João Rodrigues de Macedo stood by the bridge. The low
rectangular structure, with third story *mirador* above the sloping roof,
was the most splendid private residence in Minas Gerais. A monumental
façade of nine bays with stone pilasters at both angles faced the street and
delicate iron balustrades graced the upper windows.[2] At the door the
slave delivered a closed note to the bookkeeper and administrator of the
establishment, Vicente Vieira da Mota.[3] It was addressed to Inácio José
de Alvarenga Peixoto, who was playing cards with the opulent contractor.
The message read: 'Alvarenga, we are together, you should come at
once, [your] friend, [Carlos Correia de] Toledo.'[4] Carlos Correia was in

---

[1] 'Continuação de perguntas feitas ao...Ignácio José de Alvarenga', Rio de Janeiro, 14
January 1790, ADIM, IV, 144; 'Planta da cidade de Ouro Prêto', Manuel Bandeira, *Guia de
Ouro Prêto* (Rio de Janeiro, 1938).
[2] Robert C. Smith, Jr, 'The colonial architecture of Minas Gerais in Brazil', *The Art Bulletin*,
XXI (1939) 145–7.
[3] 'Perguntas feitas ao Padre José da Silva Oliveira', Vila Rica, 24 October 1789, ADIM, II,
276; '...por ser o dito sequestrado [Vicente Vieira da Mota] quem governava toda a sua
casa delle jurante [João Rodrigues de Macedo]', 'Termo de juramento e sequestro', Vila
Rica, 11 May 1791, ADIM, VI, 30; 'Continuação de perguntas feitas ao...Alvarenga',
Rio de Janeiro, 14 January 1790, ADIM, IV, 144.
[4] Copy and facsimile of letter in ADIM, I, 81.

Vila Rica as a guest of the Desembargador Gonzaga.[1] The message called Alvarenga to a prearranged meeting at the home of Francisco de Paula Freire de Andrade, commandant of the Dragoons. The purpose of the meeting was to foment a revolution.

When the rain ceased, Alvarenga Peixoto left the great mansion and entering the Rua Direita made his way up the hill to the home of Freire de Andrade, for whose marriage in 1782 he had composed a sonnet.[2] The lieutenant-colonel, whose illustrious if illegitimate name was one of the most distinguished in Portuguese America, and four other men waited: Dr José Álvares Maciel, son of the captain-major of Vila Rica and Freire de Andrade's brother-in-law, Padre José da Silva de Oliveira Rolim, son of the first treasurer of the Diamond District, the *alferes* Joaquim José da Silva Xavier, and Carlos Correia, vicar of São José.[3] The six men were met to formalize plans for an armed uprising against the Portuguese crown. All were Brazilian born. Between them they represented different areas of the captaincy. Oliveira Rolim was from the Sêrro do Frio, Carlos Correia from Rio das Mortes, and Alvarenga Peixoto from the São Paulo borderlands. They were the active agents of the proposed revolt.

That evening the broad strategy of the movement was coordinated. The conspirators expected the *derrama* to be imposed in mid-February. Using the general disquiet of the people the conspirators believed would follow, a popular uprising was to be instigated, under the cover of which, with the collusion of the Dragoons, the governor would be assassinated and a sovereign republic proclaimed.[4] The *alferes* Silva Xavier was to provoke a riot in Vila Rica. He would be aided by fellow conspirators who had previously converged on the town in small groups, their

---

[1] 'Perguntas feitas ao Vigário...Carlos Corrêa', Rio de Janeiro, 14 November 1789, *ADIM*, IV, 163.

[2] Location of Freire de Andrade's house, see Bandeira, *Guia*, 65–6; For sonnet see Rodrigues Lapa, *Alvarenga Peixoto*, 32.

[3] 'Continuação de perguntas feitas ao...Alvarenga', Rio de Janeiro, 14 January 1790, *ADIM*, IV, 144. Gonzaga came to the meeting, though it appears the uprising was not discussed in his presence. Captain Maximiliano de Oliveira Leite arrived and was said to be 'one of us' by Freire de Andrade. The captain was related to Maciel. There are indications that Dr José de Sá Betencourt from Sabará was present but the evidence is very sketchy.

[4] '[E]lle [Freire de Andrade] lhe [Oliveira Rolim] respondeu, que deixasse estar, que até meado de Fevereiro se havia de recolher para o Tejuco, ou com despacho, ou sem elle...que estava para se lançar a Derrama, e que o Povo se havia de oppor...' 'Perguntas feitas ao Padre José de Silva de Oliveira Rolim', 17 April 1790, Rio de Janeiro, *ADIM*, IV, 413; also 'segundas perguntas feitas ao Padre José da Silva de Oliveira Rolim', Vila Rica, 20 October 1789, *ADIM*, II, 267; 'Continuação de perguntas feitas ao Alferes Joaquim José da Silva Xavier', Rio de Janeiro, 18 January 1790, *ADIM*, IV, 49.

Conspiracy

weapons hidden under cloaks. When the Dragoons were summoned to confront the mob, Freire de Andrade was to prevaricate until the alferes had gone to Cachoeira. Entering the governor's bodyguard he was to arrest and execute Barbacena and return to Vila Rica.[1] Freire de Andrade at the head of the Dragoons would then face the multitude and demand to know what they desired. The *alferes* displaying the governor's head was to cry that they desired liberty. Forthwith a republic would be proclaimed and a declaration of independence read. Meanwhile armed confederates, summoned by the prearranged signal, 'such and such a day will be that of my baptism', would converge on Vila Rica. Two hundred men were to be quartered in the capital, a hundred dispatched to lie in ambush along the mountain road from Rio de Janeiro, and others to guard the land route from São Paulo.[2] All that remained was to await the *derrama* so that the day for the revolt could be designated. If the conspiracy was discovered all would deny any knowledge of the affair. Nothing was to be committed to paper.[3]

The critical initiative and the immediate success of the movement lay in the hands of the Dragoons, and especially Freire de Andrade and Silva Xavier. The *alferes* appears to have been given the role of persuading the cavalry and of propagandizing the movement. It was a task for which he was well suited. His part-time profession as a toothpuller gave him an excellent excuse for visiting the homes of the magnates, as well as access to levels of society where his accomplices could not venture without

---

[1] 'Sentença da alçada', 1792, Santos, *Inconfidência Mineira*, 594–5; 'Continuação de perguntas feitas ao Tenente Coronel Francisco de Paula Freire de Andrade', Rio de Janeiro, 25 January 1790, *ADIM*, IV, 217; Silva Xavier denied that he was to kill the Governor, 'Continuação de perguntas feitas ao Alferes Joaquim José da Silva Xavier', Rio de Janeiro, 4 February 1790, *ADIM*, IV, 60.

[2] 'Sentença da Alçada', 1792, Santos, *Inconfidência Mineira*, 598; 'Continuação de perguntas feitas ao...Alvarenga', Rio de Janeiro, 14 January 1790, *ADIM*, IV, 144–4; 'Perguntas feitas a José Alvares Maciel', Rio de Janeiro, 26 November 1789, *ADIM*, IV, 397–9; 'Continuação de perguntas feitas a José Alvares Maciel', Rio de Janeiro, 6 September 1791, *ADIM*, IV, 402–3; 'Continuação de perguntas feitas ao Alferes Joaquim José da Silva Xavier', Rio de Janeiro, 18 January 1789, *ADIM*, IV, 50–1; 'Segundas perguntas feitas ao Padre José da Silva de Oliveira Rolim', Vila Rica, 20 October 1789, *ADIM*, II, 268; 'Continuação de perguntas feitas ao Vigário Carlos Corrêa', Rio de Janeiro, 27 November 1789, *ADIM*, IV, 169–71. Witness, Domingos Vidal de Barbosa, Vila Rica, 13 July 1789, *ADIM*, I, 170–1.

[3] '[S]e ajustão entre todos...que se algum dia prendesse a algun, ou alguns dos socios desta conjuração, e por ella fossem perguntados, se puzessem todos em nega...' 'Perguntas feitas ao....Carlos Corrêa de Toledo e Melo', Rio de Janeiro, 14 November 1789, *ADIM*, IV, 177; José Caetano Cezar Manitti to visconde de Barbacena, Vila Rica, 13 February 1790, *AMI*, II (1953) 91; 'Ofício do Desembargador José Pedro Machado Coelho Torres ao Vice-Rei', Rio de Janeiro, 11 December 1789, *ADIM*, VI, 372–3; 'Sentença da Alçada', 1792, Santos, *Inconfidência Mineira*, 590–1.

comment.[1] Oliveira Rolim assumed responsibility for the securing of the Diamond District and the supply of 200 men armed with muskets, gunpowder, and shot from the Sêrro do Frio and Minas Novas. Alvarenga Peixoto would secure the campanha do Rio Verde where his vast landed estates lay close to the route to São Paulo. Carlos Correia guaranteed the support of São José, Bordo do Campo and Tamanduã. He would furnish horses and seek support in São Paulo through his family connections.[2] A war of three years was foreseen and the task of providing gunpowder during this period, and probably also of overseeing the exploitation of local iron, saltpetre, and salt deposits, was assigned to the son of the *capitão-mor*.[3] Little opposition seems to have been anticipated within Minas. The appropriation of the royal fifth would provide funds to pay the troops and the expenses of the campaign.[4]

All six men at the house of Freire de Andrade had pressing personal reasons for their involvement in the conspiracy. Their cohesion into a like-minded group had taken place since August 1788, the month that Dr José Álvares Maciel returned to Brazil.[5] Maciel's father had been the treasurer (*caixa*) of the three *entradas* contracts held by José Ferreira da Veiga between 1751 and 1761, and was responsible in his goods and chattels for the considerable arrears outstanding.[6] Totally dependent on his father the younger Álvares Maciel was threatened with the loss of his patrimony by Melo e Castro's orders from Lisbon.[7] The proceedings against crown debtors in Minas also adversely affected Freire de Andrade for he had married the captain-major's daughter D. Isabel Querubina de

---

[1] This excuse was used by Vicente Vieira da Mota later to explain visits of the alferes to the house of João Rodrigues de Macedo in Vila Rica. '[E] que posteriormente precisando elle testemunha Vicente Vieira do prestimo e habilidade que o dito Alferes tinha de tirar e por dentes, foi por esta razão differentes vezes a casa de João Rodrigues de Macedo...' Witness, Vicente Vieira da Mota, Vila Rica, 3 August 1789 (devassa of the viceregal commission taken in Vila Rica, will henceforth be referred to as (DRJ) to distinguish from the devassa of the Minas commission referred to henceforth as (DMG), *ADIM*, III, 334.

[2] 'Perguntas feitas a José Alvares Maciel', Rio de Janeiro, 26 November 1789, *ADIM*, IV, 399; Joaquim Silvério dos Reis to Luís de Vasconcelos e Sousa, Rio de Janeiro, 5 May 1789, *ADIM*, III, 234.

[3] '[A]o que elle Vigário [Carlos Correia] respondeu, que o mais, que duraria a guerra seriam tres annos...' 'Witness, Padre José Lopes de Oliveira, Vila Rica, 30 June 1789, (DMG), *ADIM*, I, 157; Visconde de Barbacena to Martinho de Melo e Castro, Vila Rica, 11 July 1789, *AMI*, II (1953) 67.

[4] 'Perguntas feitas ao...Freire de Andrade', Rio de Janeiro, 25 January 1790, *ADIM*, IV, 218.

[5] 'Perguntas feitas a José Alvares Maciel', Rio de Janeiro, 26 November 1789, *ADIM*, IV, 396.

[6] 'Relação dos devedores a Real Faz[enda] por contratos arrematados, extraida na fim de Dez[embro] de 1801', CCBNRJ, 1-1-6.

[7] '[S]e não acharem bens alguns, que pertencessem ao dito José Alves Maciel, filho do dito Capitão Mor por ser filho familia, e estar vivendo debaixo do Patrio poder do dito seu Pai.' 'Traslado da certidão', *ADIM*, v, 431-2.

Oliveira Maciel.[1] Dr José Álvares Maciel was twenty-seven years old in 1788, the youngest of those present at the December meeting.[2] He was also the best informed of the current situation in Europe. From the University of Coimbra he had gone to England, remained there one and a half years, traveled extensively and studied manufacturing techniques.[3] He discussed the possibility of Brazilian independence with merchants in Britain, and it was made evident to him that the failure of Portuguese America to follow the example of the North Americans was regarded with surprise, and that any initiative against Portuguese dominion would receive rapid support from individual British entrepreneurs.[4] It was in effect the same message Thomas Jefferson had relayed to the young medical student in France two years before, that the initiative lay in the hands of the Brazilians themselves.

The background of the *alferes* Silva Xavier differed markedly from that of the European educated son of one of Vila Rica's most eminent residents. A bachelor in his early forties he lived in cheap rented quarters in the town.[5] Neither oligarch nor artisan, but wedged uncomfortably between them, he possessed the ethos of the former while he followed a part-time trade more appropriate to the latter. Born in São João de'El Rei where his father served as an alderman of the municipality he was one of seven children. Following the early death of his parents, he was educated by his brother Domingos, a priest.[6] Silva Xavier had lost his properties in debt and afterwards unsuccessfully prospected and dabbled in the retail trade. He entered the Dragoons in 1775 with the rank of *alferes*, the most inferior position in the officer corps with a stipend of 72$000 *reis* per trimester.[7] Despite a dynamic personality he had progressed neither in

[1] Rodrigues Lapa, *Alvarenga Peixoto*, 32.

[2] Álvares Maciel was 28 years old in 1789, see 'Perguntas feitas a José Alvares Maciel', Rio de Janeiro, 26 November 1789, *ADIM*, IV, 396.

[3] *Ibid.*, 400.

[4] 'Continuação de perguntas feitas ao Alferes Joaquim José da Silva Xavier', Rio de Janeiro, 18 January 1790, *ADIM*, IV, 47; 'Continuação de perguntas feitas ao...Alvarenga', Rio de Janeiro, 14 January 1790, *ADIM*, IV, 138–9. Also see Visconde de Barbacena to Martinho de Melo e Castro, Vila Rica, 11 June [*sic* for 11 July 1789] *AMI*, II, (1953) 68.

[5] 'Traslado dos sequestros e mais termos que por bem delles se fizeram ao Sequestrado e Alferes Joaquim José de Silva Xavier', Vila Rica, 25 May 1789, *ADIM*, V, 319–31; 'o P[adr]e Joaquim Pereira de Magalhaes pede indenização pelo arrasamento da casa de sua propriedade, em que residia Tiradentes', *ABNRJ*, LXV (1943) 198–204; Also see *RAPM*, III (1896) 268; 'Perguntas feitas ao Alferes Joaquim José da Silva Xavier', Rio de Janeiro, 22 May 1789, *ADIM*, IV, 29.

[6] Domingos da Silva Xavier, vicar of Manaxos, Mexachalis, and Comanaxos indians, Cuyeté, 1771, *ABNRJ*, LXV (1943) 189; Santos, *Inconfidência Mineira*, 117.

[7] 'Não entram na importancia dos bens sequestrados, e avaliados ao Alferes Joaquim José da Silva Xavier, as Sesmarias e Lavras comprehendidas e inventariadas no sequestro, que lhe

rank nor remuneration by 1788.[1] He bitterly complained that despite good
service he was overlooked in promotion four times in favor of others
who were 'better looking' or who enjoyed the influence of well-placed
relatives.[2] He commanded the important Dragoons detachment patrolling
the road over the Mantiqueira Mountains during the governorship of
D. Rodrigo José de Meneses.[3] Governor Luís da Cunha Meneses removed
him from this lucrative position.[4]

Silva Xavier seems to have been especially attracted to the opulent
immigration merchant-contractors, and sought to associate himself with
them. He had received payments from Silvério dos Reis and Rodrigues de
Macedo while commandant of the Mantiqueira patrols, and Domingos de
Abreu Vieira was *padrinho* to his daughter, a relationship which implied
protection.[5] The *alferes* was a regular visitor to Abreu Vieira's house
and often played cards with him.[6] He regarded Silvério dos Reis as a
personal friend.[7] Anxious to acquire the wealth and prestige enjoyed by his
associates he was in Rio de Janeiro on leave of absence from the Dragoons
at the time of the arrival of the Visconde de Barbacena, seeking to promote
plans for supplying the city with drinking water by means of canals.[8]
He knew Rio well, having been stationed there as part of the military
forces sent from Minas Gerais to aid the defense of the city during 1778.[9]
When Dr José Álvares Maciel arrived from Europe, Silva Xavier sought

fez, por se ter conhecido, que estavam anteriormente penhoradas por um Ferreiro, cuja
execução consta agora, haver-se ultimando..."Observações...de José Caetano Cezar
Manitti, escrivão por commissão",' *ADIM*, I, 436; '[O] Alferes Joaquim José da Silva
Xavier por alcunha o Tiradentes que conheceu ainda do tempo, em que andava mascateando
por Minas Novas.... "Perguntas feitas ao...Alberto da Silva e Oliveira Rolim",' Vila
Rica, 20 February 1790, (DMG), *ADIM*, II, 460. For entry into Dragoons, see Herculano
Gomes Mathias *CCANRJ*, 26–7, and his 'Tiradentes e a cidade do Rio de Janeiro', *Anais
do Museu Histórico Nacional* (*AMHN*) XVI (1966) 100.

[1] Document 82, *ABNRJ*, LXV (1943) 194.

[2] 'Continuação de perguntas feitas ao Alferes Joaquim José da Silva Xavier, Rio de Janeiro,
18 January 1790, *ADIM*, IV, 45–6.

[3] Mathias, *CCANRJ*, 25–6; Alferes Joaq[uim] José da S[ilva] X[avier] Commandante do
camino do Rio de Janeiro, Vila Rica, 24 December 1781, [signed by] D. Rodrigo José de
Meneses, *RAPM*, II (1897) 14.

[4] 'Perguntas feitas ao Coronel José Aires Gomes', Rio de Janeiro, 6 August 1791, *ADIM*, V,
84; Santos *Inconfidência Mineira*, 128–9.

[5] Mathias, *CCANRJ*, 25–6, 'Tiradentes e a cidade do Rio de Janeiro', *AMHN*, XVI (1966) 102.

[6] Waldemar de Almeida Barbosa, *A Verdade sobre Tiradentes* (Belo Horizonte, 1965) 89.

[7] Witness, Joaquim Silvério dos Reis, Rio de Janeiro, 18 May 1789, *ADIM*, III, 253; Mathias,
ACC, III, 237, 243; Visconde de Barbacena to Martinho de Melo e Castro, Vila Rica, 11 July
1789, *AMI*, II (1953) 68.

[8] Santos, *Inconfidência Mineira*, 132; 'Perguntas feitas ao Reverendo Cônego Luís Vieira',
Vila Rica, 1 July 1789, *ADIM*, II, 119.

[9] Mathias, *CCANRJ*, 28; Herculano Gomes Mathias, 'O Tiradentes e a cidade do Rio de
Janeiro', *AMHN*, XVI (1966) 102.

Conspiracy

him out to discuss his enterprises, which the viceroy Luís de Vasconcelos e Sousa, showed little inclination to support.[1] Conversation between the two men turned instead to the potentialities of Minas, and the ease with which it could become an independent state. Silva Xavier's active commitment to a nationalist uprising seems to have dated from these conversations. He had spoken of rebellion during the rule of Governor Cunha Meneses, but this appears to have been more the result of personal pique than of any ideological conviction. On his return to Vila Rica in late August, however, staying at the *fazenda* of Colonel José Aires Gomes near Bordo do Campo, he spoke of the flourishing republic that Minas could be were it free of Portugal. He went on to attack in violent language the 'thieving governors' and their cronies who 'engrossed the offices, wealth, and positions, which should by right belong to the natives'.[2]

Alvarenga Peixoto's motivation for involvement in the plot was more immediate. Long encumbered with debts he was, by 1788, facing a critical situation. The failure of expensive hydraulic works undertaken at his numerous gold washings to produce expected dividends, combined with his abysmal record on payments had undermined his credit. Action was pending in the Lisbon *junta do comércio* for the recovery of 11,193$507 *reis* owed the estate of Dionesio Chevelier of Lisbon.[3] He remained heavily obligated to João Rodrigues de Macedo for advances originating as early as his days at Coimbra. These early loans, on which he had not even paid off the accumulated interest, had been negotiated through the contractor's brother Bento Rodrigues de Macedo, also pressing for settlement. More recently he had borrowed large sums from Joaquim Silvério dos Reis through José Pereira Marques.[4] 'To spend it and to have it is impossible', Alvarenga told a friend wistfully in 1786.[5] Two years later he was decidedly more desperate.[6] The former Pombal favorite joined

[1] 'Perguntas feitas a José Alvares Maciel', Rio de Janeiro, 26 November 1789, *ADIM*, IV, 396; 'Continuação de perguntas feitas ao Alferes Joaquim José da Silva Xavier', Rio de Janeiro, 18 January 1790, *ADIM*, IV, 46; 'Perguntas feitas ao Coronel José Aires Gomes', Rio de Janeiro, 6 August 1791, *ADIM*, V, 85.

[2] 'Continuação de perguntas feitas ao Alferes Joaquim José da Silva Xavier', Rio de Janeiro, 18 January 1790, *ADIM*, IV, 47; Witness, José Aires Gomes, Vila Rica, 28 July 1789, (DMG) *ADIM*, I, 207; Witness José Aires Gomes, Vila Rica, 30 July 1789, (DRJ) *ADIM*, III, 320. Also see Mathias, *CCANRJ*, 60.

[3] Order from the junta do comércio in CCBNRJ, 1-1-2 (56). Also see Rodrigues Lapa, *Alvarenga Peixoto*, xxvi.

[4] Rodrigues Lapa, *Alvarenga Peixoto*, xliii, xliv; 'Relação dos creditos...pertencem a Joaquim Silvério dos Reis, dividas particulares, Ignácio José de Alvarenga', CCBNRJ, 1-10-5.

[5] Inácio José de Alvarenga Peixoto to Sargento-Mor João da Silva Ribeiro de Queiros Boa Vista, 22 September 1786, Rodrigues Lapa, *Alvarenga Peixoto*, 66–7.

[6] 'No [ano] de oitenta e nove espero em Deos estar mais aliviado, e capaz de hir merecendo a sua correspondência...,' Inácio José de Alvarenga Peixoto to Sr Sargento Mor João da

the movement sometime in late 1788. The baptism of his son by Carlos Correia in São José on 8 October 1788, is the most plausible origin of the baptism sign with which the conspirators intended to notify their associates of the day chosen for the uprising.[1]

José da Silva de Oliveira Rolim, the thin scar-faced priest from Tejuco, like his friend the *alferes* had been in Rio de Janeiro at the time of the arrival of Barbacena.[2] Shortly afterwards he returned surreptitiously to Vila Rica, arriving a few days before the governor. The banishment order against him remained in force. He was living with the aged contractor of dízimos, Domingos de Abreu Vieira.[3] The unscrupulous cleric, trader in slaves and diamonds, was an influential figure in the Diamond District with a large money-lending business and an extensive clientele.[4] He had been denounced to the treasury by the investigating judge, Cruz e Silva, and was held up as an example of the rampant corruption among the influential local treasurers of the administration.[5] Oliveira Rolim was intimately linked to the hierarchy of Brazilian-born administrators and officials of the District and although he had been absent from Tejuco since 1786, and the Portuguese military had long since established their lucrative contraband monopoly under the cover of the former governor's favoritism, it was the employment of Brazilian officials which had been blamed for the chaotic conditions of the Sêrro do Frio and who were threatened by the Treasury's subsequent directive. He had sought a reversal of the banishment order from Barbacena with no success and his complaints apparently led to his invitation to join the conspiracy after conversations with Freire de Andrade, Silva Xavier, and his host Domingos de Abreu Vieira.[6]

Silva Ribeiro de Queiros, Boa Vista, 3 March 1788, Rodrigues Lapa, *Alvarenga Peixoto*, 69–70.

[1] Witness, João Dias da Mota, Vila Rica, 26 June 1789, (DMG) *ADIM*, I, 131; 'Certidão de batismo de João Damasceno, filho de Alvarenga Peixoto', M. Rodrigues Lapa, *Cartas Chilenas*, 343.

[2] For physical description of Oliveira Rolim, 'confrontações e signaes do P[adre] José da Silva de Oliveira Rolim, filho de José da Silva de Oliveira, caixa da Real Administração dos Diamantes', *AMI*, II (1953) 74; 'Perguntas feitas ao Padre José da Silva de Oliveira', Vila Rica, 19 October 1789, *ADIM*, II, 259; For comments on the scandal over José de Oliveira Rolim's ordination see comments in a letter of Martin Lopes Lobo de Saldanha, São Paulo, 15 March 1780, 'correspondência do capitão-general, Martin Lopes Lobo de Saldanha, 1774–1781', *Documentos interessantes para a história e costumes de São Paulo (DISP)* XLIII (São Paulo, 1903) 317.

[3] 'Perguntas feitas ao Padre José da Silva de Oliveira Rolim', Vila Rica, 19 October 1789, *ADIM*, II, 259.

[4] 'Autos de sequestro do Padre José da Silva', Tejuco, 26 June 1789, *ADIM*, V, 295–303.

[5] Visconde Mordomo Mor to Sr. Luis Beltrão de Gouveia de Almeida, Intendente Geral dos Dimantes, BNLCP, códice 697, 142–9, 155–6.

[6] 'Segundas perguntas feitas ao Padre José da Silva de Oliveira Rolim', Vila Rica, 20 October 1789, *ADIM*, II, 266–7.

Conspiracy

Carlos Correia de Toledo e Melo, originally from Taubaté in São Paulo, was a wealthy landed proprietor with extensive plantations, mineral workings, and numerous slaves in the comarca of Rio das Mortes.[1] An active, cultured and ambitious priest, his unceasing pursuit of emoluments had led to an abrasive dispute with the inhabitants of São Bento of Tamanduã (today Itapecerica). Rapid expansion of the frontier of settlement in Tamanduã with cattle ranches and gold washings had transformed a poverty stricken sub-parish into a flourishing community. The vicar of São José mindful of the lucrative fees for multiple religious functions and services to be obtained in the new situation, attempted to reestablish the jurisdiction of São José over the new flourishing frontier community. Meeting opposition from the local priest, and despite an unfavorable episcopal decision, he forcibly broke into the Tamanduã church and commandeered the sacrament. As a result of petitions and counter-petitions the dispute came before the highest Portuguese ecclesiastical tribunal the *Mesa da Consciência e Ordens* in Lisbon.[2] With the case pending Carlos Correia decided to go to Lisbon to defend his actions, and in 1788 intended to seek licence from the Bishop of Mariana for the voyage to Europe.[3] He dropped this plan however. The Minas clergy were one of the groups most seriously and immediately affected by Melo e Castro's instructions. Carlos Correia typified the parish priest who, in the words of the secretary of state, had by their 'excessive and intolerable demands oppressed and vexed the people', and were threatened by the 'entire and general reform' Melo e Castro instructed the governor and bishop to concert and implement.[4] The vicar of São José was a close friend of Alvarenga Peixoto. He had conducted his belated marriage to Bárbara Eliodora and baptized his sons.[5]

Francisco de Paula Freire de Andrade, illegitimate son of the second count of Bobadela and D. Maria do Bom Successo Correia de Sá e Benevides, born in Rio de Janeiro in 1756, had commanded the Dragoons for over a decade. His father and his uncle had been governors of Minas, and his mother was a member of one of the most distinguished families

---

[1] List of value of confiscations, *ADIM*, I, 433; sequestro, Carlos Correia, *ADIM*, I, 386–403; 'Traslado do sequestro do vigário Carlos Corrêa de Toledo', *ADIM*, v, 335–47.

[2] 'Mesa da consciência e ordens, consulta', 25 May 1789, AHU Minas Gerais, caixa 94; Ernesto Ennes, 'The trial of the ecclesiastics in the Inconfidência Mineira', *The Americas*, VII (October 1950) 194.

[3] 'Perguntas feitas ao Vigário da Vila de São José, Carlos Corrêa de Toledo e Melo, Rio de Janeiro, 14 November 1789, *ADIM*, IV, 162.

[4] 'Instrução para o visconde de Barbacena', Martinho de Melo e Castro, 29 January 1788, *AMI*, II (1953) 122.

[5] Rodrigues Lapa, *Alvarenga Peixoto*, xxxvii.

of the colony.[1] Melo e Castro in his instructions to Barbacena held the Dragoons and their 'abominable extortions and armed robberies' partially responsible for the disastrous state of the royal exchequer in the captaincy.[2] Whether the reform of the regular troop – and some radical restructuring was planned by Barbacena – directly threatened his position is unclear.[3] The arguments of Dr Álvares Maciel, the commandant's brother-in-law, a constant visitor to his home, may have influenced his decision to join the conspiracy.[4] The promotion of Cunha Meneses' favorites, the previous governor's dispute with the magistrates, and the actions taken against his father-in-law had also probably upset Freire de Andrade. Moreover, on 1 October 1788, the *junta da fazenda* under the presidency of Barbacena had received a report on the bloated military lists of the captaincy, and the consequent high expenditure on salaries paid to officers and soldiers – many long since retired, and many of whom probably did not exist. The junta ordered the suspension of all payments until the commissions of the troops involved could be confirmed.[5] The lists were prepared by the commandant, Freire de Andrade, and consistently during 1788 they showed forces far in excess of those which in fact existed.[6] The involvement of the commandant of the regular forces of the captaincy in the movement, however, whatever his motives, was a fact of capital significance.

Behind the activists stood more circumspect men, some of whom were not known to all of those responsible for precipitating the revolt. The body of circumstantial evidence strongly points to the involvement of Tomás Antônio Gonzaga. The former *ouvidor* of Vila Rica had the closest personal relations with both Alvarenga Peixoto and Carlos Correia.

---

[1] Santos, *Inconfidência Mineira*, 179.

[2] 'Instrução para o visconde de Barbacena', Martinho de Melo e Castro, 29 January 1788, *AMI*, II (1953) 129.

[3] For some indication of dissatisfaction among the troops see Witness, João José Nunes Carneiro, Rio de Janeiro, 20 May 1789, *ADIM*, III, 256. The aim was apparently to substitute a *Legião* in place of the regiment, *AMI*, II (1953) 44.

[4] 'Auto de perguntas feitas a Francisco de Paula Freire de Andrade', Rio de Janeiro, 16 November 1789, *ADIM*, IV, 211.

[5] Representation, junta da fazenda, Vila Rica, 9 May 1789, AHU, Minas Gerais, caixa 94.

[6] Tenente Coronel Francisco de Paula Freire de Andrade, lists of troops and placements for June, August and September 1788, in CCBNRJ, 1-1-19; 'Francisco de Paula Freire de Andrade, Regimento da Cavalaria Regular de Vila Rica', 1788, CCBNRJ, 1-1-19; According to these assessments the number of troops was given as 16,678 and 14,980 respectively, a more realistic number [400 to 500] was given by Melo e Castro in his 'instrução para o visconde de Barbacena', 29 January 1788, *AMI*, II (1953) 129. Also see Barbacena's comments on the number of troops available to him in *AMI*, II (1953) 44. Freire de Andrade had requested permission to go to Lisbon in 1785 and was apparently denied, see Luís da Cunha Meneses to Martinho de Melo e Castro, Vila Rica, 22 February 1785, APM, códice 238, 62v.

The two men were his guests in Vila Rica at the time for the meetings of December 1788.[1] He had been godfather to Alvarenga's son at the October christening in São José.[2] Moreover, he remained in Vila Rica without any means of financial support long after his appointment to the High Court of Bahia. The new ouvidor, Pedro José de Araújo Saldanha, had taken up his position in September 1788, having arrived in Minas at the same time as Silva Xavier's return from Rio de Janeiro.[3] It appears that during late 1788 and early 1789 Gonzaga was exerting his influence to establish conditions propitious for the uprising. He constantly pressured his friend the Intendent Bandeira, whose task it was to require the *derrama*, to demand the recovery of the total debt of over 500 arrobas of gold due the treasury and not simply the arrears of the past year.[4] In addition Gonzaga had taken precautions to placate his former enemies and build himself a strong party of supporters among the members of the municipal council of Vila Rica.[5]

Gonzaga, Cláudio Manuel da Costa, and the canon Luís Vieira were men who 'have ascendency over the spirits of the people' Freire de Andrade told Alvarenga.[6] Their task was to formulate the laws and constitution of the new state and provide the ideological justification for

[1] 'Perguntas feitas ao Vigário da Vila de São José, Carlos Corrêa de Toledo e Melo,' Rio de Janeiro, 14 November 1789, *ADIM*, IV, 163; According to Alvarenga, Gonzaga was present at the December meeting, 'Continuação de perguntas feitas ao...Alvarenga', Rio de Janeiro, 14 January 1790, *ADIM*, IV, 144; Silva Xavier confirmed Gonzaga's presence but said that conversation on the matter of the conspiracy had ceased on his arrival, 'Continuação de perguntas feitas ao...Silva Xavier', 18 January 1790, *ADIM*, IV, 52. Carlos Correia said he used Gonzaga's name when discussing the conspiracy, but that in fact he did not know whether he had entered or not, 'Continuação de perguntas feitas ao Vigário Carlos Corrêa...', 4 February 1790, *ADIM*, IV, 179.

[2] 'Certidão de batismo de João Damasceno, filho de Alvarenga Peixoto', Rodrigues Lapa, *Cartas Chilenas*, 343.

[3] Bacharel Pedro José de Araújo Saldanha had been appointed ouvidor on 27 March 1787, CCBNRJ, 1-1-9; For his arrival in Minas at the same time as Silva Xavier see witness, José Aires Gomes, Vila Rica, 28 July 1789 (DMG) *ADIM*, I, 207.

[4] For Gonzaga's own account of his actions see 'Continuação do auto de perguntas feitas ao Desembargador Thomás António Gonzaga', Rio de Janeiro, 3 February 1790, *ADIM*, IV, 260-1; Oliveira Rolim claimed Alvarenga had brought similar pressure to bear on Bandeira, 'Terceiras perguntas feitas ao Padre José da Silva de Oliveira Rolim', Vila Rica, 21 October 1789, *ADIM*, II, 273.

[5] Visconde de Barbacena to Luís de Vasconcelos e Sousa, Cachoeira do Campo, 25 March 1789, *AMI*, II (1953) 43; For a summary of the proof against Gonzaga see Desembargador José Pedro Machado Coelho Torres to Luís de Vasconcelos e Sousa, Rio de Janeiro, 11 December 1789 with 'a lista das pessoas...dando huma idea das prezumsoens, ou prova que rezulta contra cada huma deles', AHU, Minas Gerais, caixa 92 (47); also 'Sentença da Alçada', 1792, Santos, *Inconfidência Mineira*, 600-4.

[6] 'Continuação de perguntas feitas ao...Alvarenga', Rio de Janeiro, 14 January 1790, *ADIM*, IV, 138.

the break with Portugal. All three men were well informed of events and possessed good libraries.[1] Books and information often reached them more rapidly than official dispatches passed through the cumbersome bureaucracy from Lisbon to the captaincy secretariate. The canon Vieira's cosmopolitan collection of books contained Robertson's *Histoire de l'Amérique*, the *Encyclopédie*, as well as the works of Bielfeld, Voltaire and Condillac.[2] Cláudio Manuel da Costa was reputed to have translated Adam Smith's *Wealth of Nations*.[3] Circulating among the conspirators was the *Recueil de Loix Constitutives des États-Unis de l'Amérique*, published in Philadelphia in 1778, and which contained the Articles of Confederation and the constitutions of Pennyslvania, New Jersey, Delaware, Maryland, Virginia, the Carolinas, and Massachusetts.[4] They possessed constitutional commentaries by Raynal and Mably, and Raynal's lengthy discussion of the history of Brazil in his *Histoire philosophique et politique* was much debated.[5] Gonzaga had long been interested in jurisprudence, from the time of his treatise on the natural law, to his extensive memorials against the 'despotism' of Cunha Meneses.[6] Luís Vieira often argued against Portugal's right to dominion in America, and was a warm admirer of the North Americans' struggle for independence.[7]

[1] Unfortunately Gonzaga's books were not listed by titles, they were merely accounted for as 'quarenta e tres livros de varios autores Francezes, Portuguezes e Latinos.... Traslado do sequestro feito ao Desembargador Tomás António Gonzaga', Vila Rica, 23 May 1789, *ADIM*, IV, 211; 'Traslado dos sequestros feitos ao Doutor Cláudio Manoel da Costa', Vila Rica, 25 June 1789, *ADIM*, V, 263–5, 267, 269; 'Avaliação dos livros sequestrados, Luís Vieira', *ADIM*, I, 445.

[2] 'Avaliação dos livros sequestrados', *ADIM*, I, 458; Also see Carrato, *Igreja, Iluminismo, e Escolas Mineiras Coloniais*, 113–14; and Eduardo Frieiro, *O Diabo na Livraria do Cônego* (Belo Horizonte, Minas Gerais, 1957).

[3] According to Santos, *Inconfidência Mineira*, 237, 'esse manuscripto foi sequestrado, e perdeu-se...', This information probably came from Joaquim Norberto de Souza Silva, 'Commemoração do centenário de Cláudio Manuel da Costa', *RIHGB*, LIII pt. I (1890) 150, who cites Cônego Januário's *Parnaso Brazileiro*.

[4] 'Translado e Appensos, No. 26; neste lugar e debaixo do No. 26 vai apos aos Autos originais o livro em Francez intitulado, Recueil des Loix Constitutives des Etats Unis de l'America', AHU, Minas Gerais, caixa 92. This book also was lost, stolen, or strayed from the archives, but I have been able to locate a copy of *Recueil des Loix Constitutives des Colonies Angloises confederees sous la dénomination d'Etats-Unis de l'Amerique-Septentrionale* (Philadelphia, 1778) in the rare book collections of the Newberry Library, Chicago, which is certainly an edition of the work in the hands of the Minas conspirators, the short title page corresponding exactly to the listing in the confiscations.

[5] 'Item, le droit public de l'Europe de Mably, tres volumes em oitavo', 'avaliação dos livros ...', *ADIM*, I, 461; The Intendent Bandeira had books of Mably belonging to Cláudio Manuel da Costa, 'Termo de encerramento...', Mariana, 5 March 1791, *ADIM*, I, 466.

[6] See discussion in Chapter 4.

[7] '[F]alaram sôbre as Americas Inglezas, o que é da paixão dominante do dito Conego Luís Vieira', 'continuação de perguntas feitas ao Coronal Ignácio José de Alvarenga', Rio de Janeiro, 14 January 1790, *ADIM*, IV, 149.

Conspiracy

Cláudio Manuel da Costa and Luís Vieira were Brazilian born. Gonzaga was the son of a Brazilian and had been brought up and educated in Bahia.

Behind the activists and the ideologues was a third, more shadowy, group of men committed to the break with Portugal. Gunpowder was promised to the conspirators by Domingos de Abreu Vieira.[1] The old Portuguese contractor was closely associated with many of the principal figures in the conspiracy. Oliveira Rolim since returning from Rio de Janeiro had been his house guest in Vila Rica. He was the protector of the alferes Silva Xavier. In his financial dealings he was closely associated with Cláudio Manuel da Costa who represented him in legal questions concerning the dízimos contract. Domingos de Abreu Vieira, like his fellow taxfarmers, was heavily obligated to the royal exchequer, indeed for most of the 197,867\$375 reis contract price, and it is evident that the old, highly respected, Portuguese merchant was embroiled in the conspiracy for one reason only, because it offered a way of escaping from his debts.[2] And he was not alone. José Aires Gomes disputed the statements made by Silva Xavier at Bordo do Campo in September, but it is probable nonetheless that the conversation between the two men acted as a catalyst. José Aires Gomes was a bondman for João Rodrigues de Macedo on his dízimos contract of 1777, on which in 1787, over 280,000\$000 reis remained unpaid. Under the terms of the contract, the contractors and their partners were liable 'one for all and all for one'.[3] Alvarenga claimed later that he had been invited to enter the conspiracy first by Aires Gomes at the house of the contractor João Rodrigues de Macedo in Vila Rica during early 1789. It is more likely that the conversation with Aires Gomes took place in late September or early October when José Ayres was the guest of Rodrigues de Macedo in Vila Rica. Ayres Gomes told Alvarenga that an uprising against the crown was certain in Rio de Janeiro, and he had heard this from an officer of the Minas troop. The aid of France and

---

[1] 600 Barrils according to Freire de Andrade, 'continuação de perguntas feitas ao... Alvarenga', Rio de Janeiro, 14 January 1790, *ADIM*, IV, 142.

[2] 'Contracto dos dízimos de Minas Gerais', *AMI*, II (1953) 192; 'Addição de sequestro feito em credito e obrigações, que se acharam ao Sequestrado o Doutor Cláudio Manoel da Costa', Vila Rica, 21 March 1791, *ADIM*, I, 358.

[3] List of *fiadores* in 'relação dos devedores a Real Fazenda por contratos arrematados, extraida na fim de Dez[embro] 1801', CCBNRJ, 1-1-6; For long standing business connection between José Aires Gomes and João Rodrigues de Macedo see José Aires Gomes to João Rodrigues de Macedo, Bordo do Campo, 3 July 1780, *ABNRJ*, LXV (1943) 179–80; and 'conta corrente de José Aires Gomes com o contratador João Rodrigues de Macedo. Escrituração feita pelo guarda-livros Vicente Vieira da Mota', Borda do Campo, 6 January 1784, Mathias, *CCANRJ*, 61. For the terms of the *Dízimos Reaes* farmed by João Rodrigues de Macedo, 23 May 1777 see CCBNRJ, 1-9, 17.

foreign nations was expected.[1] Alvarenga was told a very similar story shortly afterwards by Freire de Andrade.[2]

It seems that talk of an independent state had presented at a critical juncture a panacea to the crown's debtors in the captaincy. And the activities of Abreu Vieira and Aires Gomes merely represented the tip of an iceberg. Associated with them were other more important individuals who rarely emerged in the discussion of the conspirators, but who nonetheless had a most vital concern for the success of the movement. Among them in all probability were the two great contractors João Rodrigues de Macedo and Joaquim Silvério dos Reis. Like Domingos de Abreu Vieira they were both born in Portugal, but more important, both were debtors to the royal treasury, in the case of Rodrigues de Macedo to a sum over eight times his assets.[3] Because of the special workings of the regional economy and the local tax farming system, their personal interests had become inseparable from the captaincy. More than anyone in Minas Gerais they had cause to regret the orders from Lisbon. Melo e Castro specifically named Rodrigues de Macedo and Silvério dos Reis as the most notorious debtors of the treasury, demanded the payment of arrears, and had ordered that no favors be shown and no excuses accepted.[4] And already the impact of the secretary of state's instructions had been brought home to them. During October 1788 the *junta da fazenda* ordered the confiscation of the inheritance of one of Macedo's bondsmen on his *dízimos* contract.[5]

[1] For the conflicting accounts, 'continuação de perguntas feitas ao Coronel...Alvarenga', Rio de Janeiro, 14 January 1790, *ADIM*, IV, 129; José Aires Gomes to visconde de Barbacena, Vila Rica, 1 August 1789, *ADIM*, II, 427–30; 'perguntas feitas ao Coronel José Aires Gomes', Rio de Janeiro, 6 August 1791, *ADIM*, V, 87–8.

[2] 'Perguntas feitas ao...Alvarenga', Rio de Janeiro, 11 November 1789, *ADIM*, IV, 129–30.

[3] Rodrigues de Macedo's total assets based on assessment of estate in 1805, then valued at 85,402$475 *reis.*, in 'avaliação dos bens penhorados ao João Rodrigues de Macedo', May 1805, CCBNRJ, 1–9, 28. The amount of his debts to the Royal Treasury obtained from 'relação dos contratos que se achão por pagar...' *AMI*, II (1953) 203; 'Contrato das entradas de Minas Gerais...e o que delles se esta devendo', *ibid.*, 190 'Contrato dos dízimos de Minas Gerais...e o que deles se esta devendo...', *ibid.*, 192; and from 'contas correntes extrahidas no fim de Dezembro de 1795 que mostrão o que se ficou devendo a Real Fazenda da Capitania de Minas Gerais de cada hum dos contractos da mesma Capitania', CCBNRJ, 1-1-2-1.

[4] Martinho de Melo e Castro to visconde de Barbacena, 29 January 1788, *AMI*, II (1953) 149, 153–4.

[5] Order of Junta da Fazenda to sequest estate of José João de A [?]'...ter sido sócio com João Rodrigues de Macedo e seu fiador no contrato dos Dízimos...', Vila Rica, 18 January 1789, [order dated 11 October 1788], signed by ouvidor of Sêrro Frio, Joaquim Antônio Gonzaga, CCBNRJ, 1–33, 11. A carta régia had been issued on 20 June 1788, and registered in Minas junta da fazenda, Vila Rica, 14 November 1788, setting up process for arbitration of disputes between contractors and farmers over the *dízimos* collections, 'Carta Regia

Conspiracy

There can be no doubt whatsoever that one of the most active centers of the conspiracy was the great mansion of João Rodrigues de Macedo by the bridge of São Jose in Vila Rica. Here some of the most heated discussions took place and some of the most important converts were made.[1] The opulent contractor with his vast economic interests and agents throughout the captaincy, his close personal friendships with the leading conspirators, could not have been unaware of the turn of events in a question so critical to his own interests. The outspoken canon Luís Vieira, warm admirer of the American Revolution, always stayed as his house guest during his visits to Vila Rica.[2] Alvarenga was his personal friend, card partner, and debtor, despite whose record for chronic insolvency he continued to treat with generosity during late 1788 and early 1789, even though the exchequer was threatening his own assets.[3] Rodrigues Macedo was closely associated with Cláudio Manuel da Costa and Gonzaga. Indeed he may well at this time have been supporting Gonzaga financially.[4]

Macedo, like Aires Gomes and Abreu Vieira never participated in the strategic planning of the uprising. Vicente Vieira da Mota, however, the man who in Macedo's own words 'governed all his house' is known to have discussed the situation more openly with, among others, Carlos Correia, Silva Xavier, Luís Vieira and Nicolas George.[5] Vicente Vieira's calculation of the amount that the *derrama* would require of each inhabitant, based perhaps on population figures taken from Cláudio Manuel da

sobre o Contrato dos Dízimos', APM, códice 251, 10v–11. This is also in CCBNRJ, I-9-10.

[1] For example the invitations to Alvarenga and Oliveira Lopes. For discussion of the uprising there see, witness, Vicente Vieira da Mota, Vila Rica, 22 June 1789 (DMG) *ADIM*, I, 108–12; Witness Vicente Vieira da Mota, Vila Rica, 3 August 1789 (DRJ) *ADIM*, III, 334–6.

[2] Continuação de perguntas feitas ao cônego Luís Vieira da Silva, 21 July 1790 (*sic*). This must be 21 June 1791, for the interrogation was conducted by Conselheiro Sebastião de Vasconcelos Coutinho who had not yet arrived in Rio de Janeiro in July 1790, *ADIM*, IV, 304; also see 312.

[3] See comments by Desembargador José Pedro Machado Coelho Torres, *ADIM*, VI, 403; also Desembargador José Pedro Machado Coelho Torres to Luís de Vasconcelos e Sousa, Rio de Janeiro, 11 December 1789, and 'lista das pessoas...', AHU, Minas Gerais, caixa 92 (47).

[4] Gonzaga said he had asked money only for the journey to Bahia, 'Continuação do auto de perguntas feitas ao Desembargador Tomás António Gonzaga', Rio de Janeiro, 3 February 1790, *ADIM*, IV, 259; Macedo also had financial dealings with Oliveira Rolim, see 'Sr. Francisco Roiz de Macedo em conta corrente conmigo, João Roiz de Macedo', CCBNRJ, I-1-17.

[5] 'Termo de juramento e sequestro', Vila Rica, 11 May 1791, *ADIM*, VI, 30; Also see footnote 3, p. 115 Witness, Vicente Vieira da Mota, Vila Rica, 22 June 1789, (DMG) *ADIM*, I, 108–12;12; Witness, Vicente Vieira da Mota, Vila Rica, 3 August 1789, (DRJ) *ADIM*, III, 334–6.

Costa's careful statistical history of the captaincy, was freely used by the *alferes* in his propaganda.[1] Nicolas George, a native of Waterford, who had previously lived in Setúbal and Cadiz, was a protégé of the Fiscal Beltrão, and held a position in the accountancy department of the diamond administration until removed on orders from Cunha Meneses. Vicente Vieira asked George the causes of the American Revolution. 'Bad governors and taxes imposed upon the people', the Irishman replied. And if there was an uprising in Portuguese America, George asked Vicente Vieira bluntly: 'Which party would you follow, the royalist or the republican?'[2] George's question was one which gave the crown's debtors in Minas Gerais cause for sober reflection during late 1788. Especially when the path of revolt promised instant salvation for those threatened by the massive exactions of the treasury.[3]

Aires Gomes, after his September conversation with Silva Xavier, spoke of the possibility of an uprising in Minas and Rio de Janeiro with his compadre, the Rev. José Lopes de Oliveira.[4] Later, in the house of Rodrigues de Macedo in Vila Rica, he approached the priest's brother, Colonel Francisco Antônio de Oliveira Lopes.[5] Oliveira Lopes, a tough, barely literate ex-Dragoon officer and *fazendeiro*, was related to Domingos Vidal Barbosa, the Raynal-quoting colleague of *Vendek* at Montpeillier.[6]

[1] 'Inquiração das testemunhas referidas pelo Coronel Francisco Antônio de Oliveira Lopes, como consta de suas resposta...'. *ADIM*, II, 71–2; 'continuação das perguntas feitas ao Alferes Joaquim José de Silva Xavier', 18 January 1790, *ADIM*, IV, 53; 'Notícia da capitania de Minas Gerais por Cláudio Manuel da Costa', IHGB, lata 22, doc. 13; Witness João Dias da Mota, Vila Rica, 26 June 1789 (DMG) *ADIM*, I, 130.

[2] 'Auto de perguntas feitas a Nicolao Jorge de Nasção Irlandes', Rio de Janeiro, 18 February 1791, and 'auto de segundas perguntas', *AMI*, II (1953) 213, 215–19; For Vicente Vieira's account of the conversation see, Witness, Vicente Vieira da Mota, Vila Rica, 22 June 1789 (DMG) *ADIM*, I, 111–12; and Witness, Vicente Vieira da Mota, Vila Rica, 3 August 1789 (DRJ) *ADIM*, III, 337.

[3] A similar question was proposed to Aires Gomes by Padre Lopes de Oliveira according to the former, '[S]e o Rio de Janeiro fosse invadido pelos Franceses, e mandassem Tropa de ca de Minas, e Vossa Merce fosse, como Coronel, e la vencessem os Francezes, Vossa Merce a favor de quem seria?' 'Auto de confrontação e conciliação das testemunhas o Padre José Lopes de Oliveira e o Coronel José Aires Gomes', Vila Rica, 30 October 1789, *ADIM*, II, 366.

[4] 'Compadre...(em razão de o ser, por ter baptisado uma filha delle testemunha)...', Witness, José Aires Gomes, Vila Rica, 30 July 1789 (DRJ) *ADIM*, III, 321.

[5] '[Q]ue o primeiro, que lhe falara fora José Ayres em casa de Joaquim (*sic*) Rodrigues de Macedo nesta Vila Rica', perguntas feitas ao...Francisco Antônio de Oliveira Lopes', Vila Rica, 15 June 1789, *ADIM*, II, 46.

[6] '[o] dito Doutor [Domingos Vidal Barbosa] seu Primo...' 'Inquiração.' Francisco Antônio de Oliveira Lopes, Vila Rica, 8 July 1789, *ADIM*, II, 84; Oliveira Lopes as a captain of the Dragoons had been part of the Minas force sent to Rio de Janeiro in 1778, also in this detachment was the commandant Freire de Andrade and the *alferes* Silva Xavier, Mathias, *CCANRJ*, 28.

Conspiracy

Oliveira Lopes' properties in Rio das Mortes bordered on those of the vicar of São José.[1] Suitor to his niece, Bernardina Quiteria de Oliveira Belo was the contractor Joaquim Silvério dos Reis, debtor to the crown for over 200,000$000 *reis*. Bernardina's father Colonel Luís Alves de Freitas Belo, was bondsman for Silvério's *entradas* contract.[2]

Silvério dos Reis was in Rio at the time of the arrival of the Visconde de Barbacena and must have become aware of the content of the instructions from Lisbon. He was especially displeased by the abolition of the new auxiliary regiments set up by Cunha Meneses. His prized commission came from the former governor, and along with his regiment it was now declared null and void.[3] By early 1789 Silvério had come to terms with some of the most important of his former enemies. In January he retained Cláudio Manuel da Costa as his attorney. Cláudio was well known to be Gonzaga's close friend and Silvério was probably well aware that the aged lawyer proof-read the *cartas chilenas* wherein he had been vilified.[4] But Gonzaga too had made conciliatory moves to placate his former foes. Luís Vaz de Toledo e Piza, the brother of Carlos Correia, claimed that Silvério offered him 12,000 *cruzados* to go to São Paulo to raise support for the movement.[5] By February Silvério was an active backer of the uprising, and at the review of his regiment during that month, the contractor complained openly to Luís Vaz of Lisbon's policy, and declared that 'once free, Minas could become a great Empire'.[6]

Among the three levels of support for the uprising, the activists, the ideologues, and the financial interests, the latter were in many ways the most influential. Of these men, or those that can with any certainty be identified – João Rodrigues de Macedo, Joaquim Silvério dos Reis, Domingos de Abreu Vieira, José Aires Gomes, Vicente Vieira da Mota, Dr José Álvares Maciel, possibly Luís Alves de Freitas Belo – all were

[1] 'Sequestro...Carlos Corrêa', *ADIM*, I, 387.

[2] 'Contrato das entradas de Minas Gerais arrematado a particulares...', *AMI*, II (1953) 191, Herculano Gomes Matias, 'Inconfidência e Inconfidentes', *ACC*, III, 251; Also see Mathias [name spelled differently in each place] *CCANRJ*, 72.

[3] Martinho de Melo e Castro to visconde de Barbacena, 29 January 1788, *AMI*, II (1953) 131.

[4] 'Uma obrigação passada por Joaquim Silvério dos Reis em vinte de Janeiro de mil setecentos e oitenta e nove pela qual se obrigou pagar sessenta e quatro oitavas de ouro por cada anno que o sequestrado Cláudio Manuel da Costa lhe patrocinasse as dependencias do seu contrato e particulares, Addição de sequestro feito em credito e obrigações que se achavam ao...Doutor Cláudio Manuel da Costa.' *ADIM*, I, 362.

[5] 'Perguntas feitas ao...Alvarenga', Rio de Janeiro, 11 November 1789, *ADIM*, IV, 131; 'perguntas feitas ao Sargento Mor Luís Vaz de Toledo Piza', Vila Rica, 30 June 1789, *ADIM*, II, 100.

[6] 'Continuação de perguntas feitas ao Coronel...Alvarenga', Rio de Janeiro, 14 January 1790, *ADIM*, IV, 151.

contractors, bondsmen to contractors, or like Vicente Vieira and Maciel, men whose fortunes were linked to contracts. The majority of them were born in Portugal. Together the three groups in coalition represented a formidable section of the regional power structure. In fact the alienation of the Minas plutocracy was so complete as to include Portuguese merchant-capitalists who in other circumstances might have provided the strongest support of metropolitan rule. Portugal had lost the confidence of those on whom it most relied for the continued effectiveness of its dominion in Minas Gerais. And more than that, those wealthy and influential men on whose unspoken accord the power of Lisbon at the local level always rested, were no longer satisfied merely to manipulate the administrative and fiscal system in their own interests, because it was now clear to them that such power was a delusion while they remained answerable to outside restraints and demands. It was necessary to go further, and in doing so, to cut the ties of empire.

The program of the conspiracy reflected the specific and immediate compulsions which had thoroughly alienated the magnates of Minas Gerais from the crown and forced them along the path of revolution. It also reflected the presence among their ranks of those able and distinguished magistrates, lawyers and clerics who had been forced into a reassessment of the colonial relationship by other motives, and who drew their inspiration from the example of North America, the constitutions of the American states, and the works of the Abbé Raynal. From the fragments of information that exist a crude outline of their proposals remain. The capital of the republic was to be São João d'El Rei, a decision which reflected the demographic changes taking place in the captaincy.[1] A mint was to be established and the rate of exchange fixed at 1$500 *reis* per oitava of gold.[2] This was intended to overcome the chronic shortage of circulating media in the captaincy partly caused by the alvará of December 1750 which set the rate at 1$200 *reis* per oitava for Minas Gerais while the rate everywhere else remained at 1$500 *reis*.[3] The Sêrro do Frio was to be freed from the restrictions of the diamond regulations

---

[1] José Caetano Manitti to visconde de Barbacena, Vila Rica, 12 February 1790, *AMI*, II (1953) 89.

[2] There was also some discussion on the issuance of paper money, 'perguntas feitas ao Coronel Francisco António de Oliveira Lopes', Rio de Janeiro, 21 November 1789, *ADIM*, IV, 331; Also see 'perguntas feitas ao...Oliveira Lopes', Vila Rica, 21 July 1789, *ADIM*, II, 58; and 'terceiras perguntas feitas ao Padre José da Silva de Oliveira Rolim', Vila Rica, 21 October 1789, *ADIM*, II, 273.

[3] For comments on the chronic shortage of circulating media see, 'Noticia da Capitania de Minas Gerais por Cláudio Manuel da Costa', IHGB, lata 22, doc. 13.

which were to be abolished.[1] Manufactories were to be established and
the exploitation of the iron ore deposits encouraged. A gunpowder
factory would be set up.[2] Freedom was to be granted to native born
slaves and mulattoes.[3] A University would be founded in Vila Rica.[4]
Parish priests were to levy the *dízimos* on the condition that they sustained
teachers, hospitals, and establishments of charity.[5] All women who
produced a certain number of children were to receive a prize at the
expense of the State.[6] There was to be no standing army. All citizens were
instead to bear arms and when necessary to serve in a national militia.[7]
Parliaments were to be established in each town, subordinate to a supreme
parliament (*um Parlamento principal*) in the capital.[8] For the first three
years the Desembargador Gonzaga would rule – after which time there
would be annual elections.[9] No distinctions or restrictions of dress would
be tolerated and the magnates would be obliged to wear locally manufactured products.[10] All debtors to the royal treasury would be pardoned.[11]

Several points of disagreement over policy arose among the conspirators. They were divided over the best method of dealing with the Visconde
de Barbacena. Some favored his expulsion from the captaincy. Others
wished to see his execution. The latter solution seems to have been
adopted, though both Alvarenga Peixoto and Carlos Correia were
unhappy about this. Gonzaga appears to have been in favor of the
governor's decapitation on the grounds that it was the surest means of
making the commitment to the uprising irreversible. He observed it was
essential for the governor to die first because it was necessary to place the

[1] Desembargador José Pedro Machado Coelho Torres to Luís de Vasconcelos e Sousa, Rio
de Janeiro, 11 Dezembro 1789, AHU, Minas Gerais, caixa 92 (47).
[2] 'Continuação de perguntas feitas ao Vigário...Carlos Corrêa', Rio de Janeiro, 27 November
1789, *ADIM*, IV, 173; 'Sentença da Alçada', 1792, Santos, *Inconfidência Mineira*, 594.
[3] 'Perguntas feitas a José Alvares Maciel', Rio de Janeiro, 26 November 1789, *ADIM*, IV, 398.
[4] 'Sentença de Alçada', 1792, Santos, *Inconfidência Mineira*, 591.
[5] José Caetano Manitti to visconde de Barbacena, Vila Rica 12 February 1790, *AMI*, II (1953)
89.
[6] 'Perguntas feitas ao Coronel...Oliveira Lopes', Rio de Janeiro, 21 November 1789,
ADIM, IV, 331.
[7] *Ibid.*, 331.
[8] 'Continuação de perguntas feitas ao Vigario...Carlos Corrêa', Rio de Janeiro, 27 November
1789, *ADIM*, IV, 171.
[9] José Caetano Manitti to visconde de Barbacena, Vila Rica, 12 February 1789, *AMI*, II
(1953) 89; Witness, Inácio Correia Pamplona, Vila Rica, 30 June 1789 (DMG) *ADIM*,
I, 147; See also 'ofício do...Machado Torres', Rio de Janeiro, 11 December 1789, *ADIM*,
VI, 371–80.
[10] 'Continuação de perguntas feitas ao Vigário...Carlos Corrêa', Rio de Janeiro, 27 November
1789, *ADIM*, IV, 171.
[11] Witness, Inácio Correia Pamplona, Vila Rica, 30 June 1789, (DMG) *ADIM*, I, 147;
'Sentença da Alçada', 1792, Santos, *Inconfidência Mineira*, 591.

'common good over the private, because some [who] would be neutral [would] soon follow the party [of independence] when the General was dead'.[1] Secondly, the issue of slavery became a point at issue. Maciel regarded the presence of so large a percentage of blacks in the population as a possible threat to the new state should the promise of their liberation induce them to oppose the native whites. Alvarenga, one of the greatest slaveowners among the conspirators, recommended that the slaves be granted freedom, which he held would make them the most passionate defenders of the new republic and committed to its survival. Maciel pointed out that such a solution might be self-defeating as the proprietors would be left with no one to work the mines. A compromise solution was eventually proposed and presumably agreed upon, that only the native born black and mulattoes should be freed in the interests of the defense of the state – no mention was made of compensation.[2] Thirdly, the fate of the Europeans in the captaincy was debated. Carlos Correia wished them to be eliminated, a solution opposed by Alvarenga, for he said 'sons could not be expected to rise against their fathers', and all the support possible would be needed during the early years of the republic.[3] Alvarenga could hardly have argued otherwise when so many Portuguese had thrown in their lot with the Brazilian magnates, some of them Alvarenga's personal friends and creditors. Fourthly, there was disagreement over the nature of the flag or arms of the republic. Silva Xavier suggested the adoption of a triangular symbol representing the Holy Trinity, in imitation of the allusion to Christ's five wounds on the cross in the Portuguese arms. Alvarenga disagreed and proposed an Indian breaking the chains of oppression with the inscription from Virgil: 'Libertas quae sera tamen.' The suggestion of Alvarenga seems to have been that received with most favor.[4]

The strongly regionalist emphasis of the conspirators verged at times on economic nationalism. The sentiment was most explicit in the state-

---

[1] 'Continuação de perguntas feitas ao Alferes...Silva Xavier', Rio de Janeiro, 4 February 1790, *ADIM*, IV, 60; 'Segundas perguntas feitas ao Padre José da Silva de Oliveira Rolim', Vila Rica, 20 October 1789, *ADIM*, II, 269; 'Continuação de perguntas feitas ao Vigário... Carlos Corrêa', Rio de Janeiro, 27 November 1789, *ADIM*, IV, 173; Joaquim Silvério dos Reis to Luís de Vasconcelos e Sousa, Rio de Janeiro, 11 May 1789, *ADIM*, III, 236–7; 'Auto de acareação', Rio de Janeiro, 13 July 1791, *ADIM*, IV, 193.

[2] 'Perguntas feitas a José Alvares Maciel', Rio de Janeiro, 26 November 1789, *ADIM*, IV, 398.

[3] *Ibid.*

[4] 'Continuação de perguntas feitas ao vigário...Carlos Corrêa', Rio de Janeiro, 27 November 1789, *ADIM*, IV, 171; 'Continuação de perguntas feitas ao Alferes Joaquim José da Silva Xavier', Rio de Janeiro, 18 January 1790, *ADIM*, IV, 52; 'Continuação de perguntas feitas ao Coronel...Alvarenga', Rio de Janeiro, 14 January 1790, *ADIM*, IV, 147; 'Perguntas feitas a José Alvares Maciel', Rio de Janeiro, 26 November 1789, *ADIM*, IV, 398–9.

ments of the *alferes* Silva Xavier though he was clearly not alone in his views. He praised the beauty and natu al resources of Minas as being the best in the world in words reminiscent of the Abbé Raynal's. Free and a republic like English America, Brazil could be even greater he claimed, because it was better endowed by nature. With the establishment of manufactories he said, there would be no need to import commodities from abroad.[1] Brazil, he told Freire de Andrade, was a land which had within itself all that was needed, no other country was required for its sustenance. The reason for the country's poverty despite all these riches was 'because Europe like a sponge, was sucking all the substance, and that every three years came governors, bringing a gang that they called servants, who after devouring the honor, finances, and offices that should have belonged to the natives returned happily to Portugal bloated with riches'.[2]

A discernible nativist or 'indianist' sentiment was also present in the thinking of the conspirators, represented by Alvarenga's choice of an Indian symbol for the arms of the republic. Alvarenga in fact recited his *canto genetlíaco* at the close of the December meeting.[3] The Indian sentiment was more a reflection of literary and nationalist feeling than of any desire for the type of gradiose miscegenized society envisioned by Pombal and the Duke Silva-Tarouca over a quarter of a century before. The indianist and nativist spirit of the conspiratorial discussions, however, served to broaden the objectives of the participants. Their regionalism, while dominant, was thus not exclusivist. The union of São Paulo and Rio de Janeiro was regarded by Freire de Andrade as necessary for the success of the venture, but it is uncertain what contacts were made and how far possible allies in these two captaincies were aware of the developments in Minas Gerais.[4] During Silva Xavier's stay in Rio as part of the Minas relief forces in 1778 he had become acquainted with several of the

---

[1] Witness, Vicente Vieira do Mota, Vila Rica, 22 June 1789, (DMG) *ADIM*, I, 108; Witness, Vicente Vieira da Mota, Vila Rica, 3 August 1789 (DRJ) *ADIM*, III, 334; Witness, José Aires Gomes, Vila Rica, 28 July 1789 (DMG) *ADIM*, I, 207; Witness, José Aires Gomes, Vila Rica, 30 July 1789 (DRJ) *ADIM*, III, 319–20; 'Continuação de perguntas feitas ao coronel Alvarenga', Rio de Janeiro, 14 January 1790, *ADIM*, IV, 141.

[2] 'Continuação de perguntas feitas ao Tenente Coronel...Freire de Andrade', Rio de Janeiro, 25 January 1790, *ADIM*, IV, 216; the same sentiment expressed to Witness, Padre Manuel Rodrigues da Costa, Vila Rica, 30 June 1789 (DMG) *ADIM*, I, 100.

[3] '[P]or repetir o coronel Alvarenga umas oitavas feitas ao baptisado de um filho do Excellentissimo Dom Rodrigo...' 'Continuação do auto de perguntas feitas ao Desembargador Tomás António Gonzaga', Rio de Janeiro, 3 February 1790, *ADIM*, IV, 267.

[4] 'Continuação de perguntas feitas ao Coronel Ignácio José de Alvarenga', 14 January 1790. *ADIM*, IV, 137–8.

city's wealthy merchants – clients for his dental skills.[1] Possibly by September 1788 the *alferes* was in the pay of Rio merchants, to sound out the reaction of Minas on the question of independence. During late 1788 and early 1789 he had apparently obtained some source of financial support well beyond that of his military pay.[2] Colonel José Aires Gomes shortly after talking with the *alferes* claimed that the merchants of Rio de Janeiro were behind the uprising because they desired 'freedom of commerce' and were fomenting the revolution in their 'own self interests'. They aimed to seek the support of Minas Gerais he claimed 'so that together they might make an English America'.[3]

The desire for free trade among Rio entrepreneurs was not new. Melo e Castro had been concerned over reports of plans for a direct trade with Britain some three years before. Moreover, during 1788, and coincident with the stay of the *alferes* in the city, workshops and manufactories of textiles goods had been forcibly closed down under the terms of the alvará of January 1785. Early in the year, after secret investigation into the location of looms in the city, the viceroy ordered those discovered to be dismantled and removed to the royal warehouses. During July 1788 the owners were called together and informed that their property was to be sent to Lisbon. If they so wished they would be permitted to submit letters to their correspondents in the metropolis in order that the dismantled looms might be disposed of – a concession the owners declined. In all, thirteen looms were sent by Man-of-War to Portugal.[4] In addition, the stipulations of the co-incident alvará of 1785 against contraband were evidently being more rigorously applied, causing comment as far afield as Great Britain.[5] The rise of prices in Rio, caused perhaps by shortage of

---

[1] 'Inquiração do testemunha...António Ribeiro de Avellar', Rio de Janeiro, 30 July 1791, *ADIM*, iv, 99–100; 'Perguntas feitas ao Alferes Joaquim José da Silva Xavier', Rio de Janeiro, 15 July 1791, *ADIM*, iv, 96.

[2] When valued at time of confiscation his estate was assessed at 803$226 *reis*, which did not include his property in Rio das Mortes, *ADIM*, i, 433 (see footnote 7, p. 119).

[3] Alvarenga later claimed that the alferes had confused 'liberty of commerce' with 'liberty of America'. 'Perguntas feitas ao...Ignácio José de Alvarenga Peixoto', Rio de Janeiro, 11 November 1789, *ADIM*, iv, 130; He gave a more detailed account of Aires Gomes statement, however, in the second interrogation, 'continuação de perguntas feitas ao... Alvarenga', Rio de Janeiro, 14 January 1790, *ADIM*, iv, 135–6. Domingos Vidal Barbosa had heard a very similar story, see witness, Domingos Vidal de Barbosa, Vila Rica, 13 July 1789 (DMG) *ADIM*, i, 171.

[4] Luís de Vasconcelos e Sousa to Martinho de Melo e Castro, Rio de Janeiro, 12 July 1788; 'Relação das pessoas que n'esta cidade tem teares, com declaração da qualidade dos tecidos ...Autos sobre a ordem de Sua Magestade...Autos de diligencia...' All in 'Documentos officiaes inéditos', *RIHGB*, x (2nd edition, 1870) 230–8.

[5] 'Perguntas feitas a José Alvares Maciel', Rio de Janeiro, 26 November 1789, *ADIM*, iv, 400–1.

contraband manufactures (generally cheaper than legitimate imports from Portugal), as well as by the closure of local production, was noted with concern by João Rodrigues de Macedo's correspondent in the city.[1]

Proposals for trade and commercial arrangements were noticably absent from the discussions of the Minas conspirators. As they also nowhere discussed the arrangements for the government or control of either Rio de Janeiro or São Paulo it must be assumed that they regarded the participation of these captaincies in the revolt against Portugal as being that of independent and presumably confederated states.[2] Their interest in the constitutions of the sovereign North American states and the articles of confederation among the former British colonies would point to this conclusion. If this was the case then the apparent lack of interest in international commerce is understandable. Moreover, the strong emphasis on self-sufficiency contributed to an ambivalence towards foreign trade relations and foreign support. Oliveira Lopes observed that there was no necessity whatever to invite the support of foreign powers, for they would rush to establish relations with the new state once it was established on account of its natural resources.[3] It is interesting that the conspirators did regard it as necessary to assure the merchants of Rio that after the uprising their debtors in Minas would honor obligations.[4] As to the support of São Paulo this seems to have been exaggerated. Carlos Correia's relatives in Taubaté were of little importance.[5] On the other hand both the *alferes* Silva Xavier and his commandant Freire de Andrade had contacts with officers in the military forces there.[6] Possibly it was

---

[1] José F[ernandes] Valladares, Va. de Pitangui, 24 November 1788, *ABNRJ*, LXV (1943) 180–1. This is from CCBNRJ, 1-1-21.

[2] In this connection the following use of words by Alvarenga is significant: '...estivera dizendo o dito Coronel Joaquim Silvério [dos Reis] que o Rio de Janeiro, as Minas e São Paulo brevamente haviam de ser Republicas...' 'Continuação de perguntas feitas ao coronel...Alvarenga', Rio de Janeiro, 14 January 1790, *ADIM*, IV, 153.

[3] '[N]ão havia necessidade de convidar para este fim Nação alguma Extrangeira porque logo que se verificasse projecto do levante, qualquer delles pretenderia sem duvida a alliança com a Republica em consideração ao interresante commercio, que podiam com a mesma fazer pelos preciosos generos, que possuia este Continente...' 'Continuação de perguntas ao Padre José da Silva de Oliveira Rolim', Vila Rica, 13 November 1789, *ADIM*, II, 288.

[4] '[D]eputaria a Republica envial-os ao Rio de Janeiro dizendo que se queriam, que as Minas satisfizessem o que se devia aquella Praça practicassem ali o mesmo...' 'Perguntas feitas ao coronel...Oliveira Lopes', Vila Rica, 15 June 1789, *ADIM*, II, 42. See also Witness, Domingos Vidal de Barbosa, Vila Rica, 13 July 1789 (DMG) *ADIM*, I, 171.

[5] See comments by Governor of São Paulo, Bernardo José de Lorena to Visconde de Barbacena, São Paulo, 11 July 1789, *DISP*, XLV (1924) 223–5.

[6] See Bernardo José de Lorena to Visconde de Barbacena, São Paulo, 2 February 1791, *DISP*, XLV (1924) 257; See also 'Carta de Manuel José, dirigida ao Mestre do Campo

from these sources that they expected support in the event of a successful uprising in Vila Rica.

The total abrogation of past laws and statutes was contemplated by the conspirators.[1] How far this involved an imitation of the models from North America is not clear. There is evidence of some opposition to a slavish imitation of the North American example – at least as far as the arms of the state was concerned and perhaps on more fundamental matters.[2] Some kind of written constitution was evidently intended. Despite his disparagement of democracy in his treatise, which after all was dedicated to the Marquis of Pombal, Gonzaga had been even at that early stage a firm supporter of the contractual nature of government. His experience under the government of Cunha Meneses which he referred to as 'despotic', as well as his professional self interest as a magistrate fortified these opinions. The tone of his memorials to the court during the 1780s strongly emphasized the legal and moral restraints on the actions and power of the executive. Much later an inquiry involving one of the conspirators described the intentions of the Minas movement as being to 'change the government of Minas from Monarchical to Democratic'.[3] At the time, however, as far as the evidence shows, the word democratic was never used. It is probable that the example of the American revolution was seen to be especially pertinent because the Minas conspirators saw the cause of the events in North America to be remarkably similar to their own situation. 'Nothing caused the break [between Britain and her colonies] but the great duties that were imposed', one of the conspirators claimed.[4] The group met at the house of Freire de Andrade concluded that 'the Abbé Raynal had been a writer of great vision, for he had prognosticated the uprising of North America, and the

Ignácio de Andrade Souto Mayor Rendon', and 'Carta do Capitão do Regimento de Voluntários de São Paulo', Manuel Joaquim de Sá Pinto do Rego Fortes to same, *ADIM*, III, 271–2.

[1] Joaquim Silvério dos Reis and Carlos Correia, 'auto de acareação', Rio de Janeiro, 13 July 1791, *ADIM*, IV, 193.
[2] 'Continuação de perguntas ao coronel...Alvarenga', Rio de Janeiro, 14 January 1790, *ADIM*, IV, 147.
[3] Alvarenga, according to Silva Xavier, commented that '...não queria naquella acção Cabeça, mas sim serem todos Cabeças e um Corpo Unido...' 'Continuação de perguntas feitas ao Alferes...Silva Xavier', Rio de Janeiro, 18 January 1790, *ADIM*, IV, 51; Thomas Jefferson had told Mr Jay that 'in the case of a successful revolution a republican government in a single body would probably be established'. Jefferson to Jay, Marseilles, May 4 1787, *AMI*, II (1953) 17; The reference to democracy came in a petition from Oliveira Rolim, José Bonifácio de Andrada e Silva to Dom Manuel de Portugal e Castro, Presidente, Vila Rica, 3 August 1822, *RAPM*, IX (1904) 624.
[4] 'Continuação de perguntas feitas ao Francisco da Paula Freire de Andrade', Rio de Janeiro, 29 July 1791, *ADIM*, IV, 230.

captaincy of Minas Gerais with the imposition of the *derrama* was now in the same circumstances...'[1]

Despite the proposal to emancipate native-born slaves, in itself a startling proposal for 1789, no fundamental social re-adjustments were foreseen, and even the repercussions of this action underestimated. The conspirators assumed that they could with ease control the situation that resulted. Just as many also assumed the uprising itself could be instigated, manipulated, and controlled in their own interests. Luís Vieira, saw the transfer of the court to America and the elevation of Brazil to head of the Empire as the best solution for Brazil's problems.[2] It was a suggestion reminiscent of the ideas of D. Luís da Cunha and the Duke Silva-Tarouca, but it was not the solution of a social revolutionary. Cláudio Manuel da Costa, who had sought so arduously membership of the order of Christ, rich and intensely traditionalist, would be an unlikely convert to radical social change.[3] The conservatism of the Minas conspirators was evident even in the thinking of the *alferes* Silva Xavier, the most socially insecure of the major participants in the conspiracy, and the chosen instrument of the wealthy élite in their planned revolt. The government in Lisbon, he claimed, had decided that no opulent men would be permitted to exist in the captaincy. Barbacena, he said, had brought orders from Martinho de Melo e Castro which would mean ruination for the people of Minas for none of them would be allowed to possess more than 10,000 *cruzados*.[4] He described the uprising not as a revolution but as a 'restoration'.[5] Silva Xavier's choice of the traditional symbolism of the triangle, representing the Holy Trinity, for the flag of the state was indicative of his viewpoint. But the social conservatism of the movement was hardly surprising. The Minas conspiracy was fundamentally a movement made by oligarchs in the interests of oligarchs, where the name of the people would be evoked merely in justification.

Melo e Castro's insistence on the *derrama* coupled with his attack on the crown's debtors in Minas Gerais had provided a built-in subterfuge for the magnates of the captaincy to achieve their own selfish objectives under the guise of a popular uprising. Those who had most to gain from the break with Portugal were clearly the opulent plutocrats threatened

---

[1] 'Auto de perguntas feitas ao...Freire de Andrade', Rio de Janeiro, 16 November 1789, *ADIM*, IV, 207.

[2] Witness, Vicente Vieira da Mota, Vila Rica, 22 June 1789, (DMG) *ADIM*, I, 111.

[3] Alberto Lamego, *Mentiras Históricas* (Rio de Janeiro, 1947) 113–20; Rodrigues Lapa, *Cartas Chilenas*, 28, 37. See discussion in Chapter IV above.

[4] Witness, Vicente Vieira da Mota, Vila Rica, 22 June 1789, (DMG) *ADIM*, I, 109.

[5] 'Sentença da Alçada', 1792, Santos, *Inconfidência Mineira*, 588, 593.

with the total loss of their patrimony by the proceedings of the royal exchequer. The *derrama* was a tax which fell on the whole population. As such it could be used by those interests, who themselves for years had been oppressive taxgatherers and the very agents of royal authority, to provide a respectable front for their action and attract popular support to their cause. The royal fifth was the only imposition directly administered by the crown and directly remitted to Lisbon. By insisting on the rigid observance of the 1750 gold-quota law, Melo e Castro provided the Minas magnates with the most suitable weapon to use against Portugal. By early 1789, a formidable plot had been concerted in Minas Gerais, backed by some of the captaincy's richest and most influential men, and counting on significant support among the regular troops stationed in the region. If all went as planned, and the derrama was imposed during February 1789 as anticipated, then an action would have been precipitated which threatened, at the very least, to deal a shattering blow to Lisbon's authority in Brazil.[1]

---

[1] A possible indication of the widespread commitment was the startling fall in the number of Mineiro students matriculating at the University of Coimbra. During 1786 and 1787, twelve and ten students respectively had matriculated. But in 1788 a mere three crossed to Portugal, and in 1789 none at all. It is possible that the young men of Minas were waiting, like the younger Resende Costa, whose father's estates bordered those of Carlos Correia in Rio das Mortes, for the establishment of the university in Vila Rica. 'Estudantes Brasileiros em Coimbra', *ABNRJ*, LXII (1940) 181–7, and sequestro, Carlos Correia, *ADIM*, I, 389; 'Sentença da Alçada', 1792, Santos, *Inconfidência Mineira*, 600; Witness, Domingos Vidal de Barbosa, Vila Rica, 13 July 1789 (DMG) *ADIM*, I, 172.

CHAPTER 6

SKULDUGGERY

Whoever is incapable of sustaining great enterprises should not meddle with them. It is better to die with honor than to live with dishonor.

> Extracted from a letter of warning, of unknown author, received by the conspirators, 20 May 1789, *ADIM*, I, 149.

The hand of the Almighty who regulates the just and felicitous government of Her Majesty has just defended this country if not from its ruin or total loss, at least from very grave damage irreparable for many years, and has directed my diligence in such a way that I have the glory to be able at the same time to inform Your Excellency of the great peril which the sacrilegious insolence of certain perverse men threatened and of the complete victory with which the infamous scheme in its wickedness has been for the most part overcome and discovered.

> Visconde de Barbacena to Martinho de Melo e Castro, Vila Rica, 11 July 1789, *AMI*, II, 63.

The coalition of magnates committed to an uprising in Minas was not monolithic, and the mixed backgrounds and the mixed motivations of those involved were potential weaknesses. The magnates were confident that their aims could be achieved under the cover of a popular uprising. This depended very much, however, on the stimulation of widespread discontent by the imposition of the *derrama*, and while such a reaction was highly probable, it was essentially a factor beyond their control. Moreover, the opulent entrepreneurs in the background were committed to a republic and independence not for ideological or nationalistic reasons, but because revolution seemed the best way to protect their own self interests. Hence, because the immediate threat to their interests had been created by the Portuguese authorities, it always lay within the power of Lisbon or the governor of Minas to mitigate or to remove that threat. And it also lay within the power of Lisbon or Barbacena to remove the threat to the population at large, a threat on which the oligarchs relied for the arousal of popular opposition to Portugal. In fact, the *derrama* was not imposed during February 1789 as had been expected, and during March the governor wrote to the câmara of Vila Rica announcing the suspension of the tax. He had taken this decision he said because of 'the circumstances of the captaincy' and on his own initiative. Gonzaga told the canon Luís Vieira: 'the occasion [for the uprising] has been lost'.[1]

Barbacena explained his action on 25 March in a secret letter to his uncle, the viceroy, Luís da Vasconcelos e Sousa.[2] He had been warned, he wrote, by one of the principal men of the captaincy, that a formidable conspiracy existed among the 'powerful men and magnates' of Minas Gerais who intended the forceful overthrow of the dominion of the Portuguese crown and aimed to establish a free and independent state. Tomás Antônio Gonzaga, Inácio José de Alvarenga, José da Silva de Oliveira Rolim, Domingos de Abreu Vieira, Carlos Correia de Toledo and the *alferes* Joaquim José da Silva Xavier were implicated.[3] These men Barabacena noted 'are the most capable and likely that I know for so great an evil'.[4] 'The people of any importance, or greatest stature in the captaincy', he added, 'are almost all debtors in all that they possess to Her Majesty, and only a revolution could adjust the accounts to their benefit.'[5] His position was precarious the governor told the viceroy. He was without forces for repression and suspected the Dragoons of participation in the conspiracy. Any rash action on his part might precipitate the very uprising it was essential to avoid. The 'most judicious measures and the greatest circumspection' were therefore required. He had 'resolved to dissimulate', and in the meantime to strengthen his position while awaiting the viceroy's aid and advice. As a first step he had decided to suspend the *derrama*, the imposition of which was to have provided the occasion for the revolt. A circular letter to the municipal councils of the captaincy had been issued to this effect Barbacena told Vasconcelos e Sousa. In addition, in order to quiet the misapprehensions of the Dragoons, he had let it be known that he was in no hurry to proceed

---

[1] 'Registro da carta do Ex[cellentissi]mo Senhor General sobre a suspensão da derrama, Vila Rica, 14 March 1789, visconde de Barbacene to Senhores Juiz e Officaes da Câmara de Vila Rica', *RAPM*, VII (1902) 979–80; also in AHU, Minas Gerais, caixa 57. Gonzaga's comment reported by Luís Vieira in 'Continuação de perguntas feitas ao Luís Vieira', Rio de Janeiro, 23 January 1790, *ADIM*, IV, 300.

[2] Visconde de Barbacena to Luís de Vasconcelos e Sousa, 25 March 1789, *AMI*, II (1953) 41–7; also in AHU, Minas Gerais, caixa 94.

[3] Barbacena reported that in Rio das Mortes 'some 40 people from among the most important in the comarca' were involved in the plot, but that his informant did not know their identities. In fact the participants in Rio das Mortes would have been particularly well known to Silvério dos Reis. See in this respect the anonymous denunciation to Barbacena, dated 14 October 1789, Vila de São João, in *ADIM*, III, 201–9.

[4] Barbacena also claimed that the Fiscal Beltrão was involved in the plot. There is some circumstantial evidence against him, but the viceroy dismissed the claim out of hand and no investigation or proceedings against Beltrão seem to have been instituted.

[5] Barbacena claimed Gonzaga was 'Brazilian by birth or at least by upbringing'. Gonzaga was born in Oporto but brought up in Bahia, see p. 96.

with the proposed reorganization of the regular military forces of the captaincy. He suggested to the viceroy that when the arrests were made it might be advisable to attribute the cause to some crime other than that of treason. This might dispose the people against the prisoners, especially 'if I still do not possess the force to work openly, or it seems convenient to hide from the people and foreign nations this pernicious example'.[1]

Barbacena's informant was the contractor Joaquim Silvério dos Reis. His denunciation represented, with certain understandable omissions (Silvério's own participation in the plot for example), a detailed account of the plans and dispositions of the Minas conspirators. But the governor's account of the chronology of his actions was flawed. His letter claimed that the suspension of the *derrama* was a direct result of the information received from Silvério dos Reis. This is not consistent with the facts. The denunciation was given verbally on 15 March 1789.[2] The circular letter to the câmaras mentioned in the letter to the viceroy, a copy of which was forwarded to Vasconcelos e Sousa, was dated 23 March, a week after Silvério's visit and two days before the letter to the viceroy.[3] But the letter to the câmara of Vila Rica, announcing the suspension of the *derrama* had been dated 14 March 1789. This was a day before the governor, according to his own sworn statement, had any knowledge of the plot.[4] If the decision to suspend the *derrama* occurred before 15 March, as seems to be the case, then it must have been taken on grounds other than to abort the plans of the conspirators. Should this be so, then Silvério dos Reis denunciation could not have caused the suspension. Thus, the suspension preceded the denunciation, not the opposite as Barbacena claimed.[5]

A revision of the chronology makes Silvério dos Reis' betrayal of his

[1] Visconde de Barbacena to Luís de Vasconcelos e Sousa, 25 March 1789, AHU, Minas Gerais, caixa 94.
[2] 'Luíz António Furtado de Castro do Rio de Mendonça, visconde de Barbacena...Attesto que no dia 15 de Março do anno de mil e setecentos e oitenta e nove foi a primeira vez que Joaquim Silvério dos Reis me communicou, que se achava tratada e disposta nesta capitania e na do Rio de Janeiro a rebellião que tem sido objecto e motivo desta Devassa...Vila Rica, 25 February 1791, visconde de Barbacena', *ADIM*, I, 297–8.
[3] Santos, *Inconfidência Mineira*, 432.
[4] 'Registro da carta do Ex[cellentissi]mo Senhor General sobre a suspensão da derrama, registro geral da câmara da Vila Rica, 1783–1791, Vila Rica, 14 March 1789, visconde de Barbacena to Senhores Juiz e Officiaes da Câmara de Vila Rica', *RAPM*, VII (1902) 979–80; Also copy in AHU, Minas Gerais, caixa 57, dated 14 March 1789.
[5] It is suspicious that the relevant documents are not among the records of the secretariate of the governor of Minas. For example, 'Registro de cartas, circulares, ordens e portarias do Governador a autoridades da Capitania, 1788–1797', Arquivo Público Mineiro, colonial, 1a seção, códice 259.

colleagues more explicable. The suspension of the *derrama* was a great relief to the mass of the population, but it did not remove in any way the threat that hung over the contractors for the recovery of outstanding debts. In fact the *junta da fazenda* on 5 March 1789, called Silvério to account, describing him as 'crooked, dishonest, and a falsifier'.[1] If the denunciation came after it was decided to suspend the *derrama* then Silvério had a clear and direct motive for his action. As an alternative to participation in a risky adventure, seriously weakened by the removal of its chosen occasion, he could attempt to achieve the original objective for his participation in the conspiracy – the avoidance of debt payment – by another method, that of denouncing his co-conspirators to Barbacena, and claiming as a reward for his 'loyalty' the pardoning of his debts.[2] Perfidy before the suspension would have been gratuitous. Afterwards it had motive and reason.[3]

The contention that the suspension preceded the denunciation is supported by several other pieces of evidence. On 10 March, the *alferes* Silva Xavier was given license to go to Rio de Janeiro.[4] Had the original plan been in effect on 10 March it is most peculiar that the principal activist in the proposed uprising, the man who claimed for himself the 'main role and the greatest risk', and who had been the most fervent propagandist for a republican state, even to the extent of being criticized by Cláudio Manuel da Costa for endangering the secrecy of the plans by his lack of caution, should have left the captaincy.[5] And it is certain that the *alferes* left for Rio before the plans of the conspirators were known to the governor, for Silvério dos Reis was on his way to see the governor when he met the *alferes* en route.[6] Later during this same journey Silva

---

[1] '[D]oloso, fraudulante e falsificador', [portaria de 3.3.1789 da junta da fazenda], Mathias, *ACC*, III, 234; Also Santos, *Inconfidência Mineira*, 330.

[2] Silvério dos Reis was to remind the Portuguese government constantly of this obligation during the rest of his life, see 'Requerimentos e outros papeis do coronel Joaquim Silvério dos Reis, 1789–1794', *ADIM*, VI, 299–336. Also Alberto Lamego, *Mentiras Históricas* (Rio de Janeiro, 1947) 153f.

[3] For comments on Silvério's character see Visconde de Barbacena to Luís de Vasconcelos e Sousa, Caxoeira do Campo, 25 March 1789, *AMI*, II (1953) 43–4; and Luís de Vasconcelos e Sousa to Martinho de Melo e Castro, Rio de Janeiro, 16 July 1789, *ADIM*, VI, 188.

[4] Certification, Pedro Affonço Galvão de São Martinho, Vila Rica, 10 October 1789, *ADIM*, I, 250.

[5] Witness, Joaquim Silvério dos Reis, Rio de Janeiro, 18 May 1789, *ADIM*, III, 252; He was also criticized in similar terms by Padre José Lopes de Oliveira, 'o Alferes da tropa paga Joaquim José da Silva Xavier que andava com tão pouca cautela convidando gente...', *ADIM*, VI, 304.

[6] For a detailed discussion of the timing of this meeting see Santos, *Inconfidência Mineira*, 442–3; Also very revealing are Silva Xavier's comments to Alvarenga at Cachoeira. Alvarenga was at Cachoeira to compliment the Governor (itself an interesting fact in view of

Xavier sought to talk with Colonel Luís Alves. Silvério dos Reis' future father-in-law went to great pains to avoid the *alferes*. This would suggest either that Luís Alves knew of Silvério's intention to denounce the conspiracy, or that the plans had changed sufficiently before 15 March to warrant his avoidance of Silva Xavier.[1] Moreover, the *alferes* was again speaking of his projects and of his desire to make a substantial fortune out of his enterprises in Rio. This was the reason given for his visit to the city.[2] The license to the *alferes* to leave for Rio supports the truth of Barbacena's statement that he first heard of the proposed uprising on 15 March. Had he been aware of Silva Xavier's participation before 10 March, it is extremely unlikely that he would have permitted him to leave. And if the leave of absence was granted with knowledge of the conspiracy, and hence as a conscious policy decision, then it is most unlikely that Barbacena would not have claimed credit for his action, or warned his uncle before he did of the *alferes'* presence in Rio de Janeiro. The actions of Silvério dos Reis, the journey of the *alferes* Silva Xavier, and the refusal of Luís Alves to speak with him, would all suggest that the conspiracy had been seriously disrupted and the original plan modified or abandoned before Barbacena became aware of the conspiracy on 15 March 1789.

Why then did Barbacena suspend the *derrama*? There are several factors to be considered. Firstly, at the Queen's insistence, Melo e Castro had been required to inform Barbacena that the *derrama* was to be imposed

---

the governor's comments of 25 March to the viceroy on Alvarenga's behaviour), and there met the *alferes* seeking his license: Silva Xavier proposed '...para se fazer a republica do Rio de Janeiro primeiro, que depois a de Minas com o exemplo da do Rio era mais facil, que os Povos de Minas eram uns bacamartes, faltos de espirito, e de dinheiro, e que tendo falado a muita gente, todos queriam, mas que nenhum se queria resolver a por em campo ...' 'Continuação de perguntas feitas ao...Alvarenga', Rio de Janeiro, 14 January 1790, *ADIM*, IV, 148; the *alferes* said: 'Depois disse a elle respondente [Silva Xavier] o Padre José da Silva de Oliveira Rolim, que o Coronel Ignácio José de Alvarenga dissera que o Tenente Coronel Francisco de Paula Freire de Andrade mandava dizer a elle respondente, que não falasse mais a pessoa alguma, e que as que tinha falado, se pudesse as desvanecesse; porque podia não ter effeito a sublevação e motim, e que so depois de posta a derrama se havia de ser, se a dita sublevação se fazia.' 'Continuação de perguntas feitas ao Alferes Joaquim José da Silva Xavier', Rio de Janeiro, 18 January 1790, *ADIM*, IV, 53.

[1] 'Continuação de perguntas feitas ao Alferes...Silva Xavier', Rio de Janeiro, 18 January 1790, *ADIM*, IV, 54; Witness, Luís Alves de Freitas Bello, Vila Rica, 4 August 1789 (DMG) *ADIM*, I, 229–30; Witness, Rev Padre José Lopes de Oliveira, Vila Rica, 30 June 1789 (DMG) *ADIM*, II, 160; 'Perguntas feitas ao coronel...Oliveira Lopes', Vila Rica, 15 June 1789, *ADIM*, II, 52.

[2] See Visconde de Barbacena to Luís de Vasconcelos e Sousa, Cachoeira do Campo, 25 March 1789, *AMI*, II (1953) 42. The petitions on the alferes projects had been registered in June 1788, see Archivo do Distrito Federal, vol. 2 (1895) 511, cited by Santos, *Inconfidência Mineira*, 132.

'only if the people of Minas were in a condition to support the tax'.[1] Thus, the governor had a certain room for maneuver not apparent in his general instruction. Secondly, the economic situation in Minas Gerais clearly made the imposition of the *derrama* inadvisable. Its imposition was bound to produce great hardship and discontent, and this must have been apparent to any reasonable man. Moreover, the *junta da fazenda* had stated its formal opinion that the recovery of debts was not possible, and Carlos José da Silva and the intendent Bandeira, despite their recent reprimand from Lisbon, both pointed out to Barbacena the impossibility of the demand.[2] The decision to suspend the *derrama* could have been made on the perfectly reasonable grounds of the changed economic situation in Minas Gerais. Indeed, precisely on the grounds stated in the letter to the câmara of Vila Rica on 14 March – because of the 'circumstances' of the captaincy.

If the economic conditions of Minas Gerais were the reason for the failure to impose the *derrama* then a decision of this importance was likely to have been known in advance, especially to Gonzaga through his friendship and regular meetings with the intendent Bandeira.[3] It is not certain when Gonzaga told Luís Vieira that 'the occasion [for the uprising] has been lost'. Later Luís Vieira could not recall whether the letter to the câmaras had been issued or not. Gonzaga's comment was apparently made when the canon was in Vila Rica to preach at the services of mourning for the death of the prince Dom José.[4] The heir apparent had died of

---

[1] Martinho de Melo e Castro to Visconde de Barbacena, Ajuda, 7 February 1788, AHU, códice 610, f. 610.

[2] Carlos José da Silva, [secretary of junta da fazenda] Vila Rica, 31 January 1789; Francisco Gregório Pires Monteiro Bandeira, [intendent of Vila Rica] Vila Rica, 11 February 1789, BNLCP, codice 643, f. 222. It is curious that these documents, presumably copies of the originals should be in the Pombal collection. I did not come across them in the casa dos contos collection, though it is always possible that the originals are somewhere among the documents dispersed between the Biblioteca Nacional of Rio de Janeiro, the Arquivo Nacional, and the Arquivo Público Mineiro, in Belo Horizonte, Minas Gerais.

[3] '[V]indo elle Respondente [Luís Vieira] a Vila Rica na occasião das exequias do Principe pregar nelles, encontrou com o Doutor Ignácio José de Alvarenga e o Desembargador Tomás António Gonzaga, em casa deste...e disse o...Gonzaga estes formaes palavras – a occasião para isso perdeu-se –.' 'Continuação de perguntas feitas ao Conego Luís Vieira', Rio de Janeiro, 23 January 1790, *ADIM*, IV, 300.

[4] '[E] não esta agora certo, se a carta do Governador de Minas para a suspensão da Derrama tinha ja sahido, ou não...' 'Continuação de perguntas feitas ao Cônego Luís Vieira', Rio de Janeiro, 21 July 1790 (*sic*) [this should be 1791] *ADIM*, IV, 305; '[Q]ue não tinha lembrança, qual foi primeiro se o sermão que o Cônego Luís Vieira foi fazer aos Prados, ou o que faz nas exequias do Principe; e a certeza, que pode obter e, que pelo tempo, em que, o Alvarenga esteve na Paraupeba, para onde tinha ido de Vila Rica, e que tambem o Cônego Luís Vieira esteve doente em casa de sua Mae, quando tinha ido fazer o sermão dos Prados...'

smallpox on 11 September 1788, but official mourning was not proclaimed in Minas Gerais until 20 February 1789, over five months later.[1] According to Alvarenga Peixoto, Luís Vieira preached in mid-March. This would have been before 23 March, when the governor led the viceroy and Lisbon to believe he had first suspended the *derrama*.[2] In addition the conspirators possessed a second source of information close to the governor. Dr José Álvares Maciel had been appointed tutor to the governor's children, a position which gave him residence at Cachoeira and made him an excellently placed spy.[3] The conspirators had anyway expected the announcement of the imposition for mid-February. It seems probable, therefore, that knowledge of the decision to suspend the *derrama* and possibly also of the impending letter to the câmara of Vila Rica caused the plans agreed upon in late December 1788 to be substantially altered during late February and early March 1789. This postponement of the uprising coincident with the increasing pressure on Silvério dos Reis for debt payment then led to his defection. Thus the conspiracy apparently came to the governor's attention when the original plan was already abandoned and the coalition formed during early 1789 was in disarray.

The revised chronology makes the lack of any very serious concern among the conspirators during March and April 1789 much easier to explain. Some conspirators, especially Carlos Correia, always distrusted Silvério dos Reis, but they do not seem to have become markedly more suspicious after mid-March. This would surely have been the case had Barbacena's action been a precipitous move which immediately followed

'Continuação de perguntas feitas a Vicente Vieira da Motta', Rio de Janeiro, 20 July 1790 (*sic*) [this should be 1791] *ADIM*, v, 22.

[1] 'Gemidos da Tristeza na lamentavel Perda de S.A.R. O Senhor D. José, Principe do Brasil, falecido 11 Septembro, 1788...por José Rodrigues da Costa', Lisbon, 1788, Portuguese Pamphlets, Greenlee Collection, Newberry Library, Chicago; 'Circular para todas as Câmaras', 20 February 1789, visconde de Barbacena, APM, códice 259, 4v.

[2] According to Alvarenga 'as exequias do principe, que foi pelo meio do mez de Março pouco mais ou menos, nellas veiu pregar o Cônego Luís Vieira da Silva...' 'Continuação de perguntas feitas ao...Alvarenga', Rio de Janeiro, 14 January 1790, *ADIM*, IV, 149. For Barbacena's claims see 'Assim he que veio taobem a justificarse a primeira providencia que julguei conveniente neste cazo, que foi a de participar logo a Câmara de Vila Rica a rezolução que tinha tomado de suspender o lansamento da Derrama até a decizão de S. Magde e depois as mais Câmaras da Capitania com a carta, cuja copia remetto a V Exa incluiza...', Visconde de Barbacena to Martinho de Melo e Castro, Vila Rica, 11 July 1789, *AMI*, II (1953) 69; and '...declarei que tomava sobre mim a demora, ou suspensão do lançamento até que Sua Magestade Resolvesses sobre a conta que hia darlhe por esse motivo, e assim o escrevi logo as Camaras da forma que veras na copia que remeto...', Visconde de Barbacena to Luís de Vasconcelos e Sousa, Cachoeira do Campo, 25 March 1789, *AMI*, II (1953) 44.

[3] Luíz [Antônio Furtado de Mendonça, Visconde de Barbacena] to Luís de Vasconcelos e Sousa, 6 May 1789, *AMI*, II (1953) 50.

a visit to his residence by one of the principal conspirators. The conspirators were not unaware that the governor might have heard something. Gonzaga visited Barbacena at Cachoeira sometime between 14 and 25 March 1789, and several times in the course of the conversation attempted to bring up the subject of the state of the captaincy and the suspension of the *derrama*. Gonzaga congratulated the governor on his decision observing that Minas was 'always treated like little girls in the eyes of the ministry in Lisbon', but that in reality because of its 'natural defences, resources, and the education of its people', it was the region of Portuguese America which could most easily revolt 'without the need for the slightest dependency on anyone'.[1] Barbacena was careful not to rise to the bait. Gonzaga appears to have been satisfied that the governor had no knowledge of the plot. As far as Silvério dos Reis was concerned he was considered worthy of confidences as late as May.

If the decision to suspend the *derrama* was taken on the ground stated in the letter to the câmara of Vila Rica, why did the governor claim otherwise in his correspondence with the viceroy? One can only speculate. Certainly Silvério's denunciation was acutely embarrassing to Barbacena personally. For nine months he had governed a captaincy, considered by the secretary of state to be the 'soul' of Portuguese America, in which a formidable plan for an armed uprising against the Portuguese crown had been concerted. The conspirators were so confident of success that, reputedly, laws and constitution had been formulated. The uprising moreover, had come startlingly close to realization. Indeed, had Barbacena followed the instructions of Melo e Castro to the letter the armed revolt would undoubtedly already have taken place. Its postponement had been the unintentional and, for him, fortuitous result of his decision to suspend the *derrama*. In addition Barbacena was a protégé of Melo e Castro and he was well aware of the secretary of state's mind. He knew perfectly well that the suspension of the *derrama* even on the reasonable grounds of the economic circumstances of Minas Gerais would need the strongest justification. And the problem of justifying his actions to Lisbon must have been in the forefront when composing the letter to the câmara of Vila Rica. The closeness of the timing between the letter to the câmara and the visit of Silvério dos Reis, the desire to take precautions so that his action could be viewed as a calculated act of the shrewdest policy, the coincident desire to provide a *raison d'être* for his decision on the suspen-

[1] Visconde de Barbacena to Luís de Vasconcelos e Sousa, Cachoeira do Campo, 25 March 1789, *AMI*, II (1953) 45; Visconde de Barbacena to Martinho de Melo e Castro, Vila Rica, 11 July 1789, *ibid.*, 70.

sion, must all have tempted the governor to modify his account of the chronology of events to his personal advantage. Barbacena's mis-statements in his letter to Vasconcelos e Sousa were not so important in themselves. Nor were they especially surprising in view of the damage to the governor's own reputation which would follow a recital of the truth. But the confusion they have caused to the historical record has been considerable, and in consequence of course have seriously influenced the interpretation of the Minas conspiracy.

The failure to impose the *derrama* during February 1789 seems to have led several important participants to cool in their ardour and others to withdraw from an active part in the movement. Silvério dos Reis' defection reflected the weakness of the commitment of those interests whose involvement was motivated by purely selfish considerations, as well as their desperation for relief from the staggering debts claimed by the royal exchequer. In addition, Gonzaga's comments to the canon Luís Vieira demonstrated the withdrawal of those shadowy articulators of the movement whose commitment was more ideological than material, and whose participation had been the result of careful calculation. These men clearly regarded the enterprise as having lost the most propitious moment and were apparently prepared to await another occasion. Their participation, like that of the financial interests, had been conducted throughout with the greatest circumspection and secrecy, and they apparently believed that even in the event of discovery nothing could be proved against them judicially.

The activists faced a different situation and their responses varied. Freire de Andrade now viewed the action as being too risky and confronted with insurmountable difficulties. He withdrew from Vila Rica to his estates at Caldeirão and attempted to disassociate himself from the remaining conspirators. The same may have been the attitude of his brother-in-law, Dr José Álvares Maciel.[1] Shortly afterwards Padre Oliveira Rolim left for Tejuco.[2] But Alvarenga Peixoto remained committed to the establishment of an independent state, for he believed that they were already too involved to go back, and that in the event of discovery they would all be arrested anyway. In the circumstances they

---

[1] 'Auto de continuação de perguntas feitas a Francisco de Paula Freire de Andrade', Rio de Janeiro, 29 July 1791, *ADIM*, IV, 229.

[2] '[P]orque iam estar todos na sua fazenda do Caldeirão tres ou quatro mezes; pelo que ficou o Respondente [Oliveira Rolim] despersuadido dos projectados intentos, que lhe tinham communicado e assim se retirou para o tejuco, cuidando no modo de la poder subsistir, conseguindo a permissão para isso...' 'Continuação de perguntas feitas ao Padre ...Oliveira Rolim', Rio de Janeiro, 17 April 1790, *ADIM*, IV, 418.

had no alternative but to go ahead for as he observed: '*Aut libertas, aut nihil.*' He held that 'even if an army of 10,000 men were sent against us it could not overcome our opposition'. Nothing could enter from Rio de Janeiro and São Paulo if they took preventive action. Against the invaders they would be able to employ a type of scorched earth policy by 'withdrawing the cattle and poisoning the water'. From mountain strongholds guerrilla parties could harrass the invaders.[1] Possibly the seizure of the bullion of the royal fifth would now provide the occasion for revolt.[2] The frigate from Lisbon was expected in Rio de Janeiro sometime during May.[3] The *alferes* Silva Xavier, however, by this time had little faith in the will of his associates in Minas. He dismissed Freire de Andrade as a coward (*banana*) and while in Rio de Janeiro suggested to various military officers that the action begin there with the assassination of the viceroy.[4]

The fact that the conspiracy in Minas had been reduced to a rump of its original support did not mean that the forces in favor of the administration were necessarily strengthened. Barbacena was all too aware of his weakness. But he did possess the knowledge that an important middle ground existed between himself and the activists, and if the example of Silvério dos Reis was an indicator, those who stood on that middle ground might be won over by diplomacy and tact. After mid-March Barbacena was not inactive. He had in his favor an intimate knowledge of the plot. But his actions had always to be considered in the light of his own vulnerability and his need to play for time. Both factors limited his maneuverability. He pressed home his attack at the weakest points in the coalition of disparate interests that had committed themselves to an armed uprising against the Portuguese throne during late 1788. His first move was to turn the defector Silvério dos Reis into a spy.[5] He would himself

---

[1] 'Auto de perguntas feitas ao Coronel...Oliveira Lopes', Vila Rica, 15 June 1789, *ADIM* II, 45; 'Continuação de perguntas feitas ao Vigário...Carlos Corrêa', Rio de Janeiro, 27 November 1789, *ADIM*, IV, 176; 'Auto de perguntas feitas ao coronel...Oliveira Lopes', Vila Rica, 15 June 1789, *ADIM*, II, 45. Also see Desembargador José Pedro Machado Coelho Torres to Luís de Vasconcelos e Sousa, 11 December 1789, AHU, Minas Gerais, caixa 92, (47).

[2] '[P]orque estava para chegar a esta cidade, [Rio de Janeiro] a fragata que havia de conduzir os quintos para Portugal, e que era necessario ir apresalos como entre os consocios desta sedição se tinha ajustado...' Witness, Joaquim Silvério dos Reis, 18 May 1789, Rio de Janeiro, *ADIM*, III, 253.

[3] Luíz [Visconde de Barbacena] to Vasconcelos e Sousa, Cachoeira 6 May 1789, *AMI*, II (1953) 49.

[4] Witness, Joaquim Silvério dos Reis, 18 May 1789, Rio de Janeiro, *ADIM*, III, 253.

[5] 'Determinou-se o meu General que passasse a Vila Rica...e que me fizesse parcial destes homens para descobrir mais provas o que fiz...', Joaquim Silvério dos Reis to Luís de Vasconcelos e Sousa, Rio de Janeiro, 5 May 1789, *ADIM*, III, 236.

'follow the friendships and principal associates' of the conspirators.[1] The Bishop of Mariana was informed of the nature of the conspiracy, for in the event of Barbacena's incapacitation the Bishop would automatically assume the government of the captaincy.[2] And in addition the governor consolidated support among the local Portuguese bureaucratic and military establishment. He took into his confidence, his aide-de-campe, Lieutenant-Colonel Francisco Antônio Rebêlo, and the secretary of the *junta da fazenda*, Carlos José da Silva. Rebêlo, appointed at the time of the expeditions to Rio during the late 1770s, when he raised a company at his own expense, was to act as Barbacena's personal emissary to the viceroy and later to Martinho de Melo e Castro in Lisbon.[3] Carlos José da Silva, secretary of the *junta da fazenda* of the captaincy since 1771, was among those marked out by the conspirators for elimination.[4]

Barbacena was also aware of the dispute between the magistrates of the Diamond District, Gonzaga, and the military commandants of Santo Antônio and Tejuco. The governor skilfully used these divisions to neutralize the troops. Removing the commandant of Tejuco, José de Vasconcelos Parada e Sousa, and the commandant of Santo Antônio, José de Sousa Lobo, from their lucrative positions, he appointed to these important commands two Brazilian officers implicated in the conspiracy, Captain Maximiliano de Oliveira Leite and Captain Manoel da Silva Brandão. Oliveira Leite was a cousin of Álvares Maciel, hence related by marriage to Freire de Andrade.[5] Alvarenga Peixoto complained that Brandão's promotion to 'Grand Turk of the Sêrro' led him to change his mind about joining the uprising.[6] Moreover, the two Portuguese officers were now close at hand, and as Barbacena knew of their extensive illegal activities they were no doubt under a special obligation to him. The governor's promotion of the two Brazilians was a calculated risk

[1] Luís [Visconde de Barbacena] to Luís de Vasconcelos e Sousa, Cachoeira do Campo, 11 May 1789, *AMI*, II (1953) 53.

[2] Visconde de Barbacena to Luís de Vasconcelos e Sousa, Cachoeira do Campo, 25 May 1789, *ibid.*, 46–7.

[3] Attestation, Francisco de Paula Freire de Andrade, Vila Rica, 6 January 1783, AHU, Minas Gerais, caixa 94; Attestation, Antônio de Noronha, Vila Rica, February 1780, AHU, Minas Gerais caixa 92; Attestation, D. Rodrigo José de Meneses, [n.d.] AHU, Minas Gerais, caixa 92; Luís [Visconde de Barbacena] to Luís de Vasconcelos e Sousa, 11 May 1789, *AMI*, II (1953) 53.

[4] 'Relação incluza no offício de 11 de Feb., 1790', *AMI*, II (1953) 84; Witness, Joaquim Silvério dos Reis, Rio de Janeiro, 18 May 1789, *ADIM*, III, 247.

[5] 'Maximiliano de Oliveira Leite, primo da mulher do dito Tenente Coronel [Freire de Andrade]...e dos nossos', 'Appense-se a devassa, Saldanha', *ADIM*, II, 303; For Manoel da Silva Brandão, *ADIM*, VI, 305.

[6] 'Continuação de perguntas feitas ao coronel...Alvarenga', 14 January 1790, *ADIM*, IV, 149.

for he was well aware of their participation in the conspiracy. His assumption that their greed was greater than their nationalism, however, does not appear to have been mistaken.

The governor, anxiously waiting for a reply from the viceroy, became increasingly fearful that the message had gone astray or fallen into the wrong hands. After twenty days – sufficient time for a letter to have reached Rio and a reply returned – he decided the urgency of the situation and the insecurity of his own position required he delay no further. He called Silvério dos Reis to Cachoeira and had him commit his denunciation to paper. He then furnished him with a letter of introduction and instructed the informant to present himself forthwith to the viceroy in Rio.[1] Meanwhile he considerably extended his base of support, partly as a result of his own investigations, partly through his continued exploitation of the ready-made divisions in the captaincy. Bazilio de Brito Malheiro, former crony of Parada e Sousa and Sousa Lobo, and the avowed enemy of Gonzaga and the magistrates of the Diamond District, became his spy and informant.[2] Through the good offices of José Carlos da Silva and Francisco Antônio Rebêlo, Barbacena persuaded Inácio Correia Pamplona, a wealthy merchant-landowner to engross his party. Pamplona was a friend of the vicar of São José and had long been a supply merchant for the Dragoons.[3] His title of mestre do campo was awarded for his actions as frontier pioneer and Indian fighter in Campo Grande. Pamplona who knew of the conspiracy and perhaps participated in it, was a compadre of Carlos José da Silva, secretary of the *junta da fazenda*. Like Bazilio de Brito he was heavily indebted and his creditor was Silvério dos Reis.[4]

The governor's involvement with these men, some of them like Bazilio and Silvério long notorious for unscrupulous malpractices and

---

[1] Luís [Visconde de Barbacena] to Luís de Vasconcelos e Sousa, Cachoeira do Campo, 19 April 1789, *AMI*, II (1953) 48; Joaquim Silvério dos Reis to Visconde de Barbacena, Bordo do Campo, 11 April 1789 ('escrita na Caxoeira e entregue pessoalmente no dia dezenove de April') *ADIM*, I, 6–10; denunciation also in *RAPM*, VI (1901) 199–201.

[2] 'Relação incluza no offício de 11 de Fevereiro, 1790', *AMI*, II (1953) 85.

[3] Luís [Visconde de Barbacena] to Luís de Vasconcelos e Sousa, Cachoeira do Campo, 11 May 1789, *ibid.*, 53; 'Francisco de Paula Freire de Andrade, Tenente Coronel Commandante do Regimento de Cavallaria...Certifico que tenho recibido do...Pamplona...[540] alqueires de Milho...farinha...11 Jan., 1785', CCBNRJ, 1-1-15; Francisco Xavier de Mendonça Furtado to conde de Valladeres, and Conde de Oeiras [Carvalho e Melo] to same, 10 January 1770, AHU, Minas Gerais, caixa 94; Visconde de Barbacena to Martinho de Melo e Castro, Vila Rica, 11 February 1790, AHU, Minas Gerais, caixa 92.

[4] 'Relação dos creditos...pertencem a Joaquim Silvério dos Reis, no. 4, Ignácio Corrêa Pamplona, I.138$500,' CCBNRJ, I-10-5; 'Os bens de Ignácio Corrêa Pamplona', sequested, 20 September 1771, Costa Filho, *A cana de açúcar*, 161.

bribery, involved more than the extracting of promises of loyalty to the crown. Barbacena seems to have agreed to press for special legislation from Lisbon so that Bazilio's complicated litigations might be settled in his favor.[1] Pamplona was to gain profitable returns by supplying the military forces sent from the coast.[2] Moreover, during early May, sometime about the 10th or 12th of the month, Barbacena came to an agreement with João Rodrigues de Macedo. Macedo's bookkeeper Vicente Vieira visited the governor at Cachoeira do Campo and the two men 'discussed the business of the house of Rodrigues de Macedo'. Vicente Vieira was 'to say nothing of what had passed'. The nature of the 'business' discussed is obscure, but its result was clear. Macedo was to receive complete protection from any investigation, interrogation, or implication in the conspiracy. What he gave in return can only be surmised, but positive evidence exists that Barbacena did at some time enter into financial dealings with the contractor.[3] And he had similar arrangements with Silvério dos Reis.[4] In light of the consequent behavior of Barbacena it can only be assumed that the commitments the governor entered into with the contractors and others were such that they would continue after the governor's need to compromise had passed. It was obviously in the interests of Macedo and Silvério dos Reis that this should be so, for the history of colonial empires, and of Minas Gerais in particular, were full of promises made under duress which were rapidly forgotten when European troops were at hand.

On 4 May, Barbacena received word from the viceroy. The arrival of the messenger caused a good deal of speculation and the governor deemed it wise to delay a few days before responding.[5] A gold strike in the Canastra Mountains provided an excuse for dispatching the remaining Dragoons in Vila Rica to the far southeast of the captaincy on police duties. Barbacena requested extra troops from Rio de Janeiro to replace

---

[1] See Carta Regia, Rainha, Queluz, 16 September 1790, AHU, códice 610, f. 169–70v.

[2] Credits, Pamplona for supply of farinha etc., in CCBNRJ, I-1-15.

[3] Alvarenga said Vicente Vieira told him that he had spoken to the Governor and advised him to do the same, 'Continuação de perguntas feitas ao...Alvarenga', Rio de Janeiro, 14 January 1789, ADIM, IV, 150; For Vieira's account of his meeting with the Governor see 'Perguntas feitas a Vicente Vieira da Motta', Rio de Janeiro, 19 July 1791, ADIM, V, 12; 'Continuação de perguntas feitas a Vicente Vieira da Motta', Rio de Janeiro, 20 July 1790 (*sic*) [This should be 1791] *ibid.*, 27–30. For financial dealings between the governor and Rodrigues de Macedo see 'Letra sacada por Barbacena', 1797, doc. 130, ABNRJ, LXV (1943) 296–7.

[4] 'Créditos pertenecentes ao Coronel Joaquim Silvério dos Reis do visconde de Barbacena que se entregas ao solicitador de Real Fazenda, para se apuzarem, 1796.' CCBNRJ, I-10-5.

[5] Luís [Visconde de Barbacena] to Luís de Vasconcelos e Sousa, Cachoeira do Campo, 11 May 1789, AMI, II (1953) 51.

them.[1] On the pretext that hostile Indians had been sighted near the road to Rio, the governor had already doubled the patrols and armed them with powder and shot.[2] Officially Barbacena requested two companies of infantry from the viceroy and suggested they be stationed in Vila Rica and along the road between the two capitals. This version he hoped would become known to the conspirators. In two secret letters to his uncle he stated his real intentions and needs. The small number of men mentioned was intended to make his request plausible he said. He advised that the forces dispatched be specially chosen and trustworthy, and enter the captaincy 'under some kind of dissimulation'. It was essential that they be supplied with munitions for 'in Minas the Queen possesses not one barrel of gunpowder'. The detachments should be placed along the road in strategic positions. In all events care must be taken not to warn the conspirators, even though they were now greatly disunited and weakened, 'either because of the suspension [of the *derrama*] or other causes'. He hoped the whole matter could be dealt with by mutual accord between the viceroy and himself, and without judicial inquiry. He thought it best that the leaders of the movement be removed 'without great display' from Minas and Brazil, either 'attributing the cause to some other crime, or saying nothing at all on the question'.[3] At the same time Barbacena wrote to the governor of São Paulo warning him of the plot and of possible contacts between Carlos Correia and his relatives in Taubaté.[4]

Barbacena, however, seriously miscalculated the reaction of his uncle. The viceroy acted rapidly as soon as Silvério was in his hands. Luís de Vasconcelos e Sousa was at the end of his tenure, his successor D. José de Castro, conde de Resende, having been nominated on 5 March 1789. He was also a magistrate, a member of the *casa de suplicação*, Portugal's highest court.[5] Vasconcelos e Sousa decided at once that an official investigation was essential in a case of such importance. Despite the recommendations of his nephew against judicial proceedings, on 7 May, a week after

---

[1] Visconde de Barbacena to Luís de Vasconcelos e Sousa, Cachoeira do Campo, 6 May 1789, *ibid.*

[2] Visconde de Barbacena to Martinho de Melo e Castro, Vila Rica, 11 July 1789, *AMI*, II (1953) 72.

[3] Luís [Visconde de Barbacena] to Luís de Vasconcelos e Sousa, Cachoeira do Campo, 6 May 1789, *ibid.*, 49–50.

[4] Visconde de Barbacena to Senhor Bernardo José [de Lorena], Cachoeira do Campo, 6 May 1789, *ibid.*, 50–1; also in 'Correspondência recebida e expedida pelo General Bernardo José de Lorena, Governador da Capitania de S. Paulo durante o seu Governo 1788–1797', *Documentos Interessantes para a História e Costumes de S. Paulo*, XLV (1924) 223.

[5] Letter of nomination, conde de Resende, Lisbon, 5 March 1789, AHU, Minas Gerais, caixa 92. According to Alden, *Royal Government*, 34 (footnote 23), he was with Mem de Sá (1558–72) the only other desembargador to become viceroy of Brazil.

Silvério arrived from Minas, the viceroy nominated Desembargador José Pedro Machado Torres as judge, and *ouvidor* Marcelino Pereira Cleto clerk, of a special secret court of inquiry (*devassa*). As *corpus delicti* the *devassa* used the letter Silvério dos Reis had written two days before at the viceroy's suggestion, containing a restatement of his denunciation. The magistrates were granted wide powers and military aid was placed at their disposal.[1]

Matters were coming to a head. It was already known that the mails between Minas and Rio were being searched, and friends within the military warned the *alferes* Silva Xavier that he was being followed.[2] Moreover, the time was approaching for the dispatch of the fifth to the metropolis.[3] Finding he was unable to obtain permission from the viceroy to return to Vila Rica the *alferes* resolved to go anyway, illegally, by way of São Paulo. During the evening of 8 May he went into hiding.[4] His disappearance caused considerable alarm in the viceregal palace. Patrols of soldiers were sent in search and to guard the roads out of the city. Silva Xavier's confidence in Silvério dos Reis proving his undoing. Anxious for news, he sent Father Inácio Nogueira to the house where Silvério was lodging. The contractor was unable to find out from the priest the whereabouts of the *alferes*, but he later located Nogueira's home by questioning another priest and immediately informed Vasconcelos e Sousa.[5] On 10 May, Nogueira was arrested, brought to the viceregal palace and interrogated by the viceroy. That evening, a detachment of soldiers from the European regiment of Estremoz, surrounded the house in which the *alferes* was hiding. Loaded blunderbus in hand and with letters of introduction to facilitate his journey through São Paulo, Joaquim José da Silva Xavier, nicknamed the *Tiradentes* was arrested.[6] Silvério dos Reis was also incarcerated. The viceroy considered him a man 'disposed for any evil...and perhaps the originator of those same horrific facts or projects which he now denounced'.[7]

---

[1] 'Portária do viceroi', Rio de Janeiro, 7 May 1789, *ADIM*, III, 227–8, also VI, 355–6; 'Auto de Corpo de Delicto', Rio de Janeiro, 11 May 1789, *ADIM*, III, 229–31.

[2] Witness, Pedro de Oliveira Silva, Vila Rica, 20 March 1790 (DMG) *ADIM*, I, 267 'Autos de perguntas...feitas a Simão Pires Sardinha', Lisbon, 13 August 1790, *AMI*, II (1953) 111.

[3] Witness, Joaquim Silvério dos Reis, Rio de Janeiro, 18 May 1789, *ADIM*, III, 253; Also see Luís [Visconde de Barbacena] to Luís de Vasconcelos e Sousa, Vila Rica, 6 May 1789, *AMI*, II, (1953) 49–50.

[4] 'Perguntas feitas ao Alferes...Silva Xavier', Rio de Janeiro, 22 May 1789, *ADIM*, IV, 30.

[5] Mathias, *ACC*, III, 247–9.

[6] 'Auto de exame feito em um bacamarte, que se achou ao Alferes Joaquim José da Silva Xavier', Rio de Janeiro, 12 May 1789, *ADIM*, IV, 441–2. Also see *ADIM*, I, 250.

[7] Luís de Vasconcelos e Sousa to M. de Melo e Castro, 16 July 1789, AHU, Minas Gerais, caixa 92.

Silvério's departure from Minas on the spurious pretext of compli-
menting the viceroy had caused serious concern among those who remained active in the cause of the uprising. Oliveira Lopes in particular
did not believe the reasons given for the visit to Rio. He consulted his
brother, to whom Aires Gomes had talked of the uprising in September
1788. The priest recommended an immediate denunciation to the governor.[1] Oliveira Lopes hurried to Cachoeira and made a precipitate confession. The governor instructed him to return when he had committed
a complete statement to paper – no easy task for the near illiterate
fazendeiro. He left with Barbacena a painfully wrought denunciation
dated 19 May 1789.[2] A few days before, on 13 May, Freire de Andrade
had joined the list of defectors. His denunciation was also committed to
paper.[3] Later, Freire de Andrade and his brother-in-law were both to
remain unmolested long after the governor was aware of their involvement in the plot. Maciel indeed remained at the governor's residence.
On 6 May Barbacena even praised his scientific inquiries to the viceroy,
and as late as July the *junta da fazenda* granted him funds for scientific
instruments.[4]

Maciel was to some degree a contact between the three groups of
interest involved in the Minas conspiracy. He had been an originator of
the idea, he was close to the activists, and he was the son of a contractor.
It is possible that he changed sides during early May and then brought
Freire de Andrade into the governor's growing 'loyalist' party. Evidently
Barbacena's decision not to arrest Maciel and Freire de Andrade was
taken after Silvério dos Reis had left for Rio de Janeiro, for Silvério in his
statements before the viceroy's commission of inquiry roundly implicated
both Maciel and Freire de Andrade and even cited the governor's own
statements in the process.[5] Freire de Andrade's family background alone
probably would have made the governor wary of arresting him outright,
and the suppression of the news of his involvement in the plot, at least as
far as the general public was concerned, undoubtedly would have helped
to minimize the importance of the revolutionary movement. Freire de
Andrade himself seems to have assumed that the matter would get no
further than a secret investigation. This is what he told Luís Vaz in

---

[1] Witness, Padre José Lopes de Oliveira, Vila Rica, 30 June 1789 (DMG) *ADIM*, I, 157–8.
[2] 'Auto de perguntas feitas ao Coronel...Oliveira Lopes', Vila Rica, 14 June 1789, *ADIM*,
II, 47; Francisco Antônio de Oliveira Lopes to Visconde de Barbacena, 19 May 1789,
ADIM, I, 57–9.
[3] Francisco de Paula Freire de Andrade, Vila Rica, 17 May 1789, *ADIM*, I, 54–6.
[4] 'Portária, junta da fazenda, material de pesquisa', 15 July 1789, Mathias, *CCANRJ*, 58.
[5] Witness, Joaquim Silvério dos Reis, Rio de Janeiro, 18 May 1789, *ADIM*, III, 249, 251–2.

recommending that he turn himself over to the authorities.[1] It is significant that Barbacena had consistently recommended just such a secret non-judicial inquiry to his uncle, and until that time had conducted his own proceedings in such a manner.

By 17 May, however, it was known in Minas Gerais that the *alferes* was being followed. That night Cláudio Manuel da Costa, seeing visitors off at the door of his residence in Vila Rica, was approached by a mysterious figure, who told him of the arrests in Rio de Janeiro and recommended he burn any incriminating papers.[2] On 20 May, news of the arrests and that troops were preparing to enter Minas reached the governor and several others, including Oliveira Lopes, Carlos Correia, and Alvarenga Peixoto.[3] Both the governor and the conspirators were taken by surprise, but whereas Barbacena reacted with calmness and moved rapidly onto the offensive during the following critical hours, the conspirators were thrown into panic.

Gonzaga's house was surrounded and he was arrested without incident by Colonel Francisco Antônio Rebêlo. His papers were apprehended and his personal estate confiscated.[4] The aged Domingos de Abreu Vieira was arrested at the same moment. Gonzaga was immediately sent under guard to Rio de Janeiro. Abreu Vieira was imprisoned in the Vila Rica jail where he was persuaded to write two letters of denunciation to the governor. Although he pleaded innocence, among his papers were discovered incriminating letters to him from Father Oliveira Rolim.[5] A detachment of troops under the command of Lieutenant Antônio Dias Coelho was already on the road to Rio das Mortes. Coelho, a Portuguese from Guimaraes, had been employed by Cunha Meneses in debt collecting duties in the comarca where he had been involved in disputes with Alvarenga Peixoto.[6] Accidently encountering Carlos

---

[1] Witness, Luís Vaz de Toledo, Vila Rica, 2 September 1789, (DRJ) *ADIM*, III, 416.

[2] For a detailed discussion of the episode see José Afonso Mendonça de Azevedo, in *ABNRJ*, LXV (1943) 159–62. Also see Luís [Visconde de Barbacena] to Luís de Vasconcelos e Sousa, Cachoeira, 17 May 1789, *AMI*, II (1953) 55–6.

[3] Inácio Correia Pamplona to Visconde de Barbacena, Mendanha, 27 May 1789, *ADIM*, I, 53; Luís [Visconde de Barbacena] to Luís de Vasconcelos e Sousa, Cachoeira, 25 May 1789, *AMI*, II, (1953) 57–8. Same to same, Cachoeira, 29 May 1789, *ibid.*, 59–60.

[4] Visconde de Barbacena to Senhor Desembargador Ouvidor Geral e Corregedor Pedro José de Araújo Saldanha, *ADIM*, I, 69; Visconde de Barbacena to Luís de Vasconcelos e Sousa, Cachoeira do Campo, 21 May 1789, *AMI*, II, 56–7.

[5] Domingos de Abreu Vieira to Visconde de Barbacena, Vila Rica, Cadeia, 28 May 1789; Domingos de Abreu Vieira, Cadeia, Vila Rica, 28 May 1789, *ADIM*, I, 59–62 (also see note II, 304). 'Auto de Exame, achada e separação feita nos papeis apprehendidos ao Tenente Coronel Domingos de Abreu Vieira', *ADIM*, I, 70–4.

[6] Visconde de Barbacena to Luís de Vasconcelos e Sousa, Cachoeira dos Campo, 21 May 1789, *AMI*, II, 56.

Correia en route Coelho took him into custody. He left the vicar guarded by five soldiers outside São João d'El Rei before entering the town where Alvarenga Peixoto voluntarily gave himself up.[1] Coelho searching Carlos Correia's house in São José found all in great disorder, confirming his suspicion that the priest had been in flight when apprehended.[2] Carlos Correia and Alvarenga Peixoto, like Gonzaga were immediately sent to Rio de Janeiro.

Carlos Correia, Luís Vaz and Oliveira Lopes had attempted to concert a last minute opposition before the troops from the coast reached the highlands.[3] 'It is better to die with a sword in the hand than like a leach in the mud', Luís Vaz told Oliveira Lopes when the two met clandestinely by a coppice at the foot of the mountains behind São João d'El Rei.[4] But his gallant words evaporated in confusion. The conspirators were surrounded and caught in the web the governor had woven during the previous months from his residence at Cachoeira do Campo. Carlos Correia was informed of the arrest of the *alferes* and the dispatch of troops in the house of Pamplona, his trusted friend, who for several weeks past had also been the governor's spy.[5] Oliveira Lopes, receiving the news from Rio, attempted to warn his brother, Carlos Correia, Freire de Andrade, and Oliveira Rolim. The messenger found it impossible to get through. The roads were guarded. Freire de Andrade had anyway already defected. These activities which took place after Oliveira Lopes' visit to Cachoeira probably explain his arrest and imprisonment while others who defected remained for the time being unmolested. The statement the colonel had composed for the governor was destroyed by his wife, who feared that it would incriminate him.[6]

---

[1] 'Relação incluza no offício de 11 de Fevereiro de 1790', *AMI*, II, 83; Witness, Antônio José Dias Coelho, Vila Rica, 5 August 1789 (DRJ) *ADIM*, III, 343.

[2] *Ibid.*, III, 347.

[3] For conflicting accounts of these events see, 'Continuação de perguntas feitas ao Vigário... Carlos Corrêa', Rio de Janeiro, 27 November 1789, *ADIM*, IV, 176–7; 'Auto de perguntas feitas ao Coronel...Oliveira Lopes', Vila Rica, 15 June 1789, *ADIM*, II, 50–4.

[4] *Ibid.*, II, 52 and, 'Continuação de perguntas feitas ao Sargento-Mor Luís Vaz...', Vila Rica, 23 July 1789, *ADIM*, II, 112–13.

[5] 'Auto de perguntas feitas ao Coronel...Oliveira Lopes', Vila Rica, 15 June 1789, *ADIM*, II, 50; Martinho de Melo e Castro to Visconde de Barbacena, Lisbon, 29 September 1790, *AMI*, II, 96. Witness, Inácio Correia, Pamplona, Vila Rica, 30 June 1789 (DMG) *ADIM*, I, 151–2.

[6] 'Auto de segundas perguntas feitas...Alferes Victoriano Gonçalves Velloso', Vila Rica, 6 August 1789, *ADIM*, I, 137, 139; 'Auto de terceiras perguntas feitas ao...Velloso', *ADIM*, II, 141–3; 'Continuação de perguntas feitas ao Alferes dos Pardos...Velloso', Vila Rica, 12 January 1790, *ADIM*, II, 153. For the burning of Oliveira Lopes' statement by his wife, 'Perguntas feitas ao coronel...Oliveira Lopes', Vila Rica, 15 June 1789, *ADIM*, II, 37.

By bold, rapid, and well-planned actions the Visconde de Barbacena had rounded up the conspirators without the discharge of a musket. Only Oliveira Rolim in the Sêrro do Frio escaped the net. But Barbacena had been forced to move sooner than he had anticipated, and without the troops he had requested at hand he was obliged to dispatch the leaders of the proposed uprising to Rio. Yet those not arrested were almost as significant as those who were. Álvares Maciel, Freire de Andrade, Rodrigues de Macedo, Vicente Vieira, José Aires Gomes, remained free men, despite the fact that their implication in the plot had been known to the governor for several weeks.

The apprehension of some of the captaincy's most eminent and distinguished men, however, caused widespread consternation in Minas Gerais. The initial reaction was to identify the crime as diamond smuggling, but in a matter of days the true cause was public knowledge. Alarming exaggerations of the proposals and plans of the would-be revolutionaries were bandied around.[1] Silva Xavier's preaching in favor of a republican state was widely known. Uncertainty and fear increased with the news of the property confiscations and that a *devassa* had been instituted by the viceroy. Before the end of the month the governor was forced to admit to Vasconcelos e Sousa that 'all dissembelment and secrecy are useless'.[2]

By the time the prisoners were on their way from Minas the secret inquiry in Rio had come to an inconclusive halt. Silva Xavier was first interrogated on 22 May in the fortress on Snake Island (*Ilha das Cobras*) in the Bay of Guanabara.[3] The fortress was the strongest defensive work in the harbor. John Barrow described it two years later as 'a rock about eighty feet high at the point on which the citadel stands and slanting to eight at the opposite end, its length is 300 yards; and it is detached by a narrow but very deep channel [from the mainland].'[4] The *alferes* disclaimed all knowledge of the conspiracy. 'Who was he, someone without social importance, or influence, or wealth', he asked, 'to persuade so great a people to such folly.'[5] During the second interrogation on 27 May the *alferes* admitted saying that the people of Minas were desperate

---

[1] Witness, Pedro de Oliveira, Vila Rica, 20 March 1790 (DMG) *ADIM*, I, 267–70.
[2] Luís [Visconde de Barbacena] to Luís de Vasconcelos e Sousa, Cachoeira do Campo, 25 May 1789, *AMI*, II, 57–8.
[3] 'Auto de perguntas feitas ao Alferes...Silva Xavier', Rio de Janeiro, 22 May 1789, *ADIM*, IV, 29.
[4] John Barrow, *A Voyage to Cochinchina in the years 1792 and 1793* (London, 1806) 78.
[5] 'Auto de perguntas feitas ao Alferes...Silva Xavier', Rio de Janeiro, 22 May 1789, *ADIM*, IV, 35.

because of the imposition of the *derrama*, 'which was very bad policy, for they could rise like the English provinces, especially if united with São Paulo and Rio', but this he claimed was merely conversation, and had no other significance.[1] On 30 May, he again denied the allegations.[2] In face of Silva Xavier's stout refusal to talk the viceroy decided to send the magistrates to Minas Gerais. After making a copy of the devassa, Torres and Cleto were ordered to proceed post haste to Vila Rica, to take statements from witnesses, and to return all possible speed to conclude the inquiry.[3]

The news that the devassa was underway in Rio must have caused grave concern at Cachoeira do Campo. Until the end of May the governor hoped that the whole matter could be handled without judicial inquiry. In building support he had acted on this assumption.[4] He had made promises, offered protections and rewards, and perhaps entered into financial understandings of dubious propriety, which any impartial investigation of the facts would threaten to expose and abrogate. On learning of the viceroy's action Barbacena precipitately, on 12 June, opened his own *devassa*. He appointed the *ouvidor* of Vila Rica, Araújo Saldanha, judge, and the *ouvidor* of Sabará, José César Caetano Manitti as clerk.[5] The *intendent* of Vila Rica, Bandeira, was not appointed, the governor explained to Vasconcelos e Sousa, because of the suspicion that he was involved in the plot.[6] His aspersion on Bandeira was unjustified. Bandeira, a cultured and open-minded man was a close friend of several of the leading conspirators, but there is no evidence to suggest that he joined or was ever invited to join the movement. In fact the conspirators did not hesitate to use him to further their own ends, especially in the matter of the imposition of the *derrama* for the recovery of total arrears

1 'Continuação de perguntas feitas ao Alferes...Silva Xavier', Rio de Janeiro, 27 May 1789, *ADIM*, IV, 37.
2 'Continuação de perguntas feitas ao Alferes...Silva Xavier', Rio de Janeiro, 30 May 1789, *ADIM*, IV, 41–4.
3 Luís de Vasconcelos e Sousa to Sr Desembargador José Pedro Machado Coelho Torres, Rio de Janeiro, 14 June 1789, AHU, Minas Gerais, caixa 94; Luís de Vasconcelos e Sousa to Visconde de Barbacena, Rio de Janeiro, 23 June 1789, AHU, Minas Gerais, caixa 94.
4 Luís [Visconde de Barbacena] to Luís de Vasconcelos e Sousa, Cachoeira do Campo, 11 May 1789, *AMI*, II, 53; Barbacena told the viceroy on 25 March, 'não mandei começar ainda Devassa, nem outros procedimentos mais amplos, por querer obrar de acordo com tigo, e com o teo parecer'. Luís [Visconde de Barbacena] to Luís de Vasconcelos e Sousa, *AMI*, II, 57–8.
5 He made the decision on receiving letters from the viceroy dated up to 29 May, Luís [Visconde de Barbacena] to Luís de Vasconcelos e Sousa, 2 June 1789, *AMI*, II, 58–9; 'Auto de Corpo de Delicto', Vila Rica, 14 June 1789, *ADIM*, I, 3–5ff.
6 Luís [Visconde de Barbacena] to Luís de Vasconcelos e Sousa, Vila Rica, 2 June 1789, *AMI*, II, 58.

under the quota system. Nor indeed did the conspirators refrain from discussing the possibility of his elimination during the uprising.[1] Bandeira was clearly a loyal vassal of the Portuguese crown. But he was clearly also his own man. Manitti was of different mettle and Barbacena was anxious to appoint him to the commission.[2] And Manitti, clerk of the devassa, was also pliable to the influence and wealth of those whose commitment to the uprising it was now necessary to obscure, especially Macedo with whom, like the governor, he had personal financial arrangements.[3] During the month before the arrival of the viceroy's magistrates in Vila Rica, Barbacena's men scurried with indecent haste to assure that the record show what the governor wished it to show. So rapidly were the statements taken and the prisoners interrogated that never did the Minas magistrates bother to have a notary present – essential if the proceedings were to be legally binding.[4] Manitti, a contemporary claimed, took precedence over the judge and deceived the accused with 'false promises and insinuations and if there was resistance, with the rack'.[5]

Saldanha and Manitti interrogated Cláudio Manuel da Costa on 2 July 1789.[6] Two days later he was discovered dead in his makeshift cell at the house of João Rodrigues de Macedo. An examination of the body was carried out by two doctors and the magistrates of the devassa. Their

[1] Joaquim Silvério dos Reis to Visconde de Barbacena, Bordo do Campo, 11 April 1789, *ADIM*, I, 8.

[2] Luís [Visconde de Barbacena] to Vasconcelos e Sousa. Cachoeira, 2 June 1789, *AMI*, II (1953) 58.

[3] See the revealing letter of José Caetano César Manitti to Rodrigues de Macedo, 24 September 1797, doc. 95, *ABNRJ*, LXV, (1945) 220–5.

[4] For criticism of the methods of the Minas devassa see Desembargador Torres' comments on the interrogation of Cláudio Manuel da Costa, *ADIM*, VI, 400. Of course this omission could have been deliberately contrived.

[5] 'O Ministro, que foi deputado p[ar]a Escr[iv]am da Devassa, se antepoz ao Ministro Inquiridor, e a todos os Denunciados illudio, com promessas, insinuaçõens, e se algum rezistia, com tractos…[…] Esta procedim[en]to deve cauzer admiração a q[ue]m não souber o caracter daquelle Ministro; porem a respeito da sua conducta, baste dizer, que ainda não se-lhe-conheceo a Moral.' Manuel Cardozo, 'Another document on the Inconfidência Mineira', *HAHR*, XXXII (1952) 548. Barbacena himself evidently also conducted interrogations, for example see his comments in Luíz [Visconde de Barbacena] to Luís de Vasconcelos e Sousa, Vila Rica, 3 July 1789, *AMI*, II, 61.

[6] The interrogation of Cláudio Manuel da Costa is not published in the *ADIM*. A copy of the original devassa prepared for the secretary of state Martinho de Melo e Castro is in the AHU, Minas Gerais, caixa 93. 'Auto de perguntas feitas ao Bacharel Cláudio Manuel da Costa, Dez. Pedro José Araújo de Saldanha and Bacharel José Caetano Cezar Manitti', Vila Rica, 2 July 1789. An extracted selection of his testimony is published by Santos, *Inconfidência Mineira*, 240–5; the complete testimony is available in 'Auto de perguntas feitas ao bacharel Cláudio Manoel da Costa, Commemoração do centenário de Cláudio Manuel da Costa', *RIHGB*, LIII, pt. I (1890) 156–62.

report dated 4 July, concluded that he had hanged himself.[1] On 5 July, Inácio Pamplona left Vila Rica precipitately.[2] The following day, 6 July the viceregal commission arrived in the town.[3] In a dispatch to Lisbon on 11 July the governor did not mention the death although he discussed the testimony of the prisoner.[4] He reported the 'suicide' in a separate dispatch on 15 July which enclosed the doctors' report.[5] Much later one of the doctors involved in the examination of the body claimed that a first report had stated that the cause of death was not suicide but murder. The day following the examination, he claimed, the governor's aide-de-camp, Antônio Xavier de Resende, informed him the report had been inadvertently destroyed, and advised that another be composed declaring that the prisoner had died by his own hand.[6] The death of Cláudio Manuel da Costa in the house of Rodrigues de Macedo two days before the arrival of the viceroy's judges, the strange chronology of the governor's dispatches, the flight of Pamplona, must occasion suspicion. Especially as the official story evidently carried little weight even at the time. Mass was said for the late poet, a privilege denied suicides, and the account was settled by the royal exchequer.[7]

Cláudio Manuel da Costa was an eminent lawyer, an ex-secretary to the governors of Minas, and well known in Brazil and Portugal. He was, as a contemporary observed after his death 'that great intelligence that we had in Vila Rica who in all matters knew how to find solutions'.[8] The most distinguished and famous of those arrested, he was deeply versed in the affairs of the captaincy and one of its richest and most important men. Doubts have been cast as to the authenticity of his signa-

---

[1] 'Auto de corpo de delicto e exame feito no corpo do doutor Cláudio Manuel da Costa', *ibid.*, 163–4.

[2] José Pedro Machado Coelho Torres to the viceroy, 11 December 1789, *ADIM*, vi, 375.

[3] Certification, Marcelino Pereira Cleto, Rio de Janeiro, 5 January 1790, *ADIM*, vi, 381.

[4] Visconde de Barbacena to Martinho de Melo e Castro, Vila Rica, 11 July 1789, *AMI*, ii, 66.

[5] Visconde de Barbacena to Martinho de Melo e Castro, Vila Rica, 15 July 1789, AHU, Minas Gerais, caixa 94.

[6] For identification of doctor involved and discussion of this issue see José Afonso Mendonça Azevedo, *ABNRJ*, lxv (1943) 176–7. More recently the description of the body at the time of discovery and the doctors' report has been examined by a Paulista coroner who concluded that homicide was the most likely cause of death, see Dr Nilton Sales in Jarbas Sertório de Carvalho, 'O Homicidio do Desembargador [sic] Cláudio Manuel da Costa', *Revista do Instituto Histórico e Geográfico de São Paulo*, li (1951–3), 4, 43–79. Also *ADIM*, ii, 205 ff.

[7] 'Livro de assentos dos irmãos da Irmandade de S. Miguel e Almes, do Arquivo da Matriz de N.S. do Pilar de Ouro Prêto', ['sufragado com 30 missas e pg tudo a fazareal...'] cited by Waldamar de Almeida Barbosa, *A Verdade sobre Tiradentes* (Belo Horizonte, 1965) 32.

[8] Anonymous letter, 30 September 1790 (*sic*) in fact 1789, Rio das Mortes, copy in the collections of the Museu da Inconfidência, Ouro Prêto, Minas Gerais.

ture to the deposition taken on 2 July.[1] It always lay within Manitti's power as scribe of the commission to alter the record of the proceedings. Portions of the testimony, however, especially some ambiguous words relating to the governor, would surely not have been included had the statements been manufactured. There is evidence that Manitti visited Oliveira Lopes in jail before his interrogation and told him that if he did not mention the involvement of either Pamplona or Macedo he would be treated with special consideration.[2] But it seems unlikely that Manitti would have treated the erudite lawyer in the manner he did a rustic, barely literate, ex-Dragoon. There was no need anyway to resort to such a blatant and risky malpractice as forgery. Manitti dominated the framing of the questions and it was not difficult to insure that they probed only as far as he wished them to. Thus it seems reasonable to assume that the record of Cláudio Manuel da Costa's interrogation is a faithful rendering of what he said, and on that basis to assess its implication. For if the aged poet did not commit suicide then he must have been murdered, and if he was murdered a motive is required. And if Cláudio had to be eliminated then presumably the need must have arisen between the time of his arrest and the arrival of the viceroy's commission, most probably, therefore, because of what he had said on 2 July.

Cláudio's answers to the interrogators represented the abject confession of a confused and despondent man.[3] He admitted that 'on several occasions in Gonzaga's house' the uprising was discussed in the presence of Alvarenga Peixoto and Carlos Correia. He also admitted that the matter was discussed in the house of Domingos de Abreu Vieira, and that the *alferes* Silva Xavier and Padre Oliveira Rolim had been present on these occasions. He implicated Freire de Andrade and José Álvares Maciel. The latter he said 'first suggested the case with the remembrance of England'. He claimed that he regarded these discussions as ridiculous and had never approved or aided the plans. He attributed his misfortune to 'powerful enemies' and 'divine justice'. Despite the contradictions, self pleading, apologies, and appeals to heaven, the implication of his words was clear. It was that Gonzaga, Alvarenga Peixoto, Carlos Correia, Freire de Andrade, Álvares Maciel, and Silva Xavier were associates in the

---

[1] For an examination of his signature see *ABNRJ*, LXV (1943) 173–5, where it is asserted to be a forgery. For a different opinion see Mathias, *ACC*, III, 292–4.

[2] 'Perguntas feitas ao...Oliveira Lopes', Rio de Janeiro, 21 November 1789, *ADIM*, IV, 327–8; Manuel Cardozo, 'Another Document on the Inconfidência Mineira', *HAHR*, XXXII (1952) 548.

[3] 'Translado dos Autos de Devassa, 25 Appenso, No. 4. Auto de perguntas feitas ao Bacharel Cláudio Manuel da Costa', Vila Rica, 2 July 1789, AHU, Minas Gerais, Caixa 93.

conspiracy. He had provided the most conclusive evidence to date of the existence of the plot and the relationships between the activists and the ideologues. He had incriminated his closest friend the Desembargador Gonzaga to a degree no other prisoner had done or would do. Cláudio Manuel da Costa was clearly privy to the secrets of the conspiracy. And equally important, the famous poet gave every indication of telling what he knew.

The old lawyer was exceptionally well placed to know all of those involved. What might he say when questioned by men independent of the governor's influence. That the whole truth be told was clearly not to the advantage of the conspirators or the governor, or most especially the owner of the great town house wherein Cláudio was incarcerated. To Gonzaga, Alvarenga Peixoto, Carlos Correia, the confession could not have made the slightest difference, at least between 2 July and 4 July 1789. All were imprisoned several hundred miles away in Rio de Janeiro. The governor, Macedo, Pamplona, were close at hand and their interest in seeing the truth suppressed was every day greater. And only those close to official circles would have had any idea of the contents of the prisoner's statement. All that can be said is that the suicide of Cláudio Manuel da Costa was extremely convenient, and because of the imminent arrival of the viceroy's judges its timing was especially fortuitous to those who had escaped arrest. Whatever the truth of the matter the gracious poet who for so long had dominated the cultural life and the courts of Minas Gerais was the first, perhaps the most tragic, casualty of the aborted conspiracy. The mystery surrounding his demise, and the increasing skulduggery of the proceedings in Vila Rica was representative of the quagmire into which the whole affair had sunk. And if the poet's death was deliberate, premeditated murder, and such a possibility cannot be ruled out, then it was a clear and awful warning to others of the degree to which certain parties would go to protect themselves from incrimination.

What of the governor's involvement in this matter? Surely Cláudio could not have been murdered without the connivance or at least the acquiescence of the governor? In his testimony, moreover, Cláudio said that he remembered Gonzaga told him on one occasion that 'the general . . . the visconde [de Barbacena] always said he would have the first place in the case of an uprising. And that he [Cláudio] said continuing the same witticism that in that case he did well to bring his wife and son.'[1] Did

---

[1] '[S]e bem que em certa occasião ouviu dizer ao doutor Gonzaga, segundo sua lembrança, que o general o Exmo Sr Visconde sempre dizia ter o primeiro lugar no caso de sublevação,

these ambiguous words mean that the governor was himself involved in the plot, or was the exchange between Gonzaga and Cláudio merely a joke as the poet maintained? Certainly Barbacena's behavior at various points does not bear close scrutiny. It was not unusual for conspirators against colonial regimes to harbor the delusion that local governors might be persuaded to join and possibly head an independent state. The mulatto revolutionaries in Salvador ten years later mentioned such a possibility with the governor of Bahia.[1] And Gonzaga and Barbacena knew each other better than either, or most particularly Barbacena, admitted. They had been acquainted in Portugal, and Gonzaga had composed a poem for one of the visconde's children.[2] Moreover, within a day of Gonzaga's arrest the governor had signed a letter confirming that Gonzaga had requested permission to marry.[3] Gonzaga was himself to present the governor's letter to the interrogators in Rio, to provide the excuse for his long residence in Vila Rica beyond the expiration of his official capacities and his appointment to Bahia. But Barbacena's involvement in the plot or indeed his knowledge of it before 15 March seems extremely unlikely. The governor's involvement in the skulduggery in Minas appears to have arisen after, not before, Silvério dos Reis' visit to Cachoeira, and as a result of deals and agreements entered into between 15 March and 20 May, and not from a commitment to revolution before then. How far that involvement went will probably never be known. But at the very least, it is clear that Barbacena's own account of his actions, accounts on which the historical record has been largely constructed, must be open to serious qualification. Certainly by the time the official investigations began into the conspiracy he was no longer a disinterested arbitrator. Whether he went so far as to connive at murder is impossible to determine. But it remains a possibility.

A 300-strong cavalry squadron of the viceregal bodyguard arrived in Vila Rica on 24 June and 200 infantry followed on 3 July. The troops were from the European regiments of Moura and Bragança, which

---

e que elle respondente continuando na mesma graça, disse, que fizera bem trazer mulher e filho em tal caso.' 'Auto de perguntas feitas ao bacharel Cláudio Manuel da Costa', *RIHGB*, LIII, pt. I (1890) 161.

[1] 'Denuncia pública, jurada, e necessaria, que da Joaquim José de Veiga, homen pardo...', Bahia, 27 August 1798, *ADIB*, I, 8.

[2] See M. Rodrigues Lapa in the introduction to *Obras Completas, Tomás António Gonzaga*, I, (Rio de Janeiro, 1957) xiv.

[3] Barbacena's letter was presented by Gonzaga himself to the judges, see Attestation, Barbacena, Cachoeira, 23 May 1789, *ADIM*, IV, 256. Gonzaga had certainly made such requests, both, however, interestingly enough *after* March 1789, they are to be found in AHU, Minas Gerais, caixa 92 (37).

together with that of Estremoz had been sent to Brazil in 1767 by the Marquis of Pombal.[1] On 11 July, confident that the danger was passed, Barbacena reported for the first time to Lisbon. The *derrama* had been the conspirators 'principal aid', Barbacena told Melo e Castro. Its suspension, a measure he claimed to have taken 'without the loss of a single day after the first notice', enabled him to separate the interests of the people from those of the conspirators and to 'use against my enemies, and of the state, the same weapons that they had counted on to attack me'.[2] On 16 July, the viceroy Vasconcelos e Sousa also reported to Melo e Castro. Like Barbacena he advised Lisbon that there was now no need for concern, though he recommended preventive measures be taken to safeguard the future. He informed the secretary of state of the institution of the devassa and the dispatch of the magistrates to Vila Rica. He looked forward to a speedy conclusion to their diligences.[3]

The viceroy's optimism was misplaced, though as yet he held no reason to distrust the protests of good faith and active cooperation promised on repeated occasions by his nephew.[4] But at the very moment he wrote Melo e Castro his magistrates were being prevented from taking any action or even from observing the proceedings of the Minas devassa. Not until 23 July did Barbacena grudgingly order the Minas inquiry to cease. He promised that the original record would be turned over to the viceregal commission once a copy had been taken and witnesses already called were interviewed.[5] It had been necessary for Desembargador Torres to insist that he be permitted to proceed as instructed by Vasconcelos e Sousa.[6] Ouvidor Cleto sat in on the inter-

---

[1] Anon. letter Rio das Mortes, 30 September [1789] Museu da Inconfidência, Ouro Prêto, Minas Gerais; Alden, *Royal Government*, 111–12; The Governor of São Paulo had rapidly investigated the situation in Taubaté on receiving warning from Barbacena and placed two regiments of infantry and a squadron of cavalry at the disposal of Barbacena should he require them. Bernardo José de Lorena to Barbacena, São Paulo, 11 July 1789, *DISP*, xlv (1924) 223–5.

[2] Visconde de Barbacena to Martinho de Melo e Castro, Vila Rica, 1789, 11 July [incorrectly stated here to be June] *AMI*, ii, 63–73.

[3] Luís de Vasconcelos e Sousa to Martinho de Melo e Castro, Rio, 16 July 1789, AHU, Minas Gerais, caixa 92; also in IHGB, lata 97, doc. 6.

[4] When the viceroy ordered the Rio magistrates to Minas he had not been aware of the devassa opened by Barbacena, and all the correspondence up to that date from the governor had contained pleas that they should work in accord and reiterated his intention of not establishing a devassa in deference to the viceroy's decision, Luís de Vasconcelos e Sousa to M. de Melo e Castro, Rio, 8 January 1790, AHU, Minas Gerais, caixa 92, also see *ADIM*, vi, 191–6.

[5] Visconde de Barbacena to Coelho Torres, Vila Rica, 23 July 1789, *ADIM*, vi, 388–90.

[6] Desembargador Coelho Torres to Visconde de Barbacena, Vila Rica, 18 July 1789, *ADIM*, vi, 388.

rogations of Luís Vaz, Luís Vieira, and Oliveira Lopes by Saldanha and Manitti on 23 July. Five days later the Rio magistrates began to take their own depositions from witnesses.[1] The diligences were now conducted with legal propriety but Torres and Cleto were in effect conducting a parallel inquiry, duplicating the activity of the Minas magistrates. The record was not turned over to the desembargador as promised.

The viceregal commission completed taking statements from witnesses by mid-September. Torres had Álvares Maciel and Freire de Andrade arrested and ordered that the prisoners in Vila Rica be sent at once to Rio de Janeiro. The magistrates then left to return to the coast by way of São João d'El Rei. Here, despite the governor's statements to the contrary, Torres found that Inácio Pamplona was not on a governatorial mission in the Canastra Mountains at all but resident at his fazenda. Moreover, he discovered that Pamplona had left Vila Rica precipitately one day before his own arrival there. The desembargador ordered Pamplona, whom he considered one of the principal witnesses, to appear before him. Pamplona refused, claiming that his orders from Barbacena prevented him from attending.[2]

The removal of Oliveira Lopes, Abreu Vieira, Álvares Maciel, Freire de Andrade and Luís Vaz to Rio de Janeiro was the very thing Barbacena had sought to avoid, and it upset those who had been promised preferential treatment. Barbacena did not make his promises in bad faith. He suggested in his letter of 11 July to Melo e Castro that Domingos de Abreu Vieira and Oliveira Lopes be treated with 'mercy'.[3] Circumstances, however, had seriously curtailed Barbacena's powers. Oliveira Lopes complained bitterly on being taken from his cell that 'all his confession had been made at the insinuation of Manitti'. Abreu Vieira claimed that the magistrate 'in order to make the governor's party and his own employed all the cunning and malpractice at his command'.[4] These statements became widely known in Vila Rica. The governor, anxious to avoid the damaging consequences, sent instructions after the retiring

[1] 'Continuação de perguntas feitas a...Luís Vaz', Vila Rica, 23 July 1789, *ADIM*, II, 109. 'Continuação de perguntas feitas a...Luís Vieira', Vila Rica, 23 July 1789, *ADIM*, II, 125; 'Continuação de perguntas feitas a...Oliveira Lopes', Vila Rica, 23 July 1789, *ADIM*, II, 60.
[2] 'Certidão', Marcelino Pereira Cleto, Rio de Janeiro, 5 January 1790, *ADIM*, VI, 381-4. Also see Mathias, *CCANRJ*, 58.
[3] '[Q]ue pela franqueza e sugeição com que se houverão e pela importancia dos factos que comunicarão confiados na grande bondade de S. Mag^de poderão obter em comparação dos mais Reos alguma piedade...', Visconde de Barbacena to M. de Melo e Castro, Vila Rica, 11 July 1789, *AMI*, II, 65.
[4] Manuel Cardozo, 'Another document on the Inconfidência Mineira', *HAHR*, XXXII (1952) 548.

viceregal magistrates to remove the depositions of Oliveira Lopes, Abreu Vieira, and Luís Vaz from the record.[1]

Oliveira Lopes was not so easily silenced. Once in Rio he repeated his statements before Torres and Cleto. During his first interrogation at the fortress on Snake Island he told the viceroy's inquisitors that Carlos Correia told him that Inácio Correia Pamplona and João Rodrigues de Macedo had entered the sedition. He did not mention them before, he said, because Pamplona 'did not wish to appear to be publicly involved in the matter on account of his compadre Carlos José da Silva [the secretary of the junta da fazenda] to whom he owed great obligations'. Macedo had entered the conspiracy 'in order to free himself of his debts to the treasury'. He had not said this before because Manitti came to him privately in prison at Vila Rica and told him that if he did not mention the name of the contractor, 'because of his great friendship with [Oliveira Lopes] he [Macedo] would take him under his protection and save his bacon (*o havia da por a salvo*)'.[2]

The viceroy's devassa still lacked the record of the proceedings in Minas. Yet as a result of the depositions taken in Vila Rica, and the interrogations conducted on returning to Rio, Torres possessed by the end of the year a fairly comprehensive picture of the conspiracy. The response of the prisoners to the pressure brought to bear on them varied. Some denied all knowledge or attempted to diminish the importance of the episode, following the precedent set by the alferes Silva Xavier during May. Freire de Andrade and Alvarenga Peixoto both sought to minimize the importance of what had been said.[3] Luís Vaz and Dr Álvares Maciel made abject confessions.[4] Gonzaga and the canon Luís Vieira took the offensive against the inquisitors.[5] Both were aware of their legal rights and the insubstantial nature of the evidence against them. They also knew of the inherent weakness of the crown's position as a result of the

[1] Visconde de Barbacena to José Pedro Machado Coelho Torres Vila Rica, 23 September 1789, and Visconde de Barbacena to Luís de Vasconcelos e Sousa, Vila Rica, 23 September 1789, AHU, Minas Gerais, caixa 94.

[2] 'Auto de perguntas feitas ao Coronel Francisco António de Oliveira Lopes', Rio de Janeiro, 21 November 1789, *ADIM*, IV, 327–8.

[3] 'Auto de perguntas feitas a Francisco de Paula Freire de Andrade...', Rio de Janeiro, 16 November 1789, *ADIM*, IV, 205–14; 'Auto de perguntas feitas ao Coronel Ignácio José de Alvarenga', Rio de Janeiro, 11 November 1789, *ADIM*, IV, 127–33.

[4] 'Auto de perguntas feitas ao Sargento-Mor Luís Vaz de Toledo', Rio de Janeiro, 25 November 1789; 'Auto de perguntas feitas a José Alvares Maciel', Rio de Janeiro, 26 November 1789, *ADIM*, IV, 395–401.

[5] 'Auto de perguntas feitas ao Cônego Luís Vieira', Rio de Janeiro, 20 November 1789, *ADIM*, IV, 290–8; 'Auto de perguntas feitas ao Desembargador Tomás António Gonzaga'. Rio de Janeiro, 17 November 1789, *ADIM*, IV, 247–55.

shilly shallying of Barbacena and his agents. Gonzaga denied all knowledge of the conspiracy, casting aspersions on the validity of the denunciations, especially that of Bazílio de Brito, 'a man of very bad character, his enemy...because of his arrest...and an ally of Sargent-Mor José de Vasconcelos Parada [also] his great enemy...' Moreover, there were 'clear indications', he said, to demonstrate 'why he could not have been involved'. He pointed to his Portuguese birth, his father's position, his appointment as a desembargador in Bahia, his proposed marriage, his attempts to persuade Bandeira not to impose the *derrama*.[1] Canon Luís Vieira also cast doubts on the motives behind his imprisonment. He denied knowledge of the affair beyond vague notices he heard of statements by 'an alferes, nicknamed the Tiradentes, whose proper name he did not know....'[2] Others first denied knowledge but subsequently broke under second interrogations. Carlos Correia 'again pressed by many and various methods to confess the truth' recognized 'that his guilt was entirely proved', and he forthwith confessed.[3] His statement corroborated in most details that of Álvares Maciel, though he denied the presence of Gonzaga in the conspiracy, claiming he had used his name in order to persuade others to join.

During early December Torres presented to the viceroy a private summary of the state of the investigation.[4] He was in 'no doubt whatsoever' that the plot existed and was equally certain that had it been put into effect or even begun it would have caused 'irreparable damage'. The *alferes* Silva Xavier had spread 'the seditious proposition that the mines could be independent, free, of Royal subjection, and a Republic, because they possessed all the riches, and natural resources (*producções*) and that all America could be free...' The Desembargador Gonzaga, Colonel Alvarenga, Canon Luís Vieira,. and Cláudio Manuel da Costa were 'presumed to be accomplices' and 'the directors of the fundamental social and political principles of the government (*Sistema*) and the legislation'. But the proof against them was unclear. Lieutenant-Colonel Freire de Andrade had been procured so that the troops would not be opposed to the objectives of the sedition. Secret meetings took place at his house

---

[1] *Ibid.*, 249–55. This latter point was an equivocation to say the least, see p. 125.

[2] 'Perguntas feitas ao Cônego Luís Vieira', Rio de Janeiro, 20 November 1789, *ADIM*, IV, 291.

[3] 'Continuação de perguntas feitas ao Vigário...Carlos Corrêa', Rio de Janeiro, 27 November 1789, *ADIM*, IV, 168.

[4] Desembargador José Pedro Machado Coelho Torres to Luís de Vasconcelos e Sousa, Rio de Janeiro, 11 December 1789, AHU, Minas Gerais, caixa 92 (47) published in *ADIM*, VI, 371–80.

where Álvares Maciel, Carlos Correia de Toledo, Captain Maximiliano de Oliveira Leite, Colonel Alvarenga and the *alferes* had been present. Meetings had also taken place in the house of Domingos de Abreu Vieira with Padre Oliveira Rolim, Freire Andrade and the *alferes*.

Torres appended a list of the prisoners and the state of the case against each of them.[1] As to the *alferes* there existed a great number of witnesses to his seditious statements, other witnesses had been invited by him to join the uprising, and some of those who had joined in the conventicles confessed he was the most fanatical participant. He was the first prisoner to be arrested and incarcerated in Rio. He had been found with a loaded blunderbus. But he had not confessed. As to Gonzaga, Torres observed, various witnesses asserted he had entered the conspiracy, but all referred to Carlos Correia who claimed he used Gonzaga's name to persuade the others, and that in reality he did not know whether the former *ouvidor* had entered or not. Unfortunately Torres observed, 'Dr Cláudio Manuel da Costa who had been arrested in Minas and was beginning to say something under questioning hanged himself in the prison there a few days before my arrival.' His statements, moveover, had been made without the presence of a notary or witnesses as was required if they were to be valid in law.

Desembargador Torres also drew the viceroy's attention to a list of names of men he regarded as 'important to mention'. They included João Rodrigues de Macedo. He 'could not fail to presume that he [Macedo] knew [for and perhaps patronized the project... [for] he owed great sums to the royal exchequer... [and] although he knew Alvarenga to be a great spender and swindler (*caloteiro*) was assisting him with money that already passed 40,000 *cruzados*'. Vicente Vieira 'knew something', as did Colonel Aires Gomes, and many others especially among the officers of the regiment who were related one to another or linked by marriage. 'Judicially there was no proof, because they had taken the precaution not to say anything, so as not to incriminate themselves.' The real difficulty of the matter, Torres told the viceroy, was that the conspiracy was treated only in 'words'. Those who entered it were aware that as 'events' had not occurred, their best defense was denial. All had time to take precautions, he observed. Yet many had confessed despite this. He had not proceeded with full rigor against all those implicated for he believed that 'the greater part of the inhabitants of Minas knew in a confused way

---

[1] 'Lista das pessoas que se acham presas em consequencia das noticias de que se premeditava uma conjuração, e em consequencia das diligencias judiciaes a este respeito; dando uma idea das presumpções ou prova, que resulta contra cada uma dellas...', *ADIM*, vi, 392–403.

that because of the derrama an uprising was considered, though this could not be proved judicially'. He though it advisable that precautions be taken for the future and that the number and importance of those involved be minimized.

In the meantime Vasconcelos e Sousa changed his mind over the arrest of Silvério dos Reis. The defector was consequently released. The viceroy was concerned that potential defectors might be discouraged if Silvério was seen to receive bad treatment.[1] Confident of his case Torres again interrogated those prisoners who had held out during November. Alvarenga Peixoto was the first to break under the renewed questioning. The weight of the evidence against him was overwhelming and he made a detailed, confused, and often contradictory confession on 14 January 1790.[2] Four days later the *alferes* was brought before the commission. As Torres had told the viceroy the case against the Silva Xavier was especially strong. In view of the confessions of the other conspirators further denial was pointless. But the *alferes* took a surprising course. He not only confessed to participation and propagandizing the movement, both of which was amply proved, but claimed that he and he alone had originated and conceived the entire scheme. He had done so out of desperation, he said, having been 'four times overlooked in promotion'.[3]

Silva Xavier's statement altered the whole aspect of the investigation. Whatever his motives it served to place Gonzaga in a much stronger position. Especially as the *alferes* specifically denied any knowledge of participation in the plot by the former *ouvidor*. When Gonzaga was himself interrogated on 3 February 1790 the devassa again took on the aspect of a debate. He demanded that the judge produce concrete evidence for his assertions. The insinuations against him were 'vague rumors' he claimed. He had not the spirit of a rebel and had always been a 'loyal and zealous vassal'. He again drew attention to his actions over the *derrama*. He encouraged Bandeira to impose the tax for the recovery of the total debt because as this was an impossible demand it was the surest means to obtain the total abandonment of the debt to the benefit of people and the state.[4]

---

[1] For release of Silvério and reasons for this action, Luís de Vasconcelos e Sousa to M. de Melo e Castro, Rio de Janeiro, 8 January 1790, AHU, Minas Gerais, caixa 92, also in *ADIM*, VI, 191–6.

[2] 'Continuação de perguntas feitas ao Coronel Ignácio José de Alvarenga', Rio de Janeiro, 14 January 1790, *ADIM*, IV, 134–55.

[3] 'Continuação de perguntas feitas ao Alferes Joaquim José da Silva Xavier', Rio de Janeiro, 18 January 1790, *ADIM*, IV, 44.

[4] 'Continuação de perguntas feitas ao Desembargador Tomás António Gonzaga', Rio de Janeiro, 3 February 1790, *ADIM*, IV, 256.

Conflicts and conspiracies

The devassa established by Vasconcelos e Sousa did not complete its proceedings. During February Barbacena instructed Colonel Rebêlo to take a copy of the Minas devassa to Lisbon.[1] Torres and Cleto were obliged to conclude their proceedings without seeing the original records of the proceedings in Vila Rica and to forward the uncompleted Rio devassa to the metropolis also.[2] The Minas magistrates had, in fact, resumed their investigation as soon as the viceregal commission left Vila Rica. Ostensibly the arrest of Padre Oliveira Rolim in the Sêrro do Frio provided the justification.[3] Effectively this prevented the dispatch of the record to Rio as promised, though Barbacena appears anyway to have decided against honoring his commitment of 23 July. The Minas governor's dispatch which accompanied the copy of the devassa to Lisbon was decidedly defensive in tone, and roundly chastised the viceroy's magistrates. He 'neither asked for nor required them', he complained to Melo e Castro. They had been offered every consideration and help, he claimed, but Torres and Cleto had busied themselves with insignificant matters and made no substantial discovery.[4] The governor also forwarded a resumé of the Minas devassa by Manitti and a list of those who had aided him in combating the conspiracy.[5] Among those for whom the governor solicited special favors was Francisco Antônio Rebêlo, Antônio José Dias Coelho, Manitti and Carlos José da Silva (both of whom had worked on the copies of the devassa), Araújo Saldanha, Bazílio de Brito Malheiro, José Sousa Lobo, and Vasconcelos Parada e Sousa.[6] With the exception of Rebêlo and perhaps Saldanha, it was a motley crowd, this roll call of dubious characters, the 'loyalists' of Minas Gerais.

When the content of his nephew's dispatches became known to the retiring viceroy he was understandably outraged. He wrote to the

[1] Rebêlo left Vila Rica for Lisbon 24 February 1790, arriving there 23 June. Francisco Antônio Rebêlo to D. Rodrigo de Sousa Coutinho, Vila Rica, 3 March 1789, AHU, Minas Gerais, caixa 94; a copy was also sent by second route via Bahia: Visconde de Barbacena to Martinho de Melo e Castro, Vila Rica, 20 February 1790. The governor had, in addition, written a sycophantic personal letter to the secretary of state: Visconde de Barbacena to Martinho de Melo e Castro, Vila Rica, 14 February 1790, *AMI*, II, 92.

[2] Because of the viceroy's grave illness the devassa was forwarded by his aide: Camillo Tonneles, Rio de Janeiro, 24 Feb. 1790, AHU, Minas Gerais, caixa 94.

[3] Visconde de Barbacena to Senhor Capitão Antônio José Dias Coelho, Vila Rica, 11 October 1789, *AMI*, II, 79.

[4] Visconde de Barbacena to Martinho de Melo e Castro, Vila Rica, 10 February 1790, *AMI*, II, 80–2.

[5] José Caetano César Manitti to Visconde de Barbacena, Vila Rica, 12 February 1790, *AMI*, II, 87–91.

[6] Visconde de Barbacena to M. de Melo e Castro, Vila Rica, 11 February 1790, *AMI*, II, 82–3 and 'relação incluza', *ibid.* 83–7.

governor protesting in the strongest terms his misrepresentations. He did not order the inquiry 'to extend his jurisdiction or because of his position as head of the state of Brazil' he said, 'but only in the certainty that they would both treat [the conspiracy] with common policy'. The devassa in Rio was necessary, he pointed out, because the principal defendents had been sent to Rio without previous interrogation and were imprisoned in the city's fortresses. Moreover, the aspersions against the magistrates were clearly untrue. He cited Barbacena's own dispatches to prove his point. He rejected the imputation against Coelho Torres, 'a man both disinterested and of honor'. He could hardly be accused of favoritism in his assessment of the desembargador, he told his nephew, for 'I have all and every personal reason to esteem you'.[1] The viceroy included a copy of his letter for Melo e Castro's information in a later dispatch where he criticised the 'lack of formalities...lack of observation of the law...and other negligence of good order in the proceedings [in Vila Rica]...'[2] But the issue was out of his hands. The initiative now rested in Lisbon.

Almost a full year had elapsed since the conspiracy was disrupted and weakened, and over six months since Melo e Castro had been informed of the proposed uprising. For the moment any threat to Portuguese dominion seemed thwarted. The conspirators, or some of them, had been arrested and imprisoned, and their property confiscated. Vila Rica and Minas Gerais were garrisoned by European troops. The failure of the plot had been almost accidental. It is perhaps worth recapitulating briefly the steps by which this state of affairs came about.

The *derrama* which the Minas conspirators saw as an ideal cover for their revolt had not materialized. But although the suspension was a relief to the mass of the population it had not been accompanied by a coincident suspension of the proceedings against the opulent contractors for the recovery of arrears due to the Royal Treasury. The basic motivation for the involvement of the contractors in the plot had been the avoidance of their staggering debts. In the new situation Silvério dos Reis, who early in March had been called to account by the *junta da fazenda*, saw another way out of his dilemma. He visited the governor at Cachoeira do Campo and gave him a detailed account of the plot. In return for his denunciation he expected to receive favorable treatment.

Even though the conspiracy in its original form had already been abandoned, a rump of activists remained. Barbacena feared that should

[1] Vasconcelos e Sousa to Visconde de Barbacena, 2 April 1790, *ADIM*, VI, 200–6.
[2] Vasconcelos e Sousa to M. de Melo e Castro, Rio de Janeiro, 8 May 1790, *ADIM*, VI, 198–200.

he immediately arrest those implicated he might well precipitate the revolt. Aware of the degree to which the officer corps of the Dragoons, the only military forces at his command, were embroiled in the plotting he resolved to dissimulate, build himself support within Minas, and await military aid from the viceroy in Rio de Janeiro. The governor was able to use the factionalism of the previous years to bring to his side those cronies of Cunha Meneses, Bazílio de Brito Malheiro, Sousa Lobo, Vasconcelos Parada e Sousa, who had been involved in the bitter patronage disputes with the magistrates. The ample documentation of their wrong-doings gave him special leverage over them. Flattering the avarice of the Brazilian military officers implicated in the plot, Oliveira Leite and Brandão, he bought their neutrality. To these men he added the wealthy crown debtors who had momentarily seen salvation in revolution, João Rodrigues de Macedo, Vicente Vieira da Mota, Luís Alves, perhaps Aires Gomes and Álvares Maciel, and he induced them to see a more secure future in collaboration.

He hoped that the leaders of the movement might be removed 'without great display from Minas and Brazil' either 'attributing the cause to some crime or saying nothing at all on the question'. Assuming that his uncle would act as he had suggested he made promises and entered into commitments the fulfillment of which depended on his retaining control of the situation. Winning the contractors to his side he appears to have entered into personal financial agreements. At least the bond with João Rodrigues de Macedo was strong enough to guarantee that he remained immune from prosecution, even after the viceregal cavalry and European infantry were at the governor's command and his temporary need to compromise had passed.

But Barbacena miscalculated both the speed with which events would move once Silvério dos Reis had arrived in Rio de Janeiro as well as the viceroy's reaction to the denunciation. He had consistently recommended that the matter be dealt with by mutual accord. But the prisoners had been expropriated and they were involved in treasonable activities. The arbitrary justice advised by the governor of Minas was unacceptable to the desembargador-viceroy, and he at once opened an official secret inquiry to probe the claims of his nephew and Silvério dos Reis. But almost immediately the prime suspect in the city disappeared. Vasconcelos e Sousa's subsequent arrest of Silva Xavier and of Silvério dos Reis precipitated events in Minas.

Without the forces from the coast yet at hand Barbacena could not risk holding the most active and energetic leaders of the revolutionary movement in the captaincy. He was forced to send them under guard at great speed to Rio de Janeiro. The responsibility for the conduct of the matter was, therefore, as a result irrevocably taken from him. The coincident news that the viceroy's judges were to be sent to Vila Rica forced him onto the defensive. Not only would an impartial investigation threaten to reveal the inaccuracy of his own statements in private letters to the viceroy and Lisbon, but threaten to expose the compromising agreements he appears to have made with Macedo, Pamplona and possibly others. Although Barbacena was not able to protect Oliveira Lopes and Abreu Veira, or Freire de Andrade and Álvares Maciel, once the viceroy's magistrates were in Vila Rica, João Rodrigues de Macedo was never called as a witness by either devassa, let alone interrogated.[1] This was despite the fact that meetings had taken place in his home, important participants had been invited to join the conspiracy there, and that he was at least as close to Gonzaga, Luís Vieira, Carlos Correia, and Alvarenga Peixoto as they were to one another. And others, such as Aires Gomes, Luís Alves, Vicente Vieira, Pamplona, also implicated in the testimony remained free men. Both Macedo and Pamplona, moreover, profited greatly by the supplying of services and victuals to the troops of the regiments of Moura and Bragança sent from the coast. And they were paid, Pamplona in particular, with remarkable rapidity.[2]

The viceroy's commission was not unaware of what was going on. Desembargador Torres' private report to Vasconcelos e Sousa pointed out the strong evidence against those under the governor's protection. But there was very little that could be done about it. The case anyway was difficult to prove for the conspiracy had got no further than 'words', no 'events' had occurred. Moreover, Silva Xavier had now taken the

---

[1] This point was bitterly made by Colonel Aires Gomes several years later: '...por isso q' justiça permetia que o d[it]o Macedo não fosse perguntado, nem acarcado; quando não era de presumir, que elle houvesse de deixar a sua casa a descrição de huns hospedes, que naquelle Paiz erão para ser contemplados...', Helio Vianna, 'Acrésimo aos autos de devassa da Inconfidência Mineira', Biblioteca da Ajuda, 51-VI-49, doc., 19, in *AMI*, IV (1955-7) 249.

[2] 'André Dias Sobrinho Carvalhães, Capitão Commandante da Companhia do Regimento de Infantaria de Bragança...de presente destacado nesta Capitania de Minnas Geraes... Re do Sr Me de Campo Ignácio Correya Pamplona por mão do seu caixeiro João Martins Pinto...farinha de Milho para monicio das praças abaixo mencionadas do mez de novembro proximo paçada..., 1 December 1790', CCBNRJ, I-1-15; 'João de Sousa Benevides, examinando o Documento junto do supplicante, Mestre de Campo, Ignácio Corrêa Pamplona...contadoria feita em Julho, 1789 por, 40$875 reis...24 May 1791, 171$474 *reis* 24 May 1791, 12$712 *reis*...24 May 1791, 46$472 *reis*, 31 May 1791, 275$718 *reis*... 30 September, 1789...', CCBNRJ, I-1-15; Also 'processo de cobrança...', Vila Rica, 28 August 1789, Mathias, *CCANRJ*, 54; Also see interesting list of extraordinary expenses, doc., 135, *ABNRJ*, LXV (1943) 288-90.

surprising course of claiming sole responsibility for the whole affair. As a result of the skulduggery in Vila Rica, the now acrimonious relationship between the governor and viceroy, Barbacena's misrepresentations, and the claims of the *alferes* Silva Xavier, the records on the way to the secretary of state in Lisbon only partially represented the true chronology of events and the true facts of the conspiracy.

CHAPTER 7

CRISIS

The prisoners of the Minas conspiracy were treated as rebels because they did not achieve their objective, but had they succeeded they would have been heroes.

> Interrogation of José Bernardo da Silveira Frade, Rio de Janeiro, 18 December 1794, 'Devassa ordenada pelo Viceroy, conde de Rezende', *ABNRJ*, LXI (1939) 262.

So heavy a branch cannot long remain upon so rotten a trunk...

> Robert Southey to John Rickman, Lisbon, October 1800, Robert Southey, *Journal of a Residence in Portugal 1800–1801* (editor, Rodolfo Cabral, Oxford, 1960) 137–9.

The records of the judicial proceedings with their detailed if confusing accounts of the events in Minas Gerais arrived in Lisbon during late June 1790.[1] They came under the immediate scrutiny of a newly constituted administration.[2] The post-Pombaline government had been gravely depleted by death and resignation. The Marquis of Angeja, ill and inactive in the government since 1786, died during 1788. Aires de Sá e Melo resigned in 1786. The Visconde de Vila Nova de Cerveira had been acting at the Royal Treasury for Angeja since 1783 in addition to holding his own portfolio. Melo e Castro substituted for Aires de Sá as foreign secretary also holding this position in addition to his own. After the death of Angeja, Vila Nova was made president of the Royal Treasury, and over the strong opposition of Melo e Castro, his old rival, José de Seabra e Silva became secretary of state for Home affairs (*Reino*) and Luís Pinto de Sousa Coutinho the foreign secretary (*Negócios Estrangeiros e Guerra*).[3]

[1] [E sahindo] desta capital [Vila Rica] em 24 de Fevereiro de 1790 me aprezentei nessa corte [Lisbon] em direitura ao Exmo Ministro de Estado desta repartição o Sr. Martinho de Mello e Castro...' Francisco Antônio Rebêlo to D. Rodrigo de Sousa Coutinho, Vila Rica, 3 March 1798, AHU, Minas Gerais, caixa 94.

[2] 'Ao IImo e Exmo Snr Visconde de Villa Nova de Cerveira que seu Amigo e fiel cativo Martinho de Mello e Castro remete ao S. Exa a Devaça tirada em Minas Gerais, e mais papeis que acompanhão para que lendo-a S. Exa aqueira depois mandar passar ao Sr. José de Seabra e ao Sr. Luíz Pinto; E que para servir a S. Exa fica sempre pronto, Ajuda, 28 June 1790, Martinho de Mello e Castro', AHU, Minas Gerais, caixa, 94.

[3] On Melo e Castro's threat to resign see Robert Walpole to Marquis of Carmarthen, Lisbon, 3 January 1789, PRO, FO, 63/12; For the changes in the administration, Caetano Beirão, *D. Maria I, 1777–1792* (3rd edition, Lisbon, 1944) 88, 341, 342; and Simão José da Luz Soriano, *História da Guerra Civil*...(Lisbon, 1866) I, 349–50.

The appointment of Seabra e Silva, a former protégé of Pombal who had fallen into disfavor and been banished from Portugal, was nontheless regarded by those close to Pombaline circles as 'a triumph for the memory of the late Marquis'.[1] Luís Pinto, also close to Pombal, had distinguished himself as governor of Mato Grosso, and conducted important diplomatic negotiations in London.[2] He established close relations with enlightened thinkers while in the British capital and provided William Robertson with information on South America for his famous history.[3] Both Luís Pinto and Seabra differed fundamentally in attitude from the obdurate and powerfully entrenched colonial secretary.

Luís Pinto in particular had first-hand knowledge of Brazilian conditions. Once back in Lisbon he made contact with Brazilian intellectuals, many of them students of Domingos Vandelli, one of the Italian Scholars brought into Portugal by the Marquis of Pombal as part of his educational reform program. Vandelli was especially inquisitive about Brazil's potentiality and natural resources and retained a correspondence with his students after their return to America.[4] On 31 May 1790, Luís Pinto sent two young Brazilians and a Portuguese colleague on a grand European tour of instruction at the expense of the Portuguese government. The three men, Manuel Ferreira da Câmara, a Mineiro, José Bonifácio de Andrada e Silva, a Paulista, and Joaquim Pedro Fragoso de Sequeira, were instructed to proceed to Paris where they were to take courses in physics and mineralogy. Then proceeding to Freiburg, they were to spend at least two years gaining 'all practical knowledge' of mining technology. Afterwards they were to visit the mines of Saxony, Bohemia, Hungary, and to return to Portugal via Scandinavia and Great Britain.[5]

Manuel Ferreira da Câmara, the leader of the expedition, had close links with those caught up in the events in Minas Gerais. His elder brother, José de Sá Betencourt, who graduated from Coimbra in 1787, on his

---

[1] '[Comment on] Nomeação de Seabra e Silva', 20 December 1788, BNLCP, códice 706, f. 106. Pombal had died on 5 May 1782.

[2] Soriano, *Guerra Civil*, I, 355–6.

[3] '[F]rom other quarters I have received information of great utility and importance. M. le Chevalier de Pinto the minister from Portugal to the Court of Great Britain, who commanded for several years at Matagtosso (*sic*) a settlement of the Portuguese in the interior part of Brazil...and I have often followed him as one of my best instructed guides to the natives of America.' William Robertson, *The History of America* (12th edition, 4 vols., London, 1812) I, xiv.

[4] For example José da Silva Lisboa to Domingos Vandelli, Bahia, 18 October 1781, *ABNRJ*, XXXII (1910) 494–506; For Vandelli's interest in Brazil and specifically in the problems of Mining, see his scholarly papers on gold and diamond mining in *ABNRJ*, XX (1898) 266–82.

[5] 'Instrução', Ajuda, 31 May 1790, Luís Pinto de Sousa Coutinho, Carneiro de Mendonça, *O Intendente Câmara*, 26–7.

return to Brazil had set up a laboratory at Caeté and forged some iron which he sent to colleagues in Europe. José de Sá was implicated on several occasions in the devassas. It was claimed by some that he had participated in the December meeting at the house of Freire de Andrade. He fled from Minas at the time of the arrests by way of the backlands to Bahia, where his wealthy and influential relatives possessed the great sugar mill of Ponte. His uncle had been a member of the high court of Bahia.[1] At the time that Manuel Ferreira received his instruction from Luís Pinto for the study tour of Europe, Melo e Castro had known for almost three months of his brother's suspected involvement in the conspiracy.[2]

Melo e Castro's view that 'abuses' and 'malpractices' were the cause of declining gold quotas moreover, had been publicly challenged by scientific papers read before the prestigious Academy of Sciences in Lisbon. In 1790, D. Rodrigo de Sousa Coutinho, Pombal's godson, published his 'Discourse on the true influence of mines of precious metals on the industry of the nations that possess them, and especially the Portuguese.' D. Rodrigo was related by marriage to Mathias Barbosa, one of the famous Minas pioneers, and as a result possessed *fazendas* and properties in the captaincy. In his discourse he took issue with the view that the mines were responsible for the nation's decadence, attributing the stagnation of Portugal instead to the effects of the Methuen treaty.[3] Implicitly he was preparing the way for Manuel Ferreira da Câmara's paper of 'Physical and economic observations about the extraction of gold in Brazil', where the young Brazilian made an eloquent plea for improved methods and techniques. Ferreira da Câmara recommended that Portugal's land and mining grant policies be brought into line with those of the rest of Europe. He held that the alientation of subsoil rights to individuals in return for a percentage of gold extracted was inappropriate in present circumstances. Without 'making a total revolution in the proprietory rights of the miners' it was nonetheless essential, he claimed,

---

[1] *Ibid.*, 9–10.
[2] Annotations by Melo e Castro on his copy of Barbacena's letter of 11 July 1789. He noted that José de Sá and José Álvares Maciel were both associates of the Academy of Sciences of Lisbon, AHU, Minas Gerais, caixa 94.
[3] D. Rodrigo de Sousa Coutinho, 'Memória sôbre a verdadeira influência das Minas dos Metaes preciosos na industria das nações que as possuem e especialmente da portuguêsa', *Memórias Economicas da Academia* I (1789) cited by Amzalak, *Evolução das doutrinas económicas*, 106–7, 114–18; also cited by Carneiro de Mendonça, *O Intendente Câmara*, 18–20; 'Certidão do baptismo de Dom Rodrigo de Sousa Coutinho' (1755), Marquês do Funchal, *O Conde de Linhares* (Lisbon, 1908) 186; For information on D. Rodrigo's Minas Connection, Costa Filho, *Cana de açúcar*, 92, 97, and Mawe, *Travels*, 181–2.

that some method be devised 'to reconcile the interests of the state with those of the proprietors'. He recommended that mining companies be promoted and encouraged by royal privileges. The companies should not be monopolistic, but organizations which could mobilize capital for rational exploitation. In order to provide skilled technicians and mining engineers he suggested that mining colleges be set up.[1] Both D. Rodrigo and Manuel Ferreira da Câmara were lavish in praise for the policies of Dom José I. To eulogize Dom José was tantamount to praising Pombal. The association of the Pombal ethos with the reform elements in the government, and especially the form in which it was articulated by a young Brazilian scholar who enjoyed the protection of the foreign secretary was significant. The ideas put forward by D. Rodrigo and Ferreira da Câmara in parts contradicted those held by Pombal himself, but this was less important than the fact that together they formed a thinly disguised critique of the anti-Pombaline post-1777 government, its policies, and especially its approach to the problem of Minas Gerais.

The reappearance of Pombaline influence and the presence of new ministers in the government made the arrival of the news from Brazil embarrassing for Melo e Castro. From the beginning his response was defensive. The eighty-year-old secretary of state acknowledged receipt of Barbacena's first account of the conspiracy on March 9 1790, almost a full eight months after its dispatch from Vila Rica. His first reaction was to draw an immediate connection between the proposed uprising and the proceedings instituted against the debtors of the treasury. On second thought, drawing his pen across the minute, he instead wrote a letter to the governor in more general terms, claiming that he had not had sufficient time to form an opinion.[2] Melo e Castro appears to have suspected that any close investigation of the events in Brazil would show that the conspiracy was precipitated by his policy directives of early 1788. In the delicate balance of the new administration it was not a connection he was anxious should be made, especially in light of the earlier criticism

[1] 'Memória de observações Fisico-Econômicas acêrca da extração do ouro do Brazil, por Manuel Ferreira da Câmara', Carneiro de Mendonça, *O Intendente Câmara*, 499–523.

[2] Martinho de Melo e Castro to Visconde de Barbacena, 9 March 1790. A much corrected minute of this dispatch in Melo e Castro's hand survives at the AHU. It is possible to discern under his cancelling pen strokes the original draft which read: 'He certo que a chegada de V.S. a essa Capitania não podia deixar de inquietar muito aquelles q se achavão comprien-didos nos diferentes [section obliterated] com que a Real [obliterated]... outra praticando os descaminhos e roubos. Tamben he certo que estes decapiladores da fazenda Real havião buscar os meyos para se salvar de eminente perigo que os amiaçava... 'He instead wrote 'Naõ cabendo no tempo tratar deste importante negocio com o reflexão que a gravidade delle exige...' AHU, Minas Gerais, caixa, 92.

of his strictures at court. Moreover, the need for the cooperation of Luís Pinto was acute. The *devassas* demonstrated that individual conspirators and their associates had made contact with one agent of the United States, perhaps with France, and also with merchants in Great Britain.

In fact the arrival of the news of the Minas conspiracy coincided with a critical phase in Anglo-Portuguese commercial relations. Between 1785 and 1790 the balance of trade between Portugal and Great Britain was brought almost into equilibrium. From 1791 to 1795, for the first time during the whole of the eighteenth century, Portuguese exports to Britain showed a surplus (£130,000) over British exports to Portugal (statistical appendix I, graph D). From 1783, and especially from 1788, there was rapid growth of Brazilian raw cotton re-exports from Portugal to Great Britain (statistical appendix I, graph G). Raw cotton exports to Great Britain reached 11,663 bags in 1788, and 46,628 bags valued at £582,850 in 1792.[1] Limited sources of supply for high quality cotton made the cotton wool from Lisbon especially sought after, for cotton from Pernambuco and Maranhão provided the British muslin and velveret trade in particular with the better quality cotton wool it had sought unsuccessfully in the West Indies, India and Africa. Patrick Colquoun, main advocate of the muslin manufacturers rated 'finest Brazil with the best staples of India'.[2]

An unfavorable balance with Portugal presented the British with a novel situation. 'Until we can introduce our cottons and mixed stuffs or some other articles to equalize the trade', Robert Walpole, the British envoy in Lisbon observed, 'this balance must be paid for in Gold.'[3] So radically had the terms of trade changed that not only were metropolitan Portuguese merchants forced to remit specie to Brazil, but the British were obliged to remit gold to Lisbon. Walpole told Lord Grenville in October 1791: 'It may be looked upon as a kind of Phenonemon, the remitting of money from England to Portugal; of which there has been a late example of about £10,000, and probably more may be sent; and not less so, the sending of money from Lisbon to the Brazils. Portugal by sending more goods to England than she receives, the balance must be paid for in specie. Brazil in the same manner sends a greater amount of her produce than she receives from Portugal, the balance therefore

---

[1] Harlow, *Second British Empire*, II, 282.
[2] Michael M. Edwards, *The Growth of the British Cotton Trade 1780–1815* (Manchester, 1967) 83–4; By 1820 about a quarter Lancashire's cotton wool imports came from Brazil, Arthur Redford, *Manchester Merchants and Foreign Trade 1794–1858* (Manchester, 1934) 98–9. Velveret is a variety of fustian with a velvet surface.
[3] Robert Walpole, No. 31, PRO, FO, 63/13.

must be paid in the same manner...England at present is greatly in debt to Portugal.'[1]

It was now the British who clamoured for reciprocity, a reversal of circumstances which would have gratified the subtle old Marquis of Pombal had he lived long enough to see it. Prohibition of the export of British cotton goods to Portugal seemed intolerable to the merchants of Glasgow and Manchester. As Brazilian cotton was allowed into Britain free of duty, cotton goods ought, in their opinion, to have similar privileges in Portugal. 'I need not mention to you', one Glasgow merchant wrote to another, 'the advantages which such a field of consumption in Portugal and her South American settlements would give to the manufacturers of this country, they are abundantly obvious.'[2] Since 1786 the committee of the Privy Council for trade had been seeking a new commercial treaty with Portugal.[3]

The proposals for a new commercial arrangement were presented to Luís Pinto in London during September 1786.[4] And, overoptimistically, William Fawkener was sent as an envoy extraordinary to Lisbon to negotiate the new treaty in conjunction with Walpole.[5] Between 1786 and 1788 extensive investigation continued in London into the Anglo-Portuguese commercial relationship and most especially into 'the prohibitions of Portugal upon British produce and manufactures'.[6] Both the woolen and wine merchants, as well as the cotton manufacturers, took an active interest in these developments, exerting pressure on the British government in a manner also employed over the French treaty of 1786.[7]

---

[1] Robert Walpole to Lord Grenville, Lisbon, 12 October 1791, PRO, FO, 63/14.

[2] Robert Findlay to William McDowell, Glasgow, 12 July 1793, cited by Harlow, *Second British Empire*, II, 282.

[3] 'Minute of Propositions respecting the treaty with Portugal', September 1786, Chatham Papers, PRO, 30/8/342 (2) f. 59.

[4] 'Letter to Chevalier de Pinto, enclosing propositions for regulating the commerce in general ...Portugal and Great Britain', Whitehall, 22 September 1786, PRO, BT. 5/4, 39.

[5] S. Cottrell to Marquis of Carmarthen, Committee of Council for Trade, 23 December 1786, PRO, BT, 3/1, 38.

[6] *Ibid.*, and twelve questions to Sir John Hort [British consul, Lisbon] from Committee of Council on Trade, Chatham Papers, PRO, 30/8/342 (2) 48; Lord Hawkesbury to Sir John Hort, London, 24 July 1786, Chatham Papers, PRO 30/8/342 (2); Office of committee of Privy Council for Trade, 25 June 1787, W. Fawkener, to Marquis of Carmarthen, PRO, BT, 3/1, 102.

[7] 'Messes Beachcroft, Dixon, Aislabie and Moody, wine merchants...consulted...on Portugal', 7 September 1786, PRO, BT. 5/4, 32; Council Chamber, Whitehall, 16 January, 1787 (Lord Hawkesbury, Mr Grenville, Mr Hutchinson), 'Mr. Everett...export of woollens from Great Britain to Portugal...following questions...,' *ibid.*; See also Witt Bowden 'The English manufacturers and the Commercial Treaty of 1786 with France', *AHR*, xxv (1919–20) 18–35; and R. L. Schuyler, *The Fall of the Old Colonial System* (New York, 1945) 68.

The cotton spinners and the calico and muslin manufacturers of Manchester and neighborhood, and the Borough reeve and constables of Manchester, petitioned in 1788 that an 'association for the promoting of a more extensive vend of British cotton manufactures' be established, and it was especially the cotton interests who desired the new treaty with Portugal.[1] The British objective was straightforward. To replace and expand the stipulations of the Methuen treaty was necessary, the committee of the Privy Council on trade observed in 1790, because 'woolen manufactures...were [in 1703] almost the only manufactures for which Great Britain was then distinguished: but as there are at present so many manufactures in this country which have been introduced since that period and now flourish in a great degree, and which have on that account claims to the attention and protection of Government, it would not be proper in the opinion of the committee to bring a new commercial treaty with Portugal to a conclusion without first obtaining just and reasonable conditions in favour of these manufactures'.[2]

The British desire to obtain a favorable access of their cotton goods to Luso-Brazilian markets offered a gratuitous subterfuge to the hard-pressed Portuguese administration during 1790. In September 1789, only four months after the arrest of the principal conspirators in Minas Gerais and six months before Melo e Castro's first official response to Barbacena's letter of 11 July 1789, the British envoy in Lisbon became aware of 'reports of some disturbances in the Brazils'. The notice was 'attended with such vague accounts as to the facts and even to the places, where they are said to have happened that no certain conclusion can be drawn', Walpole told London, 'but some credit is given to the account of a resistance having been made in the interior part of the country at the mines, to some order, that a new governor was encouraged to attempt to enforce...'[3] In October he reported that 'by the ships lately arrived, it seems that though there have been some local discontents they have not been carried to the excesses reported'.[4]

---

[1] Office of the Privy Council on Trade, Whitehall, 18 June 1788, W. Fawkener to Borough Reeve and Constables of Manchester, PRO, BT, 3/1, 290; Whitehall, 23 August 1788, Committee to Borough Reeve, etc., PRO, BT, 3/1, 321.

[2] Office of the Committee of the Privy Council for Trade, Whitehall, 29 November 1790, PRO, FO, 63/13.

[3] Robert Walpole to the Duke of Leeds, 19 September 1789, PRO, FO, 63/12.

[4] On 26 September the envoy returned to the rumors in his correspondence with London, observing that although the question was not yet cleared up 'the matter seems chiefly to bear upon the conduct of the secretary of the governor of Pernambuco (*sic*) in consequence of some complaint that had been made against a contractor for provisions in favour of whom, the secretary of the governor had been very active, and it is said, has paid the tribute

Walpole did not follow these rumors further. His attention was taken by another development. During May 1789 he had reminded Luís Pinto of the project for a new Anglo–Portuguese commercial treaty and the desire of the British for 'reciprocity of exchange'.[1] By 1790 the Portuguese foreign secretary became notably more flexible and receptive to the approaches of the British envoy. The committee of the Privy Council in London expressed its pleasure that 'Mr. de Pinto has...manifested a disposition to bring this negotiation to a conclusion and to make some concessions to which the ministers of Portugal had till now strongly objected.'[2] The new Portuguese flexibility, however, was shortlived. In 1791 Luís Pinto returned post haste to his previous position.[3] The Portuguese government in fact had no intention of granting the British the privileges they desired. Luís Pinto himself considered that a new commercial treaty with Britain would be 'thoroughly calamitous' (*bem funestro*) to Portugal.[4] Nor could the Portuguese government have entered into a new commercial arrangement without facing the strongest opposition from the powerfully entrenched merchant-industrial oligarchy. The *junta do comércio* had been revitalized at the same time as the government. It contained among its new members the formidable Jacques Ratton, who regarded it as his duty to defend the manufacturing interests

for his imprudence, by being assassinated by the discontented at the house of the governor'. The report appears ill founded and not relevant to the Minas affair though it was of the same rumors that Mr Walpole spoke. He did not account for the shift of location. It is interesting to speculate that if Minas were substituted for Pernambuco in this dispatch then the description of events does not appear so unlikely. Cláudio Manuel da Costa was for many years the secretary to the governors of Minas. His relationship with the opulent contractor Macedo is well known. He died under mysterious circumstances not in the house of the governor but in that of Macedo. Moreover, Cláudio Manuel da Costa's death could not fail to have aroused interest in the metropolis. He had been for many years a well known and respected figure in literary circles. What is remarkable is the speed with which the rumors were abroad in Lisbon. Robert Walpole to Duke of Leeds, Lisbon, 26 September 1789, FO, 63/12; In the Chatham Papers there is a further dispatch from Walpole to Leeds, dated 7 October 1789, where the envoy observes that 'A ship lately arrived from the Brazils brought two magistrates and a military officer, as prisoners, for having resisted some orders of the Governor at the Minas.' It is difficult to see to what and to whom this refers. Had the date been 1790 then the description might have referred to the magistrates of the special court and the new commanding officer of the regiment of Estremoz sent to Brazil in October 1790. As far as I can determine no military officers or magistrates were sent to Lisbon in either 1789 or 1790 as prisoners. Colonel Rebêlo left Vila Rica in February 1790 and did not arrive in Lisbon until June, and he was not a prisoner. Chatham Papers, PRO 30/8/342 (2) f. 182.

[1] Robert Walpole to Duke of Leeds, Lisbon, 2 May 1789, PRO, FO, 63/12.
[2] Office of the Privy Council for Trade, Whitehall, 29 November 1790, PRO, FO, 63/13.
[3] Robert Walpole to Duke of Leeds, Lisbon, 8 January 1791, PRO, FO, 63/14.
[4] Cited by Soriano, *Guerra Civil*, I, 483.

of the metropolis and oppose any concession to the British.[1] Thus it seems most likely that Luís Pinto had used the bait of the treaty to deflect any British interest in the possible emancipation of Brazil. The none-too-perceptive Robert Walpole had seen no connection between the rumors of disturbances in Minas Gerais and the sudden interest of the Portuguese government in the treaty.[2] It had been a skilful and important diplomatic achievement for the Portuguese, because during the summer of 1790, as a result of approaches to William Pitt by Francisco Miranda and the 'Mexican notables', the government in London was giving serious attention to the question of aid to Spanish American revolutionaries. Pitt himself was sufficiently impressed to be ready to commit large forces for a military assault on the Spanish Empire.[3] The bait of the treaty together with the continuing though increasingly anachronistic influence of the British Factory in Portugal, and of the wine and woolen interests in Britain, prevented the reformulation of British policy with respect to Portugal and Brazil, which the changed economic relationship demanded, and which knowledge of a formidable movement of independence in Brazil would certainly have occasioned.

The plotters in Minas apparently made no formal approach to British official circles. The conspirators were anyway suspicious of British good intentions, and their economic nationalism and the opinions of the Abbé Raynal would have made them uncomfortable partners for expansion minded British entrepreneurs. Discussion of commercial arrangements and foreign trade were largely absent from their proposals, and it was commerce and trade which was of overwhelming concern to the British. The same qualifications did not influence their attitude towards the new republic in North America, to which they looked as an example, and from which they expected support. And the United States government had been forewarned of the impending revolution in Brazil. But the Brazilians had misjudged the priorities of the new Republic in the

---

[1] 'Fiel aos principios de que me acho possuido sobre as utilidades, que resultão ao Reino do desenvolvimento da industria fabril sempre, em quanto me conservei na Real Junta, julguei meu dever votar a favor das pessoas dos proprietarios e suas justas pertençõens a benefício dos estabelecimentos', Ratton, *Recordações*, 97; For Ratton's comments on reconstitution of junta do comércio, *ibid.*, 195–212. (The other new members were Geraldo Wenceslão Braancamp de Almeida Castello Branco, Dr Domingos Vandelli, Joaquim Machado, João Roque Jorge). Ratton summed up his attitude to manufactories in the section entitled 'Sôbre as utilidades que resultão das fábricas nacionaes e da necessidade de as proteger', *ibid.*, 96–100. His comments on visit of Mr Fawkener to Lisbon, *ibid.*, 32–36.
[2] For some highly biased, but delightfully uncomplimentary comments on Walpole, see William Beckford, *Journal*, 42, 44.
[3] For Pitt's policy at this time with respect to Spanish America, see Harlow, *Second British Empire*, II, 226, 234, 236, 646.

north. Like Britain, the United States was anxious for a commercial treaty with Portugal. Jefferson and Adams, during April 1786, had negotiated and signed a treaty with Luís Pinto in London.[1] The appointment of Luís Pinto was seen by Jefferson as a hopeful sign. He wrote from Paris during March 1789 that 'the negotiation may be renewed successfully if it be the desire of our government... I think myself it is in their interest to take away all temptation to our cooperation in the emancipation of their colonies...'[2] Jefferson was more acute than Walpole in his realization of the dimensions of the issues tied in with the commercial treaty, though it is evident that he saw the immediate interests of the United States as being better served by arrangements with the metropolis than by risky adventures in South America. The United States was more interested in the trade of the metropolis than that of the colonies, and in Portuguese demand for rice and cereals Jefferson saw a market for North American production.[3]

The desire of the North Americans as well as the British for commercial concessions from Lisbon, and the optimism of both governments that such arrangements might be obtainable in view of the changed administration in Lisbon and especially the appointment of Luís Pinto as foreign secretary, gave precious diplomatic initiative to Lisbon during 1789–90. It made both the British and the North Americans unreceptive and uninquisitive about the occurrences in Brazil.

There was a further factor involved in the situation. By late 1789 the attention of all Europe was on Paris. Fortuitously for the Portuguese government, the Minas conspiracy, the arrests, and the trial of those involved, was able to pass almost unnoticed by the rest of the world. Rumors of possible French invasion had been bandied around among the conspirators, but they spoke of France of the old regime. The arrival of the news of the Minas conspiracy in Lisbon coincided with the news from France of growing revolutionary turmoil. On 19 September 1789, when Robert Walpole reported the rumors of disturbances in Minas Gerais to London he also noted that 'this court has forbid the writer of the Portuguese Gazzette to insert any more accounts of the present transactions in France...'[4] Interest in the affairs of Portugal was so slight in

---

[1] Raul d'Eça, 'Colonial Brazil as an element in the early diplomatic negotiations between the United States and Portugal, 1776–1808', *Colonial Latin America* (editor, A. Curtis Wilgus, Washington, D.C., 1936).

[2] Thomas Jefferson, Paris, 12 March 1789, *AMI*, II (1953) 21.

[3] Tableau VII, Adrien Balbi, *Variétés Politico-Statistiques sur la Monarchie Portugaise* (Paris, 1822); 'Tableau général de la valeur des merchandises importées...1796'. Adrien Balbi, *Essai Statistique sur le Royaume de Portugal et d'Algarve....* (2 vols., Paris, 1822) I, 442.

[4] Robert Walpole to the Duke of Leeds, Lisbon, 19 September 1789, PRO, FO, 63/12.

comparison and France so dominated the news in Europe that between 1790–2 not one word on Portugal made the pages of the *Annual Register* of London. The only reference to Portugal to appear in the pages of the *Gentleman's Magazine* between 1789–91 was placed there in order to provide the readers with 'a little laugh'. In Lisbon the magazine observed 'They make nothing...to fling water and piss upon you as you pass by.'[1]

Nonetheless the Lisbon government had to face the problems created by the discovery of the Minas conspiracy. By September 1790 it was no longer possible for Melo e Castro to postpone further his commentary. He clearly perceived the contradictions in the devassas which he had studied carefully. His first reaction, however, did not appear to be borne out by the evidence. Almost none of those arrested had been crown debtors, or involved in the conspiracy on those grounds. Listing the officer corps of the Dragoons, their places of birth and family relations, he noted those implicated or suspected of involvement in the plot. He observed that both José Álvares Maciel and José de Sá Betencourt were associates (*sócios*) of the Lisbon Academy of Sciences. Of the major conspirators he distinguished twelve or thirteen officers of the Dragoons or auxiliary regiments, five ecclesiastics, and eight or nine magistrates and lawyers. The importance of those involved he recognized, for they were 'of that class that by their estates, employment, and capital are considered and were reputed to be the most distinguished'. Moreover he recognized 'the vast measures' and the number of men that the conspirators claimed were available to them as being appropriate to 'those magnates...and the great number of slaves at their disposal...' But he was confused by the fact that only a comparatively small number of people had been arrested – and without opposition. He claimed that there was nothing new in the events because 'the magnates of the captaincy had always eluded the royal orders, especially over objects of the royal treasury, and most especially the Quinto'. Yet he could not deny that the magnates had intended 'a Republic, in imitation of English America'.[2]

The colonial secretary's confused response to the events in Minas was perhaps inevitable. The conspiracy challenged in a most basic way the

---

[1] *The Annual Register* (London, 1790); *The Annual Register* (London, 1791); *The Annual Register* (London, 1792); *The Gentleman's Magazine* (London, 1791) 629.

[2] This paragraph is based on a comparison between Melo e Castro's dispatch to Barbacena, Queluz, 29 September 1790 in AHU, códice 600, f. 171–86v, published in *AMI*, II, 94–107, and the documents in AHU, Minas Gerais, caixa 94, containing a list in Melo e Castro's own hand of the officers of the Minas dragoons with comments, his annotations on the letter from Barbacena of 11 July 1789, and the minutes and originals of the dispatch with changes and alterations also in his own hand.

neo-mercantilism which he had laboriously attempted to impose throughout Portuguese America since 1777. Moreover, he suspected that there existed an intimate connection between the policy and the reaction of the Minas magnates. Yet as far as the record was concerned, apart from the obvious importance of the *derrama*, the debt question did not appear to have been a preeminent cause of the proposed uprising. Thus the fact that the involvement of the financial interests had been minimized in the legal proceedings as a result of Barbacena's shilly shallying with the opulent contractors, encouraged Melo e Castro to conclude that the plot was the work of disgruntled military officers, lawyers and clerics. The conclusion was attractive to him, for it removed part of the blame for the precipitation of the conspiracy from his own shoulders, and obscured the link between his policy and the nationalistic reaction in Brazil. The interpretation moreover, made unnecessary any fundamental rethinking of his assessment of the economic situation in the captaincy. And again this was attractive. Any new evaluation would inevitably have shaken the assumptions on which he had based his massive instructions to Barbacena two years before, and would necessarily have admitted the validity of the contentions put forward by Luís Pinto and his associates at the Academy of Sciences. In fact, so far was Melo e Castro from making this mental adjustment that he chastised Barbacena for his vague remarks about the 'circumstances of the captaincy' and demanded to know what these might be. Nor could he comprehend why the conspirators represented Minas as being in a state of economic depression while they also called it an opulent country able to sustain its independence and throw off the dominion of Portugal.

The major decisions over Minas were taken during September and October 1790. The governor's behavior received mild praise and stronger censure. 'Considering the circumstances of this unheard of happening', Melo e Castro told Barbacena, 'your comportment has not unmerited the royal approval'. He found it reprehensible, however, that the plot was discussed for at least four to five months before it came to the governor's attention. Barbacena was ordered henceforth to live in Vila Rica. If he had established his residence there at the beginning the secretary of state thought it unlikely that the conspiracy would have progressed as far as it did without his knowledge. The regiment of Estremoz was ordered to Vila Rica and a new commandant, Brigader Pedro Álvares de Andrade, sent from the metropolis. In future the infantry regiments would be moved every three years. The suspension of the *derrama*, Melo e Castro pointed out, commenting on the governor's actions, while it had taken away the occasion for the uprising had not been sufficient to disanimate the conspirators or lead them to abandon the project. Almost casually he added that the backlog of arrears was 'in reality excessive to impose...and that this was sufficient reason to suspend...the derrama ...'[1] When the secretary of state's dispatch reached Vila Rica this last observation must have been received with amazement by the governor. Part of Barbacena's problems had arisen precisely because of his conviction that just such an explanation would not be 'sufficient reason' for the secretary of state. Melo e Castro's comments in this respect contradicted the whole tone and thrust of his instructions of January 1788.

Nonetheless Melo e Castro promptly rewarded those for whom the Visconde de Barbacena had requested favors. Antônio Dias Coelho was made a captain and recommended for promotion to *sargento-mor* of dragoons as being 'the best officer' of the regiment. José de Sousa Lobo and José de Vasconcelos Parada e Sousa, the former favorites of Cunha Meneses, had their commissions confirmed. Bazílio de Brito Malheiro was to be nominated either treasurer or scribe of the foundry house of Sabará or Vila Rica. In addition, a special *carta régia* was issued in his favor so that highly complicated litigations might be settled summarily by a specially appointed magistrate.[2] Manitti was to be appointed intendent of Vila Rica in place of Bandeira who was to move to the high court of Bahia. Carlos José da Silva received a pension for life of 400$000 *reis* per annum, which would pass to his wife and children (he had nine) while they lived. Pamplona received a contemptuous 'nothing'.[3]

The confusion of the devassas, the rumors of the occurrences in Minas Gerais and the fame of those arrested, also demanded some public action or demonstration and some public clarification of the case. Moreover, the continuing escalation of violence in France during the period 1789-92 while it served to deflect attention from Portuguese America also profoundly affected the frame of mind of those officials in Lisbon who decided the fate of the conspirators. The Minas movement was formulated before and without knowledge of the revolution in France, but for those who dealt with its consequences France was foremost in their thoughts. The devassas demonstrated the influence of French writers on those involved in the plot. Already in late 1789 laws had been enacted against

---

[1] M. de Melo e Castro to Visconde de Barbacena, Queluz, 29 September 1790, *AMI*, II (1953) 94–107.

[2] Carta Régia, Rainha, Queluz, 16 September 1790, AHU, códice 610, f. 169–70v.

[3] 'Offício and relação' (several pages in Barbacena's hand with annotations by Melo e Castro), AHU, Minas Gerais, caixa 92, published in *AMI*, II (1953) 84–5 and 108–9.

the 'incredible multitude of libertine and scandalous books', many of which were catalogued in the libraries of those arrested in Brazil.[1]

A special visiting court of inquiry or *alçada* was established. The device was standard practice in cases of treason or revolt. Pombal had dealt with the Oporto uprising of 1757 with a similar tribunal. The chancellor designate of the High Court of Rio de Janeiro, Desembargador Sebastião Xavier de Vasconcelos Coutinho was to head the alçada, and Antônio Gomes Ribeiro and Antônio Diniz da Cruz e Silva of the *casa de suplicação* were to accompany him from Lisbon.[2] Cruz e Silva, who conducted the investigation into the Diamond Administration, had returned to Portugal in 1787 and since then been with the High Court of Oporto.[3] The special court would meet in Rio de Janeiro. Chancellor Coutinho was instructed to ignore 'any lack of formalities...and judicial invalidities...that might exist in the devassas...and to consider only the proofs according to their merits before the natural law...' Priests were to be sentenced separately and their condemnation was to remain secret. The chancellor was given special authority over the magistrates of Minas, 'or any other captaincy'. He was to act always in accord with the viceroy and to scrupulously avoid any jurisdictional disputes. By special dispensation the court was granted all necessary jurisdiction, 'all other laws, dispositions, privileges, and orders to the contrary notwithstanding for this time only'.[4]

Despite their wide powers, however, the judges had small room for maneuver. Before they left Lisbon the guilt of the prisoners was assumed and the broad outline of the sentence agreed upon. In addition, on 15 October 1790, a secret *carta régia* was issued to Chancellor Coutinho which recommended 'clemency' for all those who had been involved in the conventicles or implicated or had knowledge of the plot.[5] The active plotters were to be banished to Angola and Benguela and those who had connived and concurred were to be banished to Mozambique. But there was an exception. The full rigor of the law would apply to that prisoner or prisoners who beyond the conventicles had 'in public and private in

---

[1] 'Ofício', 3 December 1789, cited by Rizzini, *Hypólito da Costa*, 68.

[2] 'Rainha para Sebastião Xavier de Vasconcellos Coutinho', Lisbon, 17 July 1790, *ADIM*, VII, 18–20; also in AHU, Minas Gerais, caixa 92, with copies to viceroy Resende and governor Barbacena of the same date.

[3] Rodolfo Garcia, 'Explicação', *ADIM*, VII, 10.

[4] 'Rainha para S. X. de Vasconcellos Coutinho', *ADIM*, VII, 19–22; 'Cartas que forão pelo Navio de Sua Magestade, Principe de Beira...que sahio para o Rio de Janeiro em 31 de Outobro de 1790', AHU, Minas Gerais, caixa 92.

[5] Clemency order issued 15 October 1790, 'Rainha para S. X. de Vasconcellos Coutinho', *ADIM*, VII, 225–6.

different parts' spread word of the movement. A previous draft had defined the 'different parts' as Minas and Rio de Janeiro.[1] Yet for the moment none of this was to be public knowledge. The government was preparing to stage-manage a spectacle. The alçada and the secret clemency proclamation were to form important ingredients in an elaborate and contrived scenario.

The *carta régia* of 15 October 1790 was clearly aimed at one person only, the *alferes* Silva Xavier. Why was the modest toothpuller to be made a scapegoat? In large measure he had written his own death sentence. 'Who was he, someone without social importance or influence or wealth' he asked Desembargador Torres during his first interrogation. In many respects his question revealed an important truth. Silva Xavier was not a member of the Minas plutocracy to which the other prisoners almost to a man belonged. He had sought mightily to enter but be had consistently failed. He was without influential family connections, a bachelor, a man who had spent much of his life in the shadow of more wealthy and successful protectors. Unlike Gonzaga, Cláudio Manuel da Costa, Alvarenga Peixoto, he had no reputation beyond Brazil. In fact the *alferes* was probably never fully privy to the broader schemes and objectives of the movement. From his interrogations his concerns appear to have been entirely with the immediate tactics and with the propagation of Lusophobe ideas. Important conspirators had studiously avoided associating with him. Both Gonzaga and Rodrigues de Macedo had rebuffed his attempts to talk with them and Cláudio Manuel da Costa had attempted to do so. Significantly the *alferes* had already been sacrificed by his fellow conspirators. In all the confusion of their testimony not one had denied Silva Xavier's participation, or what they claimed was his fanatical and at times reckless enthusiasm for the revolution. While many sought to diminish the importance of their colleagues' actions, no such restraint characterized their comments on the *alferes*.

But at the same time Silva Xavier was well known in Minas Gerais and Rio de Janeiro, partly because of his dental skill and healing abilities, partly as a result of the force of his personality. White, ambitious, propertyless, he was typical of many throughout Portuguese America, who sought upward mobility in the social structure and who were none too particular about how they achieved it. Silva Xavier was especially bitter for he had lost status, in as far as his father was evidently a man of position and estate. To the government in Lisbon, every day hearing more horrific

---

[1] Originals, annotated and corrected in AHU, Minas Gerais, caixa 93 (folder 40). Final version in *ADIM*, vii, 226.

stories from France, he was someone who bore all the characteristics and resentments of a revolutionary man. And he had invited martyrdom by claiming sole responsibility for the plot. The attraction that the hanging of Silva Xavier held for the Portuguese government was obvious. Few would take seriously a movement headed by a toothpuller. (The authorities after October 1790 invariably referred to the *alferes* by his nickname *Tiradentes*.) A show trial followed by the public execution of Silva Xavier offered maximum impact as a warning, while it would minimize and ridicule the objectives of the movement. He would be a perfect example to other dissatisfied colonials who might be tempted to seek too much too soon.

The situation, however, could not be manipulated so easily as had been assumed in Lisbon. The Chancellor Coutinho arrived in Rio de Janeiro at the end of 1790. He found a newly installed and suspicious viceroy, the worst inundations in living memory, and an influenza epidemic raging in the interior.[1] The general atmosphere was tense. The people were in a state of fear and uncertainty. Trade between Minas and Rio was seriously disrupted. The viceroy Resende attributed the 'decadence in part to the revolution in Minas', and Coutinho believed the disruption was caused by concern that goods sent to Minas might be confiscated or lost in reprisal.[2] The chancellor recommended privately to Lisbon that a general pardon might be helpful. He found the people of Rio 'uncontaminated', though he noted tension between Brazilians and Europeans, the former 'thinking that they possessed more talents, and were more worthy to govern than Europeans, and that the Europeans took away riches due to the native born'. He was particularly concerned about false denunciations, where for reasons of personal vendetta innocents were accused of knowledge of, or participation in the conspiracy. He proposed severe treatment for those who bore false witness.[3]

The original records of the devassa were handed over to Chancellor Coutinho on his arrival, and on 14 February 1791, he ordered that the prisoners remaining in Minas Gerais be sent to Rio. Hearing that Nicolas George was in the capital and about to sail for Europe he ordered his

---

[1] S. X. de Vasconcelos Coutinho to M. de Melo e Castro, Rio, 20 February 1791, AHU, Minas Gerais, caixa 94, published in *AMI*, II (1953) 206–7; Notes on the influenza epidemic in *RAPM*, II (1897) 7.

[2] Conde de Resende to M. de Melo e Castro, Rio, 18 January 1791, AHU, Minas Gerais, caixa 94; S. X. de Vasconcelos Coutinho to M. de Melo e Castro, 30 May 1791, AHU, Minas Gerais, caixa 94; 'Auto de perguntas feitas a Nicolao Jorge da Nação Irlandes', Rio de Janeiro, 18 February 1791, *AMI*, II (1953) 213–19.

[3] S. X. de Vasconcelos Coutinho to M. de Melo e Castro, Rio de Janeiro, 30 July 1791, AHU, Minas Gerais, caixa 94.

arrest. He did not receive the continuation of the proceedings in Minas until the end of April, and when the papers arrived they were 'almost as voluminous as the devassa'. The more glaring inconsistencies and injustices rapidly became obvious. Finding 'many points and circumstances incomplete and without clarity' he instructed Manitti in Vila Rica to arrest Vicente Vieira da Mota, José Resende da Costa (both father and son of the same name), Padre Manuel Rodrigues and José Aires Gomes. Manitti was also instructed to present himself in Rio and to require that Pamplona and Bazílio de Brito Malheiro do likewise. These men were arrested, the chancellor told Melo e Castro, because he 'found them more guilty than many of those imprisoned'. The presence of Manitti was required 'because...Saldanha the *ouvidor* of Vila Rica and judge of the Minas devassa had died, and Manitti as scribe was the only one who could reply and inform [me] over certain questions that I find without necessary explanation'.[1]

In view of the reopening of the case in Rio and especially the arrests of Vicente Vieira, the bookkeeper of João Rodrigues de Macedo, and José Aires Gomes, bondsman to the contractor, it is ironic that it was Manitti of all people who was placed in the critical role of advisor to the chancellor. The death of Saldanha, like that of Cláudio Manuel da Costa, was convenient and well timed for those who had escaped arrest in Minas Gerais and of whose interests Manitti had been a diligent protector.[2] And furthermore, the absence of the ouvidor Cleto, who in June 1791 took up a position in Bahia, led to Manitti's appointment on his arrival in Rio as assistant scribe at the chancellor's interrogations.[3] In consequence, when the interrogations were conducted during July 1791, Manitti was present throughout, to the amazement and consternation of not a few prisoners.

From the new interrogations it soon became clear that both Pamplona and Silvério dos Reis were deeply involved in the plot, and the importance of the contacts made and the discussions which had taken place in the house of Rodrigues de Macedo became every day more evident.[4] Coutinho bullied, threatened, harassed, and contradicted the prisoners

[1] *Ibid.*
[2] Saldanha died on 18 April 1791, Mathias, *CCANRJ*, 55.
[3] Marcelino Pereira Cleto took up his post at the high court in Bahia on 21 June 1791, Vilhena, *Cartas*, II, 328.
[4] 'Perguntas que mais se continuaram ao sobredito Alferes José da Silva Xavier', Rio de Janeiro, 14 April 1791, *ADIM*, IV, 62–6; During this interrogation the chancellor had asked specifically about the conversation with José Aires Gomes. Also in the course of the questioning the close connection between Silva Xavier and Silvério dos Reis, and the latter's full knowledge of the agreements made in Minas, became evident.

with frightening effectiveness. The most dramatic moment came during a confrontation between Carlos Correia and Oliveira Lopes over conflicting testimony. The presence of Manitti outraged the ex-Dragoon and he 'cried out passionately that all the testimony was false and had been prompted and tricked by promises [of Manitti]'.[1] Unfortunately for Oliveira Lopes the testimony he chose to challenge was that in the deposition he made before the viceroy's judges Torres and Cleto. The chancellor reacted violently to what he considered an attack on the 'integrity and reputation of the magistrates of Her Majesty'. Equally unfortunately for the truth was the fact that the clash had occurred over no less a matter than the involvement of Rodrigues de Macedo and Pamplona in the plot, a subject forgotten in the furor.

When two days later Oliveira Lopes was himself interrogated he withdrew his charges against Pamplona and Macedo.[2] Asked by Coutinho on what grounds he did this he replied that he 'lied without object, without reason, and simply because he wished to lie, because whoever did not lie was not of social importance (*porque quem não mento não é de boa gente*)'. The reply infuriated the chancellor, who again embarked on a lengthy diatribe against Oliveira Lopes and his imputations against the magistracy. The former Dragoon replied that 'a rustic man could say no more, nor have any more to reply'. Coutinho abrogated the whole of Oliveira Lopes' testimony as being 'so many times perjured, and beyond that attempted to sully the reputation and truth of magistrates of Her Majesty with notorious falsity'.[3] It was not magistrates in general but Manitti in particular that Oliveira Lopes had accused. The newly appointed intendent of Vila Rica was a sorry example of the propriety of the magistracy for the chancellor to so vigorously and unthinkingly defend. The dismissal of Oliveira Lopes' statements removed the only testimony against Rodrigues de Macedo, Pamplona, and not least against the malpractices of Manitti himself.

An anonymous but well-informed observer of the proceedings considered that Coutinho was deliberately misled. 'A magistrate of rectitude and uncorruptibility succumbed (without knowing it) to the cunning effects of deceit and deception. All that the prisoners produced in the

---

[1] 'Auto de continuação de perguntas feitas ao vigário…Carlos Corrêa', Rio de Janeiro, 11 July 1791, *ADIM*, IV, 181; For the confrontation between Oliveira Lopes and Carlos Correia involving Manitti, *ibid.*, 187.

[2] 'Auto de continuação de perguntas feitas ao coronel Francisco António de Oliveira Lopes', Rio de Janeiro, 13 July 1791, *ADIM*, IV, 342.

[3] 'Auto de continuação de perguntas feitas ao…Oliveira Lopes', Rio de Janeiro, 27 July 1791, *ADIM*, IV, 354–6.

interrogations respecting the insinuations, alluring promises, terror and menaces [of Manitti] was always repelled and depreciated, many times with fury because of a preconceived conviction...'[1] The situation was probably more complicated. The chancellor was being led into deep waters and he must have been aware of it. When he left Lisbon it seemed that the case was tied up, that the interrogation would be a mere formality, and the sentence rapidly arrived at. Now at each corner the most dangerous sleeping dogs were disturbed. Under interrogation Vicente Vieira declared that eight days or so before the arrest of Gonzaga he was called to Cachoeira by Barbacena, where he and the governor discussed the conspiracy and the affairs of Rodrigues de Macedo.[2] The chancellor told Macedo's bookkeeper that it was 'not credible that the governor of Minas, whose zeal and exactitude in the matter was well known would risk with him [Vicente Vieira] a secret of such importance'. Vicente Vieira, however, insisted on the truth of his statement, and furthermore told the chancellor that were he not held incommunicado he would seek an attestation to the fact from the governor. Coutinho himself seems to have been growing suspicious about the exact timing of the suspension of the *derrama*. He questioned the canon Luís Vieira very closely on the timing of his visits to Vila Rica during early 1789.[3] In particular he wished to date Gonzaga's comment that the occasion had been lost. Clearly he was not so impressed by the governor of Minas' 'zeal and exactitude' as he claimed. He later requested the attestation from Barbacena that Vicente Vieira had demanded. The governor appears to have found it prudent to ignore the petition, or at least to procrastinate to such an extent that it had still not arrived at the time of the sentencing of the prisoners in April 1792.[4]

There was certainly more going on behind the scenes than appears from the documents that survive. The new interrogations in Rio caused considerable and understandable concern in Minas Gerais. Captain Coelho, who the anonymous author of the comments on Coutinho called 'one of those monsters vomited from hell for the confusion and ruin of so many unfortunates', remained in Rio until the alçada had

[1] Manuel Cardoso, 'Another document on the Inconfidência Mineira', *HAHR*, XXXII (1952) 550.

[2] 'Auto de perguntas a Vicente Vieira da Mota', Rio de Janeiro, 19 July 1791, *ADIM*, V, 12–13; 'Continuação de perguntas...Vicente Vieira...', Rio de Janeiro, 20 July 1791, *ADIM*, V, 21f.

[3] 'Auto de continuação de perguntas feitas ao...Cônego Luís Vieira da Silva', Rio de Janeiro, 21 July 1790 (*sic*) [this should be 1791] *ADIM*, IV, 302–12.

[4] Atestation, Francisco Luís Alvares da Rocha, Rio de Janeiro, 18 February 1792, *ADIM*, V, 31–2; José de Oliveira Fagundes, *ADIM*, VII, 255–6.

finished its business.[1] João Rodrigues de Macedo was kept posted of events.[2] Coutinho himself believed some connivance had taken place between the prisoners, possibly through the guards.[3] And certain members of the tribunal do appear to have been subject to outside influences. José de Sá Betencourt paid through his aunt the substantial sum of 2 arrobas of gold in order not to be called before the court.[4] Alvarenga Peixoto was not interrogated at all by the chancellor, and he was able to correspond with his wife, who had been taken under the veiled protection of Rodrigues de Macedo.[5] Alvarenga Peixoto received special treatment, José de Resende Costa claimed later, because of his friendship with members of the tribunal, presumably with Cruz e Silva, a fellow poet and colleague at Coimbra.[6] Cruz e Silva had previously written a poem in praise of the three beautiful daughters of Dr José de Silveira e Sousa, the eldest of which, Bárbara Eliodora, was Alvarenga's wife.[7]

Melo e Castro had carefully analyzed the testimony that Gonzaga gave before the viceregal commission during the previous October. The decision to annul the judicial improprieties of the Minas devassa was clearly taken in order that the deposition of Cláudio Manuel da Costa might be used in evidence against Gonzaga. The use of Cláudio's statement was damaging to Gonzaga's stand, and he was forced to change his defense. For the first time during his interrogations he was unable to outargue his interrogator. He no longer denied all knowledge of the plot but dismissed

---

[1] Manuel Cardoso, 'Another document...', *HAHR*, xxxii (1952) 550.

[2] For example, Captain Antônio Ribeiro do Avellar to J. Rodrigues de Macedo, Rio de Janeiro, 18 May 1792, CCBNRJ, I-1-17.

[3] S. X. de Vasconcelos Coutinho to M. de Melo e Castro, Rio de Janeiro, 16 August 1791 *AMI*, II (1953) 212.

[4] Carneiro de Mendonça, *O Intendente Câmara*, 9–10.

[5] Costa Filho, *Cana de Açúcar*, 187–8; Costa Filho, 'O Engenho de Bárbara Heliodora', *Brasil Açúcareiro*, LI (1958) No. 4, 21–4; No. 5, 27–30; No. 6, 18–21; 'Bens do inconfidente Ignácio José de Alvarenga...arrematados em 30 Maio de 1795 a João Rodrigues de Macedo', CCBNRJ, 1–35, 18.

[6] José de Resenda Costa was one of the few conspirators to return to Brazil. When Robert Southey's *History of Brazil* appeared it contained some observations on the Minas conspiracy. Resende Costa translated these and added some notes in commentary among which was the observation on Alvarenga Peixoto's favorable treatment, 'Artigo traduzido da História do Brazil de Robert Southey, Vol. 3, page 978, pelo Conselheiro José de Rezende Costa.' Copy from the typescript collections on the Minas conspiracy in the Museu da Inconfidência, Ouro Prêto, Minas Gerais. Resende Costa was 74 years old at the time he made his comments on Southey's account. It is often claimed that Southey was the first to publish an account of the conspiracy, in fact Sir George Staunton had made some pertinent observations on the aborted revolt in his 'Earl Macartney's Embassy to the Emperor of China...' reprinted in *The World or the Present State of the Universe...by Cavendish Pelham* (London, 1810) vol. I, 574 (footnote).

[7] Aureliano Leite, 'A figura Feminina da Inconfidência Mineira', *RIHGB*, vol. 215 (1952) 224–5.

his conversations on the potentialities of the captaincy as being merely hypothetical. He admitted attending the December meeting at Freire de Andrade's house in Vila Rica but implied that all that had transpired was the reading 'of some stanzas' by Alvarenga Peixoto.[1] Coutinho did not know, and Gonzaga did not inform him, that the poem recited had been none other than the famous *canto genetlíaco*. Gonzaga's interrogation followed that of the other prisoners, and it had been intended no doubt as the concluding and most important confrontation of the chancellor's inquiry. Instead, while the case against Gonzaga was clearly stronger than before, so many new elements had entered the picture that the significance of the breakthrough against the subtle ex-ouvidor of Vila Rica was lost. Coutinho told Melo e Castro on 17 August that during the interrogations 'nothing essential had been discovered to alter the opinion formed on the basis of the devassas', and that he would 'proceed to the sentence with all brevity'.[2] His report to the secretary of state was equivocal, but he had very little alternative short of reopening the case to the infinite embarrassment of Melo e Castro, Barbacena, the magistrates of the various devassas, and many others. Apparently he had decided to let sleeping dogs lie.

The sentence produced by the chancellor was an impressive piece of work under the circumstances. It took him over seven months to complete. His account of the conspiracy, its objectives, and the proof against each of the prisoners was a remarkably fair and judicious summary of the case in as far as it appeared in the proceedings of the various devassas.[3] The sentence against the ecclesiastics was secret and in consequence in parts more revealing than the public case against the secular prisoners.[4] The latter, however, was itself surprisingly frank. Chancellor Countinho had chosen his words carefully. He observed pointedly that one of the measures taken as a result of Silvério dos Reis' defection had '*perhaps* been the suspension of the imposition of the derrama'.[5] Despite the designation of *Tiradentes* as first among the conspirators he did not noticeably understate the importance of the involvement in the movement of those more influential and famous men, or underplay the republican and nationalistic objectives of the proposed revolt. Indeed echoing Melo e Castro's private comments he chastised the

---

[1] 'Translado do auto de perguntas ao Dez[embargador] Tomás António Gonzaga', with marking by Melo e Castro, AHU, Minas Gerais, caixa 93.

[2] S. X. de Vasconcelos Coutinho to M. de Melo e Castro, Rio de Janeiro, 16 August 1791, *AMI*, II (1953) 212.

[3] 'Sentença da Alçada', published in full in Santos, *A Inconfidência Mineira*, 587–620.

[4] 'Carta Régia', 21 July 1790, AHU, Minas Gerais, caixa 92 (39); Sentence of the ecclesiastics published in full in *AMI*, I (1952) 73–101.

[5] 'Sentença da Alçada', Santos, *Inconfidência Mineira*, 611. Italics added.

prisoners for their 'abominable ingratitude'. The majority of them 'especially the leaders', he said, 'had enjoyed the benefits and honor of employment in Her Majesty's Service'.[1] The defense of the prisoners had been taken by Dr José de Oliveira Fagundes, a Brazilian graduate of the University of Coimbra, and the attorney of the Rio Misericórdia. His brief was conscientiously prepared. Fagundes either sought to minimize the importance of the statements made by the prisoners or he pleaded that the Queen exercise her royal prerogative of mercy. The *alferes* Silva Xavier, he claimed, should be pardoned as being insane.[2]

The reading of the sentence on 18 April 1792 in the high court chambers of Rio took an incredible eighteen hours, from eight in the morning to past two o'clock the following day. With priests, the defendants, the nine judges of the alçada, the viceroy, and guards from the regular troops with arms ready and loaded all present there was a formidable hubbub. The auxiliary regiments of the city had been mobilized and the European regiments guarded public buildings in a massive show of force.[3] The sentence decreed that *Tiradentes* should be hanged, his head cut off so that it might be taken and displayed on a high pole in the center of Vila Rica. Parts of his quartered body would be displayed at the entrance to the captaincy, and at those places he had most frequented. His home in Vila Rica was to be destroyed and the ground salted. Freire de Andrade, Álvares Maciel, Alvarenga Peixoto, Oliveira Lopes, and Luís Vaz were likewise to be hanged, beheaded and quartered.[4]

According to an eyewitness the scene that followed was 'the most tragic and comic that could be imagined...each blamed their misfortune on the excessive deposition of the others. As they had been held incommunicado for three years their desire to talk was...violent...' After four hours of mutual recrimination the prisoners were placed in heavy chains secured to the windows of the room.[5] Then dramatically as planned, the reading of the Queen's letter of clemency transformed the situation. The sentences for all but the alferes Silva Xavier were commuted to banishment.[6] The spectacle was almost done. On the morning of

---

[1] *Ibid.*, 613.   [2] The defense is published in *ADIM*, VII, 67–139.

[3] 'Memória do exito que teve a conjuração de Minas e dos factos relativos a ella. Acontecidos nesta cidade do Rio de Janeiro, desde o dia 17 até, 26 de Abril de 1792', *AMI*, II (1953) 223–4, and 'Últimos momentos dos Inconfidentes de 1789 pelo Frade que os assistio de confissão', *ibid.*, 234–43.

[4] 'Sentença da Alçada', Santos, *Inconfidência Mineira*, 615–17.

[5] 'Ultimos momentos...', *AMI*, II (1953) 238.

[6] The new sentence was given on 20 April 1792, Santos, *Inconfidência Mineira*, 619; For information in the fate of those banished to Africa see Padre Manuel R. Pombo, *Inconfidência Mineira: Conspiradores que vieram deportados para os Presidios de Angola em 1792* (Luanda,

21 April 1792, *Tiradentes*, escorted by the viceregal cavalry, was led to an outsized gallows on the outskirts of the capital. Here, about eleven o'clock in the hot sun, with the regiments drawn up in a triangle, after speeches and cheers for 'Our Most August Sovereign', the scapegoat was sacrificed.[1]

The quiet dignity with which *Tiradentes* met his death was one of the few heroic moments of a dismal misadventure. Almost a century later when Brazil eventually became a republic he was a ready made hero. As national heroes go the claim of the *alferes* of the Minas Dragoons to the title is not unjustified. Compared with his co-conspirators his behavior under interrogation was exemplary. In his enthusiasm for a republican, free, and independent Minas, none surpassed him. He claimed for himself the greatest risk, and there can be no doubt that he meant what he said. As Cláudio Manuel da Costa was reported to have observed, had there only been more men of his metal! *Tiradentes* was no angel. No man is. Yet in a history singularly lacking in noble men, Joaquim José da Silva Xavier remains an exception.

But spectacles were no substitute for policy. The euphoria over the clemency of the now mad Queen could not last. The pressing issues which had led to the confrontation between the Minas plutocracy and the government in Lisbon had not disappeared with the hanging of the toothpuller. Nor could consideration of the broader implications of the Minas conspiracy for the colonial policy of Portugal in Brazil be in-definitely postponed. The alienation of important members of the Minas élite during 1788 had proceeded from very special circumstances. The preoccupations of the magnates were determined by the intimate cohesion which had developed between their self interests and the regional economy and institutions. The economic conditions of the captaincy in the 1780s had made them a self-sufficient and locally rooted oligarchy which embraced the native-born and immigrant Portuguese. Factional disputes and struggles had concentrated around patronage, and especially over the farming of the taxes. The dictates of self interest spreading through the tentacles of extended family relationships determined patterns of conflict

Angola, 1932); Macedo had been informed privately of the arrival of the ship which would take several of the prisoners into banishment, Captain Antônio Ribeiro de Avellar to J. Rodrigues de Macedo, 18 May 1792, CCBNRJ, I-I-17; The viceroy notified the secretary of state three days later, conde de Resende to M. de Melo e Castro, Rio de Janeiro, 20 May 1792, AHU, Minas Gerais, caixa 94; Melo e Castro acknowledged the dispatch in September, M. de Melo e Castro to conde de Resende, Queluz, 20 September 1792, AHU, Minas Gerais, caixa 92 (47); The Visconde de Barbacena informed Resende that the orders of the alçada had been exactly carried out, Visconde de Barbacena to Conde de Resende, 31 May 1792, IHGB, lata 109, doc. 39.

[1] 'Ultimos momentos...'. *AMI*, II (1953) 240–3.

and alliance which permeated the institutional, bureaucratic, magisterial, and military hierarchies. The process was exaggerated by the Brazilianization of a large percentage of the officer corps of the dragoons and the appointment of men with local interests and ambitions to the magistracy. This situation, of itself dangerous to the metropolitan government, was the more so when the Brazilian-born found themselves cut out of lucrative positions and possibilities, and when those who had farmed the revenues and duties of the captaincy and who were debtors to the crown for staggering sums were unceremoniously required to pay up their arrears or face possible expropriation.

The debt position of Minas was unique. The situation in the other southern captaincies was quite the opposite. In Rio de Janeiro the vice-regal exchequer was itself the debtor.[1] This had been the result of the vast expenditures undertaken during the campaigns on the southern frontiers against the Spaniards. Out of an estimated four millions of *milreis* owed to the crown on contracts throughout Portuguese America in 1781 over two million was owed in Minas Gerais alone.[2] Minas, moreover, had benefited from no windfalls which might have mitigated the situation of the crown's debtors in the captaincy. The Jesuits had never been permitted into Minas after the 1720s (except as teachers at the seminary at Mariana). In consequence no choice properties fell into the laps of the local oligarchs on reasonable terms following the expulsion of the 'black robes' in 1759 as had happened in Bahia, Rio de Janeiro and possibly elsewhere.[3] Planters and merchants in the northeast – Pará, Maranhão, Pernambuco – although indebted as individuals to the former monopoly companies, had escaped the additional burden of contract debts as a result of the abolition of the Pombaline enterprises. For the companies themselves farmed the revenues, and they, not individuals as in Minas, were responsible for the payments to the Royal Treasury.[4] In Minas Gerais of the over two millions of *milreis* owed to the crown in the

---

[1] Dauril Alden, *Royal Government*, 350.

[2] 'Account of What is Owed to the Royal Treasury in the Different Captaincies of Brazil from the Yield of Contracts rented and administered', (*ca.* 1781), Appendix IV, *ibid.*, 507–8.

[3] The great magnate Joaquim Vicente dos Reis had obtained his estates in the captaincy of Rio de Janeiro from the alienation of Jesuit properties, see document dated 19 October 1798, in the collection of the Museu da Inconfidência, Ouro Prêto, Minas Gerais. The original acts of sequestration of these properties are in the Archive of the Museu Histórico Nacional in Rio de Janeiro, see Matias, *ACC*, III, 261. Joaquim Vicente was no relation of Silvério dos Reis. He was in fact his bitter enemy.

[4] 'Relação das dividas que se ficarão devendo a Fazenda Real da Capitania de Pernambuco ate 31 Dezembro 1773', AHU, códice 1182.

captaincy, almost a million was the responsibility of only two men, Silvério dos Reis and Rodrigues de Macedo.[1]

Melo e Castro's policy directives of 1788 had to all intents and purposes been abandoned in the aftermath of the discovery of the plot. In fact over the vital question of the administration of the royal fifth they had been abandoned by Barbacena even before he had heard of the conspiracy. Nothing constructive had replaced them and, as basically the situation which had led to the Minas conspiracy had not changed, the need for fresh initiatives was critical. Melo e Castro's policy had been based on a fundamental misconception. His failure to accept that the golden age had ended and his belief that abuses and malpractices alone had caused declining gold quotas led to dangerous and provocative decisions. But he was not wrong in assuming that the affairs of the captaincy needed reform, and the very consequences of his earlier decisions only made the need for new approaches more immediate. What Melo e Castro had not grasped was the fact that a fundamental reassessment of his approach was needed, and that the special circumstances of Minas Gerais had to be appreciated. D. Rodrigo José de Meneses had pointed the way some ten years before, and Manuel Ferreira da Câmara had put forward a rational program before the Academy of Sciences in Lisbon. Yet Melo e Castro was too old, or tired, or too pigheaded to make the mental adjustments necessary. The fault was not his entirely. The way that the conspiracy had been presented to him had camouflaged much of its motivation. Far from dealing with the broader causes of the conspiracy the decisions taken in Lisbon during 1790 had merely avoided the basic questions. The show trial and the ritual celebration of *Tiradentes'* death did not in any way tackle the basic issues, or in any way defuse, combat, or mitigate the factors which had led to revolt.

The timing and the ideology of the Minas conspiracy, moreover, had projected the movement into a very much greater context. The success of the American Revolution and the impact in Brazil of the ideas of Raynal and others meant that the magnates of Minas Gerais had articulated their opposition to Portuguese dominion in terms that challenged the colonial system in the most fundamental way. There had been uprisings far more damaging in lives and property before, but none had possessed motivations so fundamentally anti-colonial and so consciously nationalist. The proposed revolt had not materialized, but that

---

[1] 'Relação dos contratos que rematão João Roiz' de Macedo na junta da fazenda d'Minas Gerais, Carlos José da Silva, 26 January 1786'; 'Relação dos contratos...Joaquim Silvério dos Reis', AHU, Minas Gerais, caixa 94.

did not detract from the fact that an important segment of that group in society on whom the metropolitan government most relied for the exercise of its power at the local level, in one of Brazil's most important, most populous, and strategically placed captaincies, had dared to think that they might live without Portugal. Backed by the example of the North Americans and by current political theory they had questioned what had been unquestioned. The conspirators had faltered in their will, and had failed in their objectives, but they had thought new thoughts. The *status quo ante* could never be reestablished. The new mental climate was not something that could be concretely defined, but it was obvious to all, and most especially to the agents of the metropolitan government in Brazil. However material were their immediate compulsions, men in Minas Gerais had thought that they could be free, and independent, and republican, and because of that the relationships and acceptances of the past were meaningless.

And experience and failure had brought lessons. In the aftermath of the conspiracy, and during the interrogations, the ties of family and clientage had been found wanting. Luís Váz had betrayed his brother. The *alferes* Silva Xavier had been denounced by those he regarded as his friends and protectors. Professional loyalties had proved noticeably stronger, particularly between the magistrates. All were graduates of the same university, often they were colleagues and contemporaries. And where family had failed, wealth and bribery had been triumphant. The need for more formal, equal, and resilient commitments between like-minded men was self-evident. Members of the Literary Society of Rio de Janeiro, which had been founded by the former viceroy, Luís de Vasconcelos e Sousa in 1785, attempted to found a secret society where 'good faith and secrecy might be maintained among the members'. Democratically constituted, the society was to discuss 'philosophy in all its aspects'.[1] Brazilians after 1790 were clearly searching for new ways to organize confidentially and in mutual trust for agreed-upon objectives. It was not surprising that within the next decade freemasonry was to find fervent adherents throughout Brazil.[2] Melo e Castro and the intendent

---

[1] See Rizzini, *Hypólito da Costa*, 93, 95. The society had been founded by Vasconcelos e Sousa in 1786 and was a successor to the Scientific Society set up by the marquês de Lavradio in 1771; 'Devassa ordenada pelo vicerey conde de Rezende', 1794, *ABNRJ*, LXI (1939) 241–523.

[2] Masonic lodges appeared in Brazil during the early nineteenth century, first at Niterói with *Reunião* in 1801 and thereafter spread rapidly throughout Portuguese America. It is possible that Brazilian students in Europe, especially those who had been to France, had become masons earlier. Hypólito da Costa joined a Philadelphia lodge while in the United

of police in Lisbon were well aware that this might be the case. The secretary of state warned the governors in Brazil that the 'pernicious and perverse intentions of the [Jacobin] clubs formed in France was to spread the abominable and destructive principals of Liberty'.[1] The innocuous literary society of Rio with its inner secret conclave, its dedication to Raynal and Mably, and its reported sympathy for the Minas conspirators, was an all too obvious target for the nervous colonial administration. In 1794 its members were arrested, imprisoned and subjected to prolonged interrogations.[2] With the failure of Lisbon to provide constructive alternatives, arbitrary repression had replaced rational action.

By the mid 1790s it was clear to many both within and without the Portuguese government that relations between the colony and the metropolis had reached an impasse. The conspiracy in Minas had been a miserable and ignominious disaster, but so too had been Portuguese colonial policy. They had both been attempts to rationalize the changed relationships between the colony and the mother country. They had both been in formulation profoundly influenced by local social and economic compulsions. But there had been a double failure. The nationalist revolt and neo-mercantilism had proved abortive, and more than that they were seen to have been so. When Melo e Castro died in 1795, he left a profound crisis of Empire and a chronic and urgent need for new directions.

States at the turn of the century. Masonic influence has often been seen in the Minas conspiracy though the evidence is slight. It seems unlikely that had masonic organization been present it would not have been avidly exposed by the investigating commissions. A. Tenório D'Albuquerque, *A Maçonaria e a Inconfidência Mineira*, (Rio de Janeiro, n.d.) is an entirely unconvincing attempt to find masonic influences in the 1789 movement.

[1] Martinho de Melo e Castro to Sr Bernardo José de Lorena, Lisbon, 21 February 1792, 'correspondência recebida e expedida pelo General Bernardo José de Lorena', 1788–97, *DISP*, XLV (1924) 449–52.

[2] 'Devassa ordenada pelo vicerey, conde de Rezende', 1794, *ABNRJ*, LXI(1939) 241–523.

CHAPTER 8

COMPROMISE

The bulk of the people are attached to the name of their country, their religion, and their language; and I am persuaded that if the Court of Portugal had sufficient energy and activity to transplant itself to the Brazils...a mighty and brilliant empire might speedily be created in South America...

John Barrow, *A voyage to Cochinchina*... (London, 1806) 128.

I say the imaginary evils of a separation of the mother country from our alliance and ascendency would be amply compensated, and would disappear altogether before the certain and incalculable benefit attending a direct and intimate intercourse with the colonies.

Robert Fitzgerald [British Envoy in Lisbon] to Lord Hawkesbury, Lisbon, 21 October 1803, PRO, FO, 63 42.

When Martinho de Melo e Castro died on 24 March 1795, Luís Pinto de Sousa Coutinho took over as interim secretary of state for the overseas dominions.[1] Luís Pinto had direct experience of Brazil. It was at his instigation that two young Brazilians had been sent out during 1790 into a turbulent Europe to seek mineralogical and technical training that might be used for the rational development of solutions to the special problems of Minas Gerais.[2] Correspondents in Brazil urged him that in place of blind reaction the consequences of the conspiracy should be met with reform and moderation, that the peculiar debt problems of the captaincy had to be taken into account, and in particular, that Brazilians should not be prohibited from access to office and positions of responsibility.[3] As the young governor designate of Mato Grosso in 1767, Luís

[1] For report of British minister in Lisbon on the death of Melo e Castro, Robert Walpole, Lisbon, 4 April 1795, PRO, FO, 63/20; The cabinet expressed its regret in a dispatch from Downing Street, April 1795, PRO, FO, 63/20; Luís Pinto's first dispatch as secretary for the overseas dominions was dated 26 March 1795, AHU, códice 610, f. 194v-5; Death of Melo e Castro announced to Brazilian governors 30 March 1795. Luís Pinto de Sousa Coutinho to Bernardo José de Lorena, Queluz, 30 March 1795, *DISP*, XLV (1924) 464.

[2] 'Instrução', Ajuda, 31 May 1790, Luís Pinto de Sousa Coutinho, Carneiro de Mendonça, *O Intendente Câmara*, 26-7.

[3] Domingos Alves Branco Moniz Barreto, 'Observações etc., sobre a rebellião da capitania de Minas, Lisboa, 1793', manuscript volume, Biblioteca Municipal do Porto, (BMP) 11/códice no. 1123/861, and 'appendix que se promette na 5a demenstração do discurso formado sôbre a premeditada conjuração na capitania de Minas, original de Domingos Alves Branco Moniz Barreto', 189/códice no. 1054/884, *ibid*; These came from the private

Compromise

Pinto had received Pombal's eloquent advice, that 'in whatever resolution' he intended, he should employ 'prudence in deliberation, dexterity in preparation, and perseverence in execution'.[1] Of all the members of the Portuguese government he was most aware of the bankruptcy of colonial policy and of the need for rapid and conciliatory reforms.

After two months in office, on 27 May 1795, Luís Pinto forwarded a circular to the Brazilian governors.[2] It contained a startling admission of past mistakes and the promise of fundamental reforms. 'Defects of policy and fiscal restrictions had until now held back the progress of Brazil', he wrote. 'Her Majesty desiring to calm her subjects as much as possible', had taken important decisions. First it was proposed that the salt monopoly should be abolished in Brazil. Secondly, the government intended to encourage the mining and manufacture of iron, especially in Minas and São Paulo. The circular was a statement of intent, but it was to be made public to the municipal councils, whose advice was sought on the best methods to make up for the revenues lost to the crown by its action. The dispatch from Luís Pinto represented a new approach of some importance. It demonstrated, and was no doubt intended to demonstrate, that at the center of government there was a new willingness to seek a way out of the impasse. And it offered hope that an accommodation might be found between the discredited extremes of neo-mercantilism and nationalist revolt. On 25 August 1795, Luís Pinto removed the Visconde de Barbacena from office. The governor of São Paulo, Bernardo José de Lorena, was to replace him.[3]

collection of Luís Pinto, later visconde de Balsamão, presently in the Oporto Municipal Library, also in this collection, 'Copia de umas observações sôbre a necessidade de supprir com as artes e scienias mathematicas e physicas as colonias das Minas Gerais, pela dificuldade do seu actual trabalho', 170/códice no. 464.

[1] 'Carta instrutiva do marquês de Pombal a Luís Pinto de Sousa Coutinho', 1767, Marcos Carneiro de Mendonça, 'O pensamento da metropole em relação do Brasil', *RIHGB*, CCXXVII (October–December 1962) 54.

[2] Luís Pinto de Sousa Coutinho to Bernardo José de Lorena, Queluz, 27 May 1795, Arquivo do Estado de São Paulo, caixa, 63, N. Ordem 421, livro 171, f. 159–61. I am grateful to David Davidson for this reference. For a complete transcription see, Carneiro de Mendonça, *O Intendente Câmara*, 174–5. For the governor of São Paulo's reply and the results of the consultations with the câmaras, Bernardo José de Lorena to Luís Pinto de Sousa Coutinho, São Paulo, 20 April 1796, with enclosed documents, *DISP*, XLV (1924) 129–81. The original letter from Luís Pinto is also published here pp. 466–8.

[3] For Bernardo de Lorena's acknowledgement of appointment, Bernardo de Lorena to Luís Pinto de Sousa Coutinho, São Paulo, 20 April 1796, *DISP*, XLV (1924) 187. Two weeks before the official letter had been dispatched from Lisbon Jacinto Fernandes Brandão had written to the governor designate 'quanto a passagem de Vª Exª para as Minas Gerais os Snes Ministros de Estado me disserão que era necessario que V. Exª fosse, para por a direito muitas coizas que estavão fora da ordem...' Brandão to Bernardo José de Lorena, Lisbon, 12 August 1795, BNLCP, códice 643, f. 490.

Conflicts and conspiracies

To formulate and implement the reforms Luís Pinto had outlined, the Portuguese minister in Sardinia, D. Rodrigo de Sousa Coutinho was recalled to Lisbon, and in 1796 became responsible for colonial affairs.[1] D. Rodrigo was not related to Luís Pinto, though both men were in agreement over the need for reform. The new secretary of state was a close personal friend of the governor designate of Minas Gerais.[2] D. Rodrigo had impressive credentials. Son of D. Francisco Innocencio de Sousa Coutinho, who had been a governor of Angola and ambassador to Madrid, D. Rodrigo was educated by Sr Franzini, the Italian tutor of the heir apparent Dom José. Pombal, his godfather, it was widely believed, intended D. Rodrigo to exercise an influence with the prince comparable to his own relationship with Dom José I.[3] True or false it was a background that was more liability than advantage to D. Rodrigo when the death of the heir apparent, and the madness of the Queen, made Dom João effectively head of state in 1792 and Prince Regent in 1799.

A student at the College of Nobles during its early years, D. Rodrigo was enlightened and well informed. As a young man he had visited France and observed what he then called its 'parasitic and useless court' and its 'chaotic financial administration'. His sojourn in Paris strongly influenced his later approach to governmental problems in Portugal. In Paris he met the Abbé Raynal. He told Raynal that the 'population and resources of France would have made her insupportable to the rest of Europe were it not for the disorder of her financial administration'. Raynal replied that 'Providence had given France the forces but had refused her good sense. France would indeed be terrible if her natural power was matched by a just and wise administration.' D. Rodrigo writing to his sister about his conversation with Raynal asked: 'What would be better for Europe, to be a factory of the English or a slave of France? The only thing that can console us is the almost total impossibility of France reforming her system of government.'[4] D. Rodrigo was right in his analysis, but wrong in his prediction. Reform in France came

---

[1] Luís Pinto announced the appointment of D. Rodrigo de Sousa Coutinho, 9 September 1796, Luís Pinto de Sousa Coutinho to Bernardo José de Lorena, DISP, XLV (1924) 486; D. Rodrigo's first dispatch was dated, 24 September 1796, AHU, códice 610, f. 194v–195.

[2] They had been fellow students at the College of Nobles, as had the Visconde de Barbacena, Romulo de Carvalho, História da fundação do colégio Real dos Nobres de Lisboa 1761–1772, 182–6; '[S]atisfazendo assim a razão de condiscipulo e aos deveres de huma sincera amizade contrahida deste os nossos primeiros annos', D. Rodrigo de Sousa Coutinho to Bernardo José de Lorena, Arroyos, 11 October 1798, AHU, códice 610, f. 215v–16.

[3] Marquês do Funchal, O conde de Linhares, Dom Rodrigo Domingos António de Sousa Coutinho (Lisbon, 1908) 23, 186.

[4] All citations in this paragraph from D. Rodrigo to Dona Mariana de Sousa Coutinho, Fontainebleau, 4 August 1779. Funchal, Linhares, 191–4.

through revolution. And as Europe headed toward hostilities and world war, the choice between Great Britain and France, which D. Rodrigo had dreaded in 1779, was precisely that with which Portugal was faced.

Dom Rodrigo attributed the collapse of the French monarchy to its fiscal situation, and his opposition to monopolies, contracting of revenues, and his fervent support for an efficient and solvent financial administration grew from his belief that intelligent reform in Portugal was essential if similar disasters were to be avoided. The 'good administration of the royal exchequer would contribute most to the opulence and conservation of the vast overseas dominions', he wrote.[1] Taxation should not be 'arbitrary, but fixed, and all of it should enter the royal coffers with the minimum possible deduction. It should fall equally in exact proportion to the ability of those taxed to pay. An active and loyal administration was always superior to a system of farming and contracts.'[2] D. Rodrigo, at pains always to explain the reasons for his actions, was convinced that 'wise and enlightened reforms executed by intelligent men, capable of forming wise and well organized systems, the utility of which would be seen and recognized by all', would overcome the vast problems that confronted the Portuguese government.[3] He regarded the drafting of new mining legislation to be the preeminent issue on taking office, and intended that his measures 'in favor of the mines...should be based on the most liberal principals, if it is legitimate to adopt to our language the sense which the English attribute to that word'.[4]

In order to formulate the 'great plan' that he intended for Minas Gerais, the new secretary of state was able to work with a substantial body of evidence and recommendations. The municipal councils of Minas had responded at some length to Barbacena's circular announcing the suspension of the *derrama*. The câmaras were frank and offered constructive proposals for reform. The câmara of Mariana suggested that the whole of the captaincy's debt under the gold quota law be pardoned. It recommended that the *casas de fundição* be abolished and a mint reestablished in the captaincy. The value of gold should be set at 1$500 *reis* per oitava. It recommended the prohibition against gold mining in the Diamond District be revoked. The *junta da fazenda* of the captaincy ought to encourage 'societies of miners' where resources and skills might be pooled. The câmara suggested that at the cost of the state 'corporations of intelligent mechanics

---

[1] 'Plano sôbre o meio de restabelecer o crédito Público e segurar recursos para as grandes despezas', 29 October 1799, Funchal, *Linhares*, 173–9.
[2] 'Plano de fazenda', 14 March 1799, Funchal, *Linhares*, 155–68
[3] 'Discurso IV', Funchal, *Linhares*, 135.
[4] 'Discurso II', Funchal, *Linhares*, 120.

and miners in imitation of Sweden and Germany should investigate, agree and suggest methods' for overcoming mining problems.[1] The municipal council of Vila Rica also recommended that the exchange rate for gold be that of 'its just value' of 1$500 *reis* per oitava, and pointed out that although contraband was certainly a cause of diminished quotas the preeminent cause was the lack of gold produced.[2] The junta da fazenda in Vila Rica had also pondered, and the Intendent Bandeira and Carlos José da Silva each offered lengthy opinions. The fall in the quotas was, in their opinion, due both to contraband and to declining returns. They recommended that the part of the 1750 law permitting the circulation of gold dust be rescinded and specially minted provincial money circulate instead. Agents of the intendencies should be present wherever gold was extracted and 'permute the gold for money'. They too recommended that the value of gold per oitava be 1$500 *reis*.[3]

In Lisbon, Domingos Vandelli, in a memorial on the gold mines of Brazil, complained that policy had been previously 'left only in the hands of people ignorant of mineralogy to the grave prejudice of the state'. Whether gold mines were advantageous or prejudicial to Portugal he left to 'those politicians who know how to calculate the true interest of nations'. He recommended that practical experience be taken into account, especially that of scholars who might have travelled to Germany.[4] Antônio Pires da Silva Ponte, who had been denounced while a member of the border commissions in Brazil for his comments on the future of Minas, was consulted by D. Rodrigo and later embodied his thoughts in an essay on the mines. He emphasized the necessity for more training in the mathematical and physical sciences and metallurgy, because of 'the present great difficulties in extracting gold'. He criticised the fact that the value of gold in Minas Gerais was kept artificially below its value outside. He went so far as to suggest that the royal fifth be abolished and replaced with taxes on luxury goods proportional to their price. He pointed to the fact that Minas abounded in agricultural and pastoral riches, which should be encouraged. 'The royal revenues do not depend

[1] 'Causas determinantes da diminuição da contribuição das cem arrobas de ouro, appresentadas pela câmara de Marianna, Cidade de Marianna, e em Câmara, Junho 1789', *APM*, VI (1901) 143–51; In AHU, Minas Gerais, caixa 92.

[2] 'Carta da câmara de Villa Rica sôbre a derrama, Villa Rica em câmara, 5 August 1789', 5 August 1789', *RAPM*, IV (1899) 786–92.

[3] 'Ponderações da junta da Fazenda sôbre os meios de se resarcir o prejuizo da Real Fazenda com a arrecadação do quinto do ouro, 1791', *APM*, VI (1901) 153–73; In AHU, Minas Gerais, caixa 92.

[4] 'Memória...sôbre as Minas de Ouro do Brazil por Domingos Vandelli', *ABNRJ*, XX (1898) 266–78.

so much on the fifth of the gold...as in the number of consumers (*consumidores*) and inhabitants in the region.'[1] José Eloi Ottoni in a memorial on the state of the captaincy agreed that the extraction of gold was now beyond the capacities of the miners. He pointed to the absurd expense of imported iron and steel. It was most important to promote agriculture and commerce with the interior by removing all difficulties in the way of import taxes. Communications should be opened, especially along the Rio Doce and the Rio São Francisco. He did not mean to suggest that all manufactures be permitted in Brazil, but he did think it wise to allow those which provided substitutes for items which 'from negligence we buy from foreigners, iron, steel, saltpetre'.[2] Bishop Azeredo Coutinho, like Ottoni, pointed to the absurd price of iron on Minas Gerais. A quintal of iron which in Portugal cost about 3$800 *reis* he said, would in Minas Gerais be worth 19$000 *reis*, and in Goiás and Mato Grosso 28$000 *reis*. It was 'absolutely necessary' he concluded that schools of mining be immediately established in São Paulo, Minas Gerais, Goiás, Cuiabá, and Mato Grosso.[3]

For practical information D. Rodrigo mobilized a task force of erudite Brazilians in America. José Vieira Couto and José Teixeira da Fonseca Vasconcelos were instructed to collect information on salt deposits, especially in the São Francisco river valley.[4] João Manso Pereira, subsidized by local tax money, was to conduct mineralogical and metallurgical investigations and experiments in São Paulo, Minas Gerais and Rio de Janeiro.[5] Joaquim Veloso Miranda, a student of Vandelli, whose information had been used by the Italian scholar in his memorial, was appointed secretary to the governor of Minas. He was encouraged to continue his studies of the natural resources of the region, and most

---

[1] 'Memória sôbre a utilidade pública em se extrahir o ouro das Minas e os motivos dos poucos interesses que fazem os particulares que minerão actualmente no Brazil, por António Pires da Silva Pontes Leme [*sic*]', with letter to D. Rodrigo, *APM*, I (1896) 417–26.

[2] 'Memória sôbre o estado actual da capitania de Minas Gerais por José Eloi Ottoni, estando em Lisboa no anno de 1798', *ABNRJ*, xxx (1908) 303–18.

[3] 'Discurso sôbre o estado actual das Minas do Brasil', *Obras Económicas de J. J. da Cunha de Azeredo Coutinho (1794–1804) apresentação de Sérgio Buarque de Holanda* (São Paulo, 1966) 190–229.

[4] Rodrigo de Sousa Coutinho to Bernardo José de Lorena, Queluz, 18 March 1797, AHU, códice 610, f. 202v.; Also see Carneiro de Mendonça, *O Intendente Câmara*, 176–7; and 'Memória sôbre as Minas da capitania de Minas Gerais, suas descripções, ensaios, e domicílio próprio; a maneira de itinerario com hum appendice sôbre a nova lorena diamantina, sua descripção e utilidades, que d'esta paiz possa resultar ao estado, por ordem de sua alteza real, 1801, por José Vieira Couto', IHGB, lata 18, doc. 17.

[5] Rodrigo de Sousa Coutinho to Bernardo José de Lorena, Queluz, 18 March 1797, AHU, códice 610, f. 202.

especially into the deposits of saltpetre.[1] José de Sá Betencourt received a commission to investigate the copper and saltpetre deposits in Jacobina after he had forwarded a memorial on the plantation of cotton in Ilhéus, a comarca to the south of Bahia where he had lived since his escape from Minas in 1789.[2] The secretary of state was very explicit in outlining the objectives of these various investigations. He told Veloso Miranda 'that orders might perhaps be issued to the governor to establish the manufacture of gunpowder on the account of the royal exchequer...as soon as sufficient saltpetre was found'.[3] Governor Lorena was informed that the proposed ironworks would be set up on the account of the exchequer and the iron sold at reasonable prices 'equally beneficial to the royal exchequer and the inhabitants of the captaincy'.[4] When Manuel Ferreira da Câmara returned to Portugal during 1798, D. Rodrigo at once called for his views on his proposed mining legislation.[5]

By 1798 after almost three years of study and planning the first drafts of the legislation were written.[6] The proposals for Minas were of revolutionary proportions and envisioned a complete revamping of the administrative, fiscal, and organizational structure of the captaincy. Administrative distinction between the Diamond District and the captaincy was to be abolished. The royal fifth would be abandoned, and a tenth of the gold produced taken instead. Foundry houses in Minas were to be abolished and the Mint in Rio de Janeiro closed, a new Mint being established in Minas to replace them. Exchange houses would be set up to receive the gold in return for an equal value of a provincial

---

[1] Rodrigo de Sousa Coutinho to Bernardo José de Lorena, Queluz, 21 February 1797, AHU, códice 610, f. 201v. And Rodrigo de Sousa Coutinho to Joaquim Veloso de Miranda, Queluz, 18 March 1787, AHU, códice 610, f. 202v.

[2] D. Rodrigo de Sousa Coutinho to D. Fernando José de Portugal Queluz, 2 March 1798; and a letter from José de Sá Betencourt Accioli, Bahia, 7 October 1797; *Memórias Históricas e Políticas do Cel. Ignácio Accioli de Cerqueira e Silva, annotador Dr. Braz do Amaral*, (6 vols., Bahia, 1940) VI, 278 (*MHPB*) most of the references from this work will come from the documents transcribed by Dr Braz do Amaral in his extensive notes; The printed work on cotton was entitled, *Memória sôbre a plantação dos algodões e sua exportação; sôbre a decadencia da lavoura de mandiocas, no termo da villa de Camamú, comarca dos Ilhéus, governor da Bahia... Por José de Sá Betencourt* (Lisbon, 1798). There is a copy in the Greenlee collection of the Newberry Library, Chicago.

[3] Rodrigo de Sousa Coutinho to Joaquim Veloso de Miranda, Queluz, 17 September 1799, AHU, códice 611, f. 7.

[4] Rodrigo de Sousa Coutinho to Bernardo José de Lorena, 20 September 1798, AHU, códice 610, f. 212v–13v.

[5] Carneiro de Mendonça, *O Intendente Câmara*, 33–66.

[6] Numerous drafts of the future legislation were made, for some of these see AHU, Minas Gerais, caixa 57, doc. 221 (This is mistakenly dated 1780 on the folder). These projects were written between 1798–1800. The first drafts are in the name of Queen Maria, the latter in that of the Prince Regent.

coin to be made of copper and silver. Paper money was also contemplated. The establishment of the system would be financed by a loan of two million *cruzados* on which 5 per cent interest, free of tax, every six months, would be paid out of the royal revenues of the captaincy. New taxes, 'productive, but not onorous to the people', would be placed on luxury goods, slaves and taverns. The administration would be composed of the governor, a General Intendent of Minas for the captaincy (a new position), the *ouvidor* of Vila Rica, two mineralogists and two metallurgists. Mining schools would be established on the models of those at Freiburg in Saxony, and in Hungary. The ideas of the câmaras, the various memorialists, and Manuel Ferreira da Câmara were very evident in the specific proposals contained in the draft legislation.

But the proposals for Minas Gerais were no more than a part of a much broader program for imperial reconciliation which D. Rodrigo presented during 1798 to the ministers of state.[1] He intended to 'touch rapidly on the political system that it is most convenient for the Crown to embrace in order to conserve its most vast dominions, particularly those of America, that are properly the base of the greatness of the throne', he told the councillors. 'The dominions in Europe do not form any longer the capital and center [of the Portuguese Empire]' D. Rodrigo asserted. 'Portugal reduced to herself would within a very brief period be a province of Spain.' He advised that the empire should be regarded as being composed of 'provinces of the monarchy, all possessing the same honors and privileges, all reunited with the same administrative system, and all contributing to the mutual and reciprocal defense of the monarchy'. All subjects 'wherever they were born' must enjoy equal rights. Brazil itself should be divided and centralized into two great centers of power which in the north would be Pará and in the south Rio de Janeiro. It was essential, he said, to 'occupy our true natural limits', and in particular the northern bank of the Rio de la Plata. The choice of governors was important in order to maintain justice and the efficient administration of the royal exchequer, and with higher salaries, he believed, governors would have less incentive to become embroiled in business. He recommended a total division between the magistracy and the administration of the exchequer. Companies should be formed in order to exploit the mines more efficiently. The number of high courts in Brazil might be increased and the need for appeal to Lisbon be abolished.

[1] Published in full as 'Discurso de D. Rodrigo de Sousa Coutinho', Document No. 4, (1) by Marcos Carneiro de Mendonça, *O Intendente Câmara*, 277–99; This is from the coleção Linhares, BNRJ, MSS. (1) 29-13-16.

There should be a regular movement of troops between Brazil and Portugal. The rivers should be opened up to traffic and commerce. He proposed a reform of the taxation system 'in America and in Minas Gerais in particular', so that it 'should be productive but not fall heavily on the contributors, and it should not support a class of useless and unproductive men...' The contract system would be abolished because it fell unequally on the primary sources of national wealth, and because most of the money remained in the hands of the contractors, 'especially in Minas Gerais'. The *entradas* duties on Negroes, iron, steel, copper, lead, gunpowder and metropolitan manufactures, wines, and olive oil, would be removed. The fifth was to be reduced to a tenth, the circulation of gold dust was to be prohibited, and gold to be valued at 1$500 *reis* per oitava. It was necessary, he held, to distinguish between the maritime and the interior captaincies and to tackle the problems of each group separately. He opposed the division of responsibility for policies between the Treasury and the Department of Overseas Dominions.

In D. Rodrigo's bold plan for Empire the preoccupation with Minas Gerais was obvious. His specific proposals and projected reforms were couched in terms which revealed a thorough analysis of the deep-rooted problems which had led to the confrontation of the 1780s. The division of responsibility between the Treasury and the secretary of state had been in part responsible for the failure to efficiently oversee the activities of the Minas *junta da fazenda*. The local governors involvement in enterprises of dubious propriety had provoked factionalism. The magistrates responsibility in the contracting of revenues had led to Gonzaga's conflict with Cunha Meneses. The failure to move the troops had made the Minas dragoons responsive to local compulsions. The vast contract debts and the failure of the contractors to pay their arrears had been a critical factor in their involvement in the conspiracy. And in addition the plan to establish a mint in Minas Gerais, the proposals to liberalize the Diamond regulations, the proposal to value gold at 1$500 *reis* per oitava, the desire to establish mining schools, the wish to set up a gunpowder factory and exploit iron ore deposits, were all strikingly reminiscent of proposals put forward in secret conventicles ten years before in Vila Rica. Indeed at the highest level of government, many of the specific measures of the Minas conspirators had been accepted, and in 1798 they were being seriously prepared for legislative action.

But the preoccupation with Minas was almost as unbalanced as had been the government's neglect before 1788. The tension points in the colonial system which had existed in the 1780s, now squarely faced and recognized, were not the most critical and potentially dangerous ones in the 1790s. The time lag between social and economic change and policy making which so disastrously influenced Melo e Castro's interpretation of the causes of declining gold quotas, was to a lesser degree present in D. Rodrigo's attitude towards the problems of Portuguese America. His north–south division between Pará and Rio de Janeiro, and his east–west division between the interior and maritime provinces ignored tensions which ran along neither axis. In particular, he had not fully recognized the growing fear of racial revolution which would be of critical importance in determining the receptivity of Brazilians to the reforms offered by Lisbon, nor had he seen the dangers to social stability induced by the socioeconomic consequences of the sugar boom in Brazil. And while policy was being restructured in Lisbon both issues were coming to a head in the former viceregal capital of Salvador da Bahia.

The captaincy of Bahia had regained by the late eighteenth century an economic preeminence which it had lost during the early years of the century. The revival of markets for Brazilian sugar in Europe, especially after the virtual collapse of production in the French sugar colony of Saint Domingue during 1792, gave Bahia the opportunity for economic renaissance.[1] So profitable had sugar become and so high the prices fetched on the European market that according to the professor of Greek in Salvador, Luís dos Santos Vilhena, 'there is no one who does not wish to be a sugar planter'.[2] Bahia exported 746,545 arrobas of sugar to Portugal during 1798.[3] Robert Walpole, the British envoy in Lisbon, attributed the chief cause for the 'enormous prices' of all South American produce to 'the failure of the crops in the French West India Islands, partly owing to political convulsions and consequently the neglect to cultivation, and partly to the hurricanes that have lately happened'. He thought that the euphoric situation was 'probably temporary'.[4] Bishop Azeredo Coutinho, a former sugar mill proprietor from the campos de goitacas turned ecclesiastic, urged in an essay presented to the Lisbon Academy of Sciences in 1791, that full advantage be taken of the favorable market conditions provided by the 'providential' revolution of the French colonies. Voicing an opinion common to most great sugar

[1] See statistical appendix, graph I and supplement.
[2] Luíz dos Santos Vilhena, *Recopilação de noticias soteropolitanas e Basilicas, contidas em XX cartas*...(1802) (annotations by Dr Braz do Amaral, 3 vols., Bahia, 1922–35) I, 158. See Carlos Guilherme Mota 'Mentalidade Ilustrada na Colonização Portuguesa: Luís dos Santos Vilhena', *RHSP*, No. 72 (1967) 405–16.
[3] 'Exportação da Bahia para Portugal' (1798) Vilhena, *Cartas*, I, 53.
[4] Robert Walpole to Lord Grenville, Lisbon, 12 October 1791, PRO, FO, 63/14.

producers in Brazil he recommended that all restraints on production be removed and that there be no price fixing. 'The more the [price of sugar] rises, the greater becomes our production, and our commerce.'[1] Bahian prosperity did not rest exclusively on sugar. The merchants of Salvador had greatly expanded their participation in intercaptaincy shipping. The intercoastal trade in more than one respect made up for the contraction of interior commerce which Bahia like Rio de Janeiro suffered as a result of falling gold production. By the late 1780s the Minas trade with Bahia was almost exclusively confined to mule trains from Minas Novas, and cotton had largely replaced gold as cargoes.[2] Severe drought in Ceará and Paraíba meanwhile had disrupted seriously the production of salt meat in these captaincies, Bahia's traditional suppliers.[3] It was the far south of Portuguese America that provided a substitute. By the late 1790s Rio Grande do Sul was providing Bahia with over 300,000 arrobas of salt meat per annum, as well as cheese and *farinha* flour.[4] During 1800 more ships entered the port of Salvador from Rio Grande do Sul than from Lisbon.[5]

The rolled tobacco of Bahia, most of it from the Cachoeira and Manitiba regions, was the basic commodity of exchange on the West African coast, as necessary to other European slavers as to the Portuguese.[6] Some fifty vessels a year, corvettes and smaller vessels, left Bahia for Africa, four-fifths of them for the Guiné Coast and the remainder for Angola.[7] European goods and gold dust came back to Bahia with the cargoes of slaves. This clandestine commerce had outraged Melo e Castro, as had the degree of control that the merchants of Bahia exercised over the African commerce to the exclusion of metropolitan merchants.[8] The

---

[1] 'Memória sôbre o preço do açúcar', (1791), *Obras Económicas de J. J. da Cunha de Azeredo Coutinho*, 175–85. Also see Manoel Cardozo, 'Azeredo Coutinho and the Intellectual Ferment of his times', Henry H. Keith and S. F. Edwards, eds., *Conflict and Continuity in Brazilian Society* (Columbia, South Carolina, 1969) 72–103; and E. Bradford Burns, 'The Role of Azeredo Coutinho in the Enlightenment of Brazil', *HAHR*, XLIV (May 1964) 145–60. [2] Vilhena, *Cartas*, I, 50–1. [3] *Ibid.*, I, 51.

[4] 'Memória da importação dos portos do Brasil...para a Bahia', 1798, Rio Grande de S. Pedro...', *ibid.*, I, 55.

[5] 'Mappa dos Navios que entrarão e sahirão do Porto da capitánia da Bahia em 1800', IHGB, lata 55, doc. 8.

[6] José da Silva Lisboa to Domingos Vandelli, Bahia, 19 October 1781, *ABNRJ*, XXXII (1910) 505; Also see J. H. Rodrigues, *Brazil and Africa*, and Pierre Verger, *Flux et reflux de la traite des nègres entre le golfe de Bénin et Bahia de todos os santos du dix-septième au dix-neuvième siècle* (Paris/La Haye, 1968). For statistics of slave imports see statistical appendix graph H.

[7] Vilhena, *Cartas*, I, 53; Pierre Verger, *Bahia and the West Africa Trade 1549–1851* (Ibadan, 1964).

[8] 'Instrução para o Marquês de Valença', Martinho de Melo e Castro, Queluz, 10 September 1779, *ABNRJ*, XXXII (1910) 442.

Bahians always pleaded that they were forced into accepting European goods by the other slavers who needed their tobacco.[1] The contraband manufactures, however, did underprice those imported from the metropolis, and restricted the market for metropolitan goods.[2] The profitable subsidiary trade which accompanied the slave and tobacco commerce contributed to the favorable balance Bahia enjoyed with the metropolis.[3] Most of the capital obtained was sunk into the purchase of more slaves.

Martinho de Melo e Castro held that the working of the Bahian–African trade was the same as 'according to the English, French and Dutch, a free trade by the ports of Africa between those nations and the Portuguese dominions in Brazil without the intervention of the merchants of the metropolis'.[4] Admiral Donald Campbell, commandant of the Brazilian squadron of the Portuguese navy during the early years of the nineteenth century, described the people of Bahia as being 'more active in commerce than those in any other part of Brazil'. He found 'the trade [was] generally in their own hands and even their shipping of a superior quality...'[5] Indeed so conscious were the Bahians of their returned prosperity that the municipal council petitioned in 1785 that the government of Bahia be 'restituted to its ancient dignity and primacy in the viceroyalty, so justified by the dignity and primacy of this city, by the riches of its captaincy, and by its natural situation at the centre of Portuguese America'.[6]

It was not only in Bahia that the terms of trade between the metropolis and colony had changed. New as well as old commodities were enjoying high prices in European markets. Pernambuco and Maranhão between them accounted for approximately three-quarters of the raw cotton exported to Portugal from Brazil. Pernambuco also sent almost as much sugar as did Rio de Janeiro. Pernambuco's trade with the metropolis was extremely favorable to her. From Lisbon in return came manufactured

---

[1] 'Offício do Desembargador Gervasio de Almeida Paes para o Governador Marquês de Valença, no qual informa a respeito da referida devassa...', Bahia, 4 February 1783, *ibid.*, 529. [2] José da Silva Lisboa to Domingos Vandelli, Bahia, 19 October 1781, *ibid.*, 505.
[3] In 1796 the value of goods exported from Bahia to Portugal was assessed at 3702,181$721 *reis*, and the value of goods sent from Portugal to Bahia at 2069,637$404 *reis*. 'Tableau général de la valeur des marchandises importées dans le royaume de Portugal...', Balbi, *Essai Statistique*, I, 431.
[4] 'Instrucção para o marquêz de Valença', Martinho de Melo e Castro, Queluz, 10 September 1779, *ABNRJ*, XXXII (1910) 444.
[5] This observation is contained in an extensive discussion of Brazil and its various captaincies by Donald Campbell, dated London, 14 August 1804, in the Chatham Papers, PRO 30/8/345, pt. 2, f. 233. For some description of Campbell, Thomas Lindley, *Authentic Narrative of a Voyage...to Brasil* (2nd edition, London, 1808) 82–3.
[6] 'Representação do senado da Câmara da Cidade da Bahia, Bahia', 4 June 1785, *ABNRJ*, XXXII (1910) 575–6.

goods and also a substantial shipment of specie. Pernambuco was not alone in this position, for all the Brazilian ports with the exception only of Pará showed a favorable balance with the metropolis in 1796.[1]

The sending of bullion to Brazil had been viewed with considerable alarm by Melo e Castro, and it was indeed a spectacular reversal of circumstances. A mere forty years before Brazilian gold had provided the mainstay of colonial exports to Lisbon. Azeredo Coutinho's essay on the commerce of Portugal and its dominions of 1794 attempted to rationalize the new situation. 'The mother country and the colonies taken together ought to be considered like a farm of a single farmer...', he wrote. 'The owner of many estates does not care whether such and such a one procures him more revenues but he only rates the collective revenues of the whole.' If the mother country could not consume all the produce of the colonies or provide sufficient manufactures so that instead money had to be sent 'what prejudice could arise to the mother country? The more colonial products it possesses, the more it has to dispose to foreigners. Though the mother country be, in this case, made debtor to the colonies, yet it becomes, at the same time a creditor doubly consider-able in its claims upon the foreigner.'[2]

The high price of sugar, however, led planters to exploit all available land and strongly resent the obligation imposed by law to raise sub-sistence crops. Professor Luís dos Santos Vilhena condemned the failure of the great plantation owners to grow sufficient manioc, pointing out that similar circumstances in Pernambuco had recently led to famine, for there was simply no other source of supply available. D. Rodrigo José de Meneses, the former governor of Minas, had attempted as governor of Bahia during the 1780s to remedy the problems of dearth and high food prices by establishing a public granary (*cellero público*) where all manioc flour, maize, beans, and rice, were to be sold at both retail and wholesale, and he also established a public slaughter house and stock yard. For both these actions he earned the gratitude of the people of the city of Bahia, and the lasting emnity of the great sugar planters.[3]

[1] 'Tableau général...', Balbi, *Essai statistique*, I, 431.

[2] 'Ensaio Económico sôbre o commércio de Portugal e suas colónias...D. José Joaquim da Cunha de Azeredo Coutinho, Bispo em outro tempo de Pernambuco...e actualmente Bispo d'Elvas...', (Lisbon, 1816) *Obras económicas J. J. da Cunha de Azeredo Coutinho*, 59–172. There was an English translation published in 1807, *An Essay on the commerce and products of the Portuguese colonies in South America, Especially the Brazils...* (London, 1807). The quotations are taken from this edition, pp. 154–5.

[3] 'Offício do governador D. Rodrigo José de Menezes to M. de Mello e Castro', Bahia, 10 October 1785. *ABNRJ*, XXXII (1910) 586; 'Regimento para a regência do novo celleiro público', (1785) *ibid.*, 587; In an unusual gesture the camara of Bahia had requested that

Compromise

The problem was not peculiar to late eighteenth-century Bahia. In a plantation economy oriented to foreign markets, reacting to insistent overseas demand, the coexistence of booming prosperity and chronic high prices and shortages of subsistence foods was a recurrent phenomenon.[1] Salvador had a population of some 40,000 people in the 1780s, and the total for the captaincy was near 280,000.[2] Something like a quarter of the population was white.[3] Half was slave.[4] The consumption of manioc flour in the city during 1781 was over a million alqueires.[5] D. Fernando José de Portugal, successor of D. Rodrigo José de Meneses, had allowed the removal of price controls on meat and manioc flour. Vilhena held 'European ideas' responsible.[6] Such concepts, he complained, should only be applied in a place like Bahia after the most careful attention had been paid to local factors. In Europe, he pointed out, one nation in time of dearth might recourse of her neighbors for added supplies. Such mutual dependence was impossible in South America where food supplies were inelastic. Already drought in the northeast had forced Bahia and Pernambuco to seek new sources of supply in the south. But even in Rio Grande do Sul expansion was hampered by restrictive legislation and the working of the Quintella salt monopoly. The price of manioc flour, the basic subsistence food, had risen during the four years before 1798 from 640 reis per alqueire to between 1,280 and 1,600 reis.[7] Meat likewise, with heavy duties, free price, and the manipulation of the market by

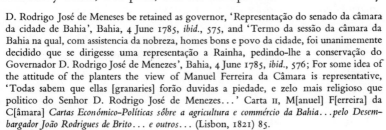

D. Rodrigo José de Meneses be retained as governor, 'Representação do senado da câmara da cidade de Bahia', Bahia, 4 June 1785, *ibid.*, 575, and 'Termo da sessão da câmara da Bahia na qual, com assistencia da nobreza, homes bons e povo da cidade, foi unanimemente decidido que se dirigesse uma representação a Rainha, pedindo-lhe a conservação do Governador D. Rodrigo José de Menezes', Bahia, 4 June 1785, *ibid.*, 576; For some idea of the attitude of the planters the view of Manuel Ferreira da Câmara is representative, 'Todas sabem que ellas [granarias] forão duvidas a piedade, e zelo mais religioso que politico do Senhor D. Rodrigo José de Menezes...' Carta II, M[anuel] F[erreira] da C[âmara] *Cartas Económico-Políticas sôbre a agricultura e commércio da Bahia...pelo Desembargador João Rodrigues de Brito... e outros...* (Lisbon, 1821) 85.

[1] Caio Prado, *A formação*, 157–8.
[2] 'Mappa da enumeração da gente e povo desta capitania da Bahia...', 5 December 1780, *ABNRJ* XXXII (1910) 480.
[3] José da Silva Lisboa to Domingos Vandelli, Bahia, October 18 1781, *ABNRJ*, XXXII (1910) 505. Vilhena put the proportion at nearer a third, Vilhena, *Cartas*, I, 49.
[4] Thales de Azevedo, *Povoamento da cidade do Salvador* (São Paulo 1955) 201.
[5] José da Silva Lisboa to Domingos Vandelli, Bahia, 1781, *ABNRJ*, XXXII (1910) 503.
[6] Vilhena, *Cartas*, II, 446.
[7] *Ibid.*, I, 159; Dauril Alden has computed the price of an alqueire of manioc flour in Rio de Janeiro (1766, 1770) at from 300 to 340 reis, Alden, *Royal Government*, 510. The price per alqueire reached 677 reis during 1787 in Rio, the highest price level between 1763 and 1800. See H. B. Johnson Jr, 'Rio de Janeiro: A Preliminary Inquiry into Money, Prices and Wages (1763–1823)'. *Colonial Roots of Modern Brazil: papers of the Newberry Library Conference* (ed. Dauril Alden, Berkeley and Los Angeles 1972).

monopolists, had resulted according to Vilhena 'in the poor of Bahia being forced to buy the most vile meat imaginable for prices more than twice what it was worth'.[1] He saw a direct connection between the removal of price controls and the 'ineffectual uprising and cruel massacre' projected by the Bahian mulatto artisans in 1798.[2]

The planned uprising in Bahia came at a critical moment, for it served to confirm fears that had been growing since 1792. The magnates of Minas Gerais believed that they could control and manipulate the popular will. They did not fear that any action that they might take against Portugal would in turn provoke and provide excuses for actions against themselves. They had talked naively about the emancipation of native-born slaves. Planning to abolish their debts to the crown, they had no intention that the debts for which they were the creditors should be similarly repudiated. After 1789 such innocence among opulent slave-owners anywhere in the Americas would have been unthinkable. The spectacular repercussions of the French Revolution in Saint Domingue had seen to that. John Barrow noted, during his visit to Rio in 1792, the change triumphant 'black power', as he called it, had wrought. 'The secret spell, that caused the Negro to tremble at the presence of the white man, is in a great degree dissolved', he wrote. 'The supposed superiority, by which a hundred of the former were kept in awe and submission by one of the latter, is no longer acknowledged.'[3] The discovery of plans for an armed insurrection by the *pardo* artisans of Bahia demonstrated what thinking whites had already begun to realize; that ideas of social equality propagated in a society where a mere third of the population was white, and where wealth and power were entirely in white hands, would inevitably be interpreted in racial terms.

The Bahian affair revealed the politicization of levels of society barely involved in the Minas conspiracy. The only racial overtones there had come from vague comments attributed to Manuel da Costa Capenema, and the evidence which linked him to the conspirators was so slight that he was absolved by the alçada.[4] The middle-aged magistrates, lawyers,

[1] Vilhena, *Cartas*, I, 128–9; Also Katia M. de Queirós Mattoso, 'Conjoncture et société au Brésil à la fin du XVIIIe siècle: Prix et Salaires às la veille de la revolution des Alfaiates, Bahia 1798', *Cahiers des Ameriques Latins*, v (January/June 1970) 33–53, especially 41. I am grateful to John N. Kennedy for bringing this important article to my attention.

[2] Vilhena, *Cartas*, II, 445–8.

[3] Barrow, *A Voyage to Cochinchina...*, 117–18. Another visitor Thomas Lindley, however, was surprised that the reaction to the events in Saint Domingue had not been stronger in Bahia.

[4] The statement attributed to him was that 'estes branquinhos do reino que nos querem tomar a terra cedo os havemos de deitar fora'. Santos, *Inconfidência Mineira*, 607, 617.

and clerics in Minas Gerais, the opulent contractors and their hangers-on, most of them members of racially exclusivist sodalities and slaveowners, contrasted markedly with the young mulatto artisans, soldiers, property-less sharecroppers, and salaried school teachers, implicated in the Bahian plot. Embittered and anti-clerical the Bahian mulattoes were as much opposed to rich Brazilians as they were to Portuguese dominion. They welcomed social turmoil, proposed the overthrow of existing structures, and sought an egalitarian and democratic society where differences of race would be no impediment to employment and social mobility. The *pardo* tailor, João de Deus, who at the time of his arrest possessed no more than 80 *reis* and eight children, claimed that 'All [Brazilians] would become Frenchmen, in order to live in equality and abundance... They would destroy the public officials, attack the monasteries, open the port... and reduce all to an entire revolution, so that all might be rich and taken out of poverty, and that the difference between white, black and brown would be extinguished, and that all without discrimination would be admitted to positions and occupations.'[1]

It was not the North American patriots that provided the example for João de Deus and his collegues. It was the sansculottes. It was not the constitutional niceties of the United States that inspired them. It was the slogans of the Paris mob. Handwritten manifestoes appeared throughout the city on 12 August, on walls, in churches and public places.[2] Addressed to the 'Republican Bahian people' in the name of the 'supreme tribunal of Bahian democracy' they called for the extermination of the 'detestable metropolitan yoke of Portugal'.[3] Clergy who preached against popular liberty were threatened. 'All citizens, especially mulattoes and blacks' were told that 'all are equal, there will be no differences, there will be

---

[1] 'Denuncia pública, jurada...que da Joaquim José da Veiga, homen pardo, forro...', 27 August 1798, *A Inconfidência da Bahia: Devassas e Sequesntros* (Biblioteca Nacional, Rio de Janeiro, 2 vols., 1931) (*ADIB*) I, 8; *MHPB*, III, 93.

[2] F. Borges de Barros, 'Cópia de vários papeis sediciosos que em alguns lugares públicos desta cidade se fixarão na manha do dia 12 de agosto de 1798, *Annais do Arquivo Público do Estado da Bahia* II (1917) 143–6; Carlos Guilherme Mota 'Ideia de Revolução no Brasil no final do século XVIII' mestrado, cadeira de historia de civilização moderna e contemporanea, Universidade de São Paulo, 1967 (I am most grateful to Professor Mota for the opportunity of using his valuable unpublished work which he has now revised and published as *Atitudes de Inovação no Brasil 1789–1801* [Lisbon, n.d.]) ; 'Autos de Devassas do levantamento e sedicão intentados na Bahia em 1798', *Anais do Arquivo Público da Bahia*, XXXV, XXXVI (1959–61). For a brief account in English see R. R. Palmer, *The Age of Democratic Revolution, The Struggle* (2 vols., Princeton, 1959, 1964) II, 513; For a first rate quanti-tative study see Katia M. de Queriós Mattoso, 'Conjoncture et société au Bresil à la fin du XVIIIe siècle: Prix et Salaires à la veille de la révolution des Alfaiates, Bahia 1798', *Cahiers des Amériques Latines*, No. 5, January–June 1970) 33–53.

[3] 'Aviso ao clero e ao povo Bahinense indouto', *MHPB*, III, 110.

freedom, equality and fraternity'.[1] Claiming widespread support the manifestoes promised the soldiers 200 *reis* a day and that the port would be open to trade of all nations, and most especially to France.[2] The 'useless câmara' was attacked for its failure to control the price of meat. 'The happy time of our liberty is about to arrive; the time when all will be brothers, the time when all will be equal.'[3] There was no equivocation over slavery: 'All black and brown slaves are to be free, so that there will be no slaves whatever.'[4] The government would be 'Democratic, free and independent'.[5]

Long before they had concerted even the most rudimentary plan the Bahian artisans had been caught redhanded. The conspirators had been identified and were under observation almost as soon as the first investigation was completed. The governor, D. Fernando José de Portugal, a desembargador of the *casa de suplicação*, had immediately instructed that the papers in the secretariate be examined to seek out any that might be in a similar hand to that of the manifestoes.[6] Almost at once suspicion fell on the mulatto Domingos de Silva Lisboa, a professional scribe. He was arrested on 16 August. Four days later, however, more manifestoes appeared. Further scrutiny of the papers and petitions in the secretariate revealed the true author to be Luís Gonzaga das Virgins, a soldier of the First Regiment of the Line. He was interrogated extrajudicially. In the meantime several denunciations had been forthcoming. The commandant of the Second Regiment was instructed to set an ambush for the conspirators at their place of rendezvous on the outskirts of the city, but he was recognized by a soldier of his regiment, and the plotters including João de Deus were forewarned and escaped. On 26 August, forty-seven would-be revolutionaries, or those suspected of being so, were arrested. Most of the prisoners, which included João de Deus, were mulattoes, and nine were slaves.[7]

Dom Fernando informed Lisbon of the discovery of the plot in October. He told D. Rodrigo de Sousa Coutinho that 'the composition

---

[1] 'Prelo', *MHPB*, III, 109.   [2] 'O povo Bahiense', *MHPB*, III, 107.
[3] 'Aviso', *MHPB*, III, 106.
[4] 'Denuncia pública...que da o capitão do regimento auxiliar dos homens pretos Joaquim José de Santa Anna...', *ADIB*, I, 13.
[5] 'Auto...para proceder a devassa pela rebelião e levantamento projectada nesta cidade, para se estabelecer no continente do Brazil, hum governo democratico', 28 August 1798, *ADIB*, I, 7.
[6] D. Fernando José de Portugal to D. Rodrigo de Sousa Coutinho, Bahia, 20 October 1798, *MHPB*, III, 121–5; For account by Braz do Amaral, *ibid.*, III, 96–7; Also Affonso Ruy, *A Primeira Revolução Social Brasileira (1798)* (São Paulo, 1942); 'Termo de conclusão', 18 October 1799, *ADIB*, II, 169–94.
[7] 'Os conspiradores que foram presos', *MHPB*, III, 99–102.

of the seditious papers, so badly organized if extremely bold and imprudent, the character and quality of the author and the principal conspirators...Luís Gonzaga, João de Deus...Lucas Dantas and Luís Pires, all four men mulattoes, [were such] that he did not consider it possible that any people of consideration, or understanding, or who had knowledge and enlightenment had entered the plot.' No formal plan for the revolution had been found among the papers confiscated, nor any letters or correspondence about it. Nonetheless he had thought it prudent to take precautions and sent military and police patrols through the city at night. He was confident that the conspiracy had been discovered in good time, though he did not underestimate the severe damage which might have followed had any action taken place, 'especially in a country with so many slaves, and in the present epoch'. He had thought it essential to institute a devassa, 'considering the example practiced in similar circumstances and recently by the viceroy...and the governor of Minas in [the case of] the uprising in that captaincy'. He requested a decision from Lisbon on the sentence.[1]

On 4 October 1798, however, D. Rodrigo had sent a severe reprimand to the governor. The last convoy from Bahia had brought rumors that 'the principal people of the city were infected with an incomprehensible madness...and were infected with the abominable French principles and with great affection for the absurd intended French constitution that varies every six months'. The cause of this state of affairs, according to the rumors, was the 'negligence of the government and the corruption of the high court which permitted the powerful to do as they pleased'. The state of the military was said to be so bad that if French troops appeared they would not be resisted and 'the principal people would unite with them'. Specifically the wealthy priest and entrepreneur Francisco Agostinho Gomes was denounced. The governor was ordered to institute an immediate inquiry into these allegations, and if true, those guilty were to be punished with the full severity of the law. 'Reward and punishment are the two poles over which the whole political machine is based', D. Rodrigo concluded, 'and in the present moment the greatest possible vigilence was necessary...'[2]

The secretary of state's letter had been drafted before news of the conspiracy reached Lisbon and when it reached Bahia the governor believed that he had been reproved unjustly. He had acted rapidly and

---

[1] D. Fernando José de Portugal to D. Rodrigo de Sousa Coutinho, Bahia, 20 October 1798, *MHPB*, III, 123.

[2] D. Rodrigo de Sousa Coutinho to D. Fernando José de Portugal, Queluz, 4 October 1798. *MHPB*, III, 95.

successfully after the posting of the manifestoes, and his efforts had been rewarded by the rapid arrest of the would be revolutionaries. There was little evidence that anyone but members of 'the lower orders' (*baixa esfera*) had been involved in the plotting. The investigation into the activities of Padre Agostinho Gomes, which the governor immediately instigated, revealed nothing beyond the fact that he was an erudite and informed man and read the English and French gazettes. D. Fernando strongly resented the fact that he should be accused of laxity simply because he 'did not act inconsiderately, without denunciations, without proof, without indications in a matter of such sensitivity and gravity, against the priest or any other person, simply because he read the English newspapers, which were not prohibited...' He pointed out to D. Rodrigo that the reading of the English papers did not make the reader a Jacobin. 'All the governors in America', he continued, 'are reprimanded either for being despots or for being indolent. If they punished without the formalities of law or due process...they merited the name of despot. If on the contrary they proceeded in conformity with the law they were held by some indiscreet and malicious people to be indolent...without remembering that there is a middle ground between the two, which I have followed, or at least wish to follow...' He repeated that he could not believe that any of the principal people of the captaincy were involved. He had no indication of this either among the business men, the men in public office or the people of property, [*homens de bem*], all of whom reacted strongly when the seditious papers appeared. Those involved in the plot were all of the lower classes (*classe ordinaria*). 'That which is always most dreaded in colonies is the slaves, on account of their condition, and because they compose the greater number of inhabitants. [It is there-fore] not natural for men employed and established in goods and property to join a conspiracy which would result in awful consequences to themselves, being exposed to assassination by their own slaves.' He did not seek 'to apologize for the inhabitants of Bahia' he told the secretary of state, he wished only 'to express his sentiments'.[1]

The causes of the Bahian affair had been an amalgam of social resentments, high food prices, and the impact of the revolutionary slogans of France. The special alienation of the mulattoes of the city came from a series of incidents in which they regarded themselves as having been insulted. A white *sargento-mor* had been appointed commandant of the

---

[1] D. Fernando José de Portugal to D. Rodrigo de Sousa Coutinho, Bahia, 13 February 1799, *MHPB*, III, 132–4. For some very pertinent comment on Father Gomes, see Lindley, *Voyage*, 66–8.

auxiliary regiment of free *pardos*, which not only crossed racial lines, but placed the mulatto regiment in an unfavorable relationship with the regiment of free blacks, the famous *Henriques*, with their black colonel-commandant. The mulatto artisans and soldiers, many of them literate, had been receptive to revolutionary ideology. But the appearance of the manifestoes with their demands for 'liberty, equality, and fraternity', and the racial composition of the conspiratorial conclave, provoked a reaction out of all proportion to the incidents themselves. The message of the projected 'cruel massacre' as Vilhena called it, was very clear. Since 1792, it had been the barely hidden concern of slave owners throughout the Americas that the revolution in the Caribbean might prove contagious. The Bahian mulattoes had provided the answer. After 1798 the question that faced all white men in Portuguese America was that posed by Admiral Campbell; Was it indeed the case that 'the transactions at St. Domingo had plainly evinced that there was no stability in the sovereignty of whites in a country necessarily worked by blacks?'[1]

The mulatto revolutionaries with their 'abominable jacobin ideas' received no moderation whatsoever in their punishment. Four of the leaders were hanged in the center of the city on 8 November 1799, and three of them, Lucas Dantas, João de Deus, and Manuel Faustus, all free mulattoes, were beheaded and quartered, parts of their severed bodies being displayed in the public places. The superintendent of health of the city sought to have the rotting flesh removed two days later on the grounds that it was a threat to the public health, but found that it was impossible without specific royal dispensation. Sixteen of the prisoners were released. Seven men, five free mulattoes and two mulatto slaves, were publicly whipped and forced to witness the executions. They with the remainder of the prisoners were as D. Rodrigo had instructed 'entirely separated from among the loyal vassals' of the Queen. Denied even the opportunity to reside in the Portuguese territories in Africa they were literally abandoned along the African coast. The defectors were rewarded with promotions and pensions.[2]

[1] Donald Campbell, London, 14 August 1804, Chatham Papers, PRO, 30/8/345, p. 2, f. 223. Question mark added.
[2] D. Fernando José de Portugal to D. Rodrigo de Sousa Coutinho, Bahia, 19 December 1799, *MHPB*, III, 105; Also in *ADIB*, I, 166; Desembargador Francisco Sabino Alvares da Costa Pinto, to D. Fernando José de Portugal, Bahia, 11 November 1799, *MHPB*, III, 106; Termo de concluzão, *ADIB*, I, 192–4; Luíz Caetano Barata, 9 November 1799, *ADIB*, II, 216–17; D. Rodrigo de Sousa Coutinho to D. Fernando José de Portugal, Queluz, 9 January 1799, *MHPB*, III, 104; *ADIB*, I, 12; Vilhena, *Cartas*, I, 254.

Conflicts and conspiracies

D. Fernando had made a vital distinction, however, while defending his actions to D. Rodrigo, and his comments underlined the change which had occurred since 1792. The sugar planters and their apologists desired 'liberty' to be sure, and the more literate of them were avid disciples of European thinkers, but the theories that appealed to them were those that articulated and provided justification for their own self interests, and these self interests D. Fernando discerned were not in conflict with the colonial relationship. The liberty that the planters most desired was the freedom Bishop Azeredo Coutinho proposed in his memorial on the price of sugar. It was the liberty 'for each to make the greatest profit from his work'.[1] Freedom for capitalist enterprise was not the freedom João de Deus had in mind. As D. Fernando saw, the firmest opponents of the demands of the Bahian mulattoes would be the Bahian planters, for it was they, not Lisbon, who had most to lose if those demands were met.

Paradoxically it was the slave revolt in the Caribbean that had added acuteness to the sugar planters demands for freedom from government interference and control, just as the events in Saint Domingue had also stimulated apprehensions about the racial balance of the population, and produced the socio-economic conditions out of which the Bahian conspiracy emerged. The 'European ideas' that Vilhena condemned as being partly responsible for creating the Bahian situation were most especially those of Adam Smith and J. B. Say. João Rodrigues de Brito and Manuel Ferreira da Câmara used both economists to document and justify their rejection of state interference to regulate production or control the prices of commodities. Rodrigues de Brito and Ferreira da Câmara had been consulted over the state of agriculture in Bahia and their responses were a clear defense of the interests of the great sugar planters. Manuel Ferreira da Câmara, speaking as proprietor of the great sugar mill of Ponte, categorically rejected all laws and regulations that restricted the liberty of the proprietors. He was violently opposed to the Inspection House which regulated the prices of sugar and tobacco, and also to the public granary. These institutions, Câmara claimed, 'had been set up out of the fantasy of those in government as obstacles to the freedom of commerce'. The granary he attributed 'to a zeal more religious than practical...' He could conceive of nothing worse than that commodities 'should be sold for less than they cost to produce or transport'. He boasted that he had not 'planted a single foot of manioc in order not to fall into the absurdity of renouncing the best cultivation of the country for the

---

[1] 'Memória sôbre o preço de açúcar' (1791), *Obras económicas*, 175–85.

worst'. Each 'must be master to do what most benefits him, and what benefits him is that which most benefits the state'.[1]

For Rodrigues de Brito the extent of the government's direction in agricultural matters could be reduced to three points: 'to the granting of liberties, facilities, and instruction'. The proprietor should not be forced to plant manioc. He opposed 'restrictions that prevented our farmers from taking their goods to the places where they could obtain most value'. He argued in favor of the removal of the prohibitions against the *commissários volantes*, the itinerant free traders outlawed by the Marquis of Pombal during the 1750s. He was strongly opposed to price fixing. Freedom should be allowed capitalist enterprise, and in order to encourage the capitalist to participate in agricultural improvement the institutional and judicial obstacles to investment should be removed. 'Intolerable inconveniences placed on the capitalist in the matters of debt collection and foreclosure should be abolished', he contended, and in particular 'foreign investment should be welcomed'.[2]

The apologists for the sugar planters were making a frontal attack on the whole concept of state regulation and government interference in economic matters. Yet the planters' demands were so closely related to their self interests that they were also limited by them. Planters desiring emancipation from government interference did not necessarily desire emancipation from the colonial relationship with Portugal. Laissez-faire for Ferreira da Câmara, Rodrigues de Brito, and Azeredo Coutinho was not synonymous with free international commercial exchange. It was this basic dichotomy that another disciple of Smith, D. Fernando José de Portugal, whose elimination of price controls in Bahia provoked Vilhena's criticism, evidently perceived in 1798. The sugar interests did not lead the demand for free international commerce for one quite simple reason. Brazilian sugar was sold in the continental European market, for which Lisbon was a logical and necessary entrepôt. Britain, the most likely candidate for any free-trade relationship outside the Luso-Brazilian commercial system, placed prohibitive duties on the importation of Brazilian sugar in the interests of its own sugar colonies in the West Indies.

The curious marriage in the writing of Azeredo Coutinho between his attack on state interference and his restatement of the basic tenets of mercantilist colonial policy was a perfect rationalization of the situation. He held up the English Navigation acts as 'a pattern of imitation to all

---

[1] Carta II, M[anuel] F[erreira] da C[âmara] *Cartas Económico-Políticas sôbre a agricultura e commércio da Bahia...pelo Desembargador João Rodrigues de Brito e outros* (Lisbon, 1821) 80–5.

[2] Carta I, João Rodrigues de Brito, *ibid.*

seafaring nations'. It was 'in the true interests of both [metropolis and colony] that the colony be permitted to carry on a direct trade with the mother country only, and they [the colonists] should not have fabrics and manufactories of their own especially of cotton, linen, wool and silk'. In fact, the interests of Brazil, defined as the interests of the great sugar planters, were not at all incompatible with those of Portugal.[1] And the point of view of the planters of the littoral, so accurately stated by Azeredo Coutinho, gained added weight during the 1790s, of course not only as a result of the sugar boom, but because of the temporary removal of any political influence from Minas Gerais, a region not dominated by an export oriented plantation economy.

There were Brazilians, however, less closely linked to the interests of the sugar planters who reacted differently to the problems of the 1790s. Among the papers confiscated from Jacinto José da Silva, one of those arrested at the time of the suppression of the Literary Society of Rio de Janeiro, were two remarkable letters from a colleague, Manuel José de Novais de Almeida, which dramatically underlined the impact of the revolt in Saint Domingue on some contemporaries. In February 1791, Dr Novais de Almeida had written enthusiastically of the 'equality of men'. But by 25 May 1792, his comments had a different tone. 'I am very worried with respect to the Americas', he told da Silva. 'What happened in [French America] demonstrates what might one day happen in ours, which God permitting I shall never see, for I am a friend of humanity. [...] Sell the slaves that you possess, have the generosity to grant them their freedom, you will have fewer enemies...'[2] For Novais de Almeida, the basic issue was slavery itself, and he was not alone in this perception. D. Fernando found it necessary to expel a Capuchin friar from Bahia during 1794 for his anti-slavery statements.[3] Professor Luís dos Santos Vilhena, observed soberly that he was 'not persuaded that the commerce in slaves is so useful as it seems'. He believed that 'Negroes were prejudicial to Brazil'.[4] A similar attitude had been expressed some years before by his colleague, José da Silva Lisboa, Professor of Philosophy in Salvador and secretary of the Bahian Inspection House. While he recognized the importance of slavery and sugar to the Bahian economy,

---

[1] *An essay on the commerce*, 55–157.
[2] 'Auto do exame que fizerão o Dez[embargador] Ou[vidor] G[eneral] do Crime Francisco Alvarez de Andrade, e o Dr. Intendent General do Ouro, Caetano Pinto de Vasconcellos Monte Negro, em todos os Papeis do Dr. Jacinto José da Silva', Rio de Janeiro, 8 January 1795, *ABNRJ*, LIX (1939) 364–70.
[3] Dom Fernando José de Portugal to Martinho de Melo e Castro, Bahia, 18 June 1794, *RIHGB*, LX, pt. I (1897) 155–7.
[4] Vilhena, *Cartas*, I, 136, 139–40.

Silva Lisboa did not believe that the number of slaves imported brought a commensurate increase in population or agricultural production. And like Vilhena he believed slavery was responsible for many of the ills of Brazilian society.[1]

The very suggestion of slave emancipation was anathema to the planters. Azeredo Coutinho regarded abolitionist sentiment sufficiently threatening to warrant a blistering attack on 'the insidious principals of the philosophic sect'. What would happen to the agriculture of Brazil and in consequence the commerce and prosperity of Portugal if slavery was abolished, he asked. For Azeredo Coutinho 'necessity has no law, because she is the origin of all law', and necessity clearly demanded the continuance of the slave trade. 'To those that accuse me of occupying myself with a study more proper to a farmer or business man than to a Bishop, it is necessary to remember that before I was a Bishop I was, as I continue to be, a citizen linked to the interest of the state.' He attacked those who 'in the depths of their studies presume to give laws to the world without having dealt at first hand with the people of whom they speak'. The Bishop's concern at the growth of emancipationist sentiment was evidently justified, for his defense of the slave was refused by the Lisbon Academy of Sciences, and he was forced to publish a French edition in London. When he sought again in 1806 to have his polemic published in Portugal, the Royal Board of Censorship denied permission, on the ground that although slavery might be tolerated in present circumstances, nothing should be said to make its elimination even more difficult.[2]

No one was advocating immediate abolition, but a small group of men were beginning to incriminate slavery for social ills in Brazil, and they were starting to think in terms of an alternative model for Brazilian development, where European immigration and free laborers would replace slavery. Vilhena's objections to slavery were not so much the result of 'humanitarian' sentiment as they were a practical response to the problem of a society where the racial balance appeared to be dangerously unstable. In fact, despite Azeredo Coutinho's calumny, those few who urged eventual emancipation of the slave, did so not because of the

---

[1] José da Silva Lisboa to Domingos Vandelli, Bahia, 18 October, 1781, *ABNRJ* (1910) 502, 505. For a brief discussion of Luso-Brazilian critics of the slave trade see Boxer, *Portuguese Seaborne Empire*, 263–4.

[2] 'Análise sôbre a justiça do comércio do resgate dos escravos da costa d'Africa (1798)' *Obras econômicas*; Sonia Aparecida Siqueira, 'A escravidão negra no pensamento do bispo Azeredo Coutinho, contribuição ao estudo da mentalidade do ultimo inquisidor geral', I, *RHSP*, XXVII (1963) 349–65, II, *RHSP*, XXVIII (1964) 141–98; D. Fernando José de Portugal significantly also supported the views of the sugar planters with respect to slavery, see D. Fernando to Martinho de Melo e Castro, Bahia, 18 June 1794, *RIHGB*, LX, pt. 1 (1897) 155–7.

humanity of Blacks, but because they wished to see Blacks eliminated. The revolution in Saint Domingue was especially important in transforming José da Silva Lisboa's vague prejudices into concrete opinions. During 1818 he expressed publicly a point of view which had been developing for over thirty years. The progress of São Paulo, he said, was due 'to the extraordinary preponderance [there] of the white race'. Rio Grande do Sul, likewise, which had become the granary of Brazil had been colonized by 'the Portuguese race, and not the Ethiopian population'. Taking the example of Madeira he asserted that 'experience had shown that once the supply of Africans has been cut off the race does not decrease and decline but becomes better and whiter...' He wished to see the cancer of slavery extirpated from the Rio de la Plata to the Amazon. 'Was the best area in America to be populated by the offspring of Africa or of Europe?' he asked. To avoid 'the horrid spectacle of the catastrophe that reduced the Queen of the Antilles to a Madagascar', Brazil should be prevented from becoming a 'Negroland'.[1]

The question of slavery raised fundamental issues about the most desirable course for Brazilian development. And during the 1790s the question of slavery was beginning to divide enlightened men. The result was a blatant paradox. Those who were the strongest supporters of laissez-faire where it involved the removal of the regulatory functions of the state, were also those most committed to the slave trade and slavery. Those who supported government interference, particularly in the control of prices and in guaranteeing sufficient supplies of subsistence food to the population, were those most opposed to the slave trade and slavery. Novais de Almeida and Vilhena saw the slave population as enemies within, and José da Silva Lisboa believed Brazil would not develop without the creation of a free labor force and the Europeanization or whitening of the population. Bishop Azeredo Coutinho saw slavery as essential to Brazilian prosperity. It was those who attacked laissez-faire where it demanded the removal of what they considered judicious government controls who would be most in favor of a free international commerce, because free trade promised to stimulate European immigration, and offered the possibility of an alliance with Great Britain against the slave trade. Yet at the same time because their very solution to Brazil's problems was based on fear of the racial composition of the Brazilian population, they would be the least likely to take any initiative that might provoke the very disaster they foresaw and sought to avoid. The

[1] José da Silva Lisboa, *Memória dos Benefícios Políticos do governo de El-Rei Nosso Senhor Dom João VI* (1818) (2nd edition, Rio de Janeiro, 1940) 160, 169–75.

division was profound. Vilhena attacked those 'European ideas' he held responsible for creating the conditions that led to the Bahian plot. Azeredo Coutinho attacked the 'humanitarians' and 'Philosophers' whose utopian concepts threatened, in his opinion, to destroy Brazilian prosperity.

With republicanism discredited by its abortion in Minas Gerais and later association with social and racial turmoil, and with Brazilians in very basic disagreement over fundamental issues, there was room for metropolitan initiatives. And for the white minority in Portuguese America, the failure of the oligarchic movement in Minas Gerais during 1789, and the threat from below revealed by the Bahian artisans in 1798, provided two powerful incentives for compromise and accommodation with the metropolis. The atmosphere was receptive to reforms that avoided the risk of social upheaval. D. Rodrigo de Sousa Coutinho sensed more acutely than most the opportunities that the situation presented, and the need to proceed with enlightened adjustment if destructive revolution was to be avoided. The severity with which he treated the Bahian mulattoes and the favors he continued to bestow on the Brazilian graduates of the University of Coimbra were indicative of his point of view. The very fear of revolution he held made it essential that 'the federative system, the most analogous to Portugal's position in the world, be conserved with the greatest firmness and pure good faith'.[1] He attacked 'the banal declamations' of those who claimed 'that in the...difficult circumstances of the moment great reforms should not be attempted and only palliatives employed'. Experience, he said 'had shown the opposite'.[2]

D. Rodrigo had employed many erudite Brazilians within the process of decision making. Others he had encouraged to undertake state-sponsored scientific expeditions in Brazil. The objective was to neutralize nationalism by diverting attention to a greater imperial commitment. He had been especially responsive to those who had been connected with the Minas conspiracy. The exiled José Álvares Maciel had forwarded a memorial on the iron mines of Angola. It was favorably received.[3] Members of the Literary Society of Rio de Janeiro, languishing in jail since 1794, were ordered released.[4] In 1800 Manuel Ferreira da Câmara

[1] 'Discurso I', 22 December 1798, Funchal, *Linhares*, 108–9.
[2] 'Plano de Fazenda', 14 March 1799, *ibid.*, 168.
[3] José Álvares Maciel to D. Rodrigo de Sousa Coutinho, 7 November 1799, AHU, Minas Gerias, caixa 94; Also see Carneiro de Mendonça, *O Intendente Câmara*, 67–70.
[4] Devassa of Literary Society, Introductory Notes, *ABNRJ*, LXI (1939) 241–5.

was nominated General Intendent of Mines in Minas Gerais and the
Sêrro do Frio.[1] Antônio Pires da Silva Ponte, also in 1800 was appointed
governor of the captaincy of Espírito Santo.[2] That Brazilians should hold
such high positions was not without precedent. But the nomination to a
new and important post, second only to the governor of Minas Gerais,
of a man whose own brother had been seriously implicated in the proposed uprising of 1789, and the appointment as a governor in Brazil of
a Brazilian whose loyalty had been gravely questioned in 1786, was little
short of revolutionary.[3] During 1801, José Bonifácio de Andrade e Silva
became General Intendent of Mines and Metals in Portugal.[4]

The Marquis of Ponte de Lima (formerly the Visconde de Vila Nova
de Cerveira), since 1788 president of the Royal Treasury, had died in
December 1800.[5] D. Rodrigo was appointed to succeed him. The
presidency of the Treasury had been created by Pombal as the linchpin of
government and Pombal's godson had at last the opportunity to implement those reforms he had long regarded as the most important, and for
which draft legislation had long been prepared. Luís Pinto's proposals
of 1795 were rapidly promulgated. The alvará of 24 April 1801, 'in favor
of the inhabitants of Brazil and the freedom of commerce', abolished the
salt and whaling contracts, promised the exploitation of saltpetre deposits
and the manufacture of gunpowder under exclusive royal direction, and
encouraged the mining and manufacture of iron.[6] In order to take hold
of the chaotic situation of the contracts, in limbo since Melo e Castro had
annulled the farms in 1788, a general administration was established in
Minas Gerais. The new administration was to assess the property of
crown debtors and to requisition all papers and financial documents
relating to past contracts. In January 1802 João Rodrigues de Macedo
and others were ordered to turn over their accounts.[7] Among the many
thousands of financial papers, personal and business correspondence, in
the business archive of Rodrigues de Macedo, existed documents which

[1] 'Carta régia', 7 November 1800, *ibid.*, p. 86; and 'instrução', *ibid.*, 87–91.
[2] *RAPM*, I (1896) 417 note. Also *ABNRJ*, LXII (1940) 145.
[3] José de Lacerda e Almeida to Martinho de Melo e Castro, 24 September 1786, AHU, Mato Grosso, maço 12.
[4] 'Carta de merce, concedendo a José Bonifácio de Andrada e Silva, o cargo de intendente geral das minas e metais do Reino, 25 August 1801', *Obras Científicas, Políticas, e Sociais de José Bonifácio de Andrada e Silva* (2 vols., Santos, 1964) III, 29.
[5] Soriano, *Historia da Guerra Civil*, II, 296–7.
[6] José da Silva Lisboa, *Synopse da Legislação principal do Senhor D. João VI* (Rio de Janeiro, 1818) 28.
[7] Rodrigo de Sousa Coutinho to junta da fazenda, 28 March 1801, Junta da fazenda to João Rodrigues de Macedo, 23 January 1801, Rodrigo de Sousa Coutinho to junta da fazenda, 21 April 1801, CCBNRJ, I-9-20; I-I-10; I-9-14.

would permit the reconstruction of those causes of the Minas conspiracy which had been kept out of the official record. Fortuitously, the archive, later moved and divided between state and national repositories, still survives.[1]

The contractors in fact received a retribution of sorts. João Rodrigues de Macedo during the last years of his life was painfully open to blackmail. Pamplona protested devout friendship but consistently excused himself from paying his debts.[2] Manitti, forced to leave Minas with the Visconde de Barbacena, suggested that in his 'dire circumstance' the sum of 1,000 réis would be appreciated for his journey to Europe.[3] Bazílio de Brito Malheiro, demanding payments, threatened that 'he knew how he [Macedo] had escaped the scaffold'.[4] During August 1803 all houses in the property of the contractor were ordered integrated with the royal patrimony.[5] Among them was the great town house in Vila Rica, scene of some of the conspiracy's most dramatic moments, and the place of Cláudio Manuel da Costa's mysterious death. During 1805 his estate to the value of 85,402$475 reis was attached by the exchequer, and when he died, on 8 October 1807, his whole property was confiscated by the Treasury.[6] Silvério dos Reis fared only slightly better. In 1794 he had been awarded the Order of Christ, conferred with the title *fidalgo da Casa Real*, and his property confiscated at the time of his arrest was restored to him. But there were conditions. The debts to the crown had first to be accounted for. Silvério, in consequence, received little from his estate, and it was not until 1809 that a pension was forthcoming from the government, a belated reward for his 'loyalty'. The opposition that he encountered in Brazil after 1790 was formidable, and he spent his last years in Maranhão. He died in São Luís on 17 February 1818.[7] The nefarious Bazílio de Brito

---

[1] The documents are now divided between the National Archive, the National Library, both in Rio de Janeiro, and the archive of the state of Minas Gerais in Belo Horizonte, Minas Gerais.

[2] Inácio Correia Pamplona to João Rodrigues de Macedo, 25 March 1797, CCBNRJ, L-8, 1-1-15.

[3] José Caetano Manitti to João Rodrigues de Macedo, 24 September 1797, *ABNRJ*, LXV (1943) 220–1.

[4] Letter of 17 August 1800, cited by Miguel Costa Filho 'O Engenho de Bárbara Heliodora', III, *Brasil Açúcareiro*, LI, (1958) No. 6, p. 18.

[5] Rodrigo de Sousa Coutinho to *junta da fazenda*, 17 August 1803, CCANRJ, 9.

[6] 'Avaliação dos bens penhorados a João Rodrigues de Macedo', 3 May 1805, CCBNRJ, I-9, 281 Notice, 13 November 1807, CCBNRJ, I-33-11.

[7] Mathias, 'Inconfidência e Inconfidentes', *ACC*, III, 254–64; 'Representação', and other documents on Silvério dos Reis, AHU, Minas Gerais, caixa 93; 'Contrato de Joaquim Silvério dos Reis', CCBNRJ, I-10-5; 'Real Decreto de 13 de Novembro em favor de Coronel Joaquim Silvério dos Reis...[and] provisão do...Real Erario...', Junta da Fazenda, 7 November 1797, CCBNRJ, I-I-6.

died in 1806. He left a curious testament. 'All the people of Minas', he complained, 'indeed in all Brazil, conceived an implacable hatred towards me after the projected conspiracy in Minas...' He advised his son to sell up and get out of the country. 'The sons of men of property that have the misfortune to be born and grow up in Brazil do not inherit from their parents the impulses of honor, but adopt totally the customs of Negroes, Mulattoes, Indians, and other ridiculous people that there are in this country... This here is a land of thieves.'[1] From the lips of Bazílio de Brito, accused murderer, defaulter, contrabandist, and blackmailer, such words came with little grace. But compared with the fate of the contractors, Tomás Antônio Gonzaga in Mozambique, married to a wealthy widow, and with an official position in the administration, was fortunate indeed.[2]

D. Rodrigo's ideas of imperial organization and his relegation of Portugal to a secondary stature in his federative scheme did not pass without opposition. Combating nationalism overseas he had underestimated nationalism at home. And his distinction between reform and revolution was not appreciated by those who saw subversion in all enlightenment philosophy. The intendent of police, Pina Manique, who had been one of the instigators of Melo e Castro's hard line metropolitan-oriented colonial policies, bitterly opposed his tolerance and preference for Brazilians. The limitations of D. Rodrigo's influence was very apparent in his failure to protect his protégé Hypólito da Costa from arrest and imprisonment for masonic activities on his return from a visit to the United States – a visit which D. Rodrigo had himself sponsored.[3] And, José Joaquim Vieira Couto, the brother of the scientist José Vieira Couto, who had come to Lisbon on behalf of the people of Tejuco, was also arrested on the instructions of the intendent of police.[4] D. Rodrigo's powers in colonial matters were severely curtailed by the division of responsibility he had criticized in 1798. He had been replaced as secretary of state for the overseas dominions by the Visconde de Anadia, a man of very different priorities. Hypólito da Costa later contrasted the two ministers with the analogy of a pair of clocks. D. Rodrigo was always fast. The Visconde de Anadia was always slow.[5]

[1] 'Testamento do...denunciante, tenente-coronel Bazílio de Brito Malheiro do Lago', Sabará, 25 October 1806. *RAPM*, I (1896) 414; Also in Francisco Antônio Lopes, 'Câmara e Cadeira de Villa Rica', *AMI*, I (1952) 196.
[2] 'Artigo traduzido...pelo...José de Rezende Costa', typescript collection, Museu da Inconfidência, Ouro Prêto, Minas Gerais.
[3] Dourado, *Hypólito*, 47–67, 83, 87; Rizzini, *Hypólito*, 9, 13.
[4] *Ibid.*, 12–13.　　　　　　　　　[5] *Ibid.*, 146.

Compromise

As a consequence of the opposition to D. Rodrigo's policies, Manuel Ferreira da Câmara remained intendent in name only and waited in vain at his *Engenho* in Bahia for instructions to continue his journey to Minas Gerais. (It was from here that he wrote his observations on the commerce and agriculture of Bahia.) The proposed legislation on which his appointment depended remained in draft. D. Rodrigo told him: 'I hope that you have that quality of obstinacy necessary to overcome the obstacles of ignorance and those who oppose the...public wellbeing.'[1]

D. Rodrigo's attack on the Quintella monopolies in America, his strongly expressed and deeply felt disapproval of the contracting of revenues in Portugal, his opposition to the control of the former royal factories by the Ferreira–Quintella–Bandeira group, brought him into headlong collision with the powerfully entrenched merchant-industrial oligarchy in Portugal. For over twenty years the priorities of the metropolis had been those of a small, bloated oligarchy, enjoying the profits of royal contracts and monopolies. D. Rodrigo clearly intended to re-establish the Treasury to the functions and preeminence it had exercised under Pombal's direction. But he enjoyed in name only the prerogatives of his godfather. He was not a Pombal, and the Prince Regent had no intention that he become one. And D. Rodrigo needed the cooperation and capital of the oligarchs, Quintella, Bandeira, Caldas, Machado, Braancamp, Ferreira, Araújo, for his projected national bank.[2]

Moreover, the designs of Portugal's continental neighbors and the war in Europe forced on Portugal the choice D. Rodrigo had foreseen in 1779 after his conversation with the Abbé Raynal. His views on the importance of Brazil made it logical that when he was consulted in 1803 on the European situation he should propose that the Prince Regent establish the seat of monarchy in America. The idea was not new or original. It was a recurrent suggestion in times of difficulty, revived during the eighteenth century by Luís da Cunha and the Duke Silva-Tarouca. It was a solution recommended by D. José Manuel de Sousa, morgado de Mateus, in 1801. D. Rodrigo told the Prince Regent that 'Portugal is not the best and most essential part of the monarchy'. In South America a mighty empire could be created, the offensive taken against the Spaniards, and natural frontiers established at the Rio de la Plata. As he saw it the Prince Regent had very little choice in the event

---

[1] Carneiro de Mendonça ,*O Intendente Câmara*, 103.
[2] Pinto de Aguiar, *Bancos no Brasil Colonial* (Bahia, 1960) 24; Macedo, *Problemas*, 222; Balbi, *Essai Statistique*, I, 402; For D. Rodrigo's attitude towards the monopolists as reported by Ratton, see *Recordações*, 109, 112, 130; D. Rodrigo was also less willing to accept without question the advice of the junta do comércio, see, for example, AHU, códice 962, f. 222-3.

of a showdown. If the French took Portugal, then the British would take Brazil. It was better to anticipate both by seizing the initiative.[1]

The Brazil plan was anathema to many. Admiral Campbell ascribed opposition to 'the French, but also the Spanish influence, and finally [to] a greater part of the nobility, who dread the idea of seeking their fortunes in a new country while they can grasp at the shadow in their own'.[2] And the plan was unthinkable to the merchants and industrialists who, unlike D. Rodrigo with his extensive Brazilian properties, had much to lose and nothing to gain by such a move. Between 1789 and 1807 the commerce of Portugal quadrupled.[3] The demand for raw cotton in France and Great Britain brought favorable balances with both nations. Wine, retaining old markets, found new ones in Europe, Africa, and North America. There was a considerable increase in trade with Spain and in the re-export of Spanish wool. Sugar during the last quarter of the eighteenth century regained continental markets, exports rising from 946,071 arrobas in 1776 to 2,509,364 arrobas in 1800.[4] During the 1790s Portuguese manufactures made up 30 per cent of the trade with the colonies and were exported to North Africa as well.[5] By the mid 1790s the Portuguese balance of trade was in surplus. These factors helped to make Lisbon the scene of an 'activity and opulence' which according to the German naturalists Spix and Martius 'raised it after London to the first commercial place in the world'.[6] The Lisbon merchants attributed their prosperity in large measure to the neutrality of Portugal. They were strongly and vocally opposed to embroilment with either side in the world conflict between Britain and France, and most especially they were opposed to alliance with England.[7]

It was unfortunate for D. Rodrigo that his many opponents could also tar him with the brush of Anglophilia. In 1801 Lord Hawkesbury had instructed the British minister in Lisbon to let it be known that 'in the

[1] Ángelo Pereira, *D. João VI, Principe e Rei* (Lisbon, 1953) I, 'quadro da situação política da europa, apresentado ao Principe por D. Rodrigo de Sousa Coutinho', 16 August 1807, 127–36. Also 'memória feita 14 April 1801', D. José [Maria de Sousa, Morgado de Mateus] *ibid.*, I, 83–91.

[2] Donald Campbell, London, 14 August 1804, Chatham Papers, PRO, 30/8/345 (2) f. 224.

[3] Macedo, *O Bloqueio Continental*, 46.

[4] Godinho, *Prix et Monnaies*, 259–76; Macedo, *Problemas*, 185–98; 'Representação dirigida por Dom Rodrigo [de Sousa Coutinho] ao Principe Regente...', 12 January 1800, Funchal, *Linhares*, 241–6. (The arroba was equal to 32 lb. or to 14.75 kilograms in metric terms.)

[5] Balbi, *Essai Statistique*, I, 440, 442.

[6] J. B. Von Spix e C. F. P. Von Martius, *Viagem pelo Brasil* (4 vols., Rio de Janeiro, 1938) I, 114.

[7] For an account of the violence of the merchants' opinions, see Robert Walpole to Lord Grenville, Lisbon, 9 September 1795, PRO, FO, 63/21.

case of invasion the British envoy was authorized to recommend that the court of Portugal embark for Brazil...and that [the British] were ready for their part to guarantee the security of the expedition and to combine with [the Prince Regent] the most efficacious ways to extend and consolidate his dominions in South America'.[1] The British had come in fact eventually to the position the French had foreseen thirty years before, *Punch's Politicks* prophetically described in 1762, and which the changed commercial relations between the countries had long made necessary. But the coincidence of the views of D. Rodrigo and the British on the need for the removal of the Prince Regent to Brazil was to prove disastrous to both. For it made the supporters of the Brazil plan and the broader imperial concept espoused by D. Rodrigo appear to support England and hence prejudice Portuguese neutrality. It gathered into a formidable opposition to the Brazil plan the majority of merchants, nobles, and pro-French elements in Portugal. When the Prince Regent consulted the Visconde de Anadia over the new legislation for Minas, which eventually had been embodied in the alvará of 13 November 1803, D. Rodrigo found his position in the government no longer tenable. Complaining that Anadia 'neither understood nor held responsibility' for the Minas legislation, he submitted his resignation, and withdrew from Lisbon to his country estates.[2]

The fall of D. Rodrigo from power, the reversal and abandonment of most of his policies, and the establishment of a ministry favorable to the French in Lisbon only hastened the British reformulation of policy. Donald Campbell, who had been forced out of the service of Portugal by the resignation of D. Rodrigo, stressed in secret correspondence with the British cabinet the 'extreme importance of preventing the French from possessing the Brazils'. 'The naval station of Cape St. Roque to Cape Frio [was] situated in the most commanding geographical position in the world...', he wrote. 'Here unlike the Cape or the Mauritius, the Enemy's Ships might cruise in an absolute line of navigation of twenty degrees extent, and of not more than three or four degrees width, as it is well known, that all outward bound Ships must, from the nature of the Trade winds, invariably pass within that distance of the coast I mention ...'[3] Campbell's comments were supported by others. John Barrow

---

[1] D. José de Almeida de Melo e Castro to Dom João, 1 September 1801, IHGB, lata 58, doc. 17.　　　　[2] Carneiro de Mendonça, *Intendente Câmara*, 113–18, 491ff.
[3] Most secret and confidential, Downing Street by Admiral Campbell, October 1803, PRO, FO, 63/42; Secret to Lord Hawkesbury, Lisbon, November 26 1803, PRO, FO, 63/42; Donald Campbell, London, 14 August 1804, Chatham Papers, PRO, 30/8/345 (2) f. 226, 236 and Chatham Papers, PRO, 30/8/342 (1) 137–41.

had observed in 1792 that 'At Rio de Janeiro alone a navy might be built, equipped, and fitted out, with every necessary for a sea voyage, sufficient to command the Southern Atlantic.'[1] If French troops reached Brazil, Admiral Campbell warned the British cabinet, they would possess the most favorable colonies in the world. 'They may establish a Navy where timber, hemp, iron and copper abounds, artificers to build and seamen to man any number, strengthening their own political and maritime powers, and weakening those of Great Britain; as there the East India trade will be more effectively cut up than even had the French the possession of Egypt.'[2]

Commercial reasoning was also an important factor in the British change of policy. The traditional commercial organization of national factories with exclusive privileges was already moribund. But in Portugal with its established and influential resident British community the realization was long in coming.[3] In 1804 Robert Fitzgerald, the British envoy, asked the question that had for several years been implicit in the situation. 'How far [was] any struggle for the preservation of Portugal – independent of her shipping of which the enemy must on no account get possession – demanded by the real interests of the British empire?' Upon a minute investigation he wrote to Lord Hawkesbury, 'it may appear that the British property within these dominions forms no object of great national importance...especially when in the opposite balance are viewed the innumerable advantages to be derived from an open unrestrained trade with the Brazils'.[4]

And the promise of commercial gain in South America also determined the British desire to see the Portuguese court in Rio de Janeiro. Since 1789 the British had been much less willing to foment revolution in South America. The reasons for caution were the same as those which had caused Brazilian whites to move away from their flirtation with republican egalitarianism. 'Revolutions in states where each individual has some interest in their welfare, are not effected without the most serious calamities', John Barrow had observed, 'what then must be the consequences in a country where the number of slaves exceeds the proprietors of the soil in at least a tenfold proportion... In promoting revolutions I trust England will never be concerned, being fully convinced that however much South America might gain by a quiet change of masters,

---

[1] Barrow, *Voyage*, 120.
[2] Donald Campbell to His Britannic Majesty's Cabinet ministers, London, 26 September 1803, PRO, FO, 63/42.
[3] Christelow, *HAHR*, xxvii (1947) 16.
[4] Robert Fitzgerald to Lord Hawkesbury, Lisbon, 21 October 1803, PRO, FO, 63/42.

she will very soon be thrown back into a state of barbarism by revolutions.'[1] Donald Campbell had made exactly the same point in 1803 to the British cabinet. 'Certain I am', he wrote, 'that should the Brazilians be precipitated into a premature effort for liberty, either by the weakness of their own government, by the imprudence of any set of individuals, or by the unqualified interference of any foreign power, they will certainly become prey to that species of anarchy, which now prevails in St. Domingo.'[2] Needless to say, where there was anarchy, there was no profitable commerce.

The monarchical solution, espoused by the British for commercial and strategic reasons, proposed by D. Rodrigo de Sousa Coutinho in the interest of Empire, was a solution also eminently acceptable to white Brazilians. The canon Luís Vieira had considered it to be the best possible solution in 1789. In 1792 Alvarenga Peixoto in an ode to Queen Maria had pleaded from his cell through the mouth of a Brazilian Indian that she visit her American subjects.[3] One of the few points to emerge from the investigation arising out of the seemingly trumped up charges against Captain Francisco de Paula Cavalcante and others in Pernambuco during 1801, was the evident concern in Brazil about what would happen if the Prince Regent did not establish himself in America in the event of the loss of Portugal.[4]

In 1789 important members of the Minas plutocracy had been prepared to move in armed rebellion against Portuguese dominion and to establish an independent republican government. After 1792 'men established in goods and property', to use the words of D. Fernando de Portugal, were wary of republicanism. The slave uprising in the Caribbean provoked fears in the minds of slaveowners throughout the Americas. The sugar boom in Brazil, in part a result of the collapse of production in Saint Domingue, brought with it social and economic problems which in turn were partly responsible for the proposed revolt of the mulatto artisans of Bahia. The Bahian manifestoes of 1798 confirmed that the slogans of the French Revolution propagated within a society structured like that of Portuguese America brought with them the risk of racial upheaval, a risk which the American Revolution had not revealed.

---

[1] Barrow, *Voyage*, 133–4.
[2] Donald Campbell, London, 14 August 1804, Chatham Papers, PRO, 30/8/345 (2) f. 260. For the impact of Saint Domingue on British policy and Spanish America, see John Lynch, 'British Policy and Spanish America 1783–1808', *Journal of Latin American Studies* I (1969) 1–30, especially p. 3.
[3] M. Rodrigues Lapa, *Alvarenga Peixoto*, lii–liii.
[4] 'Devassa de 1801 em Pernambuco' (edited by J. H. Rodrigues) *DH*, CX, 151. Also see Cardozo, 'Azeredo Coutinho', *Conflict and Continuity*, 84.

Moreover, the self-interests of the sugar planters did not necessarily lead them into opposition to metropolitan interests, and those in Brazil who might have supported ideas of economic nationalism had been discredited with the failure in Minas. But even more than the reforms and re-organization proposed by D. Rodrigo, for both chastened *Mineiros* and plantation owners, the establishment of the monarchy in Brazil was a welcome and hopeful compromise which offered political change without social disintegration.

In fact, social, economic, and political pressures had brought a remark-able cohesion of views between Brazilian whites and the British govern-ment. And despite the temporary disparagement and abandonment of D. Rodrigo's programs, the Portuguese monarchy possessed, because of his activity, a carefully thought out and highly developed blueprint for the creation of a Brazilian Empire. The dénouement was prevented by the entrenched and powerful influence of the merchant-industrial oligarchs in Portugal. It had been in their interests that neo-mercantilism had been instituted, and they were bitterly opposed to the removal of the court to Brazil. The dénouement was also prevented by the Prince Regent's horror at the idea of abandoning Europe for South America. But in late 1807, with a French army crossing the frontier and a British fleet in the Tagus, the choice foreseen by D. Rodrigo in 1779 became a reality. Dom João was forced to make a decision. At the same time the opposition in Portugal was effectively neutralized. The alternatives in November 1807 were invidious indeed. If Dom João remained the British might bombard Lisbon as they had recently bombarded Copen-hagen.[1] Certainly they would not allow the Portuguese fleet to fall into the hands of the French. And if he came to terms with Napoleon there was no guarantee that he would be permitted to retain his crown. At least the British professed to have no territorial ambitions in Portuguese America, and their attempt on Buenos Aires had been repulsed.[2] With the army of Junot marching on Lisbon even those in the government who had opposed the Brazil plan now espoused it.[3] As D. Rodrigo had also

---

[1] José Baptista Barreiros, *Correspondência inédita entre o conde da Barca e José Egidio Alvares de Almeida, secretário particular de El Rei D. João VI* (Lisbon, 1962); Ângelo Pereira, *D. João VI, Principe e Rei, a retirada da familia real para o Brasil* (Lisbon, 1953); G. S. Graham and R. A. Humphreys, *The Navy and South America* (London, 1962); Caio de Freitas, *George Canning e o Brasil* (2 vols., São Paulo, 1958) I, 9–96.

[2] For the impact of the British defeat in Buenos Aires, see 'ofícios do conde dos Arcos', IHGB, 1-4-33.

[3] The painful process by which the council of state during 1807 came to the conclusion consistently upheld by D. Rodrigo has only recently become clear thanks to the discovery (by Alan K. Manchester) of the papers of the council of state in the Arquivo Nacional, Rio

Compromise

foreseen, in the event of a showdown between the great powers over Portugal there was really very little alternative if the house of Bragança wished to survive. On 29 November 1807, a gratified Lord Strangford could write to Mr Canning from aboard the *Hibernia* at sea off the Tagus: 'I have the honour of announcing to you that the Prince-Regent of Portugal had effected the wise and magnanimous purpose of retiring from a kingdom which he could no longer retain except as a vassal of France; and that his royal highness and family accompanied by most of his ships of war and by a multitude of his faithful supporters and adherents, has this day departed Lisbon and are now on their way to the Brazils under the escort of a British fleet.'[1]

To many the New World court seemed an aberration. In a hemisphere later to be thought of as republican, the Luso-Brazilian experiment begun in 1807 was an anomaly. But the transfer of the Portuguese court to America, its warm reception, and its successful implantation, were the results of long standing tendencies and special developments which had marked the history of Portugal and Brazil since 1750. The failure of nationalist republican revolt and of neo-mercantilism during the early 1790s had allowed time for compromise solutions and for second thoughts on both sides. The decision to withdraw to Brazil, belated and forced as it was, had not been unforeseen. The idea had a venerable history, and D. Rodrigo had provided a body of legislation, planning, and a grandiose concept of Luso-Brazilian Empire ready for the new situation. 'My dear friend', D. Rodrigo wrote to José Bonifácio de Andrada e Silva from Rio de Janeiro, 'over your Brazil you may rest content, so great is its destiny.'[2] Whether or not D. Rodrigo's optimism was justified, only the future would reveal.

de Janeiro. See his article 'The Transfer of the Portuguese Court to Rio de Janeiro', *Conflict and Continuity*, 148–83, translated as 'A transferência da Corte Portuguesa para o Rio de Janeiro', *RIHGB*, CCLXXVII (October–December 1967) 3–44. Some of these documents have been published by Eneas Martins Filho, 'O conselho do estado Português e a transmigração da familia Real em 1807' (Rio de Janeiro, 1968). Additional extracts are to be found in Funchal, *Linhares*, 304–12, and in Barreiros, *Correspondência inédita...conde da Barca*.

[1] John Barrow, *The Life and Correspondence of Admiral Sir William Sidney Smith* (2 vols., London, 1848) II, 259.

[2] 'As cartas do conde de Linhares a José Bonifácio de Andrada e Silva', *RHSP*, XXVII (1963) 217–42.

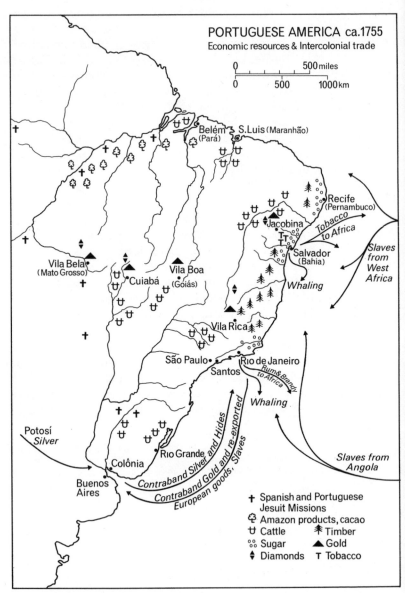

Portuguese America *ca*. 1755: Economic resources and inter-colonial trade

Maps

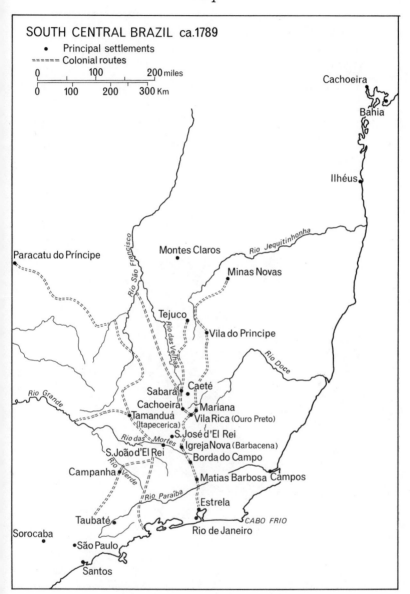

South Central Brazil *ca.* 1789: Settlements and colonial routes

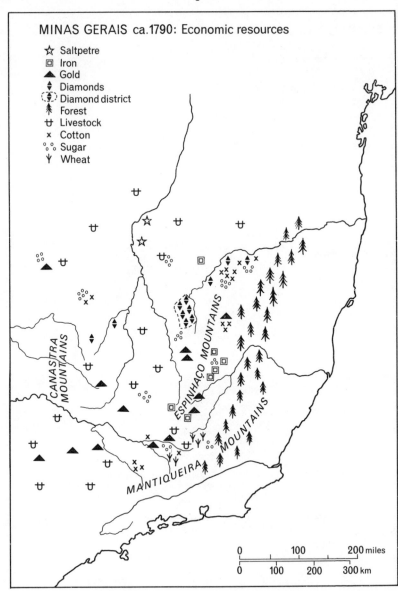

South Central Brazil *ca.* 1789: Economic resources

Portuguese colonial exports and major contraband connections *ca.* 1789

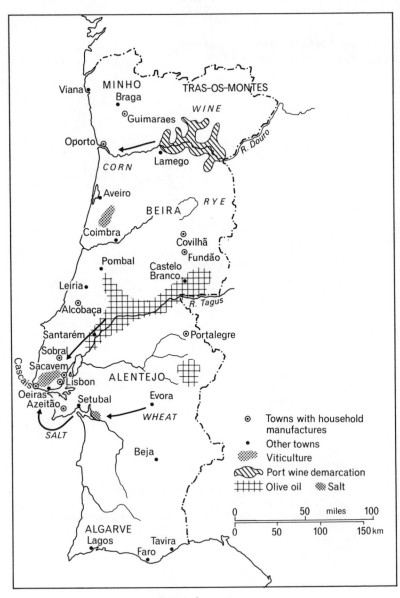

Portugal *ca.* 1760

STATISTICAL APPENDIX

1.Graphs and supplementary tables

SUPPLEMENT TO GRAPHS A AND F

Revenue Yields of the captaincy of Minas Gerais 1704–1800 (in milreis 1$000])

Note: (i) coinage in *reis* was abolished in the sixteenth century, but its multiples were retained as a money of account.

(ii) The total revenue figures given here do not necessarily represent the sum of the *dízimos* and *entradas* returns. Several other sources of income were also encompassed within this figure, especially during the second half of the century. I have not reproduced these here but they can be obtained by interested scholars from the documents in BNLCP, códice 643, ff. 204–18.

Important qualifications should be borne in mind when examining these figures.

(i) It is not clear how these figures were compiled by Carlos José da Silva, secretary of the Minas *junta da fazenda*. It would appear that they represent the amount *due* to the Royal Exchequer for the years in question rather than the amount *actually received*. For example the figure given for the *entradas*, 1776–81, the six-year period when João Rodrigues de Macedo held the contract, is 126,529 *milreis* per annum. Although this represents a sixth of the contract price of 766,726 *milreis*, in fact only a third of this contract amount had been paid to the exchequer by 1786 (see *AMI*, II [1953] 203). As contract debt increased throughout the eighteenth century the decline in real revenue was probably greater therefore than is indicated here. While rate of exchange between gold and *milreis* remained stable for much of the century, it should be remembered that in Minas the rate was artificially manipulated between 1,500 *reis* per oitava of gold and 1,200 *reis* per oitava at different periods. It is not clear whether the figures given by da Silva reflect this change or not. According to the notations on 'Mappa do rendimento que produzio o Real Quinto' in *RAPM*, VIII (1908) 575–7, the changes in rate of exchange were as follows:

1700–1713	1,500 *reis* per oitava
1713–1725	1,500 *reis* per oitava
1725 (Feb)–1730 (May)	1,200 *reis* per oitava
1730 (May–September)	1,320 *reis* per oitava
1730 (September)–1735	1,200 *reis* per oitava
1725–1751	1,500 *reis* per oitava
1751–[1803]	1,200 *reis* per oitava

(ii) The widened gap between the joint income of the *dízimos* and *entradas* and total revenues after 1761 is due to the introduction of several new sources of income then, for example the *donativos*, *terços partes dos offícios*, and so on.

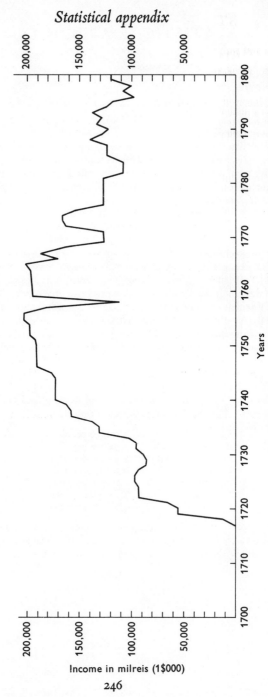

Graph A Income from the *entradas*, Minas Gerais, 1700–1800. Annual income in *milreis* (1$000). Source: 'Relação dos Rendimentos…Minas Gerais', BNLCP, códice 643, ff. 204–18.

Year	Dízimos	Entradas	Total revenue
1704	668		
1705	1,206		
1706	1,225		
1707	2,448		
1708	1,831		
1709	125		
1710	175		
1711			
1712			
1713			
1714			2,880
1715			3,141
1716	19,281		22,565
1717	46,276	1,830	49,313
1718	46,276	13,537	62,417
1719	46,613	55,134	104,337
1720	47,085	55,134	105,321
1721	40,082	65,071	108,713
1722	49,111	93,880	146,435
1723	49,111	93,880	148,080
1724	61,423	94,744	161,595
1725	78,661	97,338	181,756
1726	78,661	97,338	182,329
1727	68,018	94,751	168,721
1728	53,118	86,990	145,933
1729	47,085	86,990	139,189
1730	53,118	89,259	147,327
1731	58,607	96,069	159,688
1732	66,290	96,069	167,028
1733	66,290	104,944	175,797
1734	82,357	131,566	218,241
1735	104,852	131,566	241,025
1736	104,852	138,274	247,775
1737	97,708	158,398	260,608
1738	94,763	158,398	259,297
1739	104,642	162,420	274,918
1740	104,642	174,486	287,498
1741	104,427	174,486	287,283
1742	104,125	174,502	278,632
1743	104,125	174,550	287,681
1744	99,089	174,550	282,645
1745	92,038	178,679	281,436
1746	92,038	191,066	293,822
1747	92,038	191,066	293,701
1748	92,038	191,058	294,141
1749	92,038	191,034	293,591
1750	92,068	191,034	292,824
1751	92,111	192,585	293,294
1752	92,111	197,239	297,993
1753	80,558	197,239	286,417

Statistical appendix

Year	Dízimos	Entradas	Total revenue
1754	64,385	198,921	271,592
1755	64,385	203,967	276,631
1756	67,281	203,967	279,533
1757	71,336	181,535	257,621
1758	71.336	114,239	190,684
1759	73,405	195,739	274,318
1760	76,301	195,739	276,341
1761	76,301	195,739	275,331
1762	76,680	196,414	333,036
1763	77,211	196,414	336,902
1764	77,211	196,414	250,391
1765	79,596	201,416	358,393
1766	82,934	172,677	326,924
1767	72,335	188,261	338,170
1768	98,399	164,964	345,139
1769	62,960	126,372	268,105
1770	62,960	126,372	266,865
1771	62,962	126,372	265,494
1772	62,964	164,993	315,985
1773	62,964	166,418	311,239
1774	62,964	166,946	313,681
1775	62,964	155,220	295,996
1776	62,964	126,529	267,431
1777	39,471	126,529	242,487
1778	64,968	126 529	263,090
1779	64,968	126,529	260,631
1780	64,968	126,529	253,426
1781	64,968	126 529	253,364
1782	64,968	117,370	243,006
1783	64,968	117,370	236,318
1784	65,368	117,370	240,217
1785	65,368	124,037	240,129
1786	65,368	124,037	237,849
1787	65,368	124,037	240,588
1788	65,368	141,215	253,788
1789	82,311	129,728	257,991
1790	75,947	122,593	246,343
1791	76,269	134,547	257,422
1792	77,067	129,256	253,276
1793	72,816	139,879	259,654
1794	72,811	124,401	243,551
1795	72,831	118,676	238,031
1796	73,104	98,971	218,247
1797	73,118	117,008	237,370
1798	72,971	101,600	224,522
1799	73,525	121,298	241,363
1800	73,665	121,037	238,578

Statistical appendix

SUPPLEMENT TO GRAPH B

Emission of gold coin, Portugal (Weight in marcos)
Source: Jorge Borges de Macedo, *A situaçåó econõmica*, 167.

1752	8,003	1770	9,357
1753	17,261	1771	6,394
1754	14,886	1772	9,085
1755	10,982	1773	5,148
1756	12,680	1774	4,408
1757	12,918	1776	7,965
1758	12,558	1777	137
1759	572	1778	5,723
1760	22,849	1779	3,030
1761	13,156	1780	4,371
1762	836	1781	5,017
1764	27,732	1782	2,617
1765	8,421	1783	3,723
1766	11,118	1784	363
1767	357	1785	3,157
1768	16,752	1786	253
1769	4,850		

Note: 1 Marco = 0.23040 kilograms = 8 English ounces.

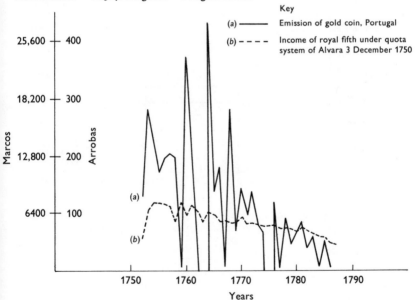

Graph B   Income from royal fifth of Minas Gerais and gold coin emission in
Portugal, 1750–86. Sources: 'Relação do rendimento do Quinto de Minas Gerais',
AHU, códice 311, annex. 15, 16, 17; Jorge Borges de Macedo, *A Situação Economica*,
p. 167; *RAPM*, VIII (1903) 575–7.

Statistical appendix

Percentage values of monetary issue, 1750–1808. Annual average value (in *reis*, with percentages)

Period	Gold	Silver	Copper
1752–1772	1,076,552.379 (95.56%)	40,979.561 (3.63%)	9,043.051 (0.80%)
1773–1792	289,660.336 (79.51%)	71,995.019 (19.76%)	2,641.782 (0.72%)
1793–1807	181,468.789 (44.55%)	223,037.962 (54.76%)	2,740.687 (0.67%)

Source: Vitorino Magalhães Godinho, *Prix et Monnaies au Portugal* (Paris, 1955) 219.

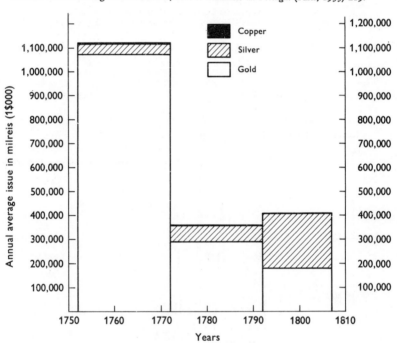

Graph C   Annual average monetary issue, 1750–1808 in *milreis* (1$000). Source: Vitorino Magalhães Godinho, *Prix et Monnaies au Portugal* (Paris, 1955) 219.

Statistical appendix

(a) *Exports from England and Wales to Portugal and imports from Portugal into England and Wales. Average annual values* (in £ thousands)

Years	Exports	Imports
1701–5	610	242
1706–10	652	240
1711–15	638	252
1716–20	695	349
1721–5	811	387
1726–30	914	359
1731–5	1,024	326
1736–40	1,164	301
1741–5	1,115	429
1746–50	1,114	324
1751–5	1,098	272
1756–60	1,301	257
1761–5	964	312
1766–70	595	356
1771–5	613	365
1776–80	525	381
1781–5	622	340
1786–90	622	597
1791–5	594	724
1796–1800	811	698

Source: Elizabeth Boody Schumpeter, *Overseas Trade Statistics*, 17–18.

b) *Origins of Portuguese exports to England, 1796–1807. Annual values* (in reis)

Year	Metropolitan Portugal	Islands	Brazil	Asia	Re-exports
1796	2,255,945.476	11,048.200	2,201,898.048	9,440.788	408,743.117
1800	2,913,868.000	14,393.000	2,758,331.814	7,029.200	1,009,214.190
1801	5,968,363.360	9,085.500	2,679,215.570	6,968.800	987,371.480
1802	3,935,087.275	3,712.000	4,045,796.050	619.400	486,955.480
1803	6,150,488.160	4,304.400	3,399,991.626	4,879.800	954,586.370
1804	3,310,050.910	–	2,807,601.074	1,946.160	1,342,894.190
1805	4,222,461.520	7,261.920	3,759,345.690	459.600	875,682.220
1806	4,710,743.560	10,150.000	2,534,011.910	2,827.680	943,383.840
1807	5,779,815.200	9,100.000	1,330,471.705	6,763.040	845,046.060

*Re-exports composed principally of Spanish money.
Source: Jorge Borges de Macedo, *O Bloqueio Continental, economia e guerra peninsular* (Lisbon, 1962) 42.

Statistical appendix

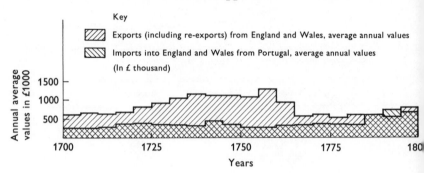

Graph D   Anglo–Portuguese   trade, 1700–1800.   Source: Elizabeth **Boody** Schumpeter, *English Overseas Trade Statistics*, pp. 17–18.

SUPPLEMENT TO GRAPH E

Gold Yield of the royal fifth (real quinto) of Minas Gerais 1714–87 in arrobas [a]

Year	Yield in arrobas [b]	Yield in arrobas [c]
1714	30	
1715	30	
1716	30	
1717	30	
1718	25	
1719	25	
1720	25	
1721	25	
1722	37	
1723	37	
1724	18	
1725	132	
1726	90	
1727	73	
1728	78	
1729	35	
1730	92	
1731	?	
1732	148	
1733	88	
1734	238	
1735	89	
1736	?	
1737	?	
1738	237	134
1739	291	132
1740	234	131
1741	?	131
1742	98	130

Statistical appendix

Year	Yield in arrobas [b]	Yield in arrobas [c]
1743	100	129
1744	280	128
1745	122	132
1746	127	130
1747	130	128
1748	5	124
1749	128	124
1750	124	
1751	124	
1752	55	
1753	107	
1754	118	
1755	117	
1756	114	
1757	110	
1758	89	
1760	93	
1761	111	
1762	102	
1763	83	
1764	100	
1765	94	
1766	132	
1767	87	
1768	84	
1769	84	
1770	92	
1771	81	
1772	82	
1773	78	
1774	75	
1775	75	
1776	76	
1777	70	
1778	72	
1779	71	
1780	65	
1781	72	
1782	65	
1783	62	
1784	58	
1785	54	
1786	49	
1787	43	

[a] 1 arroba = 14.745 kilograms = 32 pounds.

[b] According to 'Mappa do rendimento que produzio o Real Quinto do Oiro na Capitania de Minas Gerais desde o anno de 1700 a 1787 . . .' *RAPM*, VIII (1908) 575–7.

[c] According to 'Gold Yield of the capitation tax in Minas Gerais, 1735–1749' from the códice Costa Matoso, Biblioteca Municipal, São Paulo, in C. R. Boxer, *Golden Age*, 338.

Statistical appendix

Note: Only the yield in arrobas has been reprinted here, hence these figures should be regarded as approximations. The value of these figures as an indicator of total production (i.e. as 20 per cent of total production) is also highly approximate owing to contraband, fraud, and so on. In addition it must be remembered that the quinto was collected by a variety of different methods during the century. These were as follows:

1713–24	Paid by Commutation
1724–35	Paid at Mint and smelting houses
1735–49	Paid by capitation tax
1751–1803	Paid at foundry houses

(For details of these methods see C. R. Boxer, *The Golden Age of Brazil*, Chapters II, III, VII, and the relevant passages in this text on the promulgation of the alvará of 3 December 1750.)

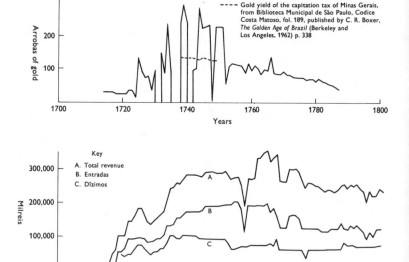

Graph E   The royal fifth of Minas Gerais 1700–87. Source: 'Mappa do rendimento que produzio o Real Quinto do Oiro na Capitania de Minas Geraes desde o anno de 1700 a 1787…' *RAPM*, VIII (1908) 575–7.

Graph F   Captaincy revenues, Minas Gerais 1700–1801. Source: 'Relação dos Rendimentos desta Capitania de Minas Gerais desde os seus descobrimentos… Carlos José da Silva', BNLCP, códice 643, ff. 204–18.

Imports of cotton wool into Great Britain, 1781–92 (in million lb)

Year	Total imports	From Brazil	From BWI	From USA
1781	5.1	0.3	3.1	
1782	11.8	0.3	6.3	
1783	9.7	0.1	6.1	
1784	11.4	0.9	6.9	
1785	18.4	1.6	8.2	
1786	19.4	2.1	7.8	
1787	23.2	2.5	9.4	
1788	20.4	2.3	12.2	0.2
1789	32.5	4.8	12.0	0.5
1790	31.4	5.5	13.2	0.4
1791	28.7	7.2	11.8	Nil
1792	34.9	7.7	12.0	0.1

Source: Michael M. Edwards, *The Growth of the British Cotton Trade 1780–1815* (Manchester, 1967) 84, 250, 251.

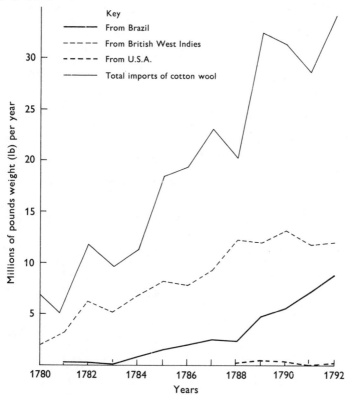

Graph G British cotton wool imports 1780–1792. Key: ———— from Brazil; ------- from British West Indies; ▬▬▬▬ from USA; ———— total imports of cotton wool. Source: Michael M. Edwards *The Growth of the British Cotton Trade 1780–1815* (Manchester, 1967) 84, 250, 251.

Goulart's estimated slave imports into Brazil by regional origin

Decade	From Costa da Mina	From Angola	Total
1701–10	83,700	70,000	153,700
1711–20	83,700	55,300	139,000
1721–30	79,200	67,100	146,300
1731–40	56,800	109,300	166,100
1741–50	55,000	130,100	185,100
1751–60	45,900	123,500	169,400
1761–70	38,700	125,900	164,600
1771–80	29,800	131,500	161,300
1781–90	24,200	153,900	178,100
1790–1800	53,600	168,000	221,600
1801–10	54,900	151,300	206,200
Total	605,500 (32.0%)	1,285,900 (68.0%)	1,891,400

Source: Philip D. Curtin, *The Atlantic Slave Trade. A Census* (Madison, Wisconsin, 1969) 207. After Mauricio Goulart, *Escravidão africana no Brasil* (São Paulo, 1950) 203–9, and David Birmingham, *Trade and Conflict in Angola: The Mbundu and Their Neighbours under the Influence of the Portuguese, 1483–1790* (Oxford, 1966) 137, 141, 154.

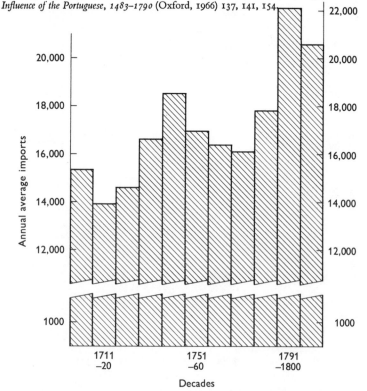

Graph H   Estimated annual average slave imports 1701–1810. Source: Philip D. Curtin, *The Atlantic Slave Trade* (Madison, Wisconsin, 1969) 207.

Statistical appendix

SUPPLEMENT TO GRAPH I

Annual average sugar prices on the Amsterdam produce Exchange, 1750–1808 (per pound in guilders)

Year	Brazilian white (powdered) sugar	Refined sugar
1750	0.23	0.34
51	0.23	0.30
52	0.23	0.30
53	0.23	0.28
54		0.29
55	0.26	0.37
56	0.32	0.37
57	0.28	0.38
58		0.44
1760		0.48
61		0.46
62	0.33	0.47
63	0.30	0.42
64	0.27	0.40
65	0.28	0.39
66	0.23	0.33
67	0.23	0.32
68	0.25	0.33
69	0.24	0.33
1770	0.24	0.33
71	0.25	0.34
72	0.23	0.33
73	0.23	0.33
74	0.23	0.33
75	0.23	0.33
76	0.23	0.34
77	0.28	0.40
78	0.33	0.43
79	0.35	0.47
1780	0.33	0.47
81	0.40	0.51
82	0.41	0.51
83	0.23	0.38
84	0.23	0.39
85	0.24	0.37
86	0.25	0.34
87	0.26	0.34
88	0.28	0.35
89	0.29	0.38

Statistical appendix

Year	Brazilian white (powdered) sugar	Refined sugar
1790	0.33	0.45
91	0.38	0.54
92	0.52	0.69
93	0.50	0.68
94	0.49	0.66
95	0.53	0.69
96	0.59	0.81
97	0.65	0.93
98	0.72	0.98
99	0.81	1.04
1800	0.50	0.81
01	0.48	0.69
02	0.34	0.54
03	0.46	0.62
04	0.48	0.61
05	0.46	0.64
06	0.37	0.60
07	0.35	0.60
08		1.54

Source: N. W. Posthumus, *Inquiry into the History of Prices in Holland* (2 vols., Leiden, 1946 1964) I, 123–4, 140–1.

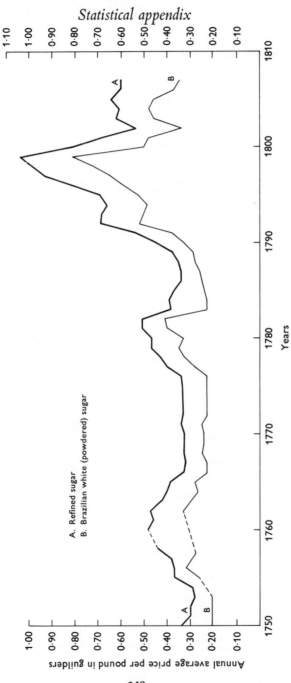

Graph I Annual average prices of refined and Brazilian white sugar on the Amsterdam produce exchange 1750–1808. Source: N. W. Posthumus *Inquiry into the history of prices in Holland* (2 vols, Leiden, 1946, 1964) I, 123–4, 140–1.

A. Refined sugar

B. Brazilian white (powdered) sugar

Annual average price per pound in guilders

Years

Statistical appendix

2. Resumé of the state of the Company of Grão Pará and Maranhão up to 1770

Principal capital of 1,164 shares		465,600$000 *reis*
Profits until the end of December 1759		323,492$804
Idem of year	1760	150,579$229
	1761	218,660$811
	1762	136,304$807
	1763	26,906$465
	1764	105,120$215
	1765	165,723$546
	1766	105,746$417
	1767	65,771$149
	1768	56,358$370
	1769	54,516$675
	1770	53,544$003

Dividend for 1760 for balance at the end of the year

1759	$10\frac{1}{2}\%$	90,792$000 *reis*
Idem 1761	6%	27,936$000
1762	7%	32,592$000
1763	8%	37,248$000
1764	$9\frac{1}{2}\%$	44,232$000
1765	$9\frac{1}{2}\%$	44,232$000
1766	10%	46,560$000
1767	11%	51,216$000
1768	$11\frac{1}{4}\%$	52,380$000
1769	$11\frac{1}{2}\%$	53,544$000
1770	$11\frac{1}{2}\%$	53,544$000
1771	$11\frac{1}{2}\%$	53,544$000

Specimen consignment for France:

Cost of 17 consignments of 4,187 sacks of cotton

for Rouen	131,470$225	
Liquid return		145,097$959
Profit		13,627$734

Cost of one consignment of 50 sacks of cotton

for Marseilles	1,503$758	
Liquid Return		1,547$223
Profit		43$465 *reis*

Source: 'Rezumo do estado da Companhia Geral do Grão Pará e Maranhão no fim do anno de 1770'; AHU, códice 1187.

Statistical appendix

3. Goods from metropolitan factories exported to the colonies by the Company of Pernambuco and Paraíba from its foundation [1759] until 1777

1760	5,338$929 *reis*
1761	8,272$066
1762	3,720$039
1763	32,744$771
1764	67,043$968
1765	19,567$233
1766	19,768$480
1767	30,643$263
1768	5,377$111
1769	9,774$978
1770	16,151$915
1771	54,994$001
1772	47,005$756
1773	56,002$607
1774	73,785$665
1775	45,457$952
1776	54,978$923
1777	31,668$656
Total	582,326$313 *reis* (*sic* for 551,653$305)

(Of this total sum goods to the value of 454,734$045 *reis* had come from the royal silk factory of Lisbon).

Source: 'Mappa de todas as fazendas que a Companhia de Geral de Pernambuco e Paraíba tem extraido das fabricas do Reino e exportado para as Conquistas desde o seu estabelecimento até 32 de Dezembro de 1777'. IHGB/AUC, 1-2-11, f. 239.

4. Brazilian contracts held by the Quintellas

Years	Period in years	Location	Type	Value to the *fazenda real* in *milreis* (1$000)
1754	1	Rio de Janeiro	*navios soltos*	38,800
1755	1	Rio de Janeiro	*navios soltos*	38,000
1757–60	3	Bahia	*dízimos*	50,300
1760–5	3	Bahia	*dízimos*	50,000
1765–71	6	Bahia	*dízimos do tobacco e mais generos*	6,700
1765–71	6	Bahia	*subsidio dos molhados*	9,130
1768–71	3	Rio de Janeiro	*azeites doces*	2,900
1772–8	6	Bahia	*subsidio dos molhados*	9,130
1770–5	6	Brazil	*sal*	42,400
1774–80	6	Bahia	*dízimos do tobacco e mais generos*	6,700
1776–81	6	Brazil	*sal*	45,600
1788–1801	13	Brazil	*sal*	48,000

Source: 'Livros dos termos de arrematações dos contratos' [Conselho Ultramarino] AHU, códices 298, 299, 306.

Statistical appendix

The Quintellas also held the Whaling contract:

1765–77	Brazilian littoral	32,000 *milreis* per annum
1777–89	Brazilian littoral	40,000 *milreis* per annum
1789–1801	Brazilian littoral	48,000 *milreis* per annum

Source: Myriam Ellis, *ACC*, I, 86, 89, 90, 100.

5. Franco–Portuguese Commerce

(a) *Origins of Portuguese exports to France, 1789–1807. Annual values* (in *reis*)

Year	Metropolis	Colonies	Re-exports
1789	66,440.070	569,540.635	1,488.218
1796	–	23,260.800	–
1800	385.000	87,531.950	2,457.600
1801	40,454.610	658,907.516	3,997.060
1802	144,911.380	3,448,080.000	47,880.605
1803	57,410.000	2,176,979.979	31,861.200
1804	66,447.790	4,300,974.282	112,134.000
1805	125,264.350	3,322,366.712	60,644.170
1806	38,525.820	5,209,217.305	145,329.160
1807	20,017.040	4,496,159.130	103,834.940

Source: Jorge Borges de Macedo, *O Bloqueio Continental, economia e guerra peninsular* (Lisbon, 1962) 39.

(b) *Exports from the ports under the direction of Rouen to Portugal and imports from Portugal, 1730–80. Annual values* (in *livres tournois*)

Year	Exports	Imports
1730	1,781,647	320,864
1732	1,383,226	141,970
1738	1,175,811	344,699
1753	1,413,307	759,751
1756	2,822,078	898,818
1766	1,977,760	1,831,780
1767	1,457,317	2,018,899
1769	1,306,326	1,444,666
1770	1,153,943	2,035,309
1771	1,034,847	1,675,725
1773	526,780	1,903,000
1774	633,905	4,053,645
1775	1,045,237	2,601,952
1776	653,781	1,871,384
1777	926,573	2,158,349
1778	995,884	2,416,485
1779	613,384	2,341,014
1780	621,399	5,798,812

Source: Pierre Dardel, *Navires et marchandises dans les ports de Rouen et du Havre au XVIII siècle* (Paris, 1963) 550–1.

Statistical appendix

6. Wine exported from Oporto in pipes 1717 to 1787 (*Annual Averages*)

1717–25	17,692
1728–37	19,234
1738–47	18,556
1748–57	15,967
1758–67	19,388
1768–77	22,143
1778–87	24,256

Source: Vitorino Magalhães Godinho, *Prix et Monnaies*, 253.

7. Population

(*a*) *Alden's adjusted totals for distribution of population of Brazil, 1772–82*

Place	Adjusted total	Per cent
Rio Negro	10,386	0.6
Pará	55,315	3.5
Maranhão	47,410	3.0
Piauí	26,410	1.7
Pernambuco	239,713	15.4
Paraíba	52,468	3.4
Rio Grande do Norte	23,812	1.5
Ceará	61,408	3.9
Bahia	288,848	18.5
Rio de Janeiro	215,678	13.8
Santa Catarina	10,000	0.6
Rio Grande de São Pedro	20,309	1.3
São Paulo	116,975	7.5
Minas Gerais	319,769	20.5
Goiás	55,514	3.5
Mato Grosso	20,966	1.3
Totals	1,555,200	100.0

Source: Dauril Alden, 'The Population of Brazil in the late Eighteenth Century: A Preliminary Survey', *HAHR*, XLIII (May, 1963) 173–201.

(*b*) *Table of the inhabitants of Minas Gerais, 1776*

Comarca	Men				Women			
	Whites	Browns	Blacks	Total	Whites	Browns	Blacks	Total
Vila Rica	7,847	7,981	33,961	49,789	4,832	8,810	15,187	28,829
Rio das Mortes	16,277	7,615	26,199	50,091	13,649	8,179	10,862	32,690
Sabará	8,648	17,011	34,707	60,366	5,746	17,225	16,239	39,210
Sêrro do Frio	8,905	8,186	22,304	39,395	4,760	7,103	7,536	19,339
Total	41,677	40,793	117,171	199,641	28,987	41,317	49,824	120,128

Statistical appendix

Comarca	Total (Men and Women)	Births	Deaths
Vila Rica	78,618	1,944	1,839
Rio das Mortes	82,781	2,795	1,660
Sabará	99,576	2,501	2,270
Sêrro do Frio	58,794	1,734	1,075
Total	319,769	8,974	6,844

Source: 'Taboa das habitantes da capitania de Minas Gerais, 1776', in 'Noticia da capitania de Minas Gerais, [attributed to] Cláudio Manuel da Costa', IHGB, lata 22, doc. 13.

(c) *Table of Population of Minas Gerais, 1821*

	Free population					
	Whites		Mulattoes		Blacks	
Comarca	Men	Women	Men	Women	Men	Women
Ouro Prêto (Vila Rica)	6,645	6,694	9,638	16,660	4,000	5,000
Sabará	11,445	10,609	21,252	21,261	6,376	7,357
Rio das Mortes	42,490	35,355	19,392	20,037	5,845	5,503
Sêrro do Frio	6,401	5,793	15,159	16,540	8,172	6,887
Paracatú	3,281	2,334	4,388	5,308	1,000	1,404
Total	70,262	60,785	69,829	79,906	25,393	26,151

Total men and women by race: 131,047   199,635   51,544
Total men and women: men 165,484; women 166,742
Total free population: 332,226

	Slave population			
	Mulattoes		Blacks	
Comarca	Men	Women	Men	Women
Ouro Prêto (Vila Rica)	1,672	1,532	15,291	(?)
Sabará	2,274	2,518	22,550	13,898
Rio das Mortes	4,581	3,723	53,506	23,185
Sêrro do Frio	3,418	1,909	11,137	8,176
Paracatú	160	90	1,631	2,176
Total	12,105	9,772	104,115	55,890

Total men and women by race: 21,887   160,005
Total men and women: men 116,270; women 65,612
Total slave population: 181,882

Statistical appendix

Comarca	Total population
Ouro Prêto (Vila Rica)	75,573
Sabará	119,520
Rio das Mortes	213,617
Sêrro do Frio	83,626
Paracatú	21,772
Total	514,108

Source: 'Noticias e Reflexões Estatisticas da Provincia de Minas Gerais por Guilherme Barão de Eschwege', *RAPM*, IV (1899) 737.

(d) *Racial breakdown of Minas population in 1776 and 1821*

	1776	1821
Blacks	166,995 (52.2%)	221,549 (41.1%)
Mulattoes	82,110 (25.7%)	171,522 (33.4%)
Whites	70,664 (22.1%)	131,047 (25.5%)

(e) *Population of Minas Gerais 1776 and 1821 by Sex*

	1776	1821
(i) *Blacks*		
Male	117,171	129,508
Female	49,824	82,041
Total	166,995	211,549
Percentage male	70.2	60.2
(ii) *Mulattoes*		
Male	40,793	81,934
Female	41,317	89,578
Total	82,110	171,512
Percentage male	49.7	47.8
(iii) *Whites*		
Male	41,677	70,262
Female	28,987	60,785
Total	70,664	121,570
Percentage male	59	57.8

(f) *Civil status of Mulatto and Black population of Minas in 1821*

Status	Mulattoes	Blacks
Free	149,635	51,544
Slave	21,887	160,005
Total	171,522	211,549
Percentage slave	14.4	75.6

Note: Tables *d, e, f*, are based on figures in table *b* and *c*.

Statistical appendix

(g) Percentages of Slaves in Minas Gerais population, 1786–1823

Year	Free	Slave	Total	Slave (%)
1786	188,712	174,135	362,847	47.9
1805	218,223	188,761	407,004	46.4
1808	284,277	148,772	433,049	34.3
1821	343,333	171,204	514,537	33.3
1823	378,620	140,365	518,985	27.0

Source: 'Documentos Diversos – População de Provincia de Minas Gerais', *RAPM*, IV (1899) 294–295.

BIBLIOGRAPHY

The most important archives used were the Pombal collection in the National Library, Lisbon (BNLCP), the Arquivo Histórico Ultramarino, Lisbon (AHU), the casa dos contos collection in the National Library, Rio de Janeiro (CCBNRJ), the archive of the Instituto Histórico e Geográfico Brasileiro, Rio de Janeiro (IHGB), the Public Archive of the State of Minas Gerais, Belo Horizonte, Minas Gerais (APM), and in London, the Public Record Office (PRO).

The Pombal collection was valuable not only for material relating to the period of the rule of the Marquis of Pombal (1750–77), but also for documents and copies of documents relating to colonial, international and domestic affairs after 1777. Especially useful and surprising were several key documents on Minas Gerais (for example, the listing of the captaincy revenues from 1700–1800, the opinion of the *junta da fazenda* on contract arrears). The casa dos contos collection was basic for the fiscal problems of Minas Gerais, as well as containing the private papers of important contractors. For official correspondence and government policy in Lisbon the codices of the AHU were essential, but a great deal of vital information also came from the caixas, organized by captaincy and containing draft correspondence, minutes, and unofficial materials of various types. The Foreign Office Papers relating to Portugal (PRO, FO) provided important details on the formation of British policy, and the papers of the Board of Trade (PRO, BT) gave some insight into the motivation behind British changes in policy. More revealing material came from the Chatham Papers in the PRO, especially the lengthy account of Brazil in the early 1800s by Donald Campbell.

Of the contemporary gazettes consulted, those which have yielded material were *The Annual Register*, *The Gentleman's Magazine*, *Gazeta de Lisboa*, *Gazetta Universale*, *Notizie del Mondo*. These were available in the Princeton University Library, and the Newberry Library, Chicago.

Historians of Brazil are especially fortunate in the substantial volume of published documentary material available. Much use has been made here of documents published in the *Revista do Instituto Histórico e Geográfico Brasileiro* (*RIHGB*), the *Revista do Arquivo Público Mineiro* (*RAPM*), *The Anais da Biblioteca Nacional*, Rio de Janeiro (*ABNRJ*), and the *Anuário do Museu da Inconfidência*, Ouro Prêto (*AMI*). The editing of these materials, however, is often careless, and not all these collections possess the excellent index prepared by Lygia Nazareth Fernandes, *Índice da Revista do Arquivo Público Mineiro* (Arquivo Nacional, Rio de Janeiro, 1966), for the *RAPM*. For Minas Gerais the casa dos contos collection in the National Archive, Rio de Janeiro, has been ably catalogued by Herculano Gomes Mathias, *A coleção da casa dos contos de Ouro Prêto, documentos avulsos* (Arquivo Nacional, Rio de Janeiro, 1966) (*CCANRJ*). A selection of the documents from the casa dos contos collection in the National Library, Rio de Janeiro was published by José Afonso Mendonça de Azevedo in *ABNRJ*, LXV (1943). Fundamental for the Minas conspiracy remains the *Autos de Devassa* (ADIM) though valuable background documentation has been published in various locations by M. Rodrigues Lapa. Both his complete works of Tomás Antônio Gonzaga, his book on Alvarenga Peixoto, and analysis of the *Cartas Chilenas* (all listed below) contain invaluable and meticulously transcribed materials. The Pombaline period possesses useful collections of published materials resulting from the activity of Marcos Carneiro de Mendonça. Both his *Correspondência inédita*, and his *O Marquês de Pombal e o Brasil* (São Paulo, 1960) have been used with profit.

Bibliography

Contemporary theses, memorials and important works of this nature were found either in their original editions or as published later in the *RAPM, RIHGB, ABNRJ*. The later publications have always been cited in full in the footnotes. The contemporary publications are listed below and were consulted either in the Ayer and Greenlee collections of the Newberry Library, the New York Public Library, the Library of Congress, or the National Libraries in Lisbon and Rio de Janeiro. An essential guide to these published materials is Rubens Borba de Morais, *Bibliografia Brasileira do Periodo Colonial* (São Paulo, 1969). A valuable and under-used repository for travel accounts on Portugal and Brazil was the Lynch collection at the Sociedade Brasileira da Cultura Inglesa in Rio de Janeiro. Four collections of laws and regimentos were valuable, the *Codigo Philippino ou Ordinações e Leis do Reino de Portugal* (Candido Mendes de Almeida, 14th edition, Rio de Janeiro, 1970), *Systema ou Collecção dos Regimentos Reaes contem os Regimentos pertenecentes a administração da Fazenda Real... por José Roberto Monteiro de Campos Coelho e Soisa* (6 vols., Lisbon, 1783), Antônio Delgado da Silva, *Collecção da Legislação Portugueza desde a ultima compilação das Ordenaçoes, regida pelo Desembargador Antônio Delgado da Silva, Legislação de 1756 a (1820)* (6 vols., Lisbon, 1830–5), *Suplemento a Collecção de Legislação Portugueza* (Lisbon 1834–47), and *Collecção das Leys, Decretos e Alvarás, que comprehende o feliz Reinado del Rey Fidelissimo D. José I, Nosso Senhor desde o anno de 1750 até o de* [1777] (4 vols., Lisbon, 1777).

For quantitative material there exist several useful published works, especially Vitorino Magalhães Godinho, *Prix et Monnaies au Portugal* (Paris, 1955). Incisive, but less systematic, are the two books of Jorge Borges de Macedo, *A situação econômica no tempo de Pombal, alguns aspectos* (Oporto, 1951) and *Problemas de História da Indústria Portuguêsa no século XVIII* (Lisbon, 1963). Little exists by way of price series for Brazil, but the work of Katia M. de Queirós Mattoso on late eighteenth century Bahia in *Cahiers des Ameriques Latins*, v (January/June, 1970) 33–53, and of H. B. Johnson Jr on Rio de Janeiro, 'A Preliminary Inquiry into Money, Prices and Wages (1763–1823)', *The Colonial Roots of Modern Brazil: Papers of the Newberry Library Conference* (ed. Dauril Aldin, Berkeley and Los Angeles, 1972), are both promising beginnings. Much relevant data used here, however, has come from such well known sources as N. W. Posthumus, *Inquiry into the History of Prices in Holland* (2 vols., Leiden, 1946, 1964), and Elizabeth Boody Schumpeter, *English Overseas Trade Statistics* (Oxford, 1960). There are two first rate recent studies of Anglo-Portuguese Trade, H. E. S. Fisher, *The Portugal Trade* (London, 1971); and of broader scope: Sandro Sideri, *Trade and Power, Informal Colonialism in Anglo-Portuguese Relations* (Rotterdam University Press, 1970).

The following lists of contemporary published and secondary materials is not exhaustive. It is composed only of works actually cited in the text and footnotes.

I. CONTEMPORARY PUBLISHED WORKS (INCLUDING CONTEMPORARY WORKS SUBSEQUENTIALLY PUBLISHED)

Ávila, Affonso (ed.) *Resíduos Seiscentistas em Minas (Textos do século do ouro e as projeções do mundo barroco)* (2 vols., Belo Horizonte, 1967).

Azeredo Coutinho, J. J. da Cunha de, *Obras Econômicas* (editor, Sérgio Buarque de Holanda, São Paulo, 1966).

Andrada e Silva, José Bonifácio de, *Obras Científicas, Políticas e Sociais* (3 vols., Santos, 1965).

Bibliography

Antonil, André João, *Cultura e Opulencia do Brasil por suas drogas e minas, texte de l'édition de 1711, traduction française et commentaire critique par Andrée Mansuy* (Paris, 1968).

Balbi, Adrien, *Essai statistique sur le royaume de Portugal et d'Algarve* (2 vols., Paris, 1822).

Variétés Politico-Statistiques sur la monarchie Portugaise (Paris, 1822).

Barrow, John, *A voyage to Cochinchina in the years 1792 and 1793...* (London, 1806).

Beckford, William, *The Journal of William Beckford in Portugal and Spain 1787–1788* (editor, Boyde Alexander, London, 1954).

Betencourt, José de Sá, *Memória sobre a plantação dos Algodões...* (Lisbon, 1798).

Bielfeld, le Baron de, *Institutions politiques* (2 vols., Leiden, 1767).

Bougainville, L. de, *A voyage round the world...in the years 1766, 1767, 1768, 1769...* (London, 1772).

Bourgoing, Jean François, *Voyage de ci-devant duc du Chatelet en Portugal...* (2 vols., Paris, 1798, 1808).

Brelin, Johan, *De passagem pelo Brasil e Portugal em 1756* (translation from the Swedish by Carlos Perição de Almeida, Lisbon, 1955).

Byron, John, *A Voyage round the World in His Majesty's Ship 'Delphin', commanded by the Honorable Commodore Byron...* (2nd edition, London, 1767).

Caldas, José Antônio, *Notícia geral de toda esta capitania da Bahia desde o seu descobrimento até o presente anno de 1759* (facsimile, Bahia, 1949).

Conceição Veloso, José Mariano, *O Fazendeiro do Brasil Melhorado na economia rural dos generos ja cultivados e de outros, que se podem introduzir e nas fábricas, que lhe são proprias, segundo o melhor, que se tem escrito a este assumpto* (10 vols., Lisbon, 1798–1806).

Costa, José Daniel Rodrigues, *Gemidos da Tristeza na lamentavel Perda de S.A.R., D. José, Principe do Brasil* (Lisbon, 1788) pamphlet.

Costigan, Arthur William, *Sketches of Society and Manners in Portugal* (2 vols., London, 1787).

Cunha, Luís da, *Instruções inéditas de D. Luís da Cunha a Marco Antônio de Azevedo Coutinho* (editors, Pedro de Azevedo and Antônio Baião, Coimbra, 1929).

Dalrymple, Major William, *Travels through Spain and Portugal in 1774* (London, 1777).

Digges, Thomas Atwood (attributed to) *Adventures of Alonso containing some striking anecdotes on the present prime minister of Portugal* (2 vols., London, 1755, in facsimile by United States Catholic Historical Society, monograph series XVIII, New York, 1943).

'Discurso preliminár, histórico, introductivo com natureza de descrição económica da comarca e cidade do Salvador...' (edited by Pinto de Aguiar as *Aspectos da economia colonial*, Bahia, 1957).

Feilding, Henry, *The Journal of a Voyage to Lisbon* (editor, Austin Dobson, Oxford, 1907).

Gonzaga, Tomás Antônio, *Obras Completas* (editor, M. Rodrigues Lapa, 2 vols., Rio de Janeiro, 1957).

Marília de Dirceu e mais poesias (editor, M. Rodrigues Lapa, Lisbon, 1944).

Gorani, José, *Portugal, a corte, e o país nos anos de 1765 a 1767* (Lisbon, 1945).

Goudar, Ange, *Relation historique du tremblement de terre...* (The Hague, 1756).

Hansard, T. C., *The Parliamentary History of England from the earliest period to the year 1803*, XV (London, 1818).

Bibliography

Keene, Sir Benjamin, *The Private Correspondence of Sir Benjamin Keene* (editor, Sir Richard Lodge, Cambridge, 1933).

King, Charles, *The British Merchant* (3rd edition, 3 vols., London, 1748).

Koster, Henry, *Travels in Brazil* (2nd edition, 2 vols., London, 1817).

Lindley, Thomas, *Authentic Narrative of a Voyage from the Cape of Good Hope to the Brazils. . . in 1802, 1803. . .* (London, 2nd edition, 1808).

Lingham, Edward James, *Vindicae Lusitanae, or An Answer to a Pamphlet entitled The Causes and Consequences of the late Emigration to the Brazils* (London, 1808) pamphlet.

Mably, Abbé de, *De la legislation ou principes des Loix* (Amsterdam, 1786).

Remarks concerning the government and laws of the United States of America (London, 1784).

Mawe, John, *Travels in the interior of Brazil* (London, 1812).

Murphy, James, *Travels in Portugal* (London, 1795).

Occasional Thoughts on the Portuguese Trade and the inexpediency of supporting the House of Bragança on the Throne of Portugal (London, 1767) pamphlet.

Punch's Politicks (London, 1762).

Ratton, Jacome, *Recordações. . .sobre occurências do seu tempo em Portugal. . .1747. . . [até] 1810.* 2nd edition (Coimbra, 1920).

Raynal, Abbé, *Histoire philosophique et politique des établissements et du commerce des Européens dans les deux Indes* (Ist edition anon., 4 vols., Amsterdam, 1770).

A Philosophical and Political History of the Settlements and Trade of the Europeans in the East and West Indies (translation, J. Justamond, 3rd edition, 5 vols., London, 1777).

The Revolution of America (London, 1781).

Rebelo da Costa, Agostinho, *Descripção topographica e histórica da cidade do Porto* (Oporto, 1787).

Recueil des Loix constitutives des colonies Angloises confederees sous la dénomination d'Etats-Unis de l'Amerique-Septentrionale (Philadelphia, 1778).

Robertson, William, *The History of America* (12th edition, 4 vols., London, 1812).

Rodrigues de Brito, João, *Memórias políticas sobre as verdadeiras bases da grandeza das nações e principalmente Portugal* (Lisbon, 1803).

(and others) *Cartas económico-políticas sobre a agricultura e comércio da Bahia* (Lisbon, 1821).

Rugendas, João Maurício, *Viagem pitoresca através do Brasil* (translation, Sérgio Milliet, 5th edition, São Paulo, 1954).

Saint-Hilaire, Auguste, *Voyage dans les Provinces de Rio de Janeiro et de Minas Gerais* (2 vols., Paris, 1830).

Say, Jean-Baptiste, *A treatise on Political Economy or the Production, Distribution, and Consumption of Wealth* (translation C. R. Prinsep, 4th American edition, Philadelphia, 1830).

Schaw, Janet, *Journal of a Lady of Quality. . .1774 to 1776* (Yale edition, Newhaven, 1934).

Shirely, William, *Observations on a pamphlet. . .* (London, 1759).

Silva Lisboa, José de, *Memórias dos benefícios políticos do Governo de El-Rei Nosso Senhor D. João VI (1818)* (2nd edition, Rio de Janeiro, 1940).

Synopse da legislação principal do Senhor D. João VI (Rio de Janeiro, 1818).

Silva Lisboa, Balthezar de, *Discurso Histórico, Político e Económico dos progressos e estado actual de Filosofia Natural Portugues. . .* (Lisbon, 1786).

Bibliography

Smith, Adam, *An Inquiry into the Nature and Causes of the Wealth of Nations* (3 vols., Edinburgh, 1811).

Southey, Robert, *Letters written during a Short Residence in Spain and Portugal* (2nd edition, Bristol, 1799).

Journal of a residence in Portugal 1800–1801 (editor, Adolfo Cabral, Oxford, 1960).

Staunton, George, *An Authentic Account of an Embassy from the King of Great Britain to the Emperor of China* (2nd edition, 3 vols., London, 1798).

Twiss, Richard, *Travels through Portugal and Spain, 1772, 1773* (London, 1775).

Vilhena, Luís dos Santos, *Recopilação de Noticias Soteropolitanas e Brasilicas (1802) contidas em XX cartas* (3 vols., Braz do Amaral's edition, Bahia, 1922–35).

II. SECONDARY MATERIALS

Abreu, Capistrano de, *Capitulos de História Colonial 1500–1800* (4th edition, edited by José Honório Rodrigues, Rio de Janeiro, 1954).

Accioli de Cerqueira e Silva, Coronel Inácio, *Memórias Históricas e Políticas de Provincia da Bahia* (6 vols., Braz do Amaral's annotated edition, Bahia, 1919–40).

Albuquerque, A. Tenório d', *A Maçonaria e a Inconfidência Mineira* (Rio de Janeiro, 1958).

Aguiar, Pinto de, *Bancos no Brasil colonial* (Bahia, 1960).

Alcochete, Nuno Daupias d', 'Lettres de Jacques Ratton à Antônio de Araújo de Azevedo, comte da Barca 1812–1817', *Bulletin des Etudes Portugaises* (2nd series, 25, 1964) 137–256.

'Lettres Famileres de Jacques Ratton (1792–1807)' *Bulletin des Etudes Portugaises* (2nd series, 23, 1961) 118–251.

Alden, Dauril, *Royal Government in Colonial Brazil, with Special Reference to the Administration of the Marquis of Lavradio, viceroy 1769–1779* (Berkeley and Los Angeles, 1968).

'The Growth and Decline of Indigo Production in Colonial Brazil: A Study in Comparative Economic History', *Journal of Economic History*, xxv (1965) 35–60.

'Manuel Luís Vieira: An entrepreneur in Rio de Janeiro during Brazil's agricultural renaissance', *HAHR*, xxxix (1959) 521–37.

'Yankee Sperm Whalers in Brazilian Waters, and the Decline of the Portuguese Whale Fisher (1773–1801)' *The Americas*, xx (1964) 267–88.

'The population of Brazil in the late Eighteenth Century', *HAHR*, xliii (1963) 173–205.

'Economic Aspects of the Expulsion of the Jesuits from Brazil: A Preliminary Report' in *Conflict and Continuity in Brazilian Society* (editors, Henry H. Keith and S. F. Edwards, Columbia, South Carolina, 1969) 25–65.

Almeida, D. José de, *ViceReinado de D. Luís d'Almeida Portugal, Marquês de Lavradio* (São Paulo, 1941).

Amazalak, Moses Bensabat, *Do estudo e da evolução das doutrinas económicas em Portugal* (Lisbon, 1928).

Azevedo, João Lúcio d', *O marquês de Pombal e a sua época* (2nd edition, Lisbon, 1922).

Estudos de história Paraense (Pará, 1893).

Os Jesuítas no Grão Pará, suas missões e a colonização (Lisbon, 1901).

Azevedo, Thales de, *Povoamento da cidade do Salvador* (2nd edition, São Paulo, 1955).

Bandeira, Manuel, *Guia de Ouro Preto* (Rio de Janeiro, 1938).

Barbosa, Waldemar de Almeida, *A Verdade sobre Tiradentes* (Belo Horizonte, 1965).

Bibliography

Barreiros, José Baptista, *Correspondência inédita entre o conde da Barca e José Egídio Alvares de Almeida, secretario particular de El Rei D. João VI* (Lisbon, 1962).

Barrow, John, *Life and Correspondence of Sir William Sidney Smith* (2 vols., London, 1848).

Bazin, Germain, *l'Architecture Religieuse Baroque au Brésil* (2 vols., Paris/São Paulo, 1956).

Aleijadinho et la sculpture baroque au Brésil (Paris, 1963).

Beirão, Caetano, *D. Maria I, 1772–1792* (3rd edition, Lisbon, 1944).

Boxer, C. R., *Race Relations in the Portuguese Colonial Empire 1415–1825* (Oxford, 1963).

Some Literary Sources for the History of Brazil in the Eighteenth Century (Oxford, 1967) pamphlet.

The Portuguese Seaborne Empire 1415–1825 (London, 1969).

The Golden Age of Brazil 1695–1750 (Berkeley and Los Angeles, 1962). *Portuguese Society in the Tropics, the municipal councils of Goa, Macão, Bahia, and Luanda* (Madison, 1965).

'Brazilian Gold and British Traders in the 17th and 18th Centuries', *HAHR*, XLIX, No. 3 (1969) 455–72.

Brown, Vera Lee, 'The relations of Spain and Portugal 1763–1777', *Smith College Studies in History*, XV (1929–30).

Bulcão Sobrinho, Antônio de Araújo de Aragão, 'O Patriarcha da liberdade Bahiana, Joaquim Inácio de Sequeira Bulcão', *RIHGB*, 217 (1952) 167–58.

Burns, E. Bradford, 'The Enlightenment in two Colonial Librareis', *Journal of the History of Ideas*, XXV (1964) 430–8.

'The role of Azeredo Coutnho in the Enlightenment of Brazil', *HAHR*, XLIV (May, 1964) 145–60.

Caetano, Marcelo, *Do conselho ultramárino ao conselho do império* (Lisbon, 1943).

Calógeras, João Padiá, *As Minas Brasil e sua legislação* (3 vols., Rio de Janeiro, 1904–5).

Câmara Municipal de Cascais, *A Real Fábrica de Lanifícios de Cascais* (Cascais, 1964).

Cardozo, Manuel, 'The Brazilian Gold Rush', *The Americas*, III, No. 2 (1946) 137–60.

'Another document on the Inconfidência Mineira', *HAHR*, XXXII (1952) 540–51.

'Azeredo Coutinho and the Intellectual Ferment of his times', in *Conflict and Continuity in Brazilian Society* (editors, Henry H. Keith and S. F. Edwards, Columbia, South Carolina, 1969) 148–83.

'Tithes in Colonial Minas Gerais', *Catholic Historical Review*, XXXVIII (1952) 175–62.

Carnaxide, visconde de (Antônio de Sousa Pedroso Carnaxide) *O Brasil na administração Pombalina* (São Paulo, 1940).

Carneiro de Mendonça, Marcos, *O Intendente Câmara, Manuel Ferreira da Câmara Bethencourt e Sá, Intendente Geral das Minas e Diamantes 1764–1835* (São Paulo, 1958).

Carrato, José Ferreira, *As Minas Gerais e os Primordios do Caraça* (São Paulo, 1963). *Ingreja, Illuminismo, e Escolas Mineiras Coloniais* (São Paulo, 1968).

Carvalho, Romulo de, *História da fundação do colégio Real dos Nobres de Lisboa 1761–1772* (Coimbra, 1959).

Chapman, A. B. Wallis, 'The commercial relations of England and Portugal 1487–1807', *Transactions of the Royal Historical Society*, 3rd series, I (1907) 157–179.

Bibliography

Cheke, Marcus, *Dictator of Portugal, a life of the Marquis of Pombal 1699–1782* (London, 1938).

Christelow, Allan, 'Economic background to the Anglo-Spanish war of 1762', *Journal of Modern History*, XVIII (1946) 22–36.

'Great Britain and the trades from Cadiz and Lisbon to Spanish America and Brazil 1759–1782', *HAHR*, XXVII (February 1947) 2–29.

Cortesão, Jaime (ed.) *Alexandre de Gusmão e o tratado de Madrid (1750)* (9 vols., Rio de Janeiro, 1950–63).

Costa Filho, Miguel, *A cana de açúcar em Minas Gerais* (Rio de Janeiro, 1963).

Cunha Saraiva, José Mendes da, *Companhia Geral de Pernambuco e Paraíba* (Lisbon, 1940).

Dardel, Pierre, *Navires et Marchandises dans les Portes de Rouen et du Havre au XVIIIe siècle* (Paris, 1963).

Dias, Luís Fernando de Carvalho, *História dos Lanifícios (1750–1834)* (3 vols., Lisbon, 1958–65).

A relação das fábricas de 1788 (Coimbra, 1955).

Dornas Filho, João, *O Ouro das Gerais e a civilização da capitania* (São Paulo, 1957).

Dourado, Mecenas, *Hipólito da Costa e o Correio Brasiliense* (2 vols., Rio de Janeiro, 1957).

Edwards, Michael M., *The Growth of the British Cotton Trade 1780–1815* (Manchester, 1967).

Ellis, Myriam, *O Monopólio do sal no Estado de Brasil 1631–1801* (São Paulo, 1955).

O Abastecimento da Capitania das Minas Gerais no século XVIII (São Paulo, 1951).

Aspectos da pesca da baleia no Brasil Colonial (São Paulo, 1959).

Ennes, Ernesto, 'The Trial of the Ecclesiastics in the Inconfidência Mineira', *The Americas*, VII (1950) 183–213.

Ferrão, Antônio, 'O marquês de Pombal e os meninos de Palhavã', *Academia das Sciencias de Lisboa, Estudos Pombalinos*, 1st series, No. 1 (Coimbra, 1923).

Fisher, H. E. S., 'Anglo-Portuguese Trade 1700–1770', *Economic History Review*, 2nd series, vol. XVI, No. 2 (1963) 219–33.

The Portugal Trade, A Study of Anglo-Portuguese Commerce 1700–1770 (London 1971).

França, José-Augusta, *Une Ville des Lumières: La Lisbonne de Pombal* (Paris, 1965).

Francis, A. D., *The Methuens and Portugal 1691–1708* (London, 1966).

Frieiro, Eduardo, *O Diabo na Livraria do Cônego* (Belo Horizonte, 1957).

Freitas, Caio de, *George Canning e o Brasil (influência da diplomacia inglesa na formação Brasileira)* (2 vols., São Paulo, 1958).

Gagé, Jean, 'Antônio de Araujo, Talleyrand et les negociations secrètes pour la "paix de Portugal" 1798–1800', *Bulletin des Etudes Portugaises* (New series, 14, 1950) 39–131.

Godinho, Vitorino Magalhães, *Prix et Monnaies au Portugal 1750–1850* (Paris, 1955).

'Le Portugal, les flottes du sucre et les flottes de l'or 1670–1770', *Annales–économies–sociétés–civilisations*, V année, No. 2 (1950) 184–97.

Hamilton, Earl J., *War and Prices in Spain 1651–1800* (Cambridge, Mass., 1947).

Harlow, Vicente T., *The Founding of the Second British Empire 1763–1793* (2 vols., London, 1952, 1964).

Kendrick, T. D., *The Lisbon Earthquake* (London, 1956).

Klein, Herbert S., 'The Colored Freedman in Brazilian Slave Society', *Journal of Social History*, III, No. I, (1969) 30–52.

Bibliography

Koebner, Richard, *Empire* (2nd edition, New York, 1961).

Kubler, George (and Martin Soria) *Art and Architecture in Spain and Portugal and their American Dominions 1500–1800* (Pelican History of Art, 1959).

Lamego, Alberto, *Mentiras Históricas* (Rio de Janeiro, 1947).

Autobiografia e inédito de Cláudio Manuel da Costa (Brussels/Paris, n.d.).

Langlans, Franz-Paul, *As corporações dos ofícios mecanicos, subsídios para a sua história com um estudo de Marcelo Caetano* (2 vols., Lisbon, 1943).

Lapa, M. Rodrigues, *As Cartas Chilenas, Um problema histórico e filológico, com prefácio de Afonso Pena Júnior* (Rio de Janeiro, 1958).

Vida e Obra de Alvarenga Peixoto (Rio de Janeiro, 1960).

Leite, Serafim, *História da Companhia de Jesús no Brasil* (10 vols., Lisbon/Rio de Janeiro, 1938–50).

Lima Júnior, Augusto de, *A capitania das Minas Gerais, origens e formação* (3rd edition, Belo Horizonte, 1965).

Livermore, Harold (ed.) *Portugal and Brazil: An Introduction* (Oxford, 1963).

'The privileges of an Englishman in the Kingdoms and Dominions of Portugal', *Atlante*, vol. 2, No. 2 (April 1954).

Lodge, Sir Richard, 'The English Factory at Lisbon', *Transactions of the Royal Historical Society*, 4th series, xvi (1933) 211–47.

Lopes, Francisco Antônio, *História da construção da Igreja do Carmo de Ouro Prêto* (Rio de Janeiro, 1942).

Álvares Maciel, no degredo de Angola (Rio de Janeiro, 1958).

Lynch, John, *Spanish Colonial Administration 1782–1810: The Intendant System in the Viceroyalty of the Rio de la Plata* (London, 1958).

'British Policy and Spanish America 1783–1808', *Journal of Latin American Studies*, 1 (1969) 1–30.

Macedo, Jorge Borges de, *A situação económica no tempo de Pombal, Alguns aspectos* (Oporto, 1951).

Problemas de História da Indústria Portuguêsa no século XVIII (Lisbon, 1963).

'Portugal e a economia "Pombalina", temas e hipoteses', *RHSP*, No. 19 (1954) 81–100.

Machado Filho, Aires da Mota, *O Negro e o Garimpo em Minas Gerais* (2nd edition, Rio de Janeiro, 1964).

Manchester, Alan K., *British Preeminence in Brazil* (Chapel Hill, 1933).

'The Transfer of the Portuguese Court to Rio de Janeiro', in *Conflict and Continuity in Brazilian Society* (editors, Henry H. Keith and S. F. Edwards, Columbia, South Carolina, 1969) 148–83.

Marchant, Alexander, 'Tiradentes in the Conspiracy of Minas', *HAHR*, xxi (1941) 239–57.

Mathias, Herculano Gomes, 'O Tiradentes e a cidade do Rio de Janeiro', *AMHN*, xvi (1966) 53–103.

'Inconfidência e Inconfidentes', *ACC*, iii, 229–99.

Mauro, Frédéric, *Le Portugal et l'Atlantique au XVIIe siècle 1570–1670* (Paris, 1960).

Mota, Carlos Guilherme, 'Mentalidade Ilustrada na colonização Portuguêsa: Luís dos Santos Vilhena', *RHSP*, No. 72 (1967) 405–416.

(ed.) *Brasil em Perspectiva* (São Paulo, 1968).

Atitudes de inovação no Brasil 1789–1801 (Lisbon, n.d.).

Nordeste 1817 (São Paulo, 1972(.

Bibliography

Moura, Americo Brasiliense Antunes de, 'Governo do Morgado de Mateus no vicereinado do conde da Cunha: S. Paulo Restaurado', *Revista do Arquivo Municipal*, LII (São Paulo, 1938) 9–155.

Novais, Fernando A., 'A proibição das manufacturas no Brasil e a política económica Portuguêsa do fim do século XVIII', *RHSP*, No. 67 (1967) 145–66.

Nunes Dias, Manuel, 'Fomento e mercantilismo: política económica Portuguesa na baixada Maranhense, 1755–1778', V Colóquio internacional de estudos Luso-Brasileiros, *Actas* (3 vols., Coimbra, 1965) II, 17–99.

'Fomento Ultramarino e mercantilismo: A Companhia Geral do Grão-Pará e Maranhão 1755–1778', I, *RHSP*, No. 66 (1966) 359–428; II, No. 67 (1966) 47–120; No. 68 (1966) 367–416; No. 69 (1967) 99–148; No. 71 (1967) 105–66; No. 73 (1968) 71–114.

'A tonelagem da frota da Companhia Geral do Grão-Pará e Maranhão', *RHSP* (January–March 1964) 113–39.

'Política Pombalina na colonização da Amazônia 1755–1778', *Studia*, 23 (Lisbon, April 1968).

'As frotas do cacao da Amazônia 1756–1773: Subsídios para o estudo do fomento ultramarino Portuguêsa no século XVIII', *RHSP*, No. 50 (April–June 1962) 363–77.

'A junta liquiditária dos fundos das Companhias do Grão-Pará e Maranhão, Pernambuco e Paraíba, 1778–1837', *Revista Portuguesa de História*, x (Coimbra, 1962) 153–201.

Oiliam José, *Historiografia Mineira* (Belo Horizonte, 1959).

Panteleão, Olga, 'A penetração comercial da Inglaterra na América Espanhola 1715–1783', *Boletim da Faculdade de Filosofia Ciências e Letras, Universidade de São Paulo* (1946).

Pares, Richard, *War and Trade in the West Indies 1739–1763* (London, 1936).

Palmer, R. R., *The Age of Democratic Revolution* (2 vols., Princeton, 1959, 1964).

Pedrosa, Manoel Xavier de Vasconcellos, 'Estudantes Brasileiros na Faculdade de Medicina de Montpellier no fim do século XVIII', *RIHGB*, 243 (1959) 35–71.

Pereira, Ángelo, *D. João VI, Principe e Rei*, vol. I, *A retirada da familia Real para o Brasil (1807)* (Lisbon, 1953).

Pereira dos Reis, P., *O Colonialismo Português e a conjuração Mineira* (São Paulo, 1964).

Pinto, Ercília, *O marquês de Pombal, lavrador e autodidacta em Souré* (Coimbra, 1967).

Pombo, Padre Manuel, *Inconfidência Mineira, conspiradores que vieram deportados para os presidios de Angola em 1792* (Luanda, Angola, 1932).

Porto, Aurélio, *História das missões orientais do Uruguai* (2 vols., Rio de Janeiro, 1943).

Posthumus, N. W., *Inquiry into the History of Prices in Holland* (2 vols., Leiden, 1946, 1964).

Prado Júnior, Caio, *A formação do Brasil contemporanêo, colônia* (7th edition, São Paulo, 1963).

Redford, Arthur, *Manchester Merchants and Foreign Trade 1794–1858* (Manchester, 1934).

Rizzini, Carlos, *Hypólito da Costa e o Correio Brasiliense* (São Paulo, 1957).

Rodrigues, José Honório, *Brazil and Africa* (translation by Richard A. Mazzara and Sam Hileman, Berkeley and Los Angeles, 1965).

Russell-Wood, A. J. R., *Fidalgos and Philanthropists: The Santa Casa de Misericórdia of Bahia, 1650–1755* (Berkeley and Los Angeles, 1968).

Bibliography

Ruy, Afonso, *A primeira revolução social Brasileira* (1798) (São Paulo, 1942).

Santos, Joaquim Felício dos, *Memorias do Distrito Diamantina da Comarca do Sêrro Frio* (3rd edition, Rio de Janeiro, 1956).

Santos, Lúcio José dos, *A Inconfidência Mineira, Papel de Tiradentes na Inconfidência Mineira* (São Paulo, 1927).

Santos, Celia Nunes Galvas Quirino dos, 'A Inconfidência Mineira', (Separata do Tomo xx dos *Anais do Museu Paulista*, São Paulo, 1966).

Santos Filho, Lycurgo, *Uma Comunidade Rural do Brasil Antigo, Aspectos da vida Patriarcal no sertão da Bahia nos séculos XVIII e XIX* (São Paulo, 1956).

Salles, Fritz Teixeira de, *Associações Religiosas no ciclo do ouro* (Belo Horizonte, 1963).

Schumpeter, Elizabeth Boody, *English Overseas Trade Statistics* (Oxford, 1960).

Schuyler, R. L., *The Fall of the Old Colonial System* (New York, 1945).

Serrão, Joel (ed.) *Dicionário de História de Portugal* (3 vols., Lisbon, 1965 to date).

Sideri, Sandro, *Trade and Power. Informal Colonialism in Anglo–Portuguese Relations* (Rotterdam University Press, 1970).

Silva Dias, Maria Odila de, 'Aspectos da ilustração no Brasil', *RIHGB*, vol. 278 (1968) 105–70.

Simonsen, Robert C., *História económica do Brasil 1500–1820* (5th edition, São Paulo, 1967).

Smith, John Athelstone, *The Marquis of Pombal* (2 vols., London, 1843).

Smith, Robert C., 'The colonial architecture of Minas Gerais in Brazil', *The Art Bulletin*, xxi (1939).

Sombra, Severino, *História Monetaria do Brasil Colonial* (Rio de Janeiro, 1938).

Soriano, Simão José da Luz, *História da Guerra Civil* (Lisbon, 1866).

Souza Silva, J. Noberto da, *História de conjuração Mineira: Estudos sobre as primeiras tentativos para a Independencia Nacional* (Rio de Janeiro, 1873).

Sousa, Manuel de Barros (Santarém, visconde de), and L. A. Rebello da Silva (eds.) *Quadro elementar das relações políticas e diplomáticas de Portugal*, Paris, 1842–1860 (18 vols., Lisbon).

Sousa, Octávio Tarquínio de, *História dos fundadores do Império do Brasil*, vol. I, *José Bonifácio* (Rio de Janeiro, 1960).

Sutherland, Lucy, S., *A London Merchant 1695–1774* (Oxford, 1933).

Torres, João Camillo de Oliveira, *História de Minas Gerais* (5 vols., Belo Horizonte, 1962).

Trindade, Cônego Raimundo, *Saõ Francisco de Assis de Ouro Prêto* (Rio de Janeiro, 1951).

Veríssimo, Inácio José, *Pombal, os Jesuitas e o Brasil* (Rio de Janeiro, 1961).

Verger, Pierre, *Bahia and the West African Trade* (Ibadan, 1964).

Flux et Reflux de la traite des negres entre le golfe de Benin et Bahia de todos os Santos du dix-septieme au dix-neuvieme siècle (Paris/The Hague, 1966).

Viveiros, Jeronimo de, *História do comércio do Maranhão 1612–1898* (2 vols., São Luis, 1964).

Vasconcellos, Sylvio de, *Vila Rica, Formação e desenvolvimento, Residencias* (Rio de Janeiro, 1956).

Walford, A. R., *The British Factory* (Lisbon, 1940).

Zemella, Mafalda, *O Abastecimento da Capitania das Minas Gerais no século XVIII* (São Paulo, 1951).

INDEX

Abreu Vieira, Domingos de, 101, 120, 122, 127, 128, 142, 157
Academia Brasilica dos Renascidos, 95
Academy of Sciences of Lisbon, 79, 114, 179, 187, 201, 213, 227
Admiralty, British, 35
Africa, trade between Brazil and, 77; between Bahia and, 214
African influence in Minas Gerais, 92; conspirators banished to, 190, 223; *see also* Angola; Mozambique; Bissau
African labor, 17, 23, 256; *see also* Slavery
Africans in Brazil, 86; in Minas Gerais, 92
Aires Gomes, Colonel José, 121, 127, 128, 130, 136, 156, 159, 193
Aimores Indians, 85
Albermarle, Lord, 35
Alçada, Special Court of Inquiry, 190, 191, 195, 198
Aleijadinho, Antônio Francisco Lisboa, sculptor and architect, 94
Alentejo, Portugal, 54
Alvará of 3 December 1750, 13, 108, 109, 113, 132, 140
Alvará of 5 January 1785, 79, 98, 107, 113, implementation in Rio de Janeiro, 136
Alvará of 24 April 1801, 230
Alvarenga Peixoto, Inácio José de, 46, 64, 69, 88, 91, 96, 98, 115, 116, 118, 191; reasons for involvement in plot, 121-2, 123, 124, 128, 129, 134, 142, 147, 149, 157; arrest, 158; implicated by Cláudio Manuel da Costa, 163; not interrogated by Vasconcelos Coutinho, 196; sentence, 198; ode to Queen, 234; *see also* Conspiracy, Minas Gerais; *Canto genetlíaco;* Bárbara Eliodora
Álvares Maciel, *see* Maciel, José Álvares
Amazon, River, 6, 29
Amazonia, 10, 16, 17, 29, 39; Portuguese claims upheld by Treaty of Madrid, 14
American Revolution, *see* United States of America
Anadia, visconde de, Secretary of State for the Overseas Dominions, 232, 235
Andrada e Silva, José Bonifácio, 82, 178, 230, 239
Angeja, Marquês de, 71, 73, 74, 177
Anglo-Americans, *see* North America, United States of America

Angola, 41, 71, 190, 206, 214
Annual Register, London, 30, 49, 187
Araújo, João Gomes de, 26
Aráujo Saldanha, Pedro José de, Ouvidor of Vila Rica, Minas Gerais, 125; appointed judge of the Minas devassa, 160, 172; death of 193
Architecture, development of in Minas Gerais, 93-4
Arriaga, Street, 76-7
Aristocracy, Pombal's policy towards, 29, 70, 31, 70; attitude towards move of the court to Brazil, 234
Articles of Confederation, former British colonies, 126, 137
Artisans, 55, 56, 59, 66, 94-5, plot of mulatto artisans of Bahia, 218, 218-23
Asia, project for Commercial Company, 18
Auxiliary regiments, 43-4, 62
Aveiro, Duke of, 30, 70
Azeredo Coutinho, José Joaquim da Cunha de, Bishop, 79, 209, 213, 216, 225-6, 227
Azevedo Coutinho, Marco Antônio de, 6
Azores, 15, 92

Bacalhão, João Marques, 26
Bahia, 5, 40, 47, 62, 77, 80, 85, 179, 213; intercoastal shipping from, 214, 215; municipal council requests reinstatement as viceregal capital, 215; population of, 217; *see also* Conspiracy, Bahia
Bandeira, José Rodrigues, 25, 26, 51
Bandeira, Jacinto Fernandes, 75
Bandeira, *see* Pires Monteiro Bandeira, Francisco Gregório
Barbacena, visconde de, Luís Antônio Furtado de Mendonça, Governor of Minas Gerais appointed, 106; instructions from Melo e Castro, 107-10; arrival in Brazil, 113-14; assassination planned by plotters, 117, 133-4; reasons for suspension of the derrama, 141, 142, 145, 148-9, 150, 153, 154, 159, 160, 164-5; reports to Lisbon on crushing of the Minas conspiracy, 172; criticized by Melo e Castro, 188-9; removed from office, 205; *see also* Conspiracy, Minas Gerais
Barbacena, Minas Gerais, *see* Igreja Nova

Index

Index

Index

Index

Index

Index

Intendent Bandeira, *see* Pires Monteiro Bandeira, Francisco Gregório
Interest Rates, 10, 42
Interlopers, 10, 19, 24; *see also Commissários volantes;* Contraband
Ipanema, São Paulo, iron mines, 40
Iron, 89, 118; experiments with, 90, 179; imports in Minas Gerais, 205; price of, 209
Iron foundry, proposals to establish in Minas Gerais, 90; proposals to establish, 205; *see also* Ferreira Pereira, Domingos
Iron mines, 40, 90, 133, 205
Itacolumí, 85
Itapecerica, *see* Tamanduá
Itinerant traders, see *Commissários volantes*

Jay, John, 80
Jacobina, 210
Jefferson, Thomas, 80, 104, 119, 186
Jesuits, 11, 14, 17, 24, 26, 27–9; expulsion, 30–1, 36; excluded from Minas Gerais, 92, 200
João V of Portugal, 1, 9
João VI of Portugal, 206
José I of Portugal, 1, 31, 58, 70, 71, 206
Juiz da Fora, Minas Gerais, 82
Junot, invasion of Portugal, 238
Junta da administração das fábricas do Reino e aguas livres, 75, 77
Junta da Fazenda (treasury boards), 44–5, 48, 64, 65, 67, 69; in Minas Gerais, 91, 99, 101, 103, 108–9, 114, 128, 151, 152, 156, 207, 245
Junta do comércio (board of trade), 24–5, 26, 40, 51, 53, 54, 56, 57, 61, 64, 75; aid to manufacturing and processing plants in Brazil, 40–1

Keene, Sir Benjamin, 1
King, Charles, quoted, 7
Kinnoull, Earl of, 34
Koster, Henry, 74

Lacerda e Almeida, José de, 83
Lavradio, Marquês de, D. Luís de Almeida Portugal, Viceroy of Brazil, 39, 46, 62, 63, 78
Leal, José Ferreira, 40, 51
Linen, 40
Lippe, Count Schaunburg-Lippe-Buckeburg, 43, 46
Lisbon, 5, 7, 10, 11, 12, 19, 30, 37, 38, 40, 54, 57, 58, 106, 107, 110, 113, 121, 123, 141, 177, 178, 181, 183, 186, 213, 215–16, 220, 235
Literary Society of Rio de Janeiro, 202, 226, 229
Lopes, Francisco José, 75
Lorena, Bernardo José de, 113, 205, 206
Loureiro, Domingos L., 40
Luís Vaz, *see* Toledo e Piza, Luís Vaz de
Lyttleton, William, 42

Mably, Abbé, 126, 203
Macedo, Bento Rodrigues de, 121
Macedo, João Rodrigues de, 67, 68, 69, 70, 88, 91, 96, 103, 105, 110, 115, 120, 121, 127, 128, 130, 137, 153, 159, 161, 191, 193, 195, 245; protection accorded by Manitti, 163; implicated in Minas Conspiracy by Oliveira Lopes, 168; involvement becomes clear in interrogations, 193; business papers to state, 230–1; blackmail of, 231
Machado, Joaquim, 75
Machado, Policarpo José, 57
Maciel, José Álvares, Capitão-mor, 104, 105, 106
Maciel, José Álvares, Dr, 82, 116, 118, 134, 147, 149, 156, 187; implicated in plot, 163; arrest, 167; confession, 168; sentenced, 198; in Angola, 229
Madeira, 228
Magistrates, 29, 46, 64, 67, 69, 96, 99, 100, 101, 103, 107–8, 110, 112, 138, 152, 155, 160, 161, 167, 172, 174, 190, 194, 202
Madrid, Treaty of, *see* Treaties
Maia e Barbalho, José Joaquim (*Vendek*), 80, 81, 104, 130
Mairinque, Baltasar João, 102
Maize, 89
Manchester, England, 60, 182, 183
Manila, 35
Manioc, prices, 216–17, 225
Manitiba, Bahia, 214
Manitti, José César Caetano, ouvidor of Sabará, appointed clerk of Minas devassa, 160; reasons for appointment, 161; conduct during the proceedings, 161, 163; makes resumé of devassa, 172; special favor requested for him by Barbacena, 172; appointed intendent of Vila Rica, 189; ordered to Rio de Janeiro, 189; loan from Macedo, 231; accused of malpractice by Oliveira Lopes, 194
Manique, Inácio de Pina, 77, 202, 232
Mantiqueira, mountains of, 84, 85, 101, 119

Index

Index

Index

Index

Index